THE CRITICAL HANDBOOK

OF THE

EEK NEW TESTAMENT

BY

EDWARD C. MITCHELL, D.D.

PRESIDENT OF LELAND UNIVERSITY, NEW ORLEANS

ILLUSTRATED BY DIAGRAMS, TABLES, AND A MAP

NEW AND ENLARGED EDITION

NEW YORK

HARPER & BROTHERS PUBLISHERS

1896

TO

THOSE MINISTERS OF THE WORD

Who have been the author's pupils, and for whose help these notes
were originally prepared, as well as to all who, like them, desire to
know "*the certainty concerning the words wherein they have been
instructed*," this handbook is affectionately inscribed.

PREFACE

HAPPILY the day is past when any respectable scholar questions the legitimacy or value of the science of Biblical Criticism. It has come to be a recognized right and duty of one who would become acquainted with the New Testament revelation to press the inquiry, reverentially but persistently: In what does this revelation consist? Are these the words which holy men of God spake or wrote as they were moved by the Holy Ghost?

The difficulties as well as the facilities attending this inquiry are beginning to be understood. The means and appliances for a critical examination of the Sacred Text are coming to be indispensable to the Christian scholar who would be thoroughly furnished unto all good works. Indeed, no good modern Commentary upon the Scriptures can be intelligently used without some acquaintance with the sources of textual criticism.

Unfortunately, the resources in this department of learning are not yet abundant, or easy of access. The few thorough and excellent treatises upon the subject are expensive, and not within easy reach of the ordinary student. They are, moreover, too extended and voluminous for the comprehension of beginners, and too minute for ready reference.

The writer, therefore, while engaged in the work of instruction, has found it necessary to prepare for his classes a brief compendium of the subject, in order that they might proceed intelligently to the work of exegesis.

The substance of this hand-book was thus prepared, at first with no thought of publication; but having been many times requested to make it available for general use, the writer has revised and enlarged the notes for the press, constructing, at the same time, a set of Tables, to serve as ready reference guides to the information most needed on the subjects discussed.

The plan of the book embraces, in the first place, a view of the present field of controversy on the subject of the Authenticity of the New Testament Scriptures, as regarded from a geographical and historical standpoint; in the presentation of which a leading object has been to familiarize the mind with the periods and the persons most often referred to in the after-work of textual criticism. This is followed by a brief discussion of the leading points in the History of the Canon, and then by a *résumé* of the subject of Textual Criticism. In this part of the work, and the Tables which accompany it, care has been taken to combine brevity with the greatest possible accuracy of statement. The best recent authorities have been consulted, and the author has received valuable aid from eminent scholars in England and America. Among these, he desires to make grateful mention of the Rev. Dr. Joseph Angus, of Regent's Park College, London, whose counsel has always been wise and useful; and of Prof. Ezra Abbot, of Cambridge, Mass., the inspiration of whose friendship it has been the writer's happiness to enjoy for many years, and whose sympathy is ever open towards any sincere effort to advance real scholarship. Though always overburdened with his own labors, which give him a recognized place in the foremost rank among Biblical critics, Dr. Abbot has yet found time to bestow much patient thought upon this little manual, giving to the whole of Part III., and the accompanying Tables, the great advantage of his careful revision, and suggesting many new points of interest and value. The author's thanks are also due to the Librarians of the *Bibliothèque Nationale* and of the *Faculté Protestante Théologique* of Paris, and especially to Mr. R. Garnett, of the British Museum, London, for much cheerful help in obtaining access to books and manuscripts.

E. C. M.

PREFACE TO THE SECOND EDITION

It is over thirty years since these notes were first prepared for dictation to successive theological classes, and fifteen years since they were published in England and America. A French edition, somewhat revised, was published in Paris in 1882. From that time a careful revision of the work has been in progress, but the materials, though accumulating, were scattered and often difficult of verification. Though repeatedly urged to issue a new edition, the author has felt constrained to withhold it until Dr. Gregory's great work on the *Prolegomena* to Tischendorf's New Testament should be completed. The publication of the last *fasciculus* of this, and the appearance of the fourth edition of Scrivener's *Plain Introduction*—the crowning work of an eminently useful life—open the way for such a summary of results as this hand-book is intended to furnish. No change in the general plan of the book has been found necessary, except the addition of a table of American manuscripts and a glossary of abbreviations and unfamiliar terms.

The discoveries of the last fifteen years, however, have more than doubled the number of known manuscripts, and much clearer light has been thrown upon the history and contents of many of them. For these discoveries and for this light the author and the public are indebted to the distinguished textual critics above mentioned, and to their industrious colaborers, whose names appear in the following pages.

E. C. M.

GROVELAND PARK, CHICAGO, *Dec.* 2, 1895.

CONTENTS

I. AUTHENTICITY OF THE NEW TESTAMENT SCRIPTURES.

TABLES AND DIAGRAMS.

Map of the Roman Empire, Showing the Localities of Early Witnesses . . . . *facing title-page*

PART I

AUTHENTICITY

OF THE

NEW TESTAMENT SCRIPTURES

AUTHENTICITY

OF THE

NEW TESTAMENT SCRIPTURES

CHAPTER I

INTRODUCTORY

§ 1. *The Question stated*

THE first question which addresses itself to the critical student of the New Testament Scriptures has reference to the authenticity and trustworthiness of the records of fact which they present.

Unless the Christ of history be genuine, and the evangelic narrative an authentic record, we have no revelation from a personal God ; we have no authoritative basis for the Christian faith.[1]

---

[1] "What is the Christianity for which we can claim and hope to establish equal validity with that of the accredited truths of science? I answer, simply and solely the genuineness of the Divine mission of Jesus Christ; that is, not of any Christ of one's own special shaping or fancy, but of the Christ of history, of the Gospels, of the Church, including of course the substantial authenticity of the evangelic narrative of what Jesus said, did, and suffered."—Dr. Andrew P. Peabody, *Christianity and Science.*

And if, according to the theories of modern rationalists, the Gospel histories are largely mythical in their character, built upon a slender basis of facts by the fertile imaginations of pious enthusiasts, and accepted by a credulous public, long after their alleged occurrence, as veritable histories,[1] then the work of critical exegesis becomes of comparatively slight importance, excepting for the detection of the fraud.

It behooves the Christian scholar, therefore, to satisfy himself at the outset whether or not these histories, and the letters and treatises connected with them, are authentic and trustworthy documents.

Without attempting any exhaustive discussion of Christian evidences, it seems appropriate to the purpose of this hand-book to furnish the student with an outline of such historical facts as furnish a basis of argument for the defence of the authenticity of the New Testament.

For this purpose our discussion will take the form of an inquiry into the theory which has been propounded in modern times, that the accepted facts of the New Testament record are "unhistorical."

§ 2. *Method of Investigation*

The simplest method of conducting such an inquiry will be to trace history up the stream, searching

---

[1] Strauss, *Leben Jesu*, §§ 13, 14. See note, p. 67.

as we go for the supposed *terra incognita* out of which must have grown the "mythical" Gospels. If we find that the links in the chain are unbroken; if it shall prove that the only possible period for the actual origin of Christianity coincides with the period claimed for it in the New Testament record, our standpoint as students of the Scripture will be vindicated. We shall then be prepared to commence a direct examination of the history of the documents which compose these records; and, in doing so, shall be but retracing our steps over familiar ground. Thus the process of inquiry into the question of authenticity will serve as an appropriate introduction to the study of the canonical and textual history of the New Testament writings.

The question before us may be thus stated: If the New Testament books are not genuine documents, and their historical statements records of fact, coming from their reputed authors, then at what period in the world's history did they originate? Obviously not *before* the time assigned to the events alluded to or recorded in them. Not certainly *since* the days of Constantine the Great, because from that time to the present the leading nations of Europe have been avowedly Christian nations, in which these books have been generally recognized as authoritative.[1]

[1] To illustrate this, let the student notice upon Table I., at the end of this hand-book, the Christian nations which once composed the Roman Empire.

Our field of inquiry, therefore, is narrowed down to the interval between the above-named periods, viz., A.D. 65–311, as affording the only possible opportunity for such a process of origination as the mythical hypothesis assumes; and the form of our question might be : *How came the Roman Empire to adopt Christianity at the close of the third century ?* How could the people assure themselves that they were not adopting a myth, instead of an historical reality ? What means had they for bridging the interval between themselves and the apostolic Church ?

To take a nearer view of this interval, let us transport ourselves in imagination to the latter period, viz., the age of Constantine, and ascertain, *first*, the extent of the Church, *secondly*, the number of New Testament books accepted, and, *thirdly*, the means which then existed for verifying them.

CHAPTER II

§ 1. *Extent of the Church in the Third Century*

LET us then take our stand at the close of the third century, and survey the position which the Christian Church held in the Roman Empire.

We find ourselves on the threshold of the reign of an avowedly Christian emperor, who carried the cross before his army, and everywhere recognized Christianity as the religion of the State. We find that at Nicomedia,[1] the eastern capital of the empire, a splendid Christian church, built in the reign of Diocletian, is standing close by the imperial residence and proudly overshadowing it,[2] and learn that such magnificent buildings for Christian worship are not uncommon throughout the empire.[3] We find in the account by Gibbon that "episcopal churches were closely planted along the banks of the Nile, on the sea-coast of Africa, in the proconsular Asia, and throughout the southern provinces of Italy;" that

---

[1] See Map of Roman Empire (Frontispiece).   [2] Gibbon, ch. xvi.

[3] Gibbon, ch. xx. See also Bingham's *Antiquities of the Christian Church*, bk. viii., ch. ii., § 3 ; Smith's *Dictionary of Christian Antiquities*, vol. i., pp. 366 and 427.

" the Bishops of Gaul and Spain, of Thrace and Pontus, reigned over an ample territory, and delegated their rural suffragans to execute the subordinate duties of the pastoral office ;" that the Bishops at this time exercising jurisdiction numbered eighteen hundred, of whom one thousand were seated in the Greek, and eight hundred in the Latin provinces of the empire; while the number of subordinate clergy may be conjectured from the circumstances that the cathedrals of Constantinople and Carthage maintained an establishment of five hundred each, and that " almost in every city the ancient churches were found insufficient to contain the increasing multitude of proselytes." [1]   In short, it is a matter of established history that the Church of the New Testament had at this period made its way, through terrific persecutions, to a foremost position in numbers, intelligence, and influence throughout the empire.[2]

[1] Gibbon, ch. xvi.

[2] About a century before, Tertullian of Carthage, in his *Apology* addressed to the Roman authorities (" Romanii imperii antistites "), probably at Carthage, had said: " We are but of yesterday, and we have filled every place among you—cities, islands, fortresses, towns, market-places, the very camp, tribes, companies, palace, senate, forum. We have left nothing to you but the temples of your gods. . . . Without arms even, and raising no insurrectionary banner, but simply in enmity to you, we could carry on the contest with you by an ill-willed severance alone.   For if such multitudes of men were to break away from you, and betake themselves to some remote corner of the world, why, the very loss of so many citizens . . . would cover the empire with shame."—*Apol.*, § 34 (Ante-Nicene Christian Library, Tert., vol. i.,

§ 2. *Estimation of New Testament books in the Third Century*

It is equally matter of history, the evidence for which we shall see hereafter, that at this time, as indeed for a century previous, that part of the New Testament comprised in what is called the First Canon (viz. the Gospels, the Acts, thirteen Epistles of Paul, the First Epistle of John and the First Epistle of Peter $= \frac{7059}{7957}$, or about $\frac{8}{9}$ of the New Testament) was generally regarded as authoritative and inspired, and co-ordinate with the Old Testament; that the copies of this collection were multiplied so numerously as to defy the whole power of the government exerted to suppress them,[1] and so sacredly preserved that many persons suffered an ignominious death rather than deliver them up.

§ 3. *Probable means then existing for verifying the Facts*

Now, in view of the mythical hypothesis, it remains for us to inquire what means of knowledge the Christian Church of the third century could have possessed, on which to found her belief—maintained

---

p. 116). And in his treatise against the Jews, he says: "The Gothic peoples, the various tribes of the Moors, all the regions of Spain, diverse nations of Gaul, and places of Britain yet inaccessible to the Romans, have submitted to Christ, as well as the Sarmatians, the Dacians, the Germans, the Scythians, and nations yet unknown."—*Adv. Jud.*, ch. vii.

[1] Gibbon, ch. xvi.

under persecution and in the face of death [1]—that the facts of the Gospel history were real and the writings authentic.

The record professes to describe portions of the life and teachings of Jesus and the twelve Apostles in the three divisions of Palestine, and the travels of Paul for the purpose of founding Churches in Syria, Asia Minor, Macedonia, Greece, and Italy; containing also letters purporting to be addressed by him to the Churches in Thessalonica, Galatia, Corinth, Rome, Ephesus, Colossæ, and Philippi, and to his brethren Timothy, Titus, and Philemon. These transactions are alleged to have taken place during the period immediately preceding A.D. 64, the date of Nero's persecution, and of the probable death of Peter and Paul.

The interval, therefore, through which Christians under Constantine must look for the facts, embraced a period of about two centuries and a half, a period even less than that which has elapsed since the settlement of America by the Pilgrim Fathers in 1620. How then, let us ask, do the citizens of the United States of America, and especially of New England, assure themselves to-day that the reported incidents in the history of their colonial ancestors were veritable facts, and not mythical in their origin?

In reply, the mind would first revert to the im-

[1] Gibbon estimates that the martyrs in the ten years of Diocletian's persecutions alone may have numbered 2000.—Chap. xvi.

probability of a whole nation being imposed upon in regard to the facts of its origin. The facts are matters of universal belief. The reality of the history as a whole has never been disputed. An intelligent public cannot be deceived about matters of this nature. If an attempt had ever been made by pretended historians to foist unhistorical records upon the public as veritable history, protests would have come from all quarters, and the controversy thus aroused would of itself have formed a prominent part of literary history. So much we should decide *a priori* without troubling ourselves to examine the question.

If pressed for further evidence of a positive character we should find it in abundance, almost without recourse to documentary sources. The scenes of Pilgrim history are full of monuments which substantiate the common report. The Rock on which the Pilgrims landed, the houses and fortifications which they erected, still exist. Their graves are preserved, and the inscriptions on their tombstones are easily legible. Their dwellings and furniture and personal property are preserved, as sacred relics, by their descendants. Indeed, the traditional history is within easy reach through family connection. Multitudes in all parts of the continent are linked by only six or seven generations to the Pilgrim Fathers. The writer's grandparents were for thirty years contemporaries of the grandchildren of his Pilgrim ancestors, and in familiar intercourse with them.

§ 4. *Comparative View of Ancient with Modern History*

Now, the entire number of the Pilgrim Fathers did not greatly exceed a hundred, and the earlier events in their history had no other witnesses excepting the " perishing sons of the forest."

On the other hand, in the New Testament Scripture, the claim is boldly set up that the actors in the scenes of Gospel history numbered many thousands, and that most of their acts were witnessed by many thousands more.

The record states that over five hundred brethren at one time saw Jesus after His resurrection, and Paul's letter to the Corinthians affirms that most of these persons were then living. It is declared in the book of the " Acts of the Apostles " that shortly after the resurrection of Jesus three thousand were converted at Jerusalem (Acts ii. 41), and that their number daily increased thereafter (Acts ii. 47). We are told that these converts were natives of different and remote countries (Acts ii. 9–11), and that they were soon driven by persecution into all parts of the empire, preaching the Word ; that Churches planted by them or others did exist in Samaria (Acts viii. 14, xv. 3), Syria (Acts ix. 19, xiii. 1, xv. 23), Phœnicia (Acts

xv. 3), Galilee (Acts ix. 31), Cilicia (Acts xv. 23, 41), Pontus, Cappadocia, Bithynia (1 Peter i. 1), and Italy (Romans i. 8). Paul himself is declared to have ministered to Churches in each of the principal cities north of the Mediterranean, from Antioch on the east to Rome on the west; and striking incidents in the early history of some of them are narrated. It is apparent, therefore, that the points of connection, and opportunities for verifying or disproving the accuracy of the record, must have been ready and abundant to Christians in the days of Constantine. The facts therein alleged, if real, were public events, and occurred in the most populous places in all parts of the empire, and at a convenient proximity to the imperial centre. If imaginary or exaggerated, the evidence of their falsity must have been within easy reach of thousands, and must have exposed their authors to universal and merited contempt.[1]

If the actors in them were numbered by thousands, the disinterested spectators of them must have been counted by tens of thousands; and the lineal descendants of both must have been living in the days of Constantine. The habits of the people were not generally so migratory as those of our own time, and the great body of the people were doubtless still living where their fathers died. If miracles were per-

[1] See Map of Roman Empire, showing localities in which the scenes of New Testament History occurred (Frontispiece).

formed by Jesus and His Apostles, the witnesses or the subjects of these miraculous works would have transmitted the facts through their children and grandchildren with concomitant circumstances and corroborative incidents. If Churches were founded by Paul and Peter and John in the various cities of the empire, most of those Churches must have been still in existence, and must have possessed tangible relics of their origin and history, such as places of worship [1] or of baptism, dwellings of pastors or leading members, etc., etc. If apostolic letters were written to different Churches, some trace of the original documents, or at least of very early copies, must have been still in existence.

If, from the beginning, disciples of Jesus had sealed their faith in Him with their blood, the memorials of their death and of the place of sepulture of many of them must have been still visible. If the Church had existed as a Church through these two centuries and a half, it must have had a literature, more or less copious, extending through the whole period. If it existed in sufficient magnitude

---

[1] The church is still standing in Scrooby, England, where the Pilgrim Fathers worshipped before A.D. 1620, and the record of the baptism of William Bradford, George Morton, and others, may still be read upon the Church Register.

The meeting-house in Hingham, Mass., U. S. A., built in 1680, is still standing and in good condition, though constructed wholly of wood.

to become an object of notice and of persecution by
the Imperial Government, the facts must have been
in some way alluded to by secular writers during the
period.

These concomitant evidences would have been
necessary from the nature of things; and a marked
deficiency of any one of them would have given occasion to all intelligent persons for great distrust, if
not for the entire rejection of the records. We
must bear in mind that the period was one of unusual intelligence. The Christian era began in the
most brilliant age of Roman literature—the Golden
Age of Augustus, the age in or near to which flourished Cæsar (died B.C. 44), Cicero (d. B.C. 43), Sallust
(d. B.C. 34), Virgil (d. B.C. 19), Horace (d. B.C. 8),
Strabo (d. after A.D. 21), Philo (*born* B.C. 20), Seneca
(*b.* B.C. 2), Ovid (d. A.D. 18), Livy (d. A.D. 17), Tacitus (*b.* A.D. 61), Plutarch (*b.* A.D. 46), Pliny (*b.* A.D.
62), and Suetonius (*b.* A.D. 70.)[1] To suppose that the
Church could have reached such a position in numbers and power as it held under Constantine, unless
the main facts of Christian history were substan-
tiated by some such corroborative circumstances as
we have mentioned, is to suppose a miracle of
human credulity and folly more stupendous than
humanity has ever witnessed, immeasurably more

[1] See synchronistical tables of ancient civilization, etc. (No. II.), at
the end of this volume.

than any or all of those miraculous occurrences which the mythical hypothesis was contrived to discredit.

Fortunately we are not left altogether to the nature of things for our evidence that these confirmatory circumstances did exist. Some of them remain to this day, and may be briefly noticed. We will adopt the inverse order to that by which they have just been cited, viz., 1, notices of secular historians; 2, the existence and testimony of a Christian literature; 3, the evidence from relics and monuments.

CHAPTER III

DATA FURNISHED BY PAGAN LITERATURE

§ 1. *What might reasonably be expected*

BEFORE proceeding to this part of the discussion, it may be proper to inquire how frequent and extended a recognition of Christians and their doings we might reasonably expect from their heathen contemporaries.

We should not look for a minute chronicler among their enemies. Even supposing the Christian Church to have occupied a distinct and prominent place among the sects at the beginning of her history, we should expect her to furnish her own historians, while the extraneous notices of her would be either controversial or of the nature of allusion and outline. Nor should we expect that these notices would accord to her all the prominence which she might justly claim.[1] Perfect accuracy of information, or

[1] Lardner illustrates this point from Roman history thus: "Many writers of great worth, and many affairs of no small importance, have long lain in obscurity, or have been totally buried in oblivion.

"It has been observed that Velleius Paterculus, a man of a good family, who flourished in the time of Tiberius, and wrote an abridgment of the Roman History, in two books, has been mentioned by no ancient writer excepting Priscian. . . . M. Annæus Seneca, father of L. A. Seneca the Philosopher, and author of divers works, has been

2

fairness of statement about opposing sects, has ever been a rare quality among men. When we add to this the remembrance that under the influence of Pagan Rome the Christian faith, however prominent, was everywhere despised and hated as a "new and pernicious superstition," whose avowed tendency and purpose was the overthrow of all existing religions and the extinction of idolatry, we should not be surprised to find both ignorance and "silence" respecting them on the part of the few writers which the Roman world at that day produced — writers many of whom filled official stations in the Roman Government.

But the Christian Church did not occupy a prominent place in the outset of its history. The uninformed are often misled by this erroneous presumption.

It is by our partiality to it, and by our historical researches, that it has been brought into the fore-

---

confounded with his son, and has been almost unknown as a writer. . . . Lucian, a subject of the Roman Empire, who has written so many things, has taken little notice of Roman authors or Roman affairs. He has a labored encomium of Demosthenes, but says nothing of Cicero. . . . Maximus Tyrius, a Platonic Philosopher, flourished in the time of Antoninus the Pious, and several of his Dissertations were written at Rome; 'nevertheless,' as Davies, one of his editors, says, ' he appears little acquainted with Roman affairs. Nay,' says he, ' I do not recollect that he has made any reference to the Roman History.' "—*Credibility*, "Heath. Test.," ch. xxii. (vol. vii., p. 305. Here and elsewhere reference is made to the London ed. of Lardner, 1838).

ground of the picture of the first three centuries. A moment's reflection will show us that Christians and their doings were of but little comparative account in making up the history of the world under the Roman Emperors. At first they were but a mere handful, springing up in a remote province, a sect of a sect, so to speak, the petty disturbances of which seldom, if ever, excited attention in the Imperial City.

Even after they had increased in numbers and extended very widely in various parts of the empire, it was some time before they were distinguished from the various sects of Judaism.

There is, therefore, but little reason to expect that a heathen historian, writing of his own time, and having no personal interest in Christians, should make very frequent allusions to them, or be very minute or accurate in his description.[1] And we

---

[1] In a history of the New England Colonies from 1630 to 1649, written by John Winthrop, the Governor, we find only very casual and indistinct allusions to Baptists as a sect, though this was a time of peculiar interest in their history; so much so that Uhden, in his *History of Congregationalists* (The New England Theocracy, Boston, 1859), devotes to them nearly the whole of the thirty pages which describe this period. Facts are mentioned, indeed, which belong to their history, relating to individuals, but only as they seem to have been forced into notice by their connection with civil government. Yet this was not the result of ignorance nor of any effort at concealment. The prominent events of Baptist history occurred under his very eyes; and, on the other hand, fairness and impartiality are qualities ascribed by all parties to the work which he wrote. Had both these circum-

should have still less reason to anticipate that literary men of the same period, whose themes are not necessarily related to Chrisianity, should go out of their way to make mention of it.

Nevertheless we shall find, upon examination, that a fair proportion of Pagan writers have in some way recognized the existence and spread of Christianity during the first two centuries.

For convenience of reference we shall enumerate these as well as Christian writers in their chronological order. It will then be easy, at the close,[1] to apply the retrospective process suggested above (ch. 1, § 2) as a method of argument.

§ 2. *Notices of Secular Historians*

Only nine secular historians have a place in history as living in the first two centuries, viz., Appian and Pausanias among the Greeks, and Livy, Paterculus, Valerius, Justin, Florus, Tacitus, and Suetonius among the Latins. Of these the first seven write

stances been reversed—had the scene of their operations for the most part been remote, and his own mind blinded by prejudice—how natural would it have been for him to avoid all allusions to them, or make such references as would throw discredit upon their account of themselves. See some striking illustrations in the *Post - Biblical History of the Jews ; from the close of the Old Testament, about the year 420 B. C. E., till the destruction of the second temple, in the year 70 C. E.,* by Rabbi Morris J. Raphall, M.A., Ph.D., 2 vols., Phila., 1856.

[1] See ch. v., § 3, *Retrospective View*, p. 64.

respecting an earlier period.   None of them records any events subsequent to the reign of Tiberius.[1]

Of the remaining two, Suetonius was a biographer, and wrote a series of brief sketches, entitled *Lives of the first twelve Cæsars*.   In his life of Claudius he has an incidental allusion which confirms Luke's account of the expelling of the Jews from Rome on account of Christian controversies,[2] and in his life of Nero he notices the cruel persecution of Christians by that emperor.[3]

Tacitus, the historian of the empire, and Consul of Rome in A.D. 97, has given a somewhat extended statement[4] respecting the numbers of Christians,

---

[1] The works of the earlier authors are as follows:

1. Appian.   A History of the World down to Augustus, who died A.D. 14.
2. Pausanias.   An Itinerary descriptive of Grecian Art, etc.
3. Livy.   History of Rome to B.C. 9.   He died A.D. 17.
4. Velleius Paterculus.   An abridgment of Roman History, nearly all lost.   He died A.D. 31.
5. Valerius Maximus.   "*Dicta et facta memorabilia*," dedicated to Tiberius, who died A.D. 37.
6. Justin.   An epitome of the history of Trogus Pompeius, who lived in the time of Augustus.
7. Lucius Annæus Florus.   An abridgment of early Roman History.   The biographers, Curtius and Plutarch, also treat of persons living before the death of Christ.

[2] Claudius Judæos, impulsore Chresto assidue tumultuantes, Româ expulit.   *Claud.* cap. 25.   Comp. Acts xviii. 1, 2.

[3] Afflicti suppliciis Christiani, genus hominum superstitionis novæ et maleficæ.   *Nero*, cap. 16.

[4] The *Annals* of Tacitus were written about the year A.D. 100.   The author, Caius Cornelius Tacitus, was at this time over forty years of age, and had been Prætor and Consul of Rome, besides filling other

their diffusion throughout the empire, and their persecution in the days of Nero. Of this statement
Gibbon (ch. xvi.) says: " The most sceptical criticism
is obliged to respect the truth of it."

posts of honor. The *Annals* were the last of his works which were
preserved; they extended from the reign of Tiberius (A.D. 14) to the
death of Nero (A.D. 68). In describing the reign of Nero, he comes to
the terrible fire at Rome, which occurred in the tenth year of Nero,
A.D. 64. After giving an account of this fire, and of the orders given
for rebuilding the city, and the methods used to appease the gods, he
goes on to say: " Sed non ope humana, non largitionibus principis, aut
deum placamentis decedebat infamia, quin jussum incendium credere-
tur. Ergo abolendo rumori Nero subdidit reos, et quæsitissimis pœnis
adfecit, quos per flagitia invisos vulgus Christianos appellabat. Auctor
nominis ejus Christus, Tiberio imperitante, per procuratorem Pontium
Pilatum supplicio adfectus erat. Repressa in præsens, exitiabilis su-
perstitio rursum erumpebat, non modo per Judæam, originem ejus
mali, sed per Urbem etiam, quo cuncta undique atrocia aut pudenda
confluunt celebranturque."

He then goes on to describe the cruel nature of the tortures to
which they were subjected, calling the victims *multitudo ingens,* " a
vast multitude," and saying that they were condemned not so much
for burning the city as for their " hatred of mankind." " Igitur pri-
mum correpti qui fatebantur, deinde indicio eorum multitudo ingens,
haud perinde in crimine incendii, quam odio humani generis convicti
sunt. Et pereuntibus addita ludibria, ut, ferarum tergis contecti, lani-
atu canum interirent, aut crucibus affixi, aut flammandi, atque ubi de-
fecisset dies, in usum nocturni luminis urerentur. Hortos suos ei
spectaculo Nero obtulerat, et circense ludicrum edebat, habitu aurigæ
permixtus plebi, vel curriculo insistens. Unde quanquam adversus
sontes et novissima exempla meritos, miseratio oriebatur, tanquam
non utilitate publica, sed in sævitiam unius, absumerentur."—*Annals,*
lib. xv., § 44. Here are allusions to the death of Christ, its time and
manner, the position He held as leader of those bearing His name, the
origin of Christianity in Judæa, and its wide and rapid spread through
that and other countries, so that even at Rome it had a great number
of adherents. They come naturally into the course of the narrative,
and their authenticity has never been disputed.

§ 3. *Notices of Pagan Writers not strictly historical*

Besides these direct historical notices, we find the growth and spread of Christianity alluded to in literary works originating in various parts of the empire.

Juvenal, a contemporary of Tacitus, has been supposed to refer to Nero's persecutions in a passage[1] in his First Satire, which Dryden thus translates:

> "But if that honest license now you take,
> If into rogues omnipotent you rake,
> Death is your doom, impaled upon a stake,
> Smeared o'er with wax, and set on fire to light
> The streets, and make a dreadful blaze by night."

He also closes his Fourth Satire with some expressions[2] about Domitian, which, from some corresponding statements in the writings of Lactantius, have been supposed to allude to that emperor's cruelty to Christians.

In A.D. 104, or 112, was written the well-known letter[3] of Pliny the Younger to the Emperor Trajan,

---

[1] "Pone Tigellinum, tæda lucebis in illa
Qua stantes ardent, qui fixo gutture fumant,
Et latum media sulcum deducit arena."
Sat. I., l. 155, sq.

[2] "Atque utinam his potius nugis tota illa dedisset
Tempora sævitiæ, claras quibus abstulit Urbi
Illustresque animas impune et vindice nullo.
Sed periit, postquam cerdonibus esse timendus
Cœperat. Hoc nocuit Lamiarum cæde madenti."
Sat. IV., l. 150, sq.

[3] Caius Plinius Cæcilius Secundus, or Pliny the Younger, Governor of the province of Bithynia in A.D. 103, or according to Merivale, A.D.

in which he describes the spread of Christianity in the north of Asia Minor, and states many interesting facts respecting the religious observances of Christians.

111 (*Hist. Emp.* ch. lxv.), was a personal friend of Tacitus, and not far from the same age. He was a man of liberal education, and fond of literary pursuits. While in Bithynia, where he spent nearly two years, he wrote frequent letters to the Emperor Trajan on various matters of business and friendship. These letters, as well as many of the answers to them, he afterwards collected and published. One of them reads as follows: "It is customary, my lord, for me to refer to you all matters concerning which I have any doubt. For who can better direct my uncertainty, or instruct my ignorance? I have never been present at any examinations of Christians. So that I know not what or how much it is customary, either to punish or inquire into their conduct. Nor have I been a little doubtful whether there should be any distinction on account of age, or whether you are pleased to have the tender in no way distinguished from the more robust; whether pardon should be awarded to repentance, or whether to him who has been a Christian at all, it shall be of no avail that he has ceased to be one; whether the name itself, even if it is without actual crimes, is to be punished, or only crimes which are found connected with the name. In the meantime, in respect to those who have been brought before me as Christians, I have pursued this course: I have inquired of them whether they were Christians. Those confessing, I again and a third time interrogated, threatening the death penalty (supplicium); such as still persisted I commanded to be led away to punishment. For I had no doubt, whatever might be the nature of their opinions, that contumacy and inflexible obstinacy ought to be punished. There were some of a like infatuation whom, because they were Roman citizens, I have noted down to be sent to the city." (We omit his mention of some who consented to supplicate the gods, and to revile the name of Christ; "none of which things, they say, can they be compelled to do who are really Christians.")

"Others, named by an informer, declared themselves to be Christians, and soon after denied it; some that they had been, but had ceased to be some three years ago, and some longer, and one or more above twenty years. All these worshipped your image and the statues

About A.D. 109 certain discourses were delivered
at Nicopolis in Epirus by Epictetus, the Stoic, and
published by Arrian, which are thought to contain
allusions to Christians under the name of Galileans.[1]

of the gods: they also cursed Christ. Moreover, they affirmed that
this was the extent of their fault or error; that they were accustomed
to assemble on a stated day, before light, and sing among themselves,
alternately, a hymn to Christ, as if God; and bind themselves by an
oath, not to any wickedness, but that they would not commit theft,
nor robbery, nor adultery, that they would not falsify their word, nor,
when called upon, deny a pledge committed to them; which things
having been enacted, it was the custom for them to separate and again
come together to partake of food, a meal eaten in common, and harm-
less, which itself they had forborne to do after my edict, by which,
according to your commands, I forbade assemblies (hetærias) to be
held. From which (account) I regarded it more necessary to ascertain what was true, and that by torture, from two maid-servants, who
were called *ministræ*. But I have discovered nothing, other than a
bad and excessive superstition; and so, suspending the trial, I have
come to consult with you.

"For the affair seems to me worthy of consultation, especially on
account of the number endangered. For many of every age, of every
rank, of both sexes even, are brought into peril, and will continue to
be. For the contagion of this superstition pervades not cities only,
but towns also, and the open country, which it seems (to me) may be
restrained and corrected. It certainly is quite evident that the temples, just now nearly desolate, have begun to be frequented, and the
sacred solemnities, after a long intermission, to be revived, and everywhere victims to be sold, of which hitherto very rarely a buyer could
be found. From which it is easy to imagine what crowds of men
might be redeemed, if there were space for repentance."—Plinii *Epist.*
lib. x. 96 (al. 97).

This epistle is followed by the answer of Trajan, which is brief and
to the point, giving the desired directions, and commending his deputy
for the course he had taken. It, however, adds nothing to our present purpose.

[1] Εἶτα ὑπὸ μανίας μὲν δύναταί τις οὕτω διατιθῆναι πρὸς ταῦτα, καὶ

Not far from the same period also flourished Dion
Chrysostomus the Sophist; from an oration by whom
to the Corinthians a passage is quoted which seems
to allude to Christians as haters of the prevailing
idolatry.[1]

All of the writers thus far mentioned were subjects of the Emperor Trajan, who reigned nineteen
years, from A.D. 98 to 117. The Emperor Hadrian
succeeded him, and from his pen we find allusions to
Christians, in letters addressed in A.D. 117 to Minucius Fundanus, Proconsul of Asia,[2] and in A.D. 134
to his brother-in-law, Servianus, the consul at Rome.

ὑπὸ ἔθους, ὡς οἱ Γαλιλαῖοι, ὑπὸ λόγου δὲ καὶ ἀποδείξεως οὐδεὶς δύναται
μαθεῖν, ὅτι ὁ Θεὸς πάντα πεποίηκε τὰ ἐν τῷ κόσμῳ.—Lib. 4, c. 7.

[1] Τίνας γὰρ οὗτοι οὐ διαβεβλήκασιν οἱ πάντα διαβάλοντες; οὐ Σω-
κράτην; οὐ Πυθαγόραν; οὐ Πλάτωνα; οὐκ αὐτὸν τὸν Δία; καὶ τὸν
Ποσειδῶ; καὶ τὸν Ἀπόλλω, καὶ τοὺς ἄλλους θεούς, Corinthiac. Or.
xxxvii.

[2] It appears, according to Eusebius, that one Serenius Granianus,
Proconsul of Asia, wrote to Hadrian that it seemed to him unjust that
the Christians should be put to death only to gratify the clamors of
the people, without trial, and without any crime being proved against
them; and that Hadrian, in answer to his appeal, wrote to Minucius
Fundanus, the successor of Granianus (whose Proconsulate was about
expiring), the following letter:

"To Minucius Fundanus: I have received a letter written to me by
Serenius Granianus, an illustrious man, whom you have succeeded. It
does not seem to me, then, that this affair should be left unexamined,
in order that the people may not be excited to commotion, and opportunity (χορηγία, expense) of evil practice be afforded to informers.
If, therefore, in respect to this demand, the people of the province are
able distinctly to make confident affirmation against the Christians,
that they also may answer before the court, let them proceed in this
way, but not by importunate demands nor clamors only. For it is far

Antoninus Pius succeeded Hadrian as emperor July 10, A.D. 138, and reigned twenty-three years. To him was addressed the *First Apology* of Justin the Martyr. In an account of this apology given by Eusebius, he records the substance of an edict issued by Antoninus, addressed to the Common Council of Asia, deprecating the persecution of Christians, and alluding to the advice given in the rescript of his father Hadrian.[1]

more proper, if any one wishes to make accusation, that you should take cognizance of it. If, therefore, any one accuses and proves anything to have been done contrary to the laws, then truly do you determine according to the degree of the crime; as (on the other hand), by Hercules, if any one prefers this (charge) for the sake of slander, let him be treated with such severity as you shall regard a just recompense." The expression "importunate demands" and "clamors" (ἀξιώσεσιν) is said to refer to a popular cry of those times, on the occasion of public shows or other assemblies, "The Christians to the lions!" by which they sometimes prevailed upon the Emperor to commit acts of persecution. This letter shows that there were then Christians in Asia, and in considerable numbers, and that they were obnoxious to the mass of the people, and is, so far as it goes, a confirmation of Christian testimony respecting the same period. This is the letter which Justin Martyr appended to his *First Apology*, addressed to Antoninus Pius. It was originally written in Latin. Eusebius translated it into Greek, and inserted it in his *History*. (1st *Apol.*, c. 69; comp. A. N. Lib. Justin, p. 66.) Its genuineness is undoubted.

[1] Euseb. lib. iv., cap. 13. The genuineness of this edict is disputed by many good critics, though Lardner was disposed to accept it.

Eusebius also records a reference to this edict of Antoninus made in the apology addressed by Melito, Bishop of Sardis, to Marcus Aurelius, the son and successor of Antoninus Pius, about the year A.D. 170. The apology is transcribed by Eusebius at some length, lib. iv., cap. 26. It contains the following passage: "Of all the Roman emperors, Nero and Domitian only, who were misled by designing men,

There are some passages in the writings of Apuleius, who flourished about A. D. 163, which are thought to indicate some knowledge of Christians and their affairs. One of these is found in his work called *The Metamorphosis; or, The Golden Ass*, in which he ascribes to the wife of his master certain vices, which are supposed to be a caricature of Christian practices.[1] Another appears in his apology for marrying Pudentilla, a rich widow, in which his accusations against her brother-in-law, who appeared against him, seem in like manner to describe a Christian from a heathen point of view.[2]

have shown enmity to our religion. From them have proceeded evil reports concerning us, that are received and propagated by the vulgar; which have often been checked by your pious ancestors, who by edicts have restrained those who have been troublesome to men of our religion, among whom is your grandfather Hadrian, who wrote, as to many others, so particularly to Minucius Fundanus, Proconsul of Asia. And your father also, at the same time that you governed all things with him, wrote to several cities that they should not give us any vexation, and among them to the Larisseans, and the Thessalonians, and the Athenians, and to all the Greeks."—*Lardner's Translation ;* ch. xiv. (vol. vii. p. 127).

[1] *Metam.* lib. ix.; Valpy, vol. ii. pp. 589–91.

"Nec enim vel unum vitium nequissimæ illi fœminæ deerat; sed omnia prorsus, ut in quandam cœnosam latrinam, in ejus animum flagitia confluxerant: scœva, sæva, virosa, ebriosa, pervicax, pertinax : in rapinis turpibus avara, in sumtibus fœdis profusa : inimica fidei, hostis pudicitiæ. Tunc spretis atque calcatis divinis numinibus, in vicem certæ religionis, mentita sacrilega præsumptione Dei quem prædicaret unicum," etc.

[2] Valpy, p. 1457. (Pp. 496, 497, Flor. ed.)

"Atque ego scio, nonnullos, et cum primis Æmilianum istum, facetiæ sibi habere, res divinas deridere. Nam, ut audio, partino Œnsium

The year A.D. 176 is the date assigned by Cave to Lucian, a native of Samosata in Syria, whose writings contain extended allusions to the faith and practices of Christians, but distorted and inaccurate, as might be expected from one whose knowledge was limited and his spirit unfriendly to them.

One of these allusions is found in his letter to Cronius concerning the death of Peregrinus Proteus,[1] a famous Cynic, who publicly burned himself to death at Olympia, about the year A.D. 166.

The translation of the passage, as given by Lardner, is as follows : " At which time he learned the wonderful doctrine of the Christians by conversing with their priests and scribes near Palestine ;[2] . . .

(percensentibus ?) qui istum novere, nulli Deo ad hoc aevi supplicavit, nullum templum frequentavit ; si fanum aliquod prætereat, nefas habet adorandi gratia manum labris admovere," etc.

[1] Ὅτεπερ καὶ τὴν θαυμαστὴν σοφίαν τῶν Χριστιανῶν ἐξέμαθε, περὶ τὴν Παλαιστίνην τοῖς ἱερεῦσι καὶ γραμματεῦσιν αὐτῶν ξυγγενόμενος. . . . (?) καὶ τί γάρ ; ἐν βραχεῖ παῖδας αὐτοὺς ἀπέφηνε, προφήτης, καὶ θιασάρκης, καὶ ξυναγωγεὺς, καὶ πάντα μόνος αὐτὸς ὤν · καὶ τῶν βίβλων τὰς μὲν ἐξηγεῖτο, καὶ διεσάφει, πολλὰς δὲ αὐτὸς καὶ ξυνέγραφε · καὶ ὡς θεὸν αὐτὸν ἐκεῖνοι ἡγοῦντο καὶ νομοθέτῃ ἐχρῶντο, καὶ προστάτην ἐπέγραφον. Τὸν μέγαν γοῦν ἐκεῖνον ἔτι σέβουσι τὸν ἄνθρωπον, τὸν ἐν τῇ Παλαιστίνῃ ἀνασκολοπισθέντα, ὅτι καινὴν ταύτην τελετὴν εἰσήγαγεν ἐς τὸν βίον. . . . . . ἔπειτα δὲ ὁ νομοθέτης ὁ πρῶτος ἔπεισεν αὐτοὺς, ὡς ἀδελφοὶ πάντες εἶεν ἀλλήλων · ἐπειδὰν ἅπαξ παραβάντες, θεοὺς μὲν τοὺς Ἑλληνικοὺς ἀπαρνήσωνται, τὸν δὲ ἀνεσκολοπισμένον ἐκεῖνον σοφιστὴν αὐτῶν προσκυνῶσι, καὶ κατὰ τοὺς ἐκείνου νόμους βιῶσι.—De Morte Peregrini, c. 11–13. Lardner, *Heath. Test.*, ch. xix. (vol. vii, pp. 279–80).

[2] Tanaquil Faber conjectures that a sentence is left out here by some Christian copyist, more pious than wise, because it contained some expressions injurious to our Saviour.

and in a short time he showed they were but children to him ; for he was a prophet, high-priest, ruler
of a synagogue, uniting all offices in himself alone.

" Some books he interpreted and explained, others
he wrote ; and they spoke of him as a god, and took
him for a lawgiver, and honored him with the title
of Master. They therefore still worship that great
man who was crucified in Palestine, because he introduced into the world this new religion. . . . Moreover, their first lawgiver has taught them that they
are all brethren, when once they have turned and re-
nounced the gods of the Greeks, and worship that
Master of theirs who was crucified, and engage to
live according to his laws."

There are also passages in a fiction of Lucian
which he denominates " *True History*," [1] where he
describes a golden city in a manner so closely resembling that in Revelation xxi., as to render it probable
that it was borrowed from it.

The same date (A.D. 176) is usually assigned to
Celsus, the opponent of Christianity, whose arguments were recorded and replied to by Origen. The
original works of Celsus are lost, but the fragments
preserved to us in the argument of Origen are very
numerous and of great value.

About eighty quotations from, or references to,

---

[1] *Vera Historia*, lib. ii., ch. 6–12.

the books of the New Testament are found in them,
chiefly the four Gospels. He says that Jesus was
represented as the Word of God; called Himself
the Son of God; was a Man of Nazareth; was the
reputed Son of a carpenter; was claimed to have been
miraculously conceived; that His coming was foretold by Magi, who saw a star in the east; that the
prediction led to the slaughter of the infants by
Herod. Allusion is made to His being carried into
Egypt; to His baptism by John, and the descent of
the dove with a voice declaring Him to be the Son
of God; to the temptation by an evil spirit; to the
choice of twelve Apostles.

He admits that Jesus wrought miracles, such as
curing the sick, multiplying loaves, raising dead persons to life, restoring sight to the blind, and healing
lameness, though he seems to ascribe these to magic.

He refers to many points in the doctrine of Christ,
as contained in the Sermon on the Mount, and to the
claim of His disciples that Jesus foretold His suffer-
ings and His resurrection. He alludes to the denial
of Peter and the betrayal of Judas, and to all the
leading incidents of the crucifixion, such as the
scourging, crowning with thorns, scarlet robe, the
drink of gall, His apparent desertion by the Father,
the darkness, and the earthquake—the last two being
spoken of as asserted by His disciples. In like manner he refers to the alleged incidents of the resurrec-

tion, saying: "We take these things from your own writings, to wound you with your own weapons." Dr. Doddridge has well said: "An abridgment of the history of Christ may be found in Celsus."

The son and successor of Antoninus Pius was Marcus Aurelius, who was Emperor of Rome from A.D. 161 to 180. He was surnamed the Philosopher, and was in many respects a good ruler. A work by him, still extant, usually entitled *Meditations*,[1] contains the following passage,[2] as translated by Casaubon:[3] "That soul which is ever ready, even now presently (if need be), to be separated from the body, whether by way of extinction, or dispersion, or continuation (in another place and estate), how blessed and happy is it! But this readiness of it must proceed, not from an obstinate and peremptory resolution of the mind, violently and passionately set upon opposition (as Christians are wont); but from a peculiar judgment, with discretion and gravity, so that others may be persuaded also, and drawn to the like example, but without any noise and passionate ex-

---

[1] Τὰ εἰς ἑαυτὸν. *De rebus suis.*

[2] Οἵα ἐστὶν ἡ ψυχὴ, ἡ ἕτοιμος, ἐὰν ἤδη ἀπολυθῆναι δέῃ τοῦ σώματος, καὶ ἤτοι σβεσθῆναι, ἢ σκεδασθῆναι, ἢ συμμεῖναι. Τὸ δὲ ἕτοιμον τοῦτο, ἵνα ἀπὸ ἰδικῆς κρίσεως ἔρχηται, μὴ κατὰ ψιλὴν παράταξιν, ὡς οἱ χριστιανοί, ἀλλὰ λελογισμένως, καὶ σεμνῶς, καὶ ὥστε καὶ ἄλλον πεῖσαι, ἀτραγῳδῶς. —*Meditationes*, lib. xi., § 3.

[3] *M. A. Antoninus, the Emperor, his Meditations concerning Himself.* Translated out of the original Greek, by Meric Casaubon, D.D. 4th ed. London, 1673.

clamations." The last expression (ἀτραγῳδως) might better have been rendered "not tragically," or "without effort to imitate tragic actors." The whole passage shows that the triumphant death of Christians was a thing not unfamiliar to "the Philosopher" or his readers.

Marcus Aurelius had a teacher of Latin whose name was Fronto, an orator and rhetorician. Only certain letters of his, and a treatise on synonyms, have come down to us; but in the *Apology* of Minucius Felix (published about A.D. 210), while denying the calumnious charge of incestuous conduct made against Christians, occurs this remark:[1] "Nor does your Fronto attest it as a positive witness, but he flings it out in the way of reproach as an orator."

Another literary man of some note during the reign of Marcus Aurelius was Ælius Aristides, the Sophist, large extracts from whose orations have been preserved by Photius. In one of these he gives an account of certain "impious men in Palestine," who would not worship the gods; which is thought by Lardner[2] and others to describe Christians, though he does not use the name

---

[1] Et de incesto convivio fabulam grandem adversum nos dæmonum coitio mentita est, ut gloriam pudicitiæ deformis infamiæ aspersione macularet. . . . Sic de isto et tuus, Fronto, non, ut affirmator, testimonium fecit, sed convicium, ut orator, adspersit.—Minuc. Felix, cap. 31, *Corpus Script. Eccles. Latinorum*, vol. ii., Vienna, 1867.

[2] Lardner, ch. xx. (vol. vii. p. 295).

3

To this period also may be referred the works of
Galen, the physician, who is said to have been born
A.D. 130, and to have died about A.D. 200. In one
passage in his writings [1] he alludes to the "school of
Moses or Christ," as one "where we must receive
laws without any reason assigned;" and in another
he says: [2] "It is easier to convince the disciples of
Moses and Christ than physicians and philosophers
who are addicted to particular sects."

During the third century, as Christianity grew
into prominence, it became the subject of labored
attack on the part of Pagan writers, and of active
persecution on the part of the government, the de-
tails of which are too voluminous to be here recorded.
We shall have to content ourselves with a mere catalogue of the principal authors who made mention of
Christianity, and those emperors who thought it necessary by special edict to recognize its growing influence upon society at large.

For fuller particulars a reference is given in each
case to the original sources, of most of which an

---

[1] Κάλλιον δ' ἂν ἦν πολλᾷ προσθεῖναι τινα, εἰ καὶ μὴ βεβαίαν ἀπό-
δειξιν, παραμυθίαν γοῦν ἱκανὴν τῷ λόγῳ περὶ τῶν ἐκτὼ ποιοτήτων, ἵνα
μήτις εὐθὺς κατ' ἀρχὰς, ὡς εἰς Μοϋσοῦ καὶ Χριστοῦ διατριβὴν ἀφιγμένος,
νόμων ἀναποδείκτων ἀκούῃ, καὶ ταῦτα ἐν οἷς ἥκιστα χρή.—De Differentia Pulsuum, Ed. Basil, iii. (p. 22).

[2] Θᾶττον γὰρ ἄν τις τοὺς ἀπὸ Μοϋσοῦ καὶ Χριστοῦ μεταδιδάξει ἢ τοὺς
ταῖς αἱρέσεσι προστετηκότας ἰατρούς τε καὶ φιλοσόφους.—De Differentia
Pulsuum, iii. (p. 34).

English translation may be found in the seventh volume of Lardner's works:

Septimius Severus (Emp. 193–211) published an edict against Christians. Spartian, *Sever.*, cap. 16, 17.

Alexander Severus (Emp. 222–235) refers approvingly to certain Christian practices, as well known, when publishing an edict about the appointment of officers in the provinces. He also gave a rescript in favor of Christians, when their right to a certain spot of ground for a church edifice was disputed by the vintners of Rome. Lampridius, cap. 45, 49. Crevier, *Hist. of Rom. Emp.*, vol. viii.

Ulpian, the lawyer (fl. A.D. 220), is said to have published a treatise, now lost, upon *The Duty of Proconsuls*, in which all edicts published against Christians were recorded. Lactantius, *Inst.*, lib. v. cap. ii.

Dion Cassius (d. A.D. 230), in his *History of the Romans*, describes the destruction of Jerusalem by Titus and Vespasian, Domitian's persecution of Christians, and Nerva's leniency towards them. Lib. lxxvi. 67, 68.

Maximin, the Thracian (Emp. 235–238), is said to have persecuted the clergy of some Churches. Sulpicius Sev., lib. ii. cap. 32.

Decius (Emp. 249–251) published edicts of persecution against Christians. Basnage, ann. 250, num. iv., v. Sulp. Sev., lib. ii. cap. 32.

Gallus (Emp. 251) is said to have persecuted Christians. Euseb. *H. E.*, lib. vii. cap. 1.

Valerian (Emp. 253–260) published several edicts of persecution. Euseb. *H. E.*, lib. vii. cap. 10.

Gallienus (Emp. 260–268) issued edicts of toleration. Euseb. *H. E.*, lib. vii. cap. 13.

Amelius, the Platonic philosopher (A.D. 263), exhibits in his writings an acquaintance with the Gospel of John. Euseb. *Præp. Evang.*, lib. xi. cap. 19.

Aurelian (Emp. 270–275) alludes to Christians in a letter to the Senate of Rome about the Sibylline books. Vopiscus, *Aurel.*, cap. 20.

Porphyry (fl. A.D. 270) wrote numerous works, among which were fifteen books *Against the Christians.* He was answered by Eusebius (20 books), Apollinarius (30 books), and Methodius (10,000 lines). Only fragments of his work remain.

Hierocles (fl. A.D. 303) wrote *Truth-loving Words against the Christians*, in two books, now lost, which were answered by Lactantius and Eusebius. See Lardner, ch. xxxix., vol. vii. pp. 474–503.

In order properly to estimate the value of Pagan testimonies to the existence of Christianity, it may be well to compare the list we have now given with the entire catalogue of writers whose works are extant upon any subject, who lived during the first three centuries. For this purpose the reader is referred to Table II., where a standard list of the principal literary men of that period may be found, taken, without alteration, from the Oxford *Chronological Tables of Ancient History*.

Few persons are aware how limited is the number of writers whose works have come down to us from that period. It may surprise many to find, upon examination of the tables, that the enumeration we have just finished nearly exhausts our present catalogue of secular writers during the first three centuries. Certainly there has been no period since when the *proportionate* number of allusions to Christianity on the part of merely literary men has been nearly as great.[1]

---

[1] It may be instructive also to compare for a moment these testimonies to the authenticity of the Christian Scriptures by Pagan authors with the testimony which exists in support of the authenticity of the Pagan writers themselves. For example, the Annals of Tacitus, from which we have quoted (page 21, note 4), are not distinctly mentioned by any writer until the fifteenth century. They exist only in one manuscript brought to light during that period. While the manuscripts of the New Testament, written from the fourth to the twelfth century, now in the possession of the Church, are numbered by thousands (see Tables VIII. and IX. in this volume), yet who questions the authenticity and genuineness of the Annals of Tacitus? [Albeit M. Jules Martha is just now (January, 1895) delivering a course of lectures at the Sorbonne, in the first of which he is defending, against some recent attacks, *The Authenticity of the Manuscript of the Annals of Tacitus.*] Indeed, in the antiquity of manuscripts there is no classic work which can compare with the New Testament, unless possibly Vergil, of whose works there is one manuscript dating from the second century. But of Cæsar's Commentaries the earliest is of the ninth; of Herodotus of the tenth; of Cornelius Nepos of the

Besides this direct form of testimony to the truth of the evangelic record, and to the facts of gospel history, on the part of writers who were not friendly to Christianity, there is an evidence, not less conclusive, because undesigned, to be derived from coincidences of statement and confirmations of their accuracy which may be found in the works of such writers as Josephus, Philo, Tacitus, Dion Cassius, Strabo, and others. This argument, which would occupy too much space for our present discussion, has been well stated by Rawlinson in his seventh Bampton Lecture upon the *Historical Evidences*. The number and variety of the confirmations of the accuracy of the sacred narrative which he has thus collected is something remarkable, especially in the case of those derived from Josephus, whose studied avoidance of all direct allusion to the Christian religion and its Founder only adds weight to these involuntary testimonies to the truth.

twelfth; and of Catullus of the fifteenth. We are informed, upon the authority of Professor Ramsay, that the correspondence of Pliny with Trajan, from which that remarkable letter from Bithynia was taken, "depends on a single manuscript of unknown age, found in Paris in 1500, apparently taken to Italy in the next few years, used by several persons before 1508, and never since seen or known. In spite of this suspicious history, the correspondence is indubitably genuine." Pliny's letters are now becoming a popular text-book in our schools.

CHAPTER IV

DATA FURNISHED BY CHRISTIAN LITERATURE

§ 1. *The Apostolic Fathers*

HAVING reviewed the notices of Christianity which appear in early Pagan literature, we now come to consider those evidences of the existence and spread of Christianity which appear in or consist of the writings of early Christians. These ancient representatives of the Christian faith it has been customary to divide into two classes: Apostolic Fathers and Christian Fathers; the former term being applicable to those who are presumed to have derived their teaching directly from some one or more of the Apostles. The works usually ascribed to "apostolical men" are the Epistle of Barnabas, the Epistles of Clement of Rome, the Epistles of Ignatius, the Martyrdom of Ignatius, the Epistle of Polycarp, the Martyrdom of Polycarp, the Epistle to Diognetus, the Shepherd of Hermas, and a fragment from Papias.[1]

The *Epistle of Barnabas* was ascribed by Clem-

---

[1] Among the best critical editions of these works are: *Patrum Apostolicorum Opera*, C. J. Hefele, Tübingen, 4th ed., 1855; *Pat. Ap. Op.*, A. R. M. Dressel, Leipsic, 1863; *Pat. Ap. Op.*, O. de Gebhardt, A. Harnack, Th. Zahn, 2d ed., Leipsic, 1876–78; *Pat. Ap. Op.*, F. X. Funk, Tübingen, 1878.

ent of Alexandria and Origen to Barnabas, the company of Paul. Many distinguished recent critics have from internal evidence rejected this theory, though not with entire unanimity.[1] All agree, however, as to its great antiquity, not later than the beginning of the second century; and it is therefore possible that the writer may have been a disciple of some Apostle. The text, until recently, was complete only in a Latin version, the Greek having many mutilations; but the discovery of the Sinaitic MS. by Tischendorf in 1859 brought to light a complete Greek copy, which has greatly added to the interest taken by scholars in this Epistle.[2] Among other things, this discovery confirms the supposition that the author of the Epistle refers to Matthew's Gospel, under the formula "as it is written."[3]

[1] Neander, Hug, Baur, Hefele, Winer, Hilgenfeld, Donaldson, Westcott, and Müller reject the authorship of Barnabas, the Levite; while Gieseler, Credner, Guericke, Bleek, and Möhler sustain it. See article "Barnabas, Epistle of," in Smith's *Dict. of Chr. Biography*, by Prof. Wm. Milligan, of the Univ. of Aberdeen, who renews the controversy in favor of Barnabas as the author.

[2] See J. G. Müller, *Erklärung des Barnabasbriefes, ein Anhang zu de Wette's Exegetischen Handbuch zum Neuen Test.*, Leipsic, 1869; also an article by Dr. Donaldson, in his *History of Christian Literature and Doctrine*. A copy of the Epistle is also contained in the same MS. with the two Epistles of Clement of Rome, discovered at Constantinople by P. Bryennios. See next paragraph, p. 41, and pp. 44, 45.

[3] At the end of ch. iv. the Latin version reads: "Adtendamus, ne quando, sicut scriptum est, multi vocati, pauci vero electi inveniamur." The Greek now proves to be προσέχωμεν, μήποτε, ὡς γέγραπται, πολλοὶ κλητοὶ ὀλίγοι δὲ ἐκλεκτοὶ εὑρεθῶμεν.

Of the two Epistles ascribed in the early Church
to *Clemens Romanus*, or Clement, Bishop of Rome,
only the first presents evidence of authenticity. This
was probably written about A.D. 97. The manuscript
of it in the library of the British Museum was until
lately the only one known to be in existence. It,
with part of the so-called Second Epistle, is subjoined to the Alexandrian Codex (A) of the New Testament. In 1875, however, Philotheos Bryennios, then
Metropolitan of Serres, in Mesopotamia, published
the whole of the two Epistles from a MS. discovered
by him in the Library of the "Most Holy Sepulchre"
in Constantinople, and in 1876 a Syrian MS. of both
Epistles was found at Paris. A Latin version of
Epistle I. was also found by Morin in 1893. In this
Epistle are found quotations from the First Epistle
of Paul to the Corinthians, and such allusions or coincidences of expression as evince an acquaintance
with other Epistles of Paul, the Epistle to the Hebrews, the Epistles of James and of Peter, and perhaps other books of the New Testament. The quotations of the words of Christ found in it correspond
substantially with passages in the first three Gospels,
but may have been derived from oral tradition. The
text of Bryennios added the missing last six chapters
(57–63) to the Epistle.

Ignatius of Antioch, called also ὁ Θεοφόρος, is
said by Eusebius to have been ordained Bishop of

Antioch, as the successor of Evodius, in A.D. 69. He held this office until his death, which occurred at Rome, where he was condemned by Trajan to be devoured by wild beasts. The year of his death has been much disputed. Some of the best recent critics adopt A.D. 115 as the probable date.

Fifteen Epistles are extant which have been ascribed to this Father, eight of which are undoubtedly spurious. The remainder have suffered many interpolations, and the question of their genuineness, even in part, has been the subject of much controversy. In 1869, the Rev. Wm. Cureton, Canon of Westminster, published a history of the controversy, in a work entitled *Corpus Ignatianum*, in which he took the ground (based in part upon a recent discovery of a Syriac version of the Epistles) that three letters— to Polycarp, to the Ephesians, and to the Romans— as found in a shorter form in the Syriac recension, are the only genuine letters of Ignatius.[1]

The Martyrdom of Ignatius is a narrative which professes to have been written by those who accompanied him on his journey to Rome, and who were witnesses of his death. The account is marked by great simplicity, and accords with the particulars

[1] For a concise history of the discussion in reference to the Epistles of Ignatius, and a *résumé* of the argument in favor of the genuineness of the Syriac recension, see Appendix B to Dr. de Pressensé's *Early Years of Christianity*. Vol. II., *The Martyrs and Apologists*. New York, 1871.

given by Eusebius and Chrysostom respecting Ignatius. Its genuineness has been disputed, but the
internal evidence is decidedly in favor of an early
date at least, if not of its full acceptance as a genuine
document.

Polycarp, Bishop of Smyrna, is believed to have
been born about A.D. 80. Irenæus says thât " Polycarp was instructed by the Apostles, and was brought
into contact with many who had seen Christ." [1]
(*Adv. Hær.*, iii. 3.) The Epistle of Polycarp to the
Philippians is a deeply interesting document, the
authenticity of which is generally admitted. It appears to have been written not long after the death
of Ignatius. It abounds in quotations from, and coincidences of expression with, the books of the New
Testament.

The martyrdom of Polycarp occurred, according
to Eusebius (*H. E.*, iv. 15), in the persecution under
the Emperors Marcus Aurelius and Lucius Verus.
It is recorded in a *Letter* from the Church at Smyrna
to the Churches of Philomelium and other places.
The narrative describes many touching incidents il-
lustrative of Polycarp's faith and constancy. When
urged to secure his release by reviling Christ, he
said : " Eighty and six years have I served Him, and
He has done me no wrong. How, then, can I revile
my King and my Saviour ?"

[1] See § 2 (10), below, p. 50.

In addition to the testimony of living witnesses of
the apostolic life and labors, other works are in existence which bear marks of equal antiquity, but whose
authorship cannot be definitely ascertained. One of
the most remarkable of these is the *Epistle* addressed
by some anonymous apostolical man to a prominent
Pagan, Diognetus (supposed by Lightfoot to be
identical with the tutor of Marcus Aurelius), in reply
to certain inquiries about Christianity. It was probably written towards the latter part of the second
century. In style and diction it ranks among the
best, and the argument exhibits throughout a high-
toned spiritual discernment. (See Semisch, in Her-
zog's *Encyl.*, Art. *Diognet.*)

Also the *Didaché* (Διδαχὴ τῶν δώδεκα αποστόλων),
or *Teaching of the* (*twelve*) *Apostles*, a work referred
to by Eusebius and others, but of which no MS. was
known to be in existence until 1873, when a copy
was discovered by Bryennios at Constantinople, in
the same precious volume which is referred to above.
It consists of sixteen chapters, the first part of which
sets forth the " way of life," and the second gives
prescriptions respecting the sacraments and other ecclesiastical usages. It appears to belong to the end
of the first or the beginning of the second century.
It is eminently scriptural, and full of interest to the
devout scholar. The octavo manuscript volume in
which it was found contains also the Epistle of Bar-

nabas, the two Epistles of Clement, Chrysostom's Synopsis of the Books of the Old and New Testaments, the Epistle of Mary of Cassobela to Ignatius, and twelve Epistles of Ignatius. The *Didaché* was published by Bryennios at Constantinople in 1883, and in 1884 it was edited, with a translation and notes, by the late President Hitchcock, assisted by Prof. Francis Brown of the Union Theol. Seminary, New York.

Mention should also be made of the *Shepherd of Hermas*, a book commonly published among the writings of the Apostolic Fathers, and conjectured by Origen to have been written by the Hermas whom Paul salutes in the Epistle to the Romans. The evidence is well-nigh conclusive that it belongs to a later period, and the most probable conjecture assigns the authorship to a brother of Pius, Bishop of Rome, A.D. 142–157. It is a collection of visions, commandments, and parables, and is chiefly valuable as showing in what way Christianity at that day was endangered by the influence of Jewish principles. It has many coincidences with, and allusions to, the language of the New Testament. (See the *Witness of Hermas to the Four Gospels*, by C. Taylor, D.D., St. John's College, Cambridge, London, 1892.)

Belonging to this period also we find the works of *Papias*, Bishop of Hierapolis in Phrygia, who flourished, according to Cave, about A.D. 110–163. In his five books, entitled *An Explication of the Oracles of the Lord*, he makes distinct reference to certain Gospels bearing the names of Matthew [1] and Mark, and to the First Epistles of Peter and of John, and alludes to the Acts and the Revelation. [2]

Besides these testimonies of Papias, we have those of others who occupied a similar position with him, preserved to us in fragments by Irenæus.

He records sentences uttered by "the elders, dis-

[1] The testimony of Papias, as recorded by Eusebius, is as follows: "Mark having become the interpreter of Peter, wrote down accurately whatsoever he remembered. It was not, however, in exact order that he related the sayings or deeds of Christ. For he neither heard the Lord nor accompanied Him. But afterwards, as I said, he accompanied Peter, who accommodated his instructions to the necessities (of his hearers), but with no intention of giving a regular narrative of the Lord's sayings. Wherefore Mark made no mistake in thus writing some things as he remembered them. For of one thing he took special care, not to omit anything he had heard, and not to put anything fictitious into the statements. This is what is related by Papias regarding Mark; but with regard to Matthew he has made the following statements: Matthew put together the oracles (of the Lord) in the Hebrew language, and each one interpreted them as best he could." In the introduction to his books Papias says: "If, then, any one who attended on the elders came, I asked him minutely after their sayings —what Andrew or Peter said, or what was said by Philip, or by Thomas, or by James, or by John, or by Matthew, or by any other of the Lord's disciples: which things Aristion and the presbyter John, the disciples of the Lord, say. For I imagined that what was to be got from books was not so profitable to me as what came from the living and abiding voice."—*Apost. Fathers.* Ante-Nicene Lib., pp. 442, 446.

[2] Upon the lives and testimony of Polycarp and Papias, see the valuable treatise of Bishop Lightfoot, *Essays on the Work Entitled Essays on Supernatural Religion*, London and New York, 1889; also his *Biblical Essays*, 1893.

ciples of the Apostles," in which allusion is made to the Gospels of Matthew and of John, and the Epistles to the Romans, Corinthians, Ephesians, and probably First Peter. (Routh, *Reliquiæ Sacræ*, I., 47 ff. Oxford, 1846.)

§ 2. *The Apologists and Martyrs.*

We now come into the period of Christian apologists, who wrote for the express purpose of defending the Christian religion against the attacks of its adversaries.

(1) First among these in the order of time is *Quadratus*, whom Eusebius calls a "disciple of the Apostles," who addressed an Apology to the Emperor Hadrian, who reigned A.D. 117–138. It is said to have been characterized by ability and sound doctrine. Only fragments of it now remain, as quoted by Eusebius. In one of these he says: "The works of our Saviour were always conspicuous, for they were real; both they which were healed and they which were raised from the dead; who were seen not only when they were healed or raised, but for a long time afterwards; not only while He dwelt on the earth, but also after His departure, and for a good while after it, insomuch that some of them have reached to our times." With Quadratus may be mentioned Aristides, an Athenian philosopher, who

addressed an apology to the Emperor Hadrian some time between 125 and 140 A.D., containing allusions to the incarnation, resurrection, and ascension of Jesus. A Syriac translation of the work has recently been discovered in the convent of St. Catharine on Mt. Sinai. These two may be called the earliest Christian apologists.

(2) *Justin*, the Philosopher and Martyr, born in Shechem (Sichem, Flavia Neapolis, Nâblus), Samaria, about A.D. 103; converted to Christianity A.D. 133; taught in Ephesus, Alexandria, and Rome, and in the intermediate cities, as an evangelist. He wrote two Apologies, the first in A.D. 147, addressed to Antoninus Pius; the second in 161–166, to Marcus Aurelius. His dialogue with the Jew, Trypho, a defence of Christianity against Judaism, was written about A.D. 150. His works contain about 200 citations from the New Testament Scriptures. A tolerably complete life of Jesus might be compiled from them. Says Rawlinson (*Hist. Ev.*, p. 215): "No one can pretend to doubt that in Justin's time the facts of New Testament history were received as simple truth, not only by himself, but by Christians generally, in whose name his apologies were addressed to the emperors."

(3) *Theophilus*, Bishop of Antioch, born A.D. 110, converted 150, died 181 (Lardner), wrote an Apology in three books addressed to Autolycus, a learned

Gentile, a Harmony of the Gospels, and some other works.[1]

(4) *Melito*, Bishop of Sardis, in Lydia, in addition to a number of works, the titles of which are given by Eusebius (*H. E.*, iv. 26) and Jerome (*De Vir. Ill.*, c. 24), wrote an Apology about A.D. 170–177, addressed to Marcus Aurelius (referred to above, p. 32, note 3), and a Treatise or Commentary on the Revelation of St. John.

(5) At about the same date, also, *Claudius Apollinaris*, Bishop of Hierapolis, addressed an Apology to the same emperor.   His other works are enumerated by Eusebius, l. iv., c. 27, and Jerome, *De Vir. Ill.*, c. 26.

(6) To about the same date may also be assigned *Tatian*, the Syrian Sophist, a disciple of Justin, who, besides numerous other treatises, wrote an *Oration to the Greeks*,[2] and a Harmony of the Gospels called *Dia Tessaron* (διὰ τεσσάρων), the Arabic text of which, with a Latin translation, was published in Rome by A. Ciasca in 1888.   An English translation now appears with introduction and notes by J. H. Hill, published (1894) by the Clarks of Edinburgh.

(7) *Dionysius*, Bishop of Corinth, wrote seven

---

[1] Published by J. C. T. Otto.   Jena, 1861.

[2] Published at Paris, 1624, in *Bibliotheca Veterum Patrum*, vol. i., pp. 160–187.   Comp. Adolph Harnack, *Texte und Untersuchungen*, I. i. 3, 1882, pp. 196–232.

Epistles, about A.D. 171–176, addressed to the Lace-
dæmonians, the Athenians, the Nicomedians, to the
Church in Gortyna (Crete), Amastris (Paphlagonia),
and the Churches throughout Pontus, to the Gnos-
sians (Crete), and to the Romans, the latter addressed
to Soter (Σωτήρ), Bishop of Rome. (Euseb., *H. E.*,
iv. 23.)   In the brief fragments which remain of the
writings of Dionysius are to be found traces of an
acquaintance with the Gospel of Matthew, the Acts,
the First Epistle to the Thessalonians, and the Apocalypse.

(8) *Athenagoras*, the Philosopher of Athens, wrote
from Alexandria about A.D. 177 an Apology inscribed
to Marcus Aurelius and Commodus, entitled *Legatio
pro Christianis*, and one called *De Resurrectione*.
(Migne, *Patrologia*, Ser. Græca, vol. vi.)

(9) To this period, 170–180, also belongs *Hegesip-
pus*, the first Church historian, " who," says Jerome,
" composed a history of the affairs of the Church,
from the Passion of our Lord to his own time."
There were five books in all, only a few fragments
of which now remain ; but the whole were in possession of Christians under Constantine, and Eusebius
quotes freely from them. (*Historia Ecclesiastica*, ii.
23 ; iii. 20, 32.)

(10) Next in the order of time may be mentioned
Irenæus, the disciple of Polycarp and Papias, who
was born about A.D. 130, in Ionia of Asia Minor, and

who succeeded the Martyr Pothinus as Bishop of
Lyons in Gaul. His bishopric extended from the
persecution under Marcus Aurelius in A.D. 177, in
which Pothinus suffered, to his own martyrdom in
A.D. 202, under Septimius Severus. His works were
numerous. The names of some of them are given
by Eusebius, lib. v. 20, 26 (see, also, Ante-Nicene Chr.
Lib., vol. v.). His work *Against Heresies* is the only
one which has come down to us entire. This consists of five books, and gives abundant testimony to
the four Gospels, the Acts of the Apostles, twelve of
Paul's Epistles, 1 Peter, 1 and 2 John, and Revelation, which last is expressly ascribed to John, the be-
loved disciple.

He says that the Four Evangelists are the four
columns of the Church . . . and sees in this number
four a peculiar appointment of the Creator of the
world. Most interesting is his own account of his
interview with Polycarp, and of that aged martyr's
testimonies to the early facts of Christianity. He
says in his letter to Florinus: "While I was yet a
boy I saw thee, in Lower Asia, with Polycarp, distinguishing thyself in the royal court, and endeavoring to gain his approbation. For those things which
then transpired I hold better in memory than such
as have happened recently; for events which happened in infancy seem to grow with the mind, and
to become part of ourselves; so that I can recall the

very place where the blessed Polycarp used to sit
and teach, his going out and his coming in, his mode
of life, his appearance, the style of his address to the
people, his familiar intercourse with St. John and
with the rest of those who had seen the Lord, and
how he remembered their sayings ; whatever he had
heard from them concerning our Lord, His miracles
and mode of teaching, Polycarp, being instructed by
those who were eye-witnesses of the Word, recounted
in strict agreement with the Scriptures." His works
were published by Erasmus at Basle in 1526. Other
editions have appeared, among the latest of which is
one by W. Wigan Harvey, Cambridge, England,
1857.

(11) Hardly less important is the testimony derived from the works of the learned *Hippolytus*, the
pupil of Irenæus (born about A.D. 170 and martyred
in A.D. 235), Bishop of Portus, at the mouth of the
Tiber, from A.D. 198 to 235, nearly forty years. He
was a voluminous writer, and the first preacher of
note in the Church of Rome after Clement. A list
of his works, somewhat imperfect, is given by Eusebius, *H. E.*, vi. 22, and Jerome, *De Vir. Ill.*, c. 61. (See
A. N. Chr. Lib., vol. ix.) In 1842 a manuscript was
discovered at Mount Athos which proves to be a
long-lost work of this Father *Against all Heresies.*
It is a work of great interest and value. Bunsen
gives extracts from it in his *Hippolytus and His*

Age. It was published first at Oxford, in 1851, by
E. Miller; and much better edited, with a Latin version, by Duncker and Schneidewin, Göttingen, 1859.
It was probably written about A.D. 225 (*Biblioth. Sac.*,
x., p. 220). In 1886 a commentary of Hippolytus on
the prophecy of Daniel came to light by the discovery and publication of the whole of the fourth book
by M. Georgiades. It treats of chapters 7–12 of the
Prophecy, and discusses the birth and death of Christ
and the history of Christmas. Hippolytus was finally banished to the mines of Sardinia, and there put
to death on account of his faith. His remains were
afterwards brought back to Portus, and a church
erected over his grave.

§ 3. *The Catechetical Schools of Alexandria and Carthage*

We now approach the period in the history of the
Church distinguished by the establishment and growing influence of the *Catechetical School of Alexandria.*

This institution, whose teachers and pupils were
among the ablest of antiquity, began to have a dis-
tinctive and recognized existence about A.D. 160, and
continued to flourish till about A.D. 395. It seems
to have originated in a mere school of catechumens.
It eventually became a fountain of profound learning and world-wide influence. The first permanent

teacher of whom we have definite knowledge was Pantænus, although Athenagoras is alleged by some to have preceded him (A.D. 160–181). Pantænus taught from 181 to about 189, and was succeeded by Clement.[1] Clement died about A.D. 220, and Origen[2] followed him (b. 186, appointed teacher 203, d. 254).

Contemporary with Clement and the Greek school was the establishment of the *Western Theological School in North Africa*, which was founded by Tertullian (b. Carthage 160, converted 190, d. 240), and originated the Latin ecclesiastical language, its teachers being Latins. Of these, Cyprian,[3] Bishop of Carthage (b. 200, converted 246, d. Sept. 14, 258), was contemporary with Origen. These were followed in both schools by a succession of eminent teachers and writers whose names and works take a prominent place in the history of the third and fourth centuries —Dionysius, Bishop of Alexandria (247–265), Gregory Thaumaturgus (244–270), Theognostus (261–280), Eusebius the Historian, Bishop of Cæsarea (270–340), Athanasius (296–373), and Didymus (314–394) of

[1] Titus Flavius Clemens Alexandrinus, born in Athens, became Christian and presbyter in Alexandria; disciple of Pantænus. His works, in 4 vols., published by William Dindorf, Oxford, 1869.

[2] Origenes Alexandrinus. Works published by C. H. E. Lommatzsch in 25 vols., Berlin, 1831–48. *Homo ille mirificus . . . qui libros innumerabiles scripsit* (Tisch. p. 1146).

[3] Thascius Cæcilius Cyprianus, Bishop of Carthage. Works published by William Hartel, Vienna, 1868.

the Greek, and Arnobius (280–330), Lactantius (260–340), Hilary (320–368), Ambrose (340–397), Augustine (354–430) of the Latin school.

Table III. presents a comparative diagram intended to illustrate the position occupied by the Christian Fathers relatively to each other in the order of time. It will be noticed that there has been no period since the beginning of the second century in which there were not living several prominent leaders of the Church, whose works are still extant. For example, during the first half of the second century seven Christian writers were contemporaneous; and during the second half of the same century no less than ten lived and wrote. All these men must have been more or less familiar with each other. Of course, the names in the *later* periods might have been greatly multiplied if space had permitted.

In Table V. the reader will find a list of references to the *canonical* books by ecclesiastical writers from the second to the fourth century; and in Table VI. a record of the authoritative judgments upon the *disputed* books by leaders of the Church in all its branches throughout the Empire during the first three centuries. If he will compare these references with what is said about the works of Tacitus on p. 37, note 1, it may help him to form a conception of the strength of Patristic testimony as an evidence of the authenticity of the Christian Scriptures. Indeed, the

classic writers can bear no comparison in the matter
of quotations or references.   There is a single possible allusion to the Annals of Tacitus in a work of
the fifth century.   Herodotus is quoted only once
for two centuries after his death.   Thucydides for
the same period is not quoted at all.   Livy was not
quoted for a century after he wrote ; and the Roman
History of Velleius Paterculus (mentioned in our list
on p. 21, note 1, as among the authors anterior to the
Christian era) has, we are informed by Dr. Salmon,
"come down to us in a single very corrupt manuscript, and the book is only once quoted by Priscian,
a grammarian of the sixth century." (See McCly-
mont, *The New Testament and its Writers*, p. 5.
New York, 1893.)

CHAPTER V

§ 1. *Evidence furnished by Heretical Writings*

PARALLEL with the evidence of a Christian literature is the testimony furnished by those who opposed
Christianity or were accused of perverting its doctrines. In the act of contending with the truth they
incidentally prove the existence of the records and
writings whose lessons they oppose or misinterpret.
Says Irenæus, in his work *Against Heresies:* " Such
is the certain truth of our Gospels that the heretics
themselves bear testimony to them, every one of them
endeavoring to prove his particular doctrines from
thence. But the Ebionites may be confuted from
the Gospel of Matthew, which alone they receive.
Marcion useth only the Gospel of Luke, and that
mutilated. Nevertheless, from what he retains, it
may be shown that he blasphemes the one only God.
They who divide Jesus from Christ, and say that
Christ always remained impassible, while Jesus suffered, prefer the Gospel of Mark. However, if they
read with a love of truth they may thence be con-
vinced of their error. The Valentinians receive the

Gospel of John entire, in order to prove their pairs of æons; and by that Gospel they may be confuted, as I have shown in the first book of this work." [1] (*Ad Hær.*, III. ii. 7, Lardner's translation.)

Our knowledge of the ancient heretical writings is derived mainly from the replies to them now found in the works of Christian Fathers, especially those of Irenæus, Tertullian, and Eusebius. If we take the latter for a guide, our list would begin with Simon Magus. Eusebius says: "From Menander, successor of Simon, proceeded two leaders of heresies, Saturninus of Antioch and Basilides of Alexandria, who set up schools of their hateful doctrine, one in Syria, the other in Egypt." (*H. E.*, iv. 7.) It is probable, however, that before Saturninus we should notice Cerinthus, who flourished, according to Le Clerc, about the year 80, though Basnage puts him at A.D. 101.

It will suffice for our present purpose merely to give a list of the more prominent (so-called) heretical writers, with their probable dates. A full account of them and their doctrines may be found in Lardner's works.

	A.D.
Simon Magus of Samaria	
Menander, the Gnostic of Samaria	
Saturninus of Antioch	about 112
Carpocrates of Alexandria	" 120

---

[1] *Works of Irenæus.* The ed. of W. Harvey, Cambridge, 1857–58, is good.

A.D.

Basilides of Alexandria	about 125
Marcion, of Pontus, disciple of Cerdon . . .	" 140
Valentinus, founder of the Valentinians . . .	" 140
Cerdon, of Rome	" 141
Leucius, or Lucian, disciple of Marcion . . .	" 145
Heracleon, the Valentinian	" 160
Theodotus, the Valentinian	" 160
Apelles, of Asia, disciple of Marcion	" 160
Marcus, founder of the Marcosians	" 160
Hermogenes, of Africa	" 170
Montanus, founder of Montanism	" 171
Cassian, the Docete	" 190
Theodotus, "the tanner," of Byzantium . . .	" 192
Praxeas, of Africa (?)	" 196
Artemon, "the Unitarian" (Lardner)	" 200

§ 2. *Evidence from Tangible Memorials*

We have said in the outset that if the facts of
Gospel history are authentic, they must have left be-
hind them tangible relics, material structures, memo-
rial stones, which would have been familiar to the
people of the days of Constantine. There is abundant evidence that such memorials did exist all over
the empire.

In the first place, the tombstones of the Martyrs,
sacredly cherished, were like mile-stones of history,
connecting the third century with apostolic times.
In the Roman Catacombs, extending beneath the
Imperial City through hundreds of miles[1] of exca-

---

[1] Mr. Spencer Northcote estimates an aggregate of 900 miles of
streets and 7,000,000 graves.

vated streets, were to be found thousands of graves
still bearing the emblems of the Christian faith, still
sacred to the memory of those who had sealed their
testimony with their blood, the date of whose martyrdom extended back to the days of cruel Nero, and of
Paul himself.

Multitudes of these still exist, and their testimony
is unequivocal. Not only the personal history of the
Martyrs, but historical scenes in the Old and New
Testaments are plainly depicted upon them. The
adoration of the Magi, their interview with Herod,
the baptism of Christ by John, the healing of the
paralytic, the turning of water into wine, the feeding
of the five thousand, the raising of Lazarus, the Last
Supper, Peter walking on the sea, Pilate washing his
hands before the people, etc. The parables of our
Lord—the Good Shepherd, the Sower, the Wise and
Foolish Virgins—are there delineated.[1]

The symbols of Christian faith—the cross (but
never the crucifix), the dove, the olive-branch, the
anchor, the fish—all yet bear witness to New Testament revelation, and in those days must have been
tenfold more significant, as the individual cases were
more familiar.

In Alexandria, also, are similar catacombs, one of
which was opened twenty-six years since (1869), and

---

[1] See Rawlinson's *Hist. Evidences.*

was visited by the writer.   There is no reason to
doubt that similar memorials of Christian and martyred dead were to be found in the days of Constantine in all parts of the empire.

We are not to forget, also, that the conversion of
Constantine marks the era of the identification of
sites and the localities of sacred scenes in Palestine
and elsewhere.   The foundations of the Church of
the Holy Sepulchre were laid in Jerusalem by Constantine in A.D. 326, and the dedication took place in
335.   The place of the nativity, the tomb of Lazarus,
the Garden of Gethsemane, the chamber of the supper, the place of baptism, and a hundred other localities dear to the Christian heart, were more or less
definitely pointed out by a reverent local tradition.
Untrustworthy and superstitious as much of that
tradition undoubtedly was, it nevertheless exhibits
the universal and unquestioning belief of the facts
which it commemorates.

We have already seen that church edifices were in
existence all over the empire, some of them very elegant.   The Churches which built them must have
had a history reaching back a century or more.   Some
of them must have had tangible and documentary
relics of primitive times.   We have allusion to something of this kind in the works of Tertullian (A.D.
160–240) of Carthage.   " Come now," he says, ad-
dressing one who had taken an erroneous view of

Scriptural salvation—"come now, thou who wilt exercise thy curiosity more profitably in the business
of thy salvation, run through the Apostolic Churches,
in which the very chairs of the Apostles still preside
—in which their authentic (or original ?) letters are
recited, sounding forth the voice and representing
the countenance of each.   Is Achaia near you, you
have Corinth.   If you are not far from Macedonia,
you have Thessalonica.   If you are near to Italy, you
have Rome, from whence, also, our assertion will be
readily confirmed." [1]

The Governors of Roman provinces were accustomed to send to Rome accounts of remarkable transactions, which were preserved in the Roman archives.
Pontius Pilate is said to have given an account of
the death and resurrection of Christ in his memoirs
of Jewish affairs, called *Acta Pilati*.

Eusebius (A.D. 315), referring to them, says:
"Our Saviour's resurrection being much talked of

---

[1] *De Præsc. Hæret.* cxxxvi. (Ante-Nicene Lib., vol. ii., p. 42).   It has
been customary to discredit these statements as extravagant and untrustworthy ; and so they may be, but there surely is no intrinsic im-
probability in the thing itself.   Papyrus manuscripts exist and are
legible to-day, which bear dates more than three thousand years old.
Documents on common paper may be found in good preservation in
nearly every town in England several hundred years older than were
these to which Tertullian refers.   The original records of the Plymouth
Colony are in the County Court-house at Plymouth, in the handwrit-
ing of Governor Bradford ; and many original letters of the Pilgrim
Fathers are extant.

throughout Palestine, Pilate informed the Emperor of it." [1]

It was the constant practice of primitive Christians, when disputing with the Gentiles, to appeal to these *Acts*, or records, thus deposited in the archives of the empire.

Thus Justin, in his first *Apology*, having quoted the prophecy (Is. xxxv. 6) of the miracles of Christ, adds, "And that He did these things you may know from the Acts of Pontius Pilate." [2]

Tertullian, after describing the crucifixion, resurrection, and ascension,[3] says : "Of all these things relating to Christ, Pilate himself, in conscience already a Christian, sent an account to Tiberius, then Emperor." Of Christ's death he writes thus : "At the same moment daylight disappeared, while the sun was at the meridian. Those who knew not that this was also predicted concerning Christ supposed it to be an eclipse. And ye still have this event related in your archives."

To this class of visible facts might be added the universally practised Christian ordinances, Baptism and the Lord's Supper, which were in some sense

---

[1] See Lardner, *Heath. Test.*, ch. ii. (vol. vi., p. 607 *seq.*). Documents purporting to be copies of these *Acts* have from time to time appeared, but are unauthentic.

[2] *Works*, Ante-Nicene Lib., vol. ii., pp. 47, 48.

[3] *Apology*, c. 21.

monumental, testifying by their perpetual recurrence, and by the uniform Christian explanation of them, to the great central truths which they were designed to commemorate.

§ 3. *Retrospective View—Concluding Remarks*

We have thus reviewed, in chronological order, the principal testimonies—Pagan, Christian, Heretical, and Monumental—to the authenticity of the sacred record, which are found to span the interval between the Christian era and the age of Constantine.

Let us now take a retrospective view, resuming the standpoint assumed in the first chapter, by the side of a believer, at the beginning of the fourth century.

We find him living in an age when "the intellectual powers of man have become almost entirely absorbed in religious controversies" (see Table II., under date A.D. 310).

We find thousands of Christian Churches all over the empire (ch. ii., p. 6), many of which claim to have had a continuous history since the Apostles founded them, with edifices, manuscript records, relics, and tombstones extending through the whole period (ch. v., p. 45). We find catechetical schools at Alexandria and Carthage, which are now over a century old, whose present teachers are the eminent Eusebius

and Athanasius among the Greeks, and Arnobius and
Lactantius among the Latins; while the Fathers tell
us of Clement and Tertullian, of Origen and Cyprian,
who have preceded them.   We find in the libraries
of these schools the works of an unbroken chain of
ecclesiastical writers extending back to the pupils of
the Apostle John.   We find a parallel succession of
heretical writings and of the controversies they have
elicited based upon the recognized authenticity of
New Testament books.   We find that a large proportion of all the Pagan writers of the period, whose
themes would permit them to do so, have taken notice of the growing power of Christianity.   We find
a history of persecution in the archives of the empire,
in the published appeals and defences of Christians,
in the annals of Christian and heathen historians, in
the Catacombs of Rome and Alexandria, and still
more indelibly recorded in the hearts of Christian
people, in the family traditions, in the precious mem-
ories of fathers and mothers, of bishops and presby-
ters, who were among the victims.

If we had found, besides all this, an ambitious
critic who undertook to set up an ingenious theory
that the historical statements of New Testament
history were fabulous, that the Roman empire was
imposed upon, that Christianity had no historical
foundation, that it was the offspring of fertile imaginations, that a "myth" had sprung up in the full

5

splendor of the first Augustan age, what should we have said to him? What would any intelligent Roman have said to him?

But ancient literature furnishes no such example of critical temerity. In all the voluminous works of controversy, of attack and defence of the Christian Religion which have come down to us from that day, not one, either Pagan or Christian, attempts to deny the reality of the main events which form the basis of Gospel history.

Such adversaries as Celsus, and Porphyry, and Hierocles, writing extensive and labored arguments against Christianity, do not think of disputing the historical character of the main facts on which it is based. They discuss the doings of Jesus and the teachings of Paul and Peter as of persons whose general historical existence and the substance of whose history nobody questions.

There is the usual amount of misrepresentation of their conduct and misconception of their doctrine, but not a word about their mythical origin. This discovery was reserved for the astute metaphysicians of the nineteenth century!

"When faith," says Rawlinson, "is a matter of life and death, men do not lightly take up with the first creed which happens to hit their fancy, nor do they place themselves openly in the ranks of a persecuted sect, unless they have well weighed the claims of the religion which it professes." It is clear that the early converts had means of ascertaining the historic accuracy of the Christian records very much beyond our own. To assume that they did not use them when so much was at stake is to deny them the average share of common-sense. It is to affirm the occurrence of a greater miracle than any recorded in the New Testament.

NOTE.—The work of Strauss, *Das Leben Jesu, kritisch bearbeitet*, appeared at Tübingen in 1835. The denial of the supernatural had its natural sequence in the denial of the historical verity of those acts and words which constitute the Christ of the New Testament, the greatest miracle of history. The Gospels, therefore, could not be records of fact, but legendary embodiments of the pious conceptions of primitive Christians. According to Strauss, the true Son of God, who was born of the Holy Spirit, who worked miracles, died and rose again, is *humanity* itself, an abstraction impossible to be realized in the actual, but nevertheless an ideal which the Christian imagination had personified in Jesus of Nazareth.

The effect of this formulation of the logical tendencies of their philosophy was somewhat startling to the friends as well as to the opponents of the extreme rationalistic school of interpretation. The field of controversy was shifted from theories to facts. A new impulse was given to historical inquiry and to critical exegesis, the fruits of which have enriched the German and English literature with many works of great value. Among these we have space only to mention a very few, such as Neander, *Das Leben Jesu Christi* (1837; English translation, New York, 1848); W. H. Mill, *On the Attempted Application of Pantheistic Principles to the Theory and Historic Criticism of the Gospels* (London, 1840–44); Norton, *On the Genuineness of the Gospels* (London, 1847).

In 1864 there appeared a second work of Strauss, entitled *Das Leben Jesu für das Deutsche Volk*, in which he found it needful to supplement his mythical theory by including wanton fraud for theological purposes, charging wilful falsification upon the promulgators of the Gospel histories.

The general theory of Strauss is reviewed in the *Bib. Sacra* for 1845 by H. B. Hackett, and in the *New Englander* for 1864 by G. P. Fisher, and the *New Life of Jesus* is discussed in the *Bib. Sacra* for 1866 by J. I. Mombert, and in the *Journal of Sac. Lit.* for 1865–66–67, by C. A. Row.

The last thirty years have produced many valuable treatises upon the life of Jesus, founded on the true historical and critical basis, such as those of De Pressensé (Paris and London, 1865), Farrar (London, 1874), Geikie (London, 1877), Edensheim (London and New York, 1886).

The student will also find profit in a careful reading of some of the special works upon the evidences of Christianity which have been referred to in the foregoing pages, such as Rawlinson's *Historical Evidences* (London, 1859 ; Boston, 1860) ; Row's *Bampton Lectures* (1877) ; *The Logic of Christian Evidences* (1880), by G. F. Wright, of Oberlin, Ohio ; and *The Authorship of the Fourth Gospel*, by Ezra Abbot, D.D., LL.D. (Boston, 1880).

PART II

HISTORY

OF THE

CANON OF THE NEW TESTAMENT

THE CANON

OF

THE NEW TESTAMENT

---

§ 1. *History of the Canonical Books*

OUR general survey of the field has demonstrated the practicability of arriving at trustworthy data for tracing the history of the New Testament books.

We may, therefore, treat them like other subjects of historical research, and proceed to a direct account of their origin and subsequent disposition.

Each of the books which now go to make up the New Testament canon was the outgrowth of circumstances in the life or labors of the author, very much as books have ever been. The Letters of Paul and other New Testament books were written at periods and for a purpose more or less plainly manifest in their tenor, or in Luke's record of the events which attended the growth of the primitive Church. This is not the place for particular discussion of these events, nor is it easy to give precise dates for the origin of any of the books, but it will be sufficient for our present purpose to indicate an approximate arrangement of dates somewhat in the following order :

		A.D.
First Epistle to Thessalonians	from Corinth,	about 53–55
Second Epistle to Thessalonians	" Corinth,	" 53–55
Epistle to Galatians. .	" Ephesus,	" 56, 57
First Epistle to Corinthians	" Ephesus,	" 57, 58
Second Epistle to Corinthians.	" Philippi,	" 57, 58
Epistle to Romans . .	" Corinth,	" 58–60
Epistle of James . .	" Jerusalem,	" 62, 63
Epistles to Ephesians, Colossians, Philemon, Philippians, Hebrews; Luke, Acts	" Rome ?	" 63–67
First Peter	" Babylon (Rome ?),	" 64
First Timothy . . .	" Macedonia,	" 64–66
Titus	" Epirus,	" 64–66
Second Timothy. . .	" Rome,	" 66–68
Second Peter	" (?)	" 67, 68
Gospel of Matthew . .	" Judæa,	" 68, 69
Gospel of Mark . . .	" Rome,	" 68, 69
Epistle of Jude . . .	" Jerusalem,	" 68–90
Gospel of John . . .	" Ephesus,	" 78–90
Revelation of St. John .	" Ephesus,	" 81–96?
First, Second, and Third Epistles of John . .	" Ephesus,	" 97–100

It thus appears that all the books which now compose the New Testament were written during the last half of the first century.

They were doubtless written upon papyrus,[1] chiefly

---

[1] 2 John 12: "Having many things to write unto you, I would not write with paper ($\chi\acute{\alpha}\rho\tau\eta\varsigma$) and ink; but I trust to come unto you,"

by the hands of amanuenses,[1] with a reed,[2] and conveyed to their several destinations by messengers. After having been publicly read in the Churches to which they were sent,[3] or by the individuals to whom they were addressed, the documents, both epistolary and historical, were multiplied by copying, the copies being sent to other Churches,[4] or purchased by individuals.[5] This work of transcription must have hastened the defacement and decay of the originals, though they were undoubtedly preserved for many years with great care.

On the other hand, the multiplication of copies and their public reading in the Churches tended to secure the sacred books from destruction or interpolation. So rapid was this diffusion, and so universal

etc. Yet parchment was in occasional though not familiar use at the time the New Testament books were written. 2 Timothy iv. 13.

[1] Rom. xvi. 22: "I, Tertius, who wrote this Epistle, salute you in the Lord."

[2] 3 John 13: "I had many things to write, but I will not with ink and pen (κάλαμος) write unto thee."

[3] 1 Thess. v. 27: "I charge you by the Lord that this Epistle be read unto all the holy brethren."

[4] Col. iv. 16: "And when this Epistle is read among you, cause that it be read also in the Church of the Laodiceans; and that ye likewise read the Epistle from Laodicea."

[5] Norton, in his work On the Genuineness of the Gospels, has made some calculations which tend to show that as many as 60,000 copies of the Gospels were circulated among Christians at the end of the second century. Vol. i., pp. 28–34 (London, 1847). Jerome (331–420) says that there was a copy of the original of the Gospel by Matthew in Hebrew in the library of Pamphilus at Cæsarea extant in his day. Catalog. Scriptor. Eccles., cap. iii.

the practice of public reading from the first, that as early as A.D. 68 we find Peter alluding to the Epistles of Paul collectively as familiar to his readers, and as classed in the same category with the Scriptures of the Old Testament.[1]

Similar allusions are found in the writings of Ignatius,[2] A.D. 109–115, and in the *Epistle of Barnabas*,[3] A.D. 71–132.

Justin the Martyr, in his *First Apology* to Antoninus Pius, in A.D. 147, has this remark: "On the day called Sunday there is an assembly of all those residing in cities and in the country, and then the memoirs (τὰ ἀπομνημονεύματα) of the Apostles or the writings of the Prophets are read as long as time permits (μέχρις ἐγχωρεῖ). Then, when the reader has finished, the President (προεστώς) delivers an exhortation to encourage the audience in imitation of these noble examples." (*Apol. I.*, c. 67.)

§ 2. *Formation of the Canon*

This collective and public use of the books of the New Testament soon grew into the formation of a

---

[1] 2 Peter iii. 16: "Which they that are unlearned and unstable wrest, as they do also the other Scriptures (ὡς καὶ τὰς λοιπὰς γραφάς), unto their own destruction."

[2] Ignatii, *Epistola ad Philadelphenses*, cap. v.

[3] The reference in this Epistle to Matt. xxii. 14, by the formula γέγραπται, "It is written," has already been alluded to in note to page 40.

" canon," or rule of discrimination between writings which were regarded as inspired or authoritative, and "those without," or "uncanonical."[1] The example of an Old Testament canon being already before them, it was natural that the Church should very early ascribe a similar rank to the records of the life and ministry of Jesus and to the didactic writings of His Apostles. Traces of such an ascription are found as early as Theophilus of Antioch, 169–181 (*ad Autolycum*, iii. 12), who mentions the Law, the Prophets, and the Gospels as of equal authority, and expressly names John as among those "moved by the Spirit," quoting John i. 1 (*ad Autol.*, ii. 22).

A somewhat remarkable evidence of the early veneration for the acknowledged New Testament writings, and their separation from all other books, appears in the controversy which arose with the heretic Marcion, about A.D. 140. This bold and influential schismatic was born in the latter part of the first century at Sinope, in Paphlagonia. His father was Bishop of the Church in that place, and he became a disciple, but was early excluded for immorality or heresy, and went to Rome, where he became a

---

[1] Westcott adopts as his definition of the Canon of Scripture: "The collection of books which forms the original and authoritative written rule of the faith and practice of the Christian Church." (Art. "Canon," *Smith's Bib. Dict.*)

teacher (140–170) and the founder of a sect.   He admitted the Epistles of Paul and a Gospel which he regarded as Pauline, though he does not name the author.   This Gospel was obviously no other than the Gospel of Luke, but mutilated by omissions and alterations to suit his peculiar doctrines.

These liberties and changes called forth a prompt and earnest protest on the part of leading Christian writers, whose discussions of the subject teem with evidence that at that time the *First Canon* (containing twenty books) was reverentially accepted by the great body of the Church.

Among the distinguished opponents of Marcion were Justin the Martyr, Irenæus, and Tertullian. See Lardner, vol. ii. pp. 126, 313, etc.   We have also independent testimony from Justin in his references to the New Testament, showing that each Gospel is distinctly recognized by him as having canonical authority.   (*Dial. c. Tryph.*, § 103; also comp. Dial. § 49 with Matt. xvii. 13; Dial. § 106 with Mark iii. 16, 17; Dial. § 105 with Luke xxiii. 46.)   Irenæus (A.D. 180), speaking of the New Testament writings as Divine, calls them the Rule or Canon of Truth, κανόνα τῆς ἀληθείας.   (*Adv. Hær.*, iii. c. 11, § 1; iv. c. 35, § 4.)

Basilides, the Gnostic of Alexandria, who wrote about A.D. 117–138, quotes from the New Testament in the same manner as from the Old, saying γέ-

γραπται and ἡ γραφή [1] (Hipp. *Adv. Hær.*, lib. vii.
cc. 10, 14), etc.   Several other Gnostic writers at this
period make similar references; showing that, to their
view, the Christian estimate of our New Testament
books was equal to that of the Old Testament.

§ 3. *Early Catalogues of the Canon*

The earliest formal catalogue of the canonical
books which has come down to us is contained in a
curious fragment discovered, A.D. 1738, by Muratori
in the Ambrosian Library at Milan.[2]

It appears from internal evidence to have been
written about A.D. 170 in Greek, and thence translated into Latin.   It is mutilated at the beginning
and end.   It commences with a reference to Mark's
Gospel, and says, " The Gospel according to Luke is
the third ;" then, after some remarks upon Luke, it
proceeds to name the Gospel of John, the Acts, and
thirteen Epistles of Paul (which latter are not given
in their present order), two Epistles of John, the
Epistle of Jude, and adds this remark : "*Apocalypses
etiam Joannis et Petri tantum recipimus quam qui-
dam ex nostris legi in ecclesia nolunt.*" [3]

---

[1] See article on the " Rendering of γραφή " in the Revised English
Version, in *The Moral Conflict of Humanity and Other Papers*, by A.
C. Kendrick, D.D., LL.D. (Philadelphia, 1894).

[2] A transcript of the document is given, with valuable notes, in
Westcott's *Canon of the New Testament*, App. C.

[3] Westcott translates this difficult passage thus : " We receive,

Equally ancient and valuable is the catalogue furnished by the older Syriac Version (called Peshitto, *simple*) of the New Testament.

It was to have been expected that the first version of the recognized New Testament writings should be in the prevailing tongue of those who were first to receive the Gospel; and this one appears to have been made before the publication or general acceptance of the Apocalypse and of Jude, 2 Peter, and 2 and 3 John, in the Church. With these exceptions, it contains the whole of our present canon (viz., four Gospels, the Acts, fourteen Epistles of Paul, First John, First Peter, and James), and *no other books*.

From the close of the second to the beginning of the fourth century the references to New Testament books, in the voluminous writings of the Christian

moreover, the *Apocalypses* of John and Peter only, which [latter] some of our body will not have read in the Church." A portion of the apochryphal "Gospel and Apocalypse of Peter" here referred to (and in § 3 below, page 81) has recently been discovered. Fragments of a manuscript, containing parts of these works, along with thirty chapters of the Greek Book of Enoch, were found in the winter of 1886–87 by workmen digging among ancient Christian graves in the town of Akmim, in Upper Egypt. The manuscript, which appears to date from about the eighth century, contains thirty-three leaves of parchment. The original work belongs somewhere about the middle of the second century. Besides confirming the reference here given, it is believed to bear remarkable testimony to the fourth gospel. See Adolph Harnack: *Bruchstücke des Evangeliums und der Apokalypse des Petrus*, Leipsic, 1893; H. B. Sweete: *The Gospel according to Peter;* also two lectures by J. A. Robinson and M. R. Jones, London, 1892.

Fathers,[1] are such as show that, without formally enumerating them, they accepted the list of the acknowledged books given in the above catalogue as authoritative and inspired, and co-ordinate with the Old Testament. We have a quaint catalogue from the writings of Origen in his seventh Homily on Joshua (*Opera* xii., p. 410, Berlin, 1831), saying, in allusion to the trumpets blown at the fall of Jericho: "When our Lord Jesus Christ came, whom Joshua (or Jesus), Son of Nun, prefigured, he sent out His Apostles as priests, bearing the trumpets of the magnificent and celestial doctrines of grace. First comes Matthew, who in his Gospel sounds the sacerdotal clarion.   Mark, also, Luke, and John, sounds each his own trumpet; then Peter blows the two trumpets of his Epistles; James, also, and Jude. Then, notwithstanding his first blasts, John sounds others in his Epistle and Apocalypse, as also Luke, when he describes the Acts of the Apostles.   Finally comes, moreover, he who said (1 Cor. iv. 9), 'I think that God hath set forth us the Apostles last;' and when he fulminates his fourteen Epistles, the walls of Jericho fall from their very foundations—all the machinations of idolatry and all the dogmas of philosophy." (See Migne, *Patrologia*, Series Græca, tom. xii. p. 858.)

[1] See Irenæus, *adv. Hær.*, ii. 28, § 2; iii. 11, § 8 sq. Clement of Alexandria, *Strom.*, vii. 3, § 14; vi. 11, § 88. Tertullian, *adv. Prax.*, 15.

Eusebius, in his *Ecclesiastical History*, vi. 25, has preserved another catalogue from the works of Origen, in which he alludes to doubts respecting the Second Epistle of Peter, the Second and Third Epistles of John, and the Epistle to the Hebrews, on which last he favors the theory that its matter was furnished by Paul, but the form produced by another hand, possibly Clement's or Luke's.[1]

§ 4. *Classification of the Canon*

In the Commentary of Origen upon John xiii. he seems to distinguish three classes of Scripture, γνήσια, μικτά, and νόθα, *genuine*, *mixed*, and *spurious*, the second of which refers to such books as are not universally acknowledged.

Eusebius has a similar classification into what he calls ὁμολογούμενα, *acknowledged*, ἀντιλεγόμενα, *contested*, and νόθα, *spurious*.

Under the first he ranks the twenty books contained in what we have called (§ 2, p. 76) the " First

---

[1] The words of Origen, as quoted by Eusebius, are as follows:

ἐγὼ δὲ ἀποφαινόμενος εἴποιμ' ἂν ὅτι τὰ μὲν νοήματα τοῦ ἀποστόλου ἐστὶν ἡ δὲ φράσις καὶ ἡ σύνθεσις ἀπομνημονεύσαντός τινος [τὰ ἀποστολικὰ καὶ ὡσπερεὶ σχολιογραφήσαντός τινος] τὰ εἰρημένα ὑπὸ τοῦ διδασκάλου. εἴ τις οὖν ἐκκλησία ἔχει ταύτην τὴν ἐπιστολὴν ὡς Παύλου, αὕτη εὐδοκιμείτω καὶ ἐπὶ τούτῳ. οὐ γὰρ εἰκῇ οἱ ἀρχαῖοι ἄνδρες ὡς Παύλου αὐτὴν παραδεδώκασι. τίς δὲ ὁ γράψας τὴν ἐπιστολήν, τὸ μὲν ἀληθὲς θεὸς οἶδεν, ἡ δὲ εἰς ἡμᾶς φθάσασα ἱστορία ὑπό τινων μὲν λεγόντων ὅτι Κλήμης ὁ γενόμενος ἐπίσκοπος Ῥωμαίων ἔγραψε τὴν ἐπιστολὴν ὑπό τινων δὲ ὅτι Λουκᾶς ὁ γράψας τὸ εὐαγγέλιον καὶ τὰς Πράξεις.

Canon," together with the Epistle to the Hebrews and the Apocalypse.

Under the second class he puts the remainder of our present canon, viz. the "five small Epistles," *i.e.* Second Epistle of Peter, James, Jude, and Second and Third Epistles of John.

The third class, or νόθα, he divides into two parts, those which may be edifying, as the Acts of Paul, Shepherd of Hermas, Revelation of Peter, Epistle of Barnabas, and the Apostolical Constitutions, and others which he calls absurd and impious, such as the Gospels of Peter, Thomas, Matthias, and the Acts of Andrew, John, and others.

It will be perceived that among the homologoumena of Eusebius are two books which we have not included in what we call the "First Canon," viz. the Epistle to the Hebrews and the Revelation.

These books seem to require a separate classification. In Italy and Western Europe, at the close of the second century, the Epistle to the Hebrews was not regarded as the work of Paul, and was therefore apparently rejected from a place in the canon, although in Alexandria it had been recognized, from the days of Pantænus, as Pauline and canonical, and this view, supported by Clement and Origen, came to prevail among the Eastern Greek Churches in the third century.

On the other hand, the Apocalypse, though gener-

6

ally received during this period, was rejected by Dionysius of Alexandria, and the distrust extended itself during the fourth century through the Churches of Syria and Asia Minor.

These circumstances have led some writers to classify these two books separately as composing a "*Second-first*" *Canon*.

The *Second Canon*, so-called, consists of the five remaining Epistles, which Eusebius denominates "antilegomena." They are all brief (constituting $\frac{222}{7959}$, or $\frac{1}{36}$, of the New Testament), and have never fully made their way to a general acceptance by the Church universal.

The complete canon of the New Testament, as now received, was ratified at the Council of Carthage, A.D. 397, and from that time has been accepted by the Latin Church, but the Syrian Churches still retained the canon of the Peshitto, while the Churches of Asia Minor seem to have occupied a mean position, as to the Canon, between the East and the West.

See Table V. for references to these books by the early Fathers, and Table VI. for early catalogues of disputed New Testament books. For a full discussion of the whole subject the student is referred to the larger work of Professor Westcott upon the Canon, or to his article on the subject in Smith's *Bible Dictionary*.

NOTE.—In addition to the works referred to under authenticity, p. 67, the following may be useful: KIRK, *The Canon of the Holy Scriptures Examined in the Light of History* (a translation and abridgment of Gaussen's work), Boston, 1862 ; DAVIDSON, *An Introduction to the Study of the New Testament, Critical, Exegetical, and Theological,* London, 1868 ; SABATIER, *Essai sur les Sources de la Vie de Jesus,* Paris, 1866 ; REUSS, *La Bible,* a new translation, with introduction and commentary, Paris, 1874, ff. ; CHARTERIS, *Canonicity,* London, 1880 ; *The New Testament Scriptures, their Claims, History, and Authority,* New York, 1882 ; M'CLYMONT, *The New Testament and its Writers,* New York and London, 1893.

Finally, and especially, see the works of WESTCOTT above referred to, viz., *An Introduction to the Study of the Gospels,* 3d ed., Cambridge, 1867 ; *The Bible in the Church,* London, 1864 ; and the *History of the Canon of the New Testament,* 5th ed., London, 1881.

A tolerably full bibliography of the subject may be found by a comparison of WINER, *Handbuch der Theologischen Litteratur,* 3d ed., Leipsic, 1838, for older works, with the article *Canon du Nouveau Testament,* by Prof. SABATIER, in the *Encyclopédie des Sciences Religieuses,* vol. ii., Paris, 1877.

PART III

—

HISTORY

OF THE

TEXT OF THE NEW TESTAMENT

HISTORY OF THE TEXT

OF THE

NEW TESTAMENT

§ 1. *Form of Manuscripts and Style of Writing*

WE have already remarked (Part II. § 1) that the New Testament books were doubtless first written upon papyrus, and that the originals disappeared very early. This material being very perishable, no copy of the New Testament upon it has come down to us except a small fragment of the First Epistle to the Corinthians. Nor indeed have we any manuscripts in the form of rolls, as in the case of the Old Testament. A few are in folio, but they are mostly in quarto or a smaller form. The material of the older class is parchment, made from the skins of sheep, goats, calves, or asses, or vellum, made from the skins of very young calves or other animals. Sometimes the sheets have been used a second time, the first writing having been erased, in which case they are called *palimpsests*. Cotton paper came into use about the tenth century, and was commonly sub-

stituted for parchment in the thirteenth ; linen paper
was also employed from the twelfth century onward.
The older manuscripts are written in uncial or capital letters, usually disconnected.[1]   At about the tenth
century appeared the cursive manuscripts (or minus-
cules) in small letters and a running hand. (See
Table VII.)

The earliest manuscripts had no divisions of words
or sentences, except to indicate the beginning of a
new paragraph, nor any accents or breathings.   The
first trace of interpunction is the use of a dot at the
top of the line, to divide sentences.   This became
frequent by the middle of the fifth century.   In the
Sinaitic and the Vatican manuscripts, about the middle of the fourth century, it is comparatively rare.

In A.D. 458 Euthalius, Deacon of Alexandria, afterwards Bishop of Sulci, in Sardinia, issued copies of
the Epistles of Paul, in which the text was divided
into short lines according to the sense ; and soon
after A.D. 460 he prepared similar copies of the Acts
and Catholic Epistles.   He called this στιχηδὸν γρά-
φειν, " writing by rows or lines."   Hence this method
of writing has been termed "stichometry."

Whether accents and breathings were introduced
a primâ manu into any of our MSS. of the New

---

[1] Uncia signifies "an inch."   The term seems to have had its origin in an expression of Jerome in his preface to Job : "Uncialibus,
ut vulgo aiunt, literis, onera magis exarata quam codices."

Testament before the seventh or eighth century is a question on which paleographers differ. It is certain that their use in earlier manuscripts was at least very unfrequent. In the uncial MSS. of the New Testament generally, and in very many of the cursives, the so-called *iota subscript* does not appear. In the earlier cursives, which have the letter at all, it is *adscript, i.e.* written in the same line with the other letters.

It results from all that has been said that the punctuation of the text, the determination of accents and breathings, the insertion of iota subscript, and the division of words in the later manuscripts are of no authority. On these points every scholar has a right to exercise his own judgment.

§ 2. *Divisions of the Text*

There is a division according to sense to be found in two manuscripts, the Codex Vaticanus (B of the fourth century) and Codex Zacynthius (Ξ of the eighth century), which is undoubtedly very ancient. According to this the New Testament is divided into sections of unequal length marked by numerals in the margin. Of these sections Matthew has 170, Mark 62, Luke 152, and John 80. In the Vatican MS. the Acts has two sets, of which the longer and more ancient numbers 36, while the more recent has 69. The first 42 of these later chapters are also found in the margin of the Codex Sinaiticus. The Pauline Epistles are, in the older notation, reckoned as one book, and they with the Catholic Epistles have also two sets of sections, with some peculiarities of arrangement, fully described by Scrivener, which go to show that the older sections were copied from some yet older document, in which the Epistle to the Hebrews preceded that to the Ephesians.

Another very ancient division of the Gospels is found in Codices Alexandrinus and Ephraemi, of the fifth century, and in later MSS. very generally, in which the sections or chapters are called τίτλοι, because a title or summary of contents is appended to the numeral which designates them. A table of these τίτλοι or chapters is also usually prefixed to each Gospel. A curious fact about them is that in each of the Gospels they commence their designation and enumeration with what should be the *second* section, apparently because the general title of the book was regarded as sufficient to designate the first. Thus the first τίτλος in Matthew, περὶ τῶν μάγων, "Concerning the Magi," begins with our second chapter. Of these τίτλοι, Matthew has 68, Mark 48, Luke 83, and John 18.

There is a division of the Acts and Epistles into κεφάλαια or chapters, to answer the same purpose as the τίτλοι of the Gospels, which is of still later date and of uncertain origin. It was used by Euthalius, and after his time became common. The Apocalypse was divided by Andreas, Bishop of Cæsarea, in Cappadocia, about A.D. 500, into twenty-four λόγοι or chapters, and each of these into three κεφάλαια or sections.

We will now notice the so-called "Ammonian (more properly Eusebian) Sections" and the "Eusebian Canons," or tables which are connected with them. The object of these sections was to facilitate the finding of the passages which in one or more of the Gospels are parallel or similar to a particular part of another. Their length, which is very unequal, is determined solely by their relation to parallel passages. Sometimes two, and in one instance (John xix. 6) three, of them are found within the limits of a single verse of our modern division. Of these sections, numbered consecutively in each Gospel, Matthew has 355, Mark 233 (as originally divided), Luke 342, and John 232, the numbers being noted in the margin. Under the number of each section in most manuscripts we find, in red ink, the number of the *canon* to which it belongs, according to the plan of Eusebius. He distributed the numbers representing these sections into ten tables, called "canons," the first of which, in four columns, gives the sections that correspond to one another in all four of the Gospels; the next three exhibit the sections parallel in three Gospels, viz. (2) Matthew,

Mark, Luke, (3) Matthew, Luke, John, (4) Matthew, Mark, John ; the next five, the sections parallel in *two* Gospels, viz. (5) Matthew, Luke, (6) Matthew, Mark, (7) Matthew, John, (8) Luke, Mark, (9) Luke, John ; while the tenth enumerates the sections *peculiar* to each single Gospel. In MSS. these tables were prefixed to the volume containing the Gospels. An example will show how they were used. Take the account of the healing of the leper, Matt. viii. 1–4. Against this passage we shall find in the margin $\xi\gamma = 63$, that being the number of the section, and *under* it $\beta = 2$, the number of the "canon" or table in which it belongs. Turning then to the second Eusebian table, we find opposite to 63 in Matthew, 18 as the parallel section in Mark, and 33 as the parallel section in Luke, which passages may readily be found by these numbers. In some MSS., to save the trouble of turning to the tables for this information, the parallel sections are noted at the bottom of the page.

The earliest MS. in which the Eusebian sections and canons are found is the Sinaitic (fourth century), where they were added, as Tischendorf thinks, not *a primâ manu*, but by a very early hand. They are also noted in the Codex Alexandrinus (fifth century). Some manuscripts have the sections without the canons.

Ammonius of Alexandria, early in the third century, prepared a Harmony of the Gospels by taking Matthew as the basis, and placing in parallel columns by the side of the text of this Gospel the similar passages in the other three Gospels. This, of course, involved a disarrangement of their text. The work of Ammonius suggested to Eusebius, as he himself tells us, the idea of accomplishing the same object by a different method; but it is to Eusebius rather than to Ammonius that the existing division into sections, as well as their arrangement in canons, should probably be ascribed.

The original authority on the whole subject is the *Epistle of Eusebius to Carpianus*, published in Tischendorf's New Testament, ed. 1859, vol. i., p. lxxiv. ff., and in many editions of the Greek New Testament. The present division of the New Testament into chapters was made by Cardinal Hugo de Sancto Caro (Hugh de St. Cher) about A.D. 1248; that into verses first appeared in Robert Stephens's edition of the Greek Testament, published at Geneva in 1551.[1] It was made by him while on a horseback journey from Paris to Lyons.

[1] See a valuable article on the division of the Greek New Testament into verses, with the variations in respect to the verse-division found "in about fifty of the principal editions," furnished for the *Prolegomena* of Tischendorf's 8th ed., by Ezra Abbott, a translation of which is published among the *Critical Essays* of Dr. Abbot (Boston, 1888) by Dr. Thayer, of Cambridge.

§ 3. *Classification of Manuscripts*

Manuscripts classified as to contents consist of (1) copies of the whole New Testament, as Codex Sinaiticus (ℵ), Codex Alexandrinus (A), and Codex Ephraemi (C), the two latter being somewhat mutilated : (2) copies of portions, such as the Gospels alone, the Acts and Catholic Epistles, the Pauline Epistles, or the Apocalypse, and (3) Lectionaries or Church Lesson books.

In three of the principal Greek MSS., Alexandrinus, Vaticanus, and Ephraemi, in the Peshitto text of the Syriac version, in the old Latin version, and in the majority of the Greek cursives, the order of the books is that given above, viz. : Gospels, Acts, Catholic Epistles, Pauline Epistles, and Apocalypse ; and this order has been adopted by the leading editors of the text—Lachmann, Tischendorf, Tregelles, and in the Westcott-Hort edition.

To this order, however, there are some noticeable exceptions.   In Codex Sinaiticus (ℵ), Montfortianus (61), Leicestrencis (69), Fabri (90), Canonici (522), Brit. Mus. King's lib. (Act. 20), and some Latin codices, the Pauline Epistles precede the Acts.   The order of our English Bible (Gospels, Acts, Pauline Epistles, Catholic Epistles, Apocalypse) appears in the canon of Muratori (A.D. 170), in the lists of Eusebius, *Eccl. Hist.*, iii. 25 (A.D. 270–340), Gregory Nazienzen (A.D. 370), Amphilochius (A.D. 370), Rufinus, and of the two councils of Carthage (A.D. 397 and 419), as well as of some later Fathers, in Codex Amiatinus of the Vulgate version, and in the Greek cursive MSS. Act. 4, 68, 119, 120, 134, 214, 215, 220, 223. It was the order adopted in the editions of the Greek New Testament published by Erasmus, Gerbelius, Cephalæus, Stephen, Beza, and the Elzevirs. As it was found in most of the editions of the Vulgate version, it became, by the decree of the Council of Trent (A.D. 1546), the established order of the Western Church.

The four Gospels are usually found in their present order, *i.e.* Matthew, Mark, Luke, and John, but in Codex Monacensis (X) the order is exactly reversed. In Codex Bezæ (D) they stand, Matthew, John, Luke, Mark; in Codex Fabri (90), John, Luke, Matthew, Mark; and in the Curetonian Syriac, Matthew, Mark, John, Luke.

Lectionaries, or Church Service books, containing extracts for daily service throughout the year, are taken either from the Gospels, and called *Evangelistaria*—see Table IX., E. (1), or from the Acts and Epistles, and called *Apostoli* or *Praxapostoli*. A full table of Greek Church Lessons may be found in Scrivener's *Introduction*, 4th ed., pp. 80–89. The whole number of manuscripts (including Lectionaries) now known to exist is about 3600, of which only about 100 are uncials, and the rest cursives. Most of the latter class have not been collated.

§ 4. *Uncial Manuscripts*

Table VIII. in this hand-book presents a list of the Uncial Manuscripts, so far as at present known, arranged in the order of their probable date, with their designation, present place of deposit, contents and history.   A fuller account of these, and of nearly all known New Testament manuscripts, may be found in Gregory's *Prolegomena* to Tischendorf's 8th ed. of the Greek New Testament, published (in Latin), at Leipsic, 1884–1894, pp. 1428.   A less complete and accurate, but very helpful compendium in English, is the 4th edition of Scrivener's *Introduction to the Criticism of the New Testament*, edited, since the decease of the author, by Rev. Edward Miller (2 vols., London and New York, 1894, pp. 418, 428).   We can afford space here only for a brief notice of a few of the principal uncials.

א. Codex Sinaiticus was discovered by Professor Tischendorf, in 1859, at the convent of St. Catherine, on Mount Sinai, where forty-three leaves of the Septuagint, which afterwards proved to be a part of the same manuscript, had been found by him in 1844. It consists of $346\frac{1}{2}$ leaves of thin yellowish vellum, made from the finest skins of antelopes (as Tischendorf thinks), $13\frac{1}{2}$ inches by $14\frac{7}{8}$ inches in size; 199

leaves contain portions of the Septuagint version.
There are four columns on a page of forty-eight lines
each, except in the poetical books of the Old Testament, which are written in στίχοι, and have but two
columns each. The forty-three leaves of the Sinaitic
MS., discovered by Tischendorf in 1844, were published by him at Leipsic in 1846, under the name of
Codex Friderico-Augustanus. Adding these to the
199 leaves already mentioned, the Sinaitic MS. contains the following parts of the Septuagint : 1 Chron.
ix. 27–xix. 17 ; Ezra, ix. 9–x. 44 ; Nehemiah, Esther,
Tobit, Judith, 1st and 4th Maccabees, Isaiah, Jere-
miah, Lam. i. 1–ii. 20 ; the last nine of the Minor
Prophets, viz. Joel to Malachi, inclusive ; and the
poetical books, in the following order : Psalms, Proverbs, Ecclesiastes, Canticles, Wisdom of Solomon,
Ecclesiasticus (or Wisdom of Siracides), Job. In addition to the above, a small fragment of a leaf, containing Gen. xxiv. 9, 10, 41–43, was picked up by
Tischendorf in 1853, and published in vol. ii. of his
Monumenta (1857), p. 321 ; and parts of two leaves
found by Abp. Porfiri, in the binding of certain
MSS., were published by Tischendorf in his *Appendix codicum celeb. Sin. Vat. Alex.*, 1867, pp. 3–6.
These contain Gen. xxiii. 19–xxiv. 4 ; xxiv. 5–8 ; 9,
10 ; 10–14 ; 17, 18, 19 ; 25–27 ; 30–33 ; 36–41 ; 41–
43 ; 43–46 ; Num. v. 26–30 ; vi. 5, 6 ; 11, 12 ; 17, 18 ;
22–27 ; vii. 4, 5 ; 12, 13 ; 15–20. The remaining 147½

7

leaves contain the whole New Testament, the Epistle of Barnabas, and a part of the Shepherd of Hermas. On the margin of the New Testament part are the so-called Ammonian sections and Eusebian canons, apparently not by the original scribe, but, as Tischendorf thinks, by a contemporary hand. The τίτλοι are wanting. There are numerous corrections, some of which seem to have been by the original scribe, and others by a contemporary reviser, whom Tischendorf designates אᵃ; others were made by two writers of the sixth century (אᵇ), and many by a later hand belonging to the seventh century (אᶜ); besides which are corrections of a still later date. In all, Tischendorf finds in the New Testament the work of ten different correctors. In the order of New Testament books the Pauline Epistles precede the Acts and Catholic Epistles, the Epistle to the Hebrews following 2 Thessalonians.

Through the munificence of the Emperor of Russia, a beautiful edition of the MS., printed in fac-simile type, was published at St. Petersburg in 1862, in four folio volumes. The edition was limited to 300 copies, 100 of which were given to Tischendorf, and were mostly put on sale, while the remainder were distributed as presents by the Russian Government. In 1863, the New Testament part of the MS., together with the Barnabas and Hermas, was published by Tischendorf at Leipsic, in quarto, in ordinary Greek type, but representing the MS. line for line, and with the Prolegomena somewhat enlarged ; and in 1864 (with the date 1865) appeared Tischendorf's *Novum Testamentum Græce. Ex Sinaitico codice . . . Vaticana itemque Elzeviriana lectione notata.* A supplement to this, containing corrections, was prefixed to his *Responsa ad Calumnias Romanas ;* Lips., 1870.

A. CODEX ALEXANDRINUS was placed in the British Museum at its formation in 1753. It was originally sent as a present from Cyril Lucar, Patriarch of Constantinople, to Charles I., and was probably brought from Alexandria by him. It is a quarto, thirteen inches high and ten broad, consisting of 773 leaves, of which 639 belong to the Old Testament, each page being divided into two columns of fifty lines each.

Some of the reasons for assigning its date to the fifth century are thus stated by Scrivener: "The presence of the canons of Eusebius (A.D. 268–340 ?) and of the Epistles to Marcellinus by the great Athanasius, Patriarch of Alexandria (300 ?–373), before the Psalms, place a limit in one direction, while the absence of the Euthalian divisions of the Acts and Epistles, which came into vogue very soon after A.D. 458, and the shortness of the ὑπογραφαί, appear tolerably decisive against a later date than A.D. 450."

This MS. contains the whole of the Old Testament, except that part of a leaf has been torn out, so that Gen. xiv. 14–17, xv. 1–5, 16–19, xvi. 6–9, are wanting; also one leaf containing 1 Sam. xii. 18–xiv. 9, and nine leaves containing Ps. xlix. (l.) 20–lxxix. (lxxx.) 11. It is the basis of the editions of the LXX., by Grabe (Oxford, 1707–1720), Breitinger (Zurich, 1730–1732), and Field (1859). The Old Testament text was published in facsimile type, under the editorship of H. H. Baber, London, 1816– 1828, four vols. fol. The New Testament part of the MS. was published in facsimile type by C. G. Woide, London, 1786, fol.; in ordinary type by B. H. Cowper, London, 1860, 8vo, and a beautiful photo- graphic facsimile has been issued by the Trustees of the British Museum (1880). Woide's *Notitia Co- dicis Alexandrini*, with notes by G. L. Spohn, Leips., 1790, 8vo, is useful.

In the New Testament the following portions are wanting: Matt. i. 1–xxv. 6; John vi. 50–viii. 52; 2 Cor. iv. 13–xii. 7: unfortunately, also, many letters have been cut away from the edges of the leaves in binding. The MS. contains also the First Epistle of Clement (three leaves wanting), and a part of the Second.

The text of this manuscript in the Gospels agrees much more frequently with that of the later (in dis- tinction from the earlier) uncials than it does in the rest of the New Testament.

B. CODEX VATICANUS is a quarto volume in the

Vatican Library, numbered 1209. It appears in the earliest catalogue of the library in 1475, and was very probably placed there at the foundation of the library by Pope Nicholas V. in 1448. It consists of 759 leaves of thin vellum, 142 of which belong to the New Testament. The text has three columns on a page, and forty-two lines to the column, with no intervals between words except at the end of a paragraph. It contains the New Testament complete down to Hebrews ix. 14, breaking off in the middle of a word, $\kappa\alpha\theta\alpha$-. The rest of the Epistle to the Hebrews and the Apocalypse are written in a comparatively recent hand. In the Old Testament it wants the larger part of the Book of Genesis (the MS. begins Gen. xlvi. 28, $\pi o\lambda\iota\nu$), Ps. cv. (cvi.) 27–cxxxvii. (cxxxviii.) 6, and the Books of Maccabees. It was the main foundation of the Roman edition of the Septuagint (1586, in corrected copies 1587), which has been the basis of most subsequent editions; e.g., those of Pearson (1665), Bos (1709), Holmes and Parsons (1798–1827), and Tischendorf (1850, 6th ed. 1880).

Formerly textual critics had to depend mainly for their knowledge of the New Testament text of this MS. on the imperfect collations of Bartolocci (1669, first used by Scholz, 1830–36), Mico (for Bentley, published by Ford, 1799), and Birch (1788–1801). The text of the whole manuscript was first published by Cardinal Mai, Rome, 1857, in five vols., folio (the New Testament also separately by Vercellone, 1859); but this edition was unsatisfactory, and was wholly superseded by the magnificent edition, in facsimile type, published by Vercellone, Cozza, Sergio, and Fabiani, the concluding volume of which was published in 1881. Then, in 1889, appeared the photographic facsimile, produced under the care of the Abbate Cozza-Luzi.

In reference to this MS. the following works still have value : Tischendorf, *Novum Testamentum Vaticanum*, Leipsic, 1867, and *Appendix ad Novum Test. Vat.* (1869), in which he reviews the Roman edition (1868) of the New Testament part of the MS. See, also, Tischendorf's *Appendix Codicum celeberrimorum, Sin., Vat. Alex.* (1867), and *Responsa ad Calumnias Romanas* (1870). In the Prolegomena to Tischendorf's *Novum Test. Vat.*, edited by Dr. Caspar René Gregory, will be found the best account of the MS. from a palæographical point of view. He adduces plausible arguments to show that the scribe D, who wrote six leaves of the New Testament part of the Sinaitic MS., is identical with the scribe who wrote the New Testament in the Vatican MS. He would assign both MSS. to about the middle of the fourth century.

See, also, Ezra Abbot, *Comparative Antiquity of the Sinaitic and Vatican MSS.*, in the *Journal of the American Oriental Society,* vol. x., pp. 189–200; republished in a posthumous volume edited by Prof. J. H. Thayer, entitled, *The Authorship of the Fourth Gospel, and other Critical Essays,* Boston, 1888.

The Vatican MS. has corrections by a contemporary scribe, whom Tischendorf designates in his eighth edition of the New Testament by B^2, and by another of the tenth or eleventh century, B^3, who retouched the faded ink of the MS. throughout, and supplied accents and breathings, except when words were accidentally repeated.

In a critical point of view, the text of this MS. seems on the whole decidedly superior to that of any other of our New Testament codices. So judge Tregelles, Westcott and Hort, Lightfoot and Weiss. Next in value is the Sinaitic, to which Tischendorf is disposed to give the preference. But it must not be supposed that every reading which they both support is genuine. A very different view of the character of these MSS. is taken by Burgon and McClellan, who regard them as singularly vicious and corrupt. In regard to the omissions of Cod. B., see § 10, 5, p. 123; for facsimile, see Table VII.

C. CODEX EPHRAEMI is a palimpsest MS. in the National Library of Paris (No. 9), containing portions of the Old Testament on 64 leaves, and of the New on 145 leaves. In the twelfth century the ancient

writing was effaced to receive certain Greek works
of Ephraem, the Syrian Father. In the sixteenth
century it was brought to Florence from the East,
probably by Andrew John Lascar, and was brought
into France by Queen Catherine de Medici. In
1834 an attempt was made to restore the original
writing by the use of a chemical preparation, which
has defaced the vellum with stains of various colors.
It was collated by Wetstein in 1716, and a fine edition was published by Tischendorf in 1843–45. The
entire Epistles of 2 John and 2 Thessalonians are
lost. Of the rest of the New Testament the following portions remain : Matthew i. 2–v. 15 ; vii. 5–xvii.
26 ; xviii. 28–xxii. 20 ; xxiii. 17–xxiv. 10 ; xxiv. 45–
xxv. 30 ; xxvi. 22–xxvii. 11 ; xxvii. 47–xxviii. 14 ;
Mark i. 17–vi. 31 ; viii. 5–xii. 29 ; xiii. 19–xvi. 20 ;
Luke i. 2–ii. 5 ; ii. 42–iii. 21 ; iv. 25–vi. 4 ; vi. 37–vii.
16 or 17 ; viii. 28–xii. 3 ; xix. 42–xx. 27 ; xxi. 21–
xxii. 19 ; xxiii. 25–xxiv. 7 ; xxiv. 46–53 ; John i. 3–
41 ; iii. 33–v. 16 ; vi. 38–vii. 3 ; viii. 34–ix. 11 ; xi. 8–
46 ; xiii. 8–xiv.–7 ; xvi. 21–xviii. 36 ; xx. 26–xxi. 25 ;
Acts i. 2–iv. 3 ; v. 35–x. 42 ; xiii. 1–xvi. 36 ; xx. 10–
xxi. 30 ; xxii. 21–xxiii. 18 ; xxiv. 15–xxvi. 19 ; xxvii.
16–xxviii. 4 ; James i. 1–iv. 2 ; 1 Peter i. 2–iv. 5 ; 2
Peter i. 1–1 John iv. 2 ; 3 John 3–15 ; Jude 3–25 ;
Rom. i. 1–ii. 5 ; iii. 21–ix. 6 ; x. 15–xi. 31 ; xiii. 10–1
Cor. vii. 18 ; ix. 6–xiii. 8 ; xv. 40–2 Cor. x. 8 ; Gal. i.
20–vi. 18 ; Ephes. ii. 18–iv. 17 ; Phil. i. 22–iii. 5 ; Col.

i. 1–1 Thess. ii. 9; Hebrews ii. 4–vii. 26; ix. 15–x. 24; xii. 15–xiii. 25; 1 Tim. iii. 9–v. 20; vi. 21–Philemon, 25; Apoc. i. 2(?)–iii. 19; v. 14–vii. 14; vii. 17–viii. 4; ix. 17–x. 10; xi. 3–xvi. 13; xviii. 2–xix. 5.

Tischendorf assigns the MS. to a date somewhat before the middle of the fifth century, regarding it (with Hug) as a little older than the Alexandrine. It has been manipulated by two different correctors, one (C^2) of the sixth century, the other (C^3), a Byzantine scribe, who prepared it for church use in the ninth century. This scribe changed the reading ὅς, in 1 Tim. iii. 16, to θεός.

The typographical errors of Tischendorf's edition of the New Testament part (1843) are corrected in the volume containing the Old Testament fragments (1845). Tischendorf's *Prolegomena* discuss thoroughly all questions of interest pertaining to the MS. For facsimile, see Table VII.

D. Codex Bezae, a Greek and Latin manuscript of the Gospels and Acts, belongs to the University Library at Cambridge, England. It was presented to the library, in 1581, by Theodore Beza. It is a quarto volume, ten inches by eight, with one column on a page, each left-hand page having the Greek text, and the right-hand the corresponding Latin. It has thirty-four lines to the page, which are arranged in στίχοι.

The MS. has had eight or nine correctors besides

the original scribe, extending through several centuries. The text is peculiar, preserving in many
cases the primitive reading, where it has been lost in
the mass of later MSS., but, on the other hand, defaced with many corruptions. "No known MS. contains so many bold and extensive interpolations (six
hundred, it is said, in the Acts alone), countenanced,
where they are not absolutely unsupported, chiefly
by the Old Latin and the Curetonian versions."
(Scrivener.)

The following passages are wanting: viz., *in the
Greek*, Matthew i. 1–20; vi. 20–ix. 2; xxvii. 2–12;
John i. 16–iii. 26; Acts viii. 29–x. 14; xxi. 2–10, 15–
18; xxii. 10–20, 29–xxviii. 31; *and in the Latin*,
Matt. i. 1–11; vi. 8–viii. 27; xxvi. 65–xxvii. 1; John
i. 1–iii. 16; Acts viii. 20–x. 4; xx. 31–xxi. 2, 7–10;
xxii. 2–10; xxiii. 20–xxviii. 31.

The MS. was published in magnificent style, in facsimile type, by Thomas Kipling, Cambridge, 1793, 2
vols. fol. Only 250 copies were printed. It is an
uncritical edition, placing the readings of later hands
in the text, and of the first hand in the notes. For
all ordinary purposes it is completely superseded
by the excellent edition of F. H. Scrivener, *Bezae
Codex Cantabrigiensis*, Cambridge, 1864, 4to, printed
in ordinary type, but representing the MS. line for
line. The Introduction to this edition is exceedingly
thorough and valuable. He regards the MS. as writ-

ten early in the sixth century, probably in Gaul.
Mr. J. Rendel Harris, in a very interesting treatise
on the Codex Bezae, printed in the second volume
of the Cambridge *Texts and Studies*, entitled "A
study of Codex Bezae," suggests that the Greek text
may have been made up from the Latin. (Cambridge, 1891, pp. viii. and 272.) Compare an article
in the *Guardian*, London, 1892 (May 18 and 25) [by
William Sanday(?)]. See, also, F. H. Chase, *The Old
Syriac Element in the Text of Codex Bezae*, London,
1893. For a notice of the Latin text, see Table X.
in this hand-book, and Tisch. *Prolegomena*, p. 954.
For two remarkable interpolations in Codex D, of
considerable length, see the large critical editions of
the Greek Testament, on Matthew xx. 28, and Luke
vi. 5. For facsimile, see Table VII.

It will appear by examination of Table VIII., at
the close of this volume, that a large accession to
the list of Uncial MSS. has been made since the
first edition of this hand-book was published (1880).
Nearly forty new names are now inserted, mostly of
fragments — one of which (T^g) is of the fourth century — but some contain considerable portions of
the several books of the New Testament. Codex $\aleph$,
however (of the sixth century), has the four gospels,
though with many leaves lost. For these additions
to our critical apparatus, together with the much
larger accession to the list of cursives, we are greatly

indebted to Dr. Gregory, of Leipsic, whose completion of Tischendorf's *Prolegomena* is a monument
of scholarly labor.   As yet the more recently discovered Uncials appear scattered in the several supple-
ments and in the *Addenda et Emendanda* of the
Prolegomena, so that our list, as now published in
Table VIII., is the only complete arrangement of
them all in order.   The full description of each MS.,
however, can be found only in the *Prolegomena*
itself, though the larger part of them are given in
Scrivener's Introduction (4th ed., London, 1894).

§ 5. *Cursive Manuscripts*

Of over 2000 manuscripts in the cursive (or minuscule) character, written in and after the tenth century, a very large majority have not been thoroughly
collated.   We shall have space only to notice carefully a few of the most important.   For a full list
see Table IX.[1]

1. *Codex Basileensis,* A. N. IV. 2, is an illuminated
manuscript at Basle, which has been assigned to the
tenth century.   It is an octavo, of 297 leaves, with

---

[1] The list in Table IX. is practically an index to that of the *Prolegomena* of Tischendorf, to which the reader is referred for full and
accurate particulars.   For the convenience of those who have access
only to Scrivener's Introduction, the numbers adopted by Scrivener
are appended in all cases (which are numerous) where they differ
from Tischendorf.   Not all of the manuscripts, however, are to be
found in Scrivener.

thirty-eight lines to the page. It has the τίτλοι, and contains prologues before the several books. It has also a Calendar of the Daily Lessons throughout the year. It has been collated by Wetstein, C. L. Roth, and Tregelles. It contains the Gospels, Acts, and Pauline Epistles, but is especially valuable only in the Gospels. See facsimile, Table VII.

13. *Paris* (once *Regius*) 50 is a quarto of the twelfth century, highly valued by Kuster (referred to as *Paris* 6). It has the Daily Lesson Calendar. It, and 69, 124, 346, are regarded by some as transcripts of one archetype, whose text is not lower in value than the uncial Codex D.[1] It contains the Gospels with the following omissions: Matthew i. 1–ii. 20; xxvi. 33–52; xxvii. 26–xxviii. 9; Mark i. 20–45; John xvi. 19–xvii. 11; xxi. 2–25.

22. *Paris* (once *Regius*) 72 (formerly Colbertinus 2467) is a quarto of the eleventh century, which has some remarkable readings, though the manuscript is very imperfectly known. It contains the Gospels, except Matthew i. 1–ii. 2; John xiv. 22–xvi. 27. It eminently deserves a new collation.

33. *Paris* 14 is a folio of the eleventh century, called also Codex Colbertinus 2844, and, by Mill, Colbertinus 8. It contains some of the Prophets and all the New Testament except the Apocalypse.

---

[1] See Ferrar and Abbott, *Collation of Four Important Manuscripts of the Gospels* (Dublin, 1877).

(It is numbered 13 in Acts, and 17 in the Pauline Epistles.)   The text is one of the most valuable, resembling Codd. B, D, L more than any other cursive. Carefully collated by Tregelles in 1850.   Mutilated : Mark ix. 31–xi. 11 ; xiii. 11–xiv. 50 ; Luke xxi. 38– xxiii. 26.   Scrivener has a facsimile.

38. Of the Apocalypse, No. 579 in the Vatican Library at Rome, is an octavo manuscript of the fifteenth (Scrivener, thirteenth) century, on cotton paper, but has a text of remarkable value.   Collated by Birch, but much more thoroughly by B. H. Alford.

40. Of the Acts (Pauline Epp. 46, Apoc. 12), in the Vatican Library at Rome (*Alexandrino - Vat.* 179), is a quarto manuscript of the eleventh century, which, containing the labors of Euthalius on the Acts and Epistles, was made by L. A. Zacagni the basis of his edition of the Prologues, etc., of Euthalius, published in his *Collectanea Mon. Vet. Ecclesiæ Gr. et Lat.*, Rome, 1698.   Tischendorf called it " Codex admodum insignis."   The latter part of Titus (from iii. 3), Philemon, and the Apocalypse are in a later hand.

47. Of the Pauline Epistles (*Bodl. Roe* 16), is a folio manuscript of the eleventh and twelfth centuries, with a text much resembling that of Codex A. After Mill, Tregelles thoroughly collated it for his edition of the New Testament.   It has a catena, used by Cramer.   *Catenæ*, vols. v. and vi.

61. *Codex Montfortianus* is a manuscript whose chief interest has grown out of its connection with the famous passage 1 John v. 7 and the printed text of Erasmus. It is an octavo manuscript at Trinity College, Dublin, belonging to the fifteenth or six-teenth century. Erasmus refers to it as "Codex Britannicus." It appears to have been the work of three or four successive scribes. It contains the whole New Testament, the Acts and Catholic Epis-tles being numbered 34, the Pauline Epistles 40, and the Apocalypse 92, as they appear in our tables of cursive manuscripts. Dr. Dobbin, the last collator, thinks that the Acts and Epistles were transcribed from Codex 33 of the Acts (No. 39 of the Pauline Epistles), and the Apocalypse from Codex 69 (see below). The part containing the Acts and Catholic Epistles was probably written after the year 1500, and the text of the Three Heavenly Witnesses bears marks of having been translated from the Latin. See Tregelles, *Text. Crit.* pp. 213–217.

61. Of the Acts is the designation now given to a cursive copy of the Acts discovered by Tischendorf in Egypt in 1853, and sold to the British Museum in 1854 (B. M. Addit. 20,003). It was formerly called lo^ti, *i.e. Londinensis Tischendorfianus.* It is dated April 20, 1044. Collated by Tischendorf, Tregelles, and Scrivener. 297 verses are wanting, viz. ch. iv. 8–vii. 17; xvii. 28–xxiii. 9.

69. Of the Gospels (Acts 31, Paul 37, Apoc. 14) is *Codex Leicestrensis,* a folio of the fifteenth century, partly on parchment and partly on paper, now in the Library of the Town Council of Leicester. It is written on 212 leaves of 38 lines to the page. It has been collated by Mill, Tregelles, and Scrivener. The latter says of it, "No MS. of its age has a text so remarkable as this; less, however, in the Acts than in the Gospels." Scrivener has a facsimile, v. i., p. 343. It contains the whole New Testament, except Matthew i. 1–xviii. 15; Acts x. 45–xiv. 17; Jude 7– 25; Apoc. xviii. 7–xxii. 21. See J. R. Harris, *The Origin of the Leicester Codex.* London, 1887.

157. Of the Gospels in the Vatican Library at Rome (*Cod. Urb.-Vat.* 2) is an octavo manuscript of the twelfth century, regarded by Birch as the most important MS. of the New Testament in the Vatican, except Codex B. Very beautifully written on vellum, with ornaments and pictures in vermilion and gold.

209. Of the Gospels (Acts 95, Paul 108, Apoc. 46) in the Library of St. Mark at Venice (*Venet.* 10) is an octavo manuscript of the eleventh or twelfth century, the text of which in the Gospels is of remarkable value, resembling that of Codex B. The Apocalypse is in a later hand. Codex 205 in the Gospels is perhaps a copy of this MS. or was transcribed from the same archetype.

The above notices may serve as illustrations of the character and use of cursive manuscripts. See, also, the article "New Testament," in the *American* edition of Smith's *Bible Dictionary* (which contains valuable notes by the late Prof. Ezra Abbot, of Cambridge), and Scrivener's *Plain Introduction to the Criticism of the New Testament.*

§ 6. *Versions of the New Testament.*

Next to the authority of MSS. in determining the text of the New Testament is the evidence furnished by certain ancient translations, made for the benefit of Christian converts unable to understand the original Greek. Some of these versions were from a text much older than any now existing.

Of course the weight of this evidence is much impaired by the difficulty of estimating the degree in which the idioms of a language or the habits of a translator may have caused him to deviate from the exact structure of the Greek sentence. Moreover, we have the disadvantage of being obliged to reach the *version* through copies more or less remote from the original, and correspondingly liable to corruption ; and in the case of some versions (*e. g.* the Egyptian, Ethiopic, etc.), the acquaintance of scholars with the languages themselves has been confessedly imperfect. Nevertheless, after these allowances are made, the value of versions is still considerable,

8

and in the matter of determining the authenticity of whole clauses or sentences inserted or omitted by Greek MSS. it is sometimes very great. In any case they are mainly valuable as witnesses to the text, and not as models of translation or guides to interpretation. The Peshitto Syriac, however, is regarded as, on the whole, a translation of remarkable fidelity and excellence ; and the Vulgate has high merit.

Table X. presents a succinct view of the versions available for critical purposes in the order of the date. For a good discussion of the subject the student is referred to the article "Versions, Ancient," by S. P. Tregelles, in Smith's *Bible Dictionary*, to which must be added, for the Syriac Versions, Dr. Isaac H. Hall's Appendix to Murdock's *Translation of the Syriac New Testament* [6th ed., Boston, 1894], and for the Latin versions, the elaborate article "Vulgate," by Prof. Westcott, in Smith's *Bible Dictionary*, and especially the recent work of Samuel Berger, *Histoire de la Vulgate pendent les Premiers Siècles du Moyen Age.* Paris, 1893.

§ 7. *New Testament Citations by the Christian Fathers*

Among the sources of evidence for determining the text of the New Testament we come to notice finally that derived from citations of passages made by early ecclesiastical writers, commonly spoken of as the Christian Fathers.

For convenience of reference to these Fathers a complete list of them is subjoined (Table XII., Parts i.–ii.), with a descriptive designation and the time when they flourished, in assigning which the authority of Cave has usually been followed.

The evidence furnished by patristic citations is subject to drawbacks similar to those which affect the versions of Scripture. Our text of the writings of the Fathers is itself more or less uncertain, and their citations are often loosely made from memory, or, if originally made *verbatim*, are liable to have been altered by subsequent correctors. Yet, as corroborative testimony in regard to readings which are already supported by manuscript authority, they have considerable value. Special importance is attached to them in cases where a discussion has arisen among the early Fathers respecting variations in the reading of the manuscripts, cases which are not unfrequent as early as the days of Origen, Eusebius, and Jerome.

The Greek Fathers most important for textual criticism are, in the *second* century, Justin Martyr (quotations generally free) and Irenæus (for the most part preserved only in an old Latin version); for the end of the *second* or the earlier part of the *third*, Clement of Alexandria, Hippolytus, and, far above all others, ORIGEN; for the *fourth*, Eusebius, Athanasius, Cyril of Jerusalem, Didymus of Alexandria, Epiphanius (quotations often free and text corrupt), Basil the Great, and Chrysostom (text considerably corrupted by copyists); in the *fifth*, Cyril of Alexandria and Theodoret; in the beginning of the *sixth*, Andreas of Cæsarea (for the Apocalypse); in the *seventh*, Maximus the Confessor; in the *eighth*, Joannes Damascenus; in the *ninth*, Photius; in the *tenth*, Œcumenius; in the *eleventh*, Theophylact; and near the beginning of the *twelfth*, Euthymius Zigabenus, the last three being commentators.

The early Latin Fathers are of value in criticism mainly as indicating by their citations the readings of the Old Latin version or versions, for which they are, in many parts of the New Testament, our principal authority. Of these the most important are, for the end of the *second* century and later, Tertullian, whose quotations have been completely collected by Rönsch, *Das Neue Test. Tertullians* (Leipsic, 1871); for the *third* century, Cyprian and Novatian; for the *fourth*, Lucifer of Cagliari, Hilary of Poitiers, Ambrosiaster or Hilary the Deacon, Ambrose, Rufinus, and especially Jerome (Hieronymus); for the *fifth*, Augustine; and for the *sixth*, Primasius (valuable only in the Apocalypse).

§ 8. *Textual Criticism*

The process of endeavoring to ascertain the orig-

inal reading in any given passage, by a comparison
of manuscript and other authorities, is attended with
certain difficulties which require experience and skill
to overcome.   It does not come within the scope of
this treatise to attempt an exhaustive discussion of
the principles which underlie the work.   We can
only hope to give an outline of the nature of the
process, and refer the student to the special treatises
on the subject, and to critical editions of the Greek
New Testament, as those of Griesbach, Tischendorf,
and Westcott and Hort, for a fuller discussion.   The
subject is one of deep interest, but involving a great
variety of complications.   With all the labors of
critical editors in the past, from Mill and Bentley in
the last century to Westcott and Hort in the present,
there are still questions in regard to method and
praxis of criticism upon which leading scholars differ.
It is evident that all our progress is only towards a
substantial and not a literal agreement; but every
step towards a correct knowledge of the sacred originals is *progress*, the value of which cannot be overestimated.

§ 9. *The Nature of Various Readings*

Since no manuscripts are extant which date earlier
than the fourth century, it is obvious that all now
existing are the result of transcriptions from previous copies, and are liable to such variations and im-

perfections as are incident to all copies in manuscript. Of course these variations multiply with the increase of number of different manuscripts, and with the lateness and frequency of their transcription.

The variations are of different kinds:

1. In the first place, there are two whole paragraphs of some importance which are wanting in some or many of the best MSS. and other ancient authorities, viz.: Mark xvi. 9–20 and John vii. 53–viii. 11.

2. There are shorter passages which may have crept into the text from the margin. Among them is the famous interpolation in 1 John v. 7, 8. So also, probably, John v. 4 (the angel at the Pool of Bethesda), and the doxology in Matthew vi. 13; and perhaps the account of the bloody sweat (Luke xxii. 43, 44). Scrivener thinks that Acts viii. 37, "If thou believest with all thine heart," etc., may have been derived from some Church ordinal, and that the last clauses of Rom. viii. 1 and Gal. iii. 1 are glosses of the transcriber.

3. Frequently a clause is lost by what is called *Homœoteleuton* (ὁμοιοτέλευτον), where two clauses happen to end with the same word, and the transcriber's eye passes from one to the other. Omissions from this cause occur in the Sinaitic MS. in the New Testament—according to Scrivener, no fewer than one hundred and fifteen times—though many of them are supplied by a later hand.

4. Words are sometimes mistaken one for another where they differ in only one or two letters. This is specially liable to occur in uncial MSS., where several letters closely resemble each other, and the words are not spaced.

5. Numerous variations have arisen from the tendency to assimilate one Gospel to another by bringing in clauses in one Gospel which belong in the same connection to another evangelist. Thus the prophecy about the parting of the garments, found in Matt. xxvii. 35, was probably borrowed from the parallel passage in John xix. 24. So, also, Acts ix. 5, 6 has been interpolated from the two other accounts of Paul's conversion, Acts xxvi. 14, 15, and xxii. 10. This, however, should rather be charged to Erasmus following the Vulgate, as the spurious addition does not seem to be found in any Greek MS.

6. Sometimes copyists have attempted to improve upon their originals in citations from the Old Testament, copying the passage more fully or more accurately than the author thought it necessary. See, for example, the critical editions on Matt. ii. 18; xv. 8; Luke iv. 18; Rom. xiii. 9; Heb. xii. 20.

7. Several variations in the older copies arise from abbreviations and other peculiarities in the modes of writing. Prominent among these is the remarkable passage, 1 Tim. iii. 16 (see Scrivener, 4th ed. vol. ii. pp. 390–395), where the difference between OC and

ΘС (ὅς and θεός) consists only in the presence or absence of two horizontal strokes.[1] We give a facsimile of the passage in Table VII.

[1] Briefly stated, the principal authorities for the different readings are as follows (see Tables for explanations where needful) :

1. In favor of ὅς : ℵ A (see below), C, F, G, and the following cursive MSS., 17, 33 (see p. 109), 73 (12th cent.), 181 (13th cent.). *Versions:* Goth., Æth. (ed. Platt), Philox. Syr. marg., and, with a relative pronoun which may represent either ὅς or ὅ, Copt., Sahidic, Pesh. Syr., Philox. Syr. text (so White, but Ward doubts this), Æth. (Polygl.), Arm., Erpenian Arabic, and a MS. Arabic version in the Vatican. *Quotations* or *References:* Origen, Basil, Epiphan., Jerome, Theod. Mopsuest., Cyr. Alex., Eutherius of Tyana, Gelasius (or Macarius of Jerusalem), Pope Martin I., Apollinarius, Chrysostom, Nestorius, and others.

2. In favor of θεός : ℵ[e] (a corrector of the twelfth century), A (corrected by a modern hand), C[c] (corrected in the ninth century), D[c] (corrected in the ninth century), K, L, P, and the great mass of cursive MSS. ; Arabic of the Polyglot, Slavonic, and Georgian versions (all these versions are of little or no authority) ; Greg. Nyss., Didymus, pseudo-Athanasius, Macedonius, Euthalius (?), Theod. Stud., Theophyl. ; and *probably* pseudo-Dionysius Alexandrinus, Theodoret, Severus, Joannes Damascenus, Photius.

3. In favor of ὅ : D, Old Lat. and Vulg. *quod ;* other ancient versions *may* have read ὅ, but not probably (see above); on the other hand, the Old Lat. and Vulg. may have *read* ὅς, but have rendered *quod* for the sake of the grammar. The Latin Fathers (except Jerome) generally read *quod ;* in one place pseudo-Chrysostom has ὅ.

The evidence was fully reviewed by Dr. W. Hayes Ward, in an article in the *Bibl. Sacra* for January, 1865. The reading of A *a primâ manu* has been disputed ; and Scrivener is disposed to believe it to have been ΘС ; but the matter has been very carefully examined by Wetstein, Porson, Tregelles, Tischendorf, Bishop Ellicott, Alford, and Sir Frederick Madden, who agree that the primitive reading was ὅς. B does not contain the Epistle.

As to the critical question, if θεός were the original reading, it would be difficult to explain how all the leading ancient versions, representing widely separated regions, should have dropped so important a word, and have substituted a relative pronoun. The reading ὅς has

8. Besides these prominent causes of variation there are slips of the pen, trifling varieties in spelling, interchange of synonymous words, omission or insertion of pronouns and particles, with occasional attempts at correction of words whose sense seems obscure, which go to make up the sum of those various readings whose number looks so large.

§ 10. *Rules of Judgment in Critical Cases*

While, therefore, the testimony of the most ancient manuscripts is always decisive where it is harmonious, which is true of the great bulk of Scripture, it is obvious that there will yet remain a wide margin for the exercise of critical judgment in cases where the leading authorities differ.

The number of these unsettled points would be alarming if their character in the main were not so unimportant. That number has been estimated by thousands, but being chiefly orthographical or verbal, or at most grammatical, the instances are few in

the best ancient authority; it is the more difficult reading, and best explains the origin of the others. It is adopted by Griesbach, Lachmann, Tischendorf, Tregelles, Westcott and Hort, Scrivener, Alford, Ellicott, Wordsworth, T. S. Green, Olshausen, Wiesinger, Huther, Meyer, De Wette. For a more extended discussion of this subject, see Burgon: *Revision Revised*, pp. 424–501, and the reply to it by Bishop Ellicott and Archdeacon Palmer, London, 1882. See, also, *Appendix J* of an interesting monograph upon Cod. 700 (604 Scrivener) of the Gospels, published in London, 1890, by Mr. H. C. Hoskier, of New York city.

which they affect the sense or bear upon any important fact or doctrine.

Nevertheless, the work of the conscientious critic is not done until all possible accuracy is reached, and the clearest possible light thrown upon what yet remains necessarily doubtful.

To aid in this work certain principles of judgment have been laid down upon which critical scholars are pretty well agreed:

1. In the first place it has become established as a rule that *conjectural* emendations are to be discarded. Unless respectable external authority can be found for a reading, it should not be admitted, however plausible may seem the arguments in its favor.

2. All scholars have agreed to adopt Bengel's prime canon, *Proclivi scriptioni præstat ardua*, "To an easy reading prefer the harder." Copyists were more likely to relieve a hard construction than to make an easy one difficult.

3. We may next mention the canon of Griesbach, *Brevior lectio præferenda est verbosiori*, "The briefer reading must be preferred to the longer."

The reasonableness of this rule results from the tendency of scribes to incorporate marginal notes or fuller parallel passages, or to amplify Old Testament quotations. And yet it must be modified by the consideration that words and clauses are sometimes omitted to remove difficulties (see Bengel's canon), or through Homœoteleuton.

4. Another more comprehensive principle may be thus stated : That reading is probably genuine from which the origin and diffusion of the others may be most readily explained. In practice this will usually be found to cover Nos. 2 and 3. We may say still more generally : In every question of textual criticism we have to consider what supposition will best explain all the facts in the case. We cannot settle these questions by any mechanical rules.

5. In estimating the value of the evidence of different MSS. their peculiar characteristics must be taken into account. Thus Codex D has special weight where it omits, as its general tendency is to add. Some would apply the reverse of this rule to Codex B. But when Scrivener (4th ed., vol. i., p. 120) quotes Dr. Dobbin as finding in B no fewer than 2556 cases of omissions of words or whole clauses, the fact will be less "startling" when we know, what Scrivener and McClellan (*New Testament,* vol. i., p. xxv., note) do not tell us, that his "standard of comparison" is no ancient or critical text, but "Elzevir, 1624"! See *Dublin Univ. Mag.,* Nov. 1859, p. 621. The question whether what Dr. Dobbin calls "omissions" in B are not rather, in a large majority of cases, *interpolations* in Elz. 1624, cannot be thus disposed of by a cool assump-

.tion.   See Westcott and Hort, *New Testament*, vol. ii., pp. 234–237.

6. Manuscripts differ also in the value of their testimony in different parts of the New Testament, some having a much better text of the Gospels than of the Epistles, and *vice versa*, e.g. A of the Gospels is quite inferior to A of the rest of the New Testament.   And, in general, experience and critical judgment are needful accurately to weigh the comparative value of manuscripts.

The editors of our latest critical text of the New Testament believe that the surest progress towards trustworthy presumptions is to be found in the historical study of documents, to reach what is called "Genealogical Evidence," as well as in weighing the "Internal evidence of *groups* of documents."   For an account of the methods for working out these problems, see the Introduction to Westcott and Hort's *Greek Testament*, or Dr. B. B. Warfield's *Textual Criticism of the New Testament*.

The whole subject seems to be well summed up by Dr. Hort, where he says (Introduction, § 83): "Textual criticism fulfils its task best, that is, is most likely to succeed ultimately in distinguishing true readings from false, when it is guided by a full and clear perception of all the classes of phenomena which directly or indirectly supply any kind of evidence, and when it regulates itself by such definite methods as

the several classes of phenomena suggest when pa-
tiently and circumspectly studied."

7. With all the help in the work of textual criticism which a knowledge of these facts and principles
may give, it is yet quite obvious that most students
of Scripture will be mainly dependent upon the critical judgment and skill of experts in this particular
department of sacred learning. The materials are so
difficult of access, and the labor of collating manuscripts, and of acquiring sufficient critical skill to
weigh them rightly, is so enormous, that Biblical
scholars will usually find it wiser simply to learn
how to make discriminating use of the materials
which critical editors have furnished to their hand.

The Christian world are under profound obliga-
tions to the few men who, having special gifts for
this kind of investigation, have been prompted by a
love of the truth to consecrate their lives to unre-
quited toil in this direction, and whose labors have
already brought forth fruits of incalculable value to
the Church of Christ.

The student will find the whole subject of textual
criticism discussed at length in the works of Scrivener, Tregelles, and Westcott and Hort, above referred to, and in the Art. "New Testament" in
Smith's *Bible Dictionary.* See, also, Schaff's *Com-
panion to the Greek Testament and the English Version* (New York, 1891); and Scrivener's *Six Lectures*

on the Text of the New Testament and the Ancient MSS. which Contain It (London, 1875); also, Ezra Abbot's *Notes on Scrivener's Plain Introduction*, edited by Dr. Thayer, of Cambridge, Mass., 1885. A useful contribution to the literature of the subject is the entertaining volume of the Rev. G. E. Merrill, *The Parchments of the Faith* (Philadelphia, 1894).

As the New World is not abundantly provided with critical material in the shape of original manuscripts of the New Testament, the author has thought it might be helpful to the readers of this manual to indicate the localities in America where such material may be found. He has accordingly prepared, in Table XI., a list of such manuscripts as have come to his knowledge, including those already catalogued in Tischendorf's *Prolegomena*, with brief descriptions of them. That they are not more numerous is a thing to be regretted. Dr. Gregory, the distinguished editor of the *Prolegomena*, himself an American, appends to his account of five American codices of the Vulgate version the following admonitory suggestion: "Sine dubio exstant in America codices alii. Ii tamen viri Americani, quibus sinus nummis resonat, qui etiam Europam, Asiam, Africam semper denuo percurrunt, adhuc minus codices manu scriptos quam libros in cunabulis quae dicunt typis expressos amant."

PART IV

CHARTS AND TABLES

TABLE I

CHRISTIAN NATIONS OF EUROPE

FORMED OUT OF THE DIVISION OF THE ROMAN EMPIRE

(See p. 5.)

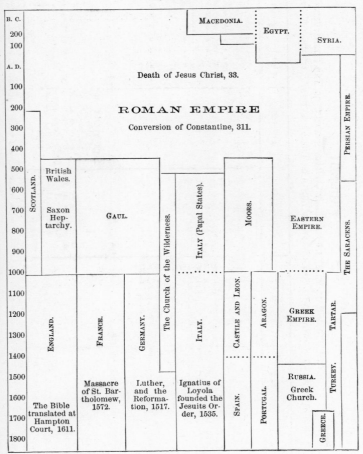

TABLE II

SYNCHRONISTICAL TABLES OF ANCIENT CIVILIZATION, SCIENCE, AND LITERATURE *

FROM THE " ANNALES ANTIQUITATIS. CHRONOLOGICAL TABLES OF ANCIENT HISTORY." OXFORD, 1835. TABLE XV., p. 36

DATE.	CIVILIZATION IN GENERAL.	POETRY AND RHETORIC.	PHILOSOPHY.	PHYSICS.	HISTORY.	DATE.
B.C. 50		B.C.	B.C.	B.C.	B.C.	B.C. 50
40		Virgil, the greatest epic and didactic poet of Rome, d. 19 B.C., aged 51. Horace, the great lyric poet, patronized by Mæcenas, d. 8 B.C., aged 57. Ovid, died in banishment at Tomos, A.D. 17, aged 59. Tibullus and Propertius. *Elegies.* Phædrus. *Fables.*			Livy, the celebrated historian, born at Padua, flourished under Augustus, and died at Rome, A.D. 19, aged 75.	40
30	AGE OF AUGUSTUS: the golden period of Roman Literature — Mæcenas—the poets Virgil, Horace, Ovid—the historian Livy — Varro the critic. The Greek language adopted at Court.				Valerius Maximus. *Celebrated actions and sayings of the Romans and other illustrious persons.* Velleius Paterculus, historian. Strabo, the great geographer, born about 60 B.C., still living A.D. 14.	30
20						20
10						10
0						0
A.D. 10	BIRTH OF CHRIST.	A.D.	A.D.	A.D.	A.D.	A.D. 10
20				15 Celsus, the Roman Hippocrates, whose system he transplanted to Rome.		20
30			30 Philo, an Alexandrine Jew. He was much attached to the philosophy of Plato.	30 Seneca—*Quæstiones Naturales.*	30 Pomponius Mela, wrote a geographical compendium.	30
40						40

* These tables are presented here simply as an appeal to recognized authority for the names of writers known to have flourished during the first three centuries. The dates are given just as they are found in the Oxford tables, which do not always conform to those assigned by the best recent authorities, and hence are not always in accord with those found in the body of this work.

DATE	CIVILIZATION IN GENERAL.	POETRY AND RHETORIC.	PHILOSOPHY.	PHYSICS.	HISTORY.	DATE
A.D.	A.D.	A.D.	A.D.	A.D.	A.D.	A.D.
50		50 LUCAN, heroic poem on the civil wars of Cæsar and Pompey. PERSIUS. *Satires.* PETRONIUS. *Satires.* SENECA. *Tragedies.*	30 SENECA, moral philosopher. His pupil, NERO, ordered him to be bled to death, 65 A.D.			50
60				60 PLINY the Elder, killed by an eruption of Vesuvius, 79 A.D.		60
70					70? QUINTUS CURTIUS. *History of Alexander the Great.* FLAVIUS JOSEPHUS, b. 37, d. 93. *Antiquities and Wars of the Jews.*	70
80	81? DOMITIAN introduces the censorship.	80 JUVENAL. *Satires.* VAL. FLACCUS. *Argonauts.*				80
90	98 *The last flourishing period of Roman culture under* TRAJAN *and* ADRIAN.	90 SILIUS ITALICUS, historical poet. MARTIAL, epigrammatist. STATIUS, the *Thebaid, etc.* QUINTILIAN, rhetorician, wrote under DOMITIAN. DIO CHRYSOSTOM, of *Prusa,* orator.	90 PLUTARCH, moralist and biographer, died about 140 A.D. EPICTETUS, the Stoic, a Phrygian slave. His *Morals.*		90 TACITUS, contemporary with Trajan. Philosophical historian. SUETONIUS. Adrian's Secretary. *Lives of the Twelve Cæsars.* FLORUS. An *Epitome of Roman History.* PLUTARCH of Chæronea, was contemporary with Trajan, and died about 140. PTOLEMY, geographer, etc., in the reign of Adrian and Antoninus Pius.	90
100	133 The great historians: PLUTARCH. TACITUS. SUETONIUS. *The great Ulpian library.* Public schools in all the provinces. Jurisprudence flourishes. Edifices — the Forum Trajani. Triumphal arches. Baths.	100 PLINY the Younger. *Panegyrics and Epistles.*				100
110						110
120						120
130						130
140						140
150				150 GALEN of *Pergamus,* celebrated physician at Rome. PTOLEMY of Alexandria, the greatest astronomer of antiquity. He also left a treatise on *Geography.*		150
160		160 LUCIAN, witty satiric dialogues. He died under COMMODUS. APULEIUS, satirical romance of the *Golden Ass* (the beautiful episode of *Psyche*).	160 APULEIUS, miscellaneous philosophical treatises. THE ANTONINES, sometimes called the Philosophic Emperors. — The latter, Marcus, was a strict disciple of the Stoics.			160
170					170? PAUSANIAS, the first writer of travels, wrote *Description of Greece.* APPIAN, historian under Trajan and the Antonines. ARRIAN. *Alexander's Expedition — India, e'c.* AULUS GELLIUS. *Noctes Atticæ,* fragments from ancient writers.	170
180						180
190						190

DATE.	CIVILIZATION IN GENERAL.	POETRY AND RHETORIC.	PHILOSOPHY.	PHYSICS.	HISTORY.	DATE.
A.D. 200	A.D. *Decline of Roman civilization*, from the death of MARCUS AURELIUS.		A.D.		A.D.	A.D. 200
210			210 DIOGENES LAERTIUS—*Lives of the Philosophers.*		JUSTIN. Abridgment of Trogus Pompeius' *History.*	210
220					DIO CASSIUS (b. 155). Only fragments of his great *History* from ÆNEAS to ALEXANDER SEVERUS exist.	220
230					ÆLIAN. Various history.	230
240					HERODIAN. *Roman History*, in eight books. He flourished between 180 and 235 A.D.	240
250			250 LONGINUS, philosopher and critic (treatise *On the Sublime*), d. 273.			250
260						260
270						270
280						280
290						290
300					300 D. Scriptores, *Historiæ Augustæ*: SPARTIANUS, CAPITOLINUS, TREBELLIUS, VOPISCUS, GALLICANUS, LAMPRIDIUS. 44 Lives, from Adrian to Caracalla.	300
310	312 From the time of CONSTANTINE the intellectual powers of man became almost entirely absorbed in religious controversies.					310
320						320
330						330

132

TABLE III

COMPARATIVE DIAGRAM, SHOWING WHAT CHRISTIAN WRITERS WERE CONTEMPORANEOUS *

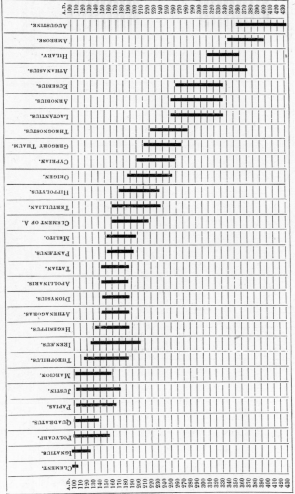

* For the uses of this table see Part I., ch. 4, §3, page 55 of this book.

133

TABLE IV

LIST OF WITNESSES OR ACTORS IN THE SCENES OF CHRISTIAN HISTORY

Grouped in connection with localities in which they lived, labored, or wrote, and with which their names have been associated in the history of the first three centuries. The period to which their respective testimonies chiefly relate is given approximately in the third column. See Map at the beginning of the volume.

LOCALITIES.	WITNESSES.	A.D.
SYRIA. Scene of life and crucifixion of Jesus; also of Paul's conversion. Seat of Apostolic Church, centre of Missions to the Gentiles.	CHRIST, Apostles, Evangelists.	30–70
	Paul, Apostle to the Gentiles.	36–64
	Barnabas, the Apostle.	36–72
	Evodius.	50–69
	Ignatius.	69–115
	Saturninus, the Gnostic.	110–120
	Justin, Apologist and Martyr.	133–150
	Hadrian, the Emperor.	117–138
	Theophilus, Bishop of Antioch.	150–181
	Lucian.	176–180
	Paul of Samosata, Bishop of Antioch.	260–273
	Tatian.	172–174
	Methodius, Bishop and Martyr.	290–300
	Pamphilus, Presbyter of Cæsarea.	294–309
	Eusebius, Bishop of Cæsarea.	260–340
	The Church at Jerusalem and Antioch.	36–300
ASIA MINOR. Paul's birthplace and early residence. Scene of first, second, and third missionary labors. John's later home.	Paul.	40–58
	Barnabas.	45–48
	Timothy.	47–96
	Silas.	51–54
	Luke.	51–58
	Titus.	57–59
	John, the Apostle.	70–100
	Cerinthus, the Jew.	70–100
	Polycarp, Bishop and Martyr of Smyrna.	100–155
	Hadrian, the Emperor.	117–138
	Papias, Bishop of Hierapolis.	110–163
	Pliny Secundus, Governor of Bithynia.	104–112
	Irenæus, Bishop of Lyons.	177–202
	Marcion, the Heretic.	130–
	Justin, Apologist and Martyr.	140–
	Melito, Bishop of Sardis.	177–?
	Claudius Apollinaris, Bishop of Hierapolis.	172–?
	Aristides, the Sophist.	130–180
	Theodotus, the Gnostic.	160–170
	Artemon.	200–
	The Churches at Ephesus, Smyrna, Hierapolis, and in Galatia.	52–300
MACEDONIA and GREECE. Scene of Paul's second and third journeys. Seat of the Corinthian Church, and of Paul's labors for eighteen months.	Paul.	52–65
	Silas.	52–54
	Luke.	52–54
	Timothy.	52–58
	Titus.	57–59
	Clement of Rome (Epistles). (†102)	–95
	Epictetus, the Stoic.	109–
	Dion, the Sophist orator at Corinth.	109–
	Quadratus of Athens.	126–
	Aristides of Athens, Apologist.	130–
	Dionysius.	170–176
	The Churches at Philippi, Thessalonica, Berœa, and Corinth.	53–300

LOCALITIES.	WITNESSES.	A.D.
ITALY. Scene of Paul's imprisonment and place of writing his later Epistles.	Paul.	61–66
	Peter (?).	61–66
	Linus, Bishop of Rome.	67–78
	Suetonius, Historian.	70–130
	Clement, Bishop of Rome.	91–102
	Tacitus, Historian.	55–117
	Juvenal, Satirist.	80–120
	Ignatius, Martyr.	109–115
	Diognetus (?), to whom Epistle is addressed.	130–
	Pius.	142–157
	Hadrian, Emperor.	117–138
	Cerdo.	140–
	Polycarp.	155–
	Justin.	150–
	Soter.	171–
	Celsus.	175–
	Irenæus.	177–
	Hegesippus, the Church historian.	170–180
	Galen.	130–201
	Hippolytus.	198–235
	Dion Cassius.	155–230
	Aurelian.	212–276
	The Church in Rome.	53–300
EGYPT. Scene of the flight into Egypt, and residence of certain persons who were converted on the day of Pentecost.	Hadrian, Emperor.	117–138
	Basilides.	125–140
	Carpocrates.	120–
	Valentinus.	130–160
	Heracleon.	150–
	Justin, Martyr.	138–140
	Athenagoras.	177–
	Catechetical School of Alexandria.	166–395
	Pantænus.	181–190
	Clement.	190–218
	Origen.	185–254
	Dionysius.	247–265
	Gregory Thaum.	244–270
	Theognostus.	261–280
	Amelius.	263–
	Porphyry.	233–305
	Athanasius.	296–373
	Hierocles.	300–
AFRICA. Birthplace of Simon and Manaen. Residence of certain Pentecostal converts.	Apuleius, the philosopher.	160–170
	Hermogenes.	170–
	Praxeas (?).	196–
	Tertullian.	190–240
	Catechetical School of Carthage.	200–430
	Cyprian.	246–258
	Arnobius.	280–330
	Lactantius.	280–330
	Hilary.	320–368
	Ambrose.	340–397
	Augustine.	354–430

TABLE V

REFERENCES TO THE CANONICAL BOOKS BY THE FATHERS AND THEIR OPPONENTS

	Clement of Rome.	Peshito Version.	Ignatius.	Papias.	Elders of Irenæus.	Barnabas, Epist.	Polycarp, Ep. to Phil.	Basilides.	The Ophites.	Valentinus.	Heracleon.	Epistle to Diognetus.	Marcion.	Justin Martyr.	Ptolemæus.	Hermas, Shepherd.	Irenæus.	Church at Smyrna.	Theophilus.	Canon of Muratori.	Melito.	Apollinaris.	Tatian.	Hegesippus.	Church at Vienna.	Athenagoras.	Clement of Alexand.	Tertullian.	Theodotus.	Hippolytus.	Origen.	Cyprian.	Eusebius.
Matthew	a	o	a	a	a	a	a	a	a	a	a	o		a	a	o	a	o	a	a?		a	a		o	a	a	a	a	a	a	a	a
Mark		o		a		a		a	a	a	a	o	o	a	a		a		a?	a		a?			o	c?	a	a	a	a	a	a	a
Luke	a	o	a	a	a		a	a	a	a	a	o	a	a	a	a	a	o	a	a		a?	a	o	o	a	a	a	a	a	a	a	a
John	c?	o	a				a	a	a	a	a	o	a	a?	a		a		a	a		a		o	o		a	a	a	a	a	a	a
Acts	a	o			a		a		a	a		o	a?	a			a	a	o	a			a?	o	c?	a	a	a		a	a	a	a
Ep. to Romans	a	o	a		a		a	a	a			o	a	o	a	a	a		o	a			a		c?	a	a	a	a	a	a	a	a
1 Ep. to Corinth.	a	o	a		a	a	a	a	a			o	a	o	a		a	a	o	a					o	o	a	a	a	a	a	a	a
2 Ep. to Corinth.		o					a	a	a			o	a	c?		a	a		o	a					o	a	a	a	a	a	a	a	a
Ep. to Galatians	a	o					a			a			a	o	a?		a			a							a	a		a	a	a	a
" Ephesians		o	a									o	a	o	a		a			a			a?				a	a	a	a	a	a	a
" Philippians		o					a						a	o			a		o	a			a?		o		a	a		a	a	a	a
" Colossians		o					a			a			a	c?			a		o	a					o	c?	a	a	a	a	a	a	a
1 Ep. to Thess.	a	o					a		a		a		o	o			a			a							a	a		a	a	a	a
2 Ep. to Thess.		o					a						o				a		o	a					o		a	a		a	a	a	a
1 Timothy		o				a		a				o	o			o	a			a							a	a		a	a	a	a
2 Timothy		o				a	a						o				a		o	a							a	a		a	a	a	a
Titus	a	o					a						a?				a			a							a	a		a	a	a	a
Philemon	c?	o			a?					a		o				o	a		o	a	o		a				a	a		a			a
1 Peter	c?		a	a			a	a				o		c?			a			a					o		a	a	a	a	a	a	a?
1 John		o		a			o	a	a	a		o	o				a	a	o						o		a	a		a	a		a?
Hebrews	o	o				a	c			a			o			o	o		o		o				o		a	a?			a	a	a?
James	o	o															a?			a							a				a?		a?
2 Peter	o																			a	c?	a					a	a			a?		a?
2 John																	o			a													a?
3 John																				a													a?
Jude				a													a?			a							a	a				a	a?
Revelation					a			a	a					a		c	a		a?		a	a	a	a	a	a	a	a		a	a	a	a

ABBREVIATIONS.—(a) alluded to, acknowledged, or quoted; (c) containing coincidences of expression, showing familiarity with; (o) omission, or opposition to its admission into the Canon; (?) doubt, or lack of absolute certainty about the reference indicated.

136

TABLE VI

CATALOGUES OF DISPUTED BOOKS

CONDENSED BY PERMISSION FROM WESTCOTT'S LIST, IN SMITH'S "DICTIONARY OF THE BIBLE"

	Epistle to Hebrews.	Jude.	James.	2 and 3 John.	2 Peter.	Apocalypse.
I. CONCILIAR CATAL.						
[Laodicea] (A.D. 366)..	Q	Q	Q	Q	Q	
Carthage (A.D. 397)...	Q	Q	Q	Q	Q	Q
Apostolic (Council Quinisext).........	Q	Q	Q	Q	Q	
II. ORIENTAL CATAL.						
(a) Syria:						
The Peshito Version..	Q		Q			
Junilius.............	Q	?	?	?	?	?
Joann. Damasc.......	Q	Q	Q	Q	Q	Q
Ebed Jesu...........	Q		Q			
(b) Palestine:						
Eusebius............	Q	?	?	?	?	?
Cyril of Jerusalem († A.D. 386).........	Q	Q	Q	Q	Q	
Epiphanius..........	Q	Q	Q	Q	Q	Q
(c) Alexandria:						
Origen..............	Q	?	?	?	?	?
Athanasius († A.D. 373)	Q	Q	Q	Q	Q	Q
(d) Asia Minor:						
Gregory Naz. (A.D. 389)...............	Q	Q	Q	Q	Q	
Amphilochius (A.D. 380)...............	Q	?	?	?	?	?

	Epistle to Hebrews.	Jude.	James.	2 and 3 John.	2 Peter.	Apocalypse.
(e) Constantinople:						
Chrysostom........	Q		Q			
Leontius...........	Q	Q	Q	Q	Q	Q
Nicephorus........	Q	Q	Q	Q	Q	?
III. OCCIDENTAL CAT.						
(a) Africa:						
Cod. Claromontanus.	U	Q	Q	Q	Q	Q
Augustine..........	Q	Q	Q	Q	Q	Q
(b) Italy:						
Canon of Muratori..		Q		U		Q
Philastrius.........		Q	Q	Q	Q	Q
Jerome.............	Q	Q	Q	Q	Q	Q
Rufinus............	Q	Q	Q	Q	Q	Q
Innocent...........	Q	Q	Q	Q	Q	Q
[Gelasius]..........	Q	Q	Q	Q	Q	Q
Cassiodorus (Vet. Trans.)...........	Q		Q			Q
(c) Spain:						
Isidore of Seville....	Q	Q	Q	Q	Q	Q
Cod. Baroc. 206.....	Q	Q	Q	Q	Q	Q

Q=Direct quotation.   ?=An expression of doubt.   U=Uncertain reference.

TABLE VII

FACSIMILES OF MANUSCRIPTS

1. CODEX SINAITICUS.
2. —— VATICANUS.
3. —— ALEXANDRINUS.
4. —— BEZÆ.
5. —— ROSSANENSIS.
6. —— EPHRÆMI.
7. EVANGELIUM, 302ª.
8. CODEX BASILEENSIS.
9. —— CLAROMONTANUS.
10. —— LAUDIANUS.
11. —— COLBERTINUS.
12. —— LEICESTRENSIS.
13. —— PURPUREUS.
14. —— AMIATINUS.
15. —— LENOX LIBRARY VULGATE.

FACSIMILES OF MANUSCRIPTS

Specimen of the Codex Sinaiticus, containing 1 Tim. iii. 16:

και ομολογουμε | *νως μεγα εστιν* | *το της ευσεβειας* | *μυστηριον ος ε* | *φανερωθη εν σαρ* | *κι· εδικαιωθη εν* | $\overline{πνι}$ *ωφθη αγγελοις* | *εκηρυχθη* *εν ε* | *θνεσιν επιστευ* | *θη εν κοσμω·* | *ανελημφθη εν* | *δοξη.*

KΛIOMOΛOΓOYMe
NWCMEΓΛECTIN
TOTHCEYCEBEIΛC
MYCTHPIONOCE
ΦANEPWΘENᴄᴘ
KI·EΔIKΛIWΘEN
ΠNIWΦΘHΛΓΓΕλοιᶜ
EKHPYXΘENE
ΘNECINEΠICTEY
ΘHENKOCMW·
ΛNEΛHMΦΘHEN
ΔOΞH

140

SPECIMEN OF THE CODEX VATICANUS, CONTAINING MARK XVI. 3-8.

[*Reduced from Dean Burgon's photograph of the whole page. By permission*].

μῖν τὸν λίθον ἐκ τῆσ
| θύρασ τοῦ μνη-
μείου | καὶ ἀνα
βλέψασαι θεω|ροῦ-
σιν ὅτι ἀνακεκύ |
λισται ὁ λιθοσ ἦν
γὰρ | μέγασ σφό-
δρα καὶ ἐλ | θοῦσαι
ἐισ τὸ μνημεῖ | ον
εἶδον νεανίσκον |
καθήμενον ἐν τοῖσ
| δεξιοῖσ περιβε-
βλημέ | νον στολὴν
λευκὴν | καὶ ἐξε-
θαμβήθησαν | ὁ δὲ
λέγει αὐταῖσ μὴ |
ἐκθαμβεῖσθε ᾿ιν ζη-
τει | τε τὸν ναζα-
ρηνὸν τὸ– | ἐσταυ-
ρωμένον ἠγέρ|θη
ὀυκ ἔστιν ὧδε ἴδε
| ὁ τόποσ ὅπου
ἔθηκα | αὐτὸν ἀλλα
ὑπάγετε | ἐιπατε
τοῖσ μαθηταῖσ |
αὐτοῦ καὶ τῶ πέ-
τρω | ὅτι προάγει
ὑμᾶσ ἐισ | τὴν γα-
λιλάιαν ἐκεῖ αὐ
| τὸν ὄψεσθε κα-
θὼσ εἶ | πεν ὑμῖν
καὶ ἐξελθοῦ | σαι
ἔφυγον ἀπὸ τοῦ |
μνημέιου εἶχεν
γὰρ | αὐτὰσ τρό-
μοσ καὶ ἔκ | στασισ
καὶ ὀνδενὶ ὀυ | δὲν
εἶπον ἐφοβοῦν | το
γάρ :

Κατὰ
Μάρκον.

SPECIMEN OF CODEX ALEXANDRINUS, CONTAINING 1 TIM. III. 16.

By permission from the photograph in the Astor Library.

142

Codex Alexandrinus, 1 Tim. iii. 14–iv. 1.—*Copy of the facsimile in modern Greek letters.*

The specimen commences with 1 Tim. iii. 14, and extends to chapter iv., verse 1. It is mutilated on the left side, but the missing words are supplied in the following transcript of the passage. The famous letters ΘC in verse 16 have become indistinct by frequent handling, so that experts would now be no longer able to form decisive judgments upon the point in controversy, viz.: whether the — over them and the — in the O are *a prima manu* or by a later hand.

Ταῦτά σοι γράφω ἐλπίζων ἐλθεῖ
ν πρός σὲ ἐντάχει · ἐὰν δὲ βραδύνω
ἵνα ειδῃ ς πῶς δεῖ ἐν οἴκῳ θεοῦ [ῶ] ἀνασ
τρέφεσ θαι · ἥτις ἐστὶν ἐκκλησία
θυ ζῶ ντος · στύλος καὶ ἑδραίωμα
τῆςαλ ηθείας · καὶ ὁμολογον
μέν ως ς μέγα ἐστὶν τὸ τῆς εὐσε
βεία ς μυστήριον · ΟС ἐφανερώ
θηὲ ν σαρκὶ ἐδικαιώθη ἐν πνεύματι [ΠΝΙ-]
ὤφ θη ἀγγέλοις ἐκηρύχθη ἐν
ἐθ νεσιν ἐπιστεύθη ἐν κόσμῳ
ἀ νελημφθη ἐν δόξῃ ·
Τὸ δὲ πνεῦμα ῥητῶς λέγει ὅτι ἐν ὑστέρ **4**:ο1
ο ις καιροῖς αποστήσονταί τι
ς τῆς πίστεως,ὡς προσέχοντες

143

ΚΔ ∴ ΙΔΩΝ ΔΕ ΤΟΥΣ ΟΧΛΟΥΣ ΑΝΕΒΗ ΕΙΣ ΤΟ ΟΡΟΣ
ΚΑΙ ΚΑΘΙΣΑΝΤΟΣ ΑΥΤΟΥ ΠΡΟΣΗΛΘΟΝ ΑΥΤΩ

ΚΕ ∴ ΟΙ ΜΑΘΗΤΑΙ ΑΥΤΟΥ ΚΑΙ ΑΝΟΙΞΑΣ ΤΟ ΣΤΟΜΑ ΑΥΤΟΥ
ΕΔΙΔΑΣΚΕΝ ΑΥΤΟΥΣ ΛΕΓΩΝ

ΚΣ ∴ ΜΑΚΑΡΙΟΙ ΟΙ ΠΤΩΧΟΙ ΠΝΙ ΟΤΙ ΑΥΤΩΝ ΕΣΤΙΝ
Η ΒΑΣΙΛΕΙΑ ΤΩΝ ΟΥΡΑΝΩΝ

uidens autem turbas ascendit in montem
et sedente eo accesserunt ad eum
discipuli eius et aperiens os suum
docuit eos dicens
beati pauperes sptu quoniam ipsorum est
regnum caelorum

144

πονηρου οτι | σου εστιν η βα | σιλεια και η δυ | ναμις και η δο | ξα εις
τους αιω | νας αμην. | Εαν γαρ αφητε | τοις αν[θρωπ]οις τα | παραπ-
τωματα.

EV MATTHAEI VI 13 14
(COD FOL 26ᵃ)

SPECIMEN OF THE CODEX EPHRÆMI, CONTAINING 1 TIM. III. 15, 16.

ωμα της αληϑειασ · | Και ομολογουμενωσ μεγα εστιν το της ευσεβειασ μυ | ϲτηριον · ̅ϑ̅[εο]ϲ εφανερωϑη εν σαρκι · εδικαιωϑη εν πν[ευματ]ι.

TRANSCRIPTION OF THE FACSIMILE OF EVANGELIUM 30
UPON THE OPPOSITE PAGE.

πλήσαντες σπόγγον
ὄξους καὶ ὑσσώπῳ
περιθέντες, προ
σήνεγκαν αὐτοῦ τῷ
στόματι. ὅτε οὖν
ἔλαβε τὸ ὄξος ὁ ι̅υ̅
εἶπε · Τετέλεσται
καὶ κλίνας τὴν κε
φαλὴν, παρέδωκε
τὸ πν̅α̅. Οἱ οὖν Ἰου
δαῖοι ἵνα μὴ μείνῃ
ἐπὶ τοῦ σταυροῦ τὰ
σώματα ἐν τῷ σα
ββάτῳ · ἐπεὶ παρα
σκευή ἦν · ἦν γὰρ με
γάλη ἡ ἡμέρα ἐκεί
νου τοῦ σαββάτου,
ἠρώτησαν τὸν Πι
λάτον, ἵνα κατεαγῶ
σιν αὐτῶν τὰ σκέ
λη καὶ ἀρθῶσιν ·
ἦλθον οὖν οἱ στρατι

146

ῶται · καὶ τοῦ μὲν πρώτου
κατέαξαν τὰ σκέλη
καὶ τοῦ ἄλλου τοῦ συσ
ταυρωθέντος αὐ τῷ ·
ἐπὶ δὲ τὸν ι̅ν̅ ἐλθόν
τες · ὡς εἶδον αὐτὸν
ἤδη τεθνηκότα, οὐ
κατέαξαν αὐτοῦ τὰ
σκέλη · ἀλλ᾽ εἰς τῶν στρα
τιωτῶν λόγχῃ αὐτοῦ
τὴν πλευρὰν ἔνυξε ·
καὶ εὐθέως ἐξῆλθεν
αἷμα καὶ ὕδωρ · καὶ ὁ
ἑωρακὼς μεμαρτύ
ρηκε · καὶ ἀληθινὴ
ἐστιν ἡ μαρτυρία αὐτοῦ ·
κἀκεῖνος οἶδεν ὅτι
ἀληθῆ λέγει, ἵνα ὑμεῖς
πιστευσητε · ἐγένετο
γὰρ ταῦτα, ἵνα ἡ γρα
φὴ πληρωθῇ · Ὀστοῦν
ὸν συντριβήσεται ἀπ᾽ [αυτου.

SPECIMEN PAGE OF EVANGELIUM 302ᵃ (belonging to Rev. R. A. Benton, of Sewickley, Pa.), containing John xix. 29, πλήσαντες σπόγγον —ἀπ'[αυτου 36. This is a part of one of the twelve "gospels of the holy passion" (τῶν ἁγίων παθῶν), viz., No. 9. John xix. 25–37, or for the 9th hour of the vigil of Good Friday (τῆς ἁγιας παραμονῆς).

SPECIMEN OF THE CODEX BASILEENSIS, OF THE TENTH CENTURY, CONTAINING LUKE I. 1, 2, NEARLY AS IN ALL GREEK TESTAMENTS.

εὐαγγέ[λιον] κατὰ λουκᾶν:

ἐπειδήπερ πολλοὶ ἐπεχείρησαν ἀνατάξασθαι | διήγησιν περὶ τῶν πε-
πληροφορημένων | ἐν ἡμῖν πραγματων. καθὼς παρέδοσαν ἡμῖ | οἱ
ἀπαρχῆς αὐτόπται καὶ ὑπηρεται γενόμενοι.

Ḥ ΑΓΑΠΗ
ΟΥΔΕΠΟΤΕΕΚΠΙΠΤΕΙ +

Codex CLAROMONTANUS: Sixth Century; Greek Text.—1 Cor. xiii. 8.

ἡ ἀγάπη | οὐδέποτε ἐκπίπτει

,CARITAS
NUMQUAMEXCIDET

Codex CLAROMONTANUS: Sixth Century; Latin Text.—1 Cor. xiii. 8.

caritas | numquam excidet

THNEKKΛHCIΛN
TOΥKΥ

Codex LAUDIANUS: Sixth Century; Greek Text.—Acts xx. 28.

την εκκλησιαν | του κ[υριο]υ

148

Codex COLBERTINUS: Eleventh Century; the "Queen of the Cursives."—Luke i. 8, 9.

ξει τῆσ ἐφημερίασ αὐτοῦ ἔναντι τοῦ κ[υρίο]υ κατὰ τὸ ἔθοσ τῆσ ἱερατειασ. ἔλαχεν τοῦ θυμιᾶ

Codex LEICESTRENSIS: Fourteenth Century.—1 Tim. iii. 16.

τῆσ εὐσεβε(θ)ίασ μυστήριον· ὁ θ[εὸ]σ ἐφανερώθη ἐν σαρ· κι· ἐδικαιώθη ἐν πνεύματι· ὤφθη ἀγγέλοις·

Codex SINAITICUS: Fourth Century.—John i. 18.

νογενης θ[εὸ]ς [ο ων corr.] εις τον

This extract shows that the words μονο-γενὴς θεός, which are retained in the Re-viser's Text (W–H.), are found in the text of codex ℵ a prima manu. The interpolation of ὁ ὤν, above the line, is by ℵᶜ (a third hand). The MS. evidence in support of the reading is thus given by W–H.: "Text ℵ* (omitting ὁ ὤν) B. C. L. (33) syr. vg.hl. mg (me apparently)."

Codex PURPUREUS: Sixth Century.—John xv. 20.

του λογου ου

Codex AMIATINUS, A.D. 541: the oldest known MS. of the Vulgate.—Acts vii. 6. Locutus est autem d[eu]s

Codex LAUDIANUS, Latin Text, Sixth Century.—Acts xx. 28.

149

TABLE VIII

UNCIAL MANUSCRIPTS

(Index at the end of the Table)

TABLE VIII

UNCIAL MANUSCRIPTS OF THE NEW TESTAMENT

CLASSIFIED IN THE ORDER OF THEIR CENTURIES, WITH PRESENT LOCALITY, CONTENTS, AND HISTORY

In this table the uncials are arranged, within their respective centuries, in alphabetical order. For an alphabetical arrangement of *all* the uncials see page 168. The titles here given are those assigned by Tischendorf, unless otherwise noted. They usually indicate the present place of deposit. The small capital letters A, C, P, R, attached to the signs of certain MSS. indicate that they contain ACTS, CATHOLIC EPISTLES, PAULINE EPISTLES, or REVELATION. "F—S. in Scr." means "Facsimile in Scrivener, 4th Edition, Volume I." For other abbreviations see Glossary.

CENTURY.	SIGN.	TITLE OF CODICES.	PRESENT PLACE OF DEPOSIT.	CONTENTS.	EDITOR, WITH PLACE AND DATE OF PUBLICATION.	REMARKS.
IV	א	Sinaiticus.	St. Petersburg.	New Testament entire.	Tischendorf: St. Petersburg, 1862. fol. Leipsic, 1863. 4to. Leipsic, 1865 (1864). 8vo.	See page 96, Table VII., and Tisch. Proleg., pp. 345–354.
	B	Vaticanus.	Library of the Vatican, Rome. No. 1209.	New Testament entire to Hebrews ix. 14 καθα. Includes the Catholic Epistles, but wants 1st and 2d Timothy, Titus, Philemon, and Revelation.	Card. Mai, Rome, 1857. 4to. Vercellone, Rome, 1859. 8vo. Tisch., Leipsic, 1867. 4to, with App. 1869. Vercellone and Cozza, Rome, 1868. fol. Cozza–Luzi, Rome, 1889. 4to.	See page 100, Table VII., and Tisch., pp. 358–366.
	T^{wg} T_{Paul}	Parisiensis.	Egyptian Museum, Louvre, Paris. No. 7332.	Four words from 1 Tim. vi. 2, and about 20 from 1 Tim. iii. 15, 16.	Theodore Zahn. Erlangen, 1884.	1 T m. iii. 16 ω εφανερωϑη and και ε[δικαιωϑη]. *Vide* Zahn, *Forschungen*, etc., vol. ii., p. 277. See Tisch., p. 441. "*Saec. iv–vi?*" Tisch.

152

Century.	Sign.	Title of Codices.	Present Place of Deposit.	Contents.	Editor, with Place and Date of Publication.	Remarks.
V	ℶ^act_Paul	**Romæ Vaticanus.** Once Basil 100—before that Patiriensis 27.	Library of the Vatican at Rome. Gr 2061.	Fragments of the Acts and of the Catholic and Pauline Epistles.	P. Batiffol. (1890?)	The MS. has 316 leaves, of which 21 are palimpsest. It was brought from the monastery of St. Mary of Patirium, a suburb of Rossana, in Calabria. Discovered in the Vatican by Batiffol in 1887. Tisch., pp. 447, 448.
	A	**Alexandrinus.**	British Museum, London.	New Testament entire except Matt. i.—xxv. 6 ὁ νυμφιος ἔρχεται; John vi. 50 ινα—viii. 52 και συ; 2 Cor. iv. 13 ἐπιστευσα—xii. 6 ἐξ ἐμοῦ, inclusive.	Woide, London, 1786. Cowper, London, 1860. Brit. Museum. Photographic facsimiles, Lond, 1879, 1880.	See page 103. Table VII, and Tisch, p. 354. See, also, Scrivener, 4th ed, vol. i, p. 97.
	C	**Ephræmi.**	National Library of Paris, No. 9.	All the New Testament books except 2 Thess. and 2 John, but with many lacunae.	Tisch., Leipsic, 1843. (Old Testament fragments, 1845.)	See page 79, Table VII, and T.sch., p. 366.
	I^act I^Paul	**Petropolitanus.** (Tischendorfianus II. In Murat's Catalogue, number, ed VI. i. (1) (2) (3); iii. (7—12); ii. (4) (5) (6). Fragments1, 2, and 5 Scrivener.)	Imperial Library. St. Petersburg.	*Fragment 1.* John xi. 50—xii. 9; xv. 12—xvi. 2; xix. 11—24. *Frag. 2.* Matt. xiv. 13—16, 19—23; xxiv. 37—xxv. 1; xxv. 32—45; xxvi. 31—45; Mark ix. 14—22; xiv. 58—70. *Frag. 5.* Acts xxviii. 8—17; 1 Cor. xv. 53—xvi. 9; Tit. i. 1—13, with lacuna.	Tisch., *Mon. Sac. In. edita*, vol. i. Leipsic, 1855.	The sign *I* represents seven different fragments of palimpsest MSS., three of which belong to the fifth century, and the rest to the sixth and seventh; for which see below. "*Textus est optimæ notæ.*" See Tisch., pp. 378, 415, 431.
	I^b	**Londinensis.**	British Museum Library, Add. MSS. 17,136.	John xiii. 16, 19, 20, 23, 24, 26, 27. John xvi. 7. 8, 9, 12, 13, 15, 16, 18, 19, with lacuna.	Tisch., *Mon. Sac. In. edita*, vol. ii. Leipsic, 1857.	Four leaves of a 16mo volume brought from the Nitrian Desert, a palimpsest containing the hymns of Severus in Syriac. Scrivener (4th Ed.) calls it N^b. See Tisch., p. 379.

Century.	Sign.	Title of Codices.	Present Place of Deposit.	Contents.	Editor, with Place and Date of Publication.	Remarks.
V (Continued.)	Q	Guelpher-bytanus.	Weissenburg, 64.	Twelve fragments of 247 verses from Luke and John.	Knittel, Brunswick, 1762. Tisch., *Monum. Sac. Inedita,* vol. iii. Leipsic, 1860.	Palimpsest consisting of 13 leaves. See Tisch. Proleg., p. 388.
	Q^P	Porfirianus Chiovensis.	Library of Abp. Porfiri at St Petersburg.	Fragments of 1 Cor. i., vi., vii.		A papyrus manuscript brought by Porfiri from the East. Examined by Tisch., 1862. See Tisch. Proleg., p. 434.
	T^a	Romæ Borgianus I.	Library of the Propaganda, Rome.	Luke xxii. 20 — xxiii. 20; John vi. 28—67; vii. 6—viii. 31 with lacuna.	Giorgi, Rome, 1789 (John). B. H. Alford, and Tisch., collated the fragment of Luke.	The fragment (T^a) contains 177 verses; "*est optimæ notæ.*" See Tisch., p. 391.
	T$_{woi}$	Olim Woidii.	Oxford (?) (Once C. G. Woide's.)	(T$_{woi}$) Luke xii. 15—xiii. 32 αυτοις πο; John viii. 33—42 γαρ εκ του.	T$_{woi}$, Ford, App. Cod. Alex., Oxon., 1799.	The Greek text is accompanied by a version in the Thebaic dialect. Tisch., Proleg., pp. 392, 439.
	T^7	Sinaiticus.	Convent of St. Catherine, Mt. Sinai.	Matt. xiv. 28—31.	J. Rendel Harris. *Bib. Frag. from Mt. Sinai.* London, 1890. No. 7.	See Tisch., p. 1308.
	T^{10}	Sinaiticus.	Convent of St. Catherine.	Matt. xxv. 15—37; xxvi. 17—39; xxviii. 11—20. Mark i. 11—22; ii. 21—iii. 3; iii. 27—iv. 4; v. 9—20.	J. R. Harris, *Bib. Frag.,* pp. xi., xii., and 27—44. No. 10.	A palimpsest fragment of 9 leaves. See Tisch., p. 1308.
	T^{14}	Sinaiticus.	Convent of St. Catherine.	1 Cor. i. 25—27; ii. 6—8; iii. 8—10; iii. 20.	J. R. Harris, *Bib. Fragm.,* No. 14, pp. xiii., and 54—56.	Seven papyrus fragments. See Tisch., p. 1308.
VI	D	Bezæ.	University Lib., Cambridge. (Nn ii. 41.)	Gospels and Acts except Matt. i. 1—20; vi. 20—ix. 2; xxvii. 2—12; John i. 16—iii. 26; Acts viii. 29—x. 14; xxi. 2—10, 15—18; xxii. 10—20, 29—xxviii. 31.	Kipling, in facsimile type, Cambridge, 1793. Scrivener, in ordinary type, Cambridge, 1864, cf. J. R. Harris, *Texts and Studies,* vol. ii., Camb., 1891.	Matt. iii. 7—16, Mark xvi. 15—20, John xviii. 14—xx. 13, are supplied by a later hand (9th century?). Stichometric and Græco-Latin. "It is, to the best of our belief, substantially a Western text of Cent. II., with occasional readings probably due to cent. IV." W—H, § 202. See Table VII. See Tisch., pp. 360, 954.

CENTURY.	SIGN.	TITLE OF CODICES.	PRESENT PLACE OF DEPOSIT.	CONTENTS.	EDITOR, WITH PLACE AND DATE OF PUBLICATION.	REMARKS.
VI *(Continued.)*	D^P	**Claromontanus.**	National Lib., Paris, 107.	All of Paul's Epistles except Rom. i. 1—7, 27—30; 1 Cor. xiv. 13—22.	Tischendorf, Leipsic, 1852.	Procured by Beza at Clermont (Oise), near Beauvais. Rom. i. 27—30; and 1 Cor. xiv. 13—22, have been supplied by *early* hands. F—S. in Scr., p. 124. See Tisch., p. 419.
	E^A	**Laudianus** 35.	Bodleian Library, Oxford.	Acts entire except xxvi. 29 Ευξαιμην to xxviii. 26 λέγων.	Hearne, Oxford, 1715. Tischendorf, *M.S.L.*, vol. ix., Leipsic, 1870.	Presented to University of Oxford in 1636 by Abp. Laud. Stichometric and Graeco-Latin. See Tisch., p. 410. F—S. in Scr., p. 121.
	H^P	**Coislinianus.** (Scrivener.)	(*a.*) Twenty-one leaves. Nat. Lib., Paris, 202. (*b.*) Two leaves, Imp. Lib., St. Petersburg. Muralt xlv. (*c.*) Two leaves, Moscow, SS. 60 (LXI.), and one in the Roumian't Museff Museum at Moscow. (*d.*) Four leaves belonging to Abp. Porfiri, and the Archimandrite Antony. (*e.*) Nine leaves found in the binding of MSS. at Mt. Athos, one of which is in the Paris Lib., containing Gal. iv. 30—v. 5. (*f.*) Two leaves in the Nat. Lib. at Turin, B. 1—5.	(*a*) 1. Cor. x. 22—29; xi. 9—16, Col. i. 26—ii. 8; ii. 20—iii. 4; 1 Tim. iii. 7—13; Titus i. 1—3; i. 15—ii. 5; iii. 13—15; Heb. ii. 11—16; iii. 13—18; iv. 12—15—xii. 10—15; xiii. 24, 25. (*b*) (St. Petersburg.) Gal. iv. 4—10; ii. 9—14; Col. iii. 11—13. (*c*) (Moscow.) Heb. i. 3—8; x. 1—3; 3—7, 32—38. (*d*) (Antony.) Cited by Tisch. on 2 Cor. iv. 2—7; 1 Thess. ii. 9—13; iv. 5—11. (Porfiri.) Col. iii. 4—11. (Mt. Athos.) 2 Cor. x. 8—12; x. 18—xi. 6; xi. 12—xii. 2; Gal. i. 1—4; i. 14—17; iv. 30—v. 5. (Turin.) 1 Tim. vi. 9—13; 2 Tim. ii. 1—9.	*a* and *b* Montfaucon. *Bibliotheca Coisliniana* (Paris, 1715), p. 261 ff. *c* In facsimile by Sabas, *Specimina Palæographica,* Moscow, 1863. *d* (Antony.) Cited by Tisch. critical edition. *e Archives des Missions scientifiques et littéraires,* 3e ser. tom. iii., pp. 420—429. Paris, 1876.	Of this MS. 40 leaves are now known, nearly all found in the *binding* of MSS. which belonged originally to the Monastery of St. Athanasius at Mt. Athos. The 12 leaves in the National Library at Paris, with two others now at St. Petersburg, came from the library of Bp. Coislin of Metz. The 2 Moscow leaves were first described by Matthæi in his *N. Test. Gr. et Lat.* on Heb. x. 1, but have since been published in facsimile by Sabas in his *Specimina Palæographica,* Moscow, 1863. Scrivener describes them (p. 185) under the name O. The contents of the 4 leaves belonging to Abp. Porfiri and the Archimandrite Antony are known only by Tischendorf's citations in his 8th critical edition. The MS. is stichometric, and its text is of much value. In the final subscription to the Epistles it purports to have been "compared with the copy in the Library at Cæsarea, written by the hand of the holy martyr Pamphilus." In 1888 the Paris Lib. received 9 other leaves of this codex, containing Col. i. 26—ii. 8; ii. 20—iii. 4; Heb. xii. 10—15; xiii. 24, 25, and fragm. of 1 Tim. One of the St. Petersburg leaves has, upon its other side, an impression of a lost leaf containing Col. iii. 11, καὶ ιουδ—αλλήλων iii. 13. See Tisch. 429 and 448.

155

CENTURY.	SIGN.	TITLE OF CODICES.	PRESENT PLACE OF DEPOSIT.	CONTENTS.	EDITOR, WITH PLACE AND DATE OF PUBLICATION.	REMARKS.
VI (Continued.)	I	Petropolitanus. (Tischendorfianus II. Fragments 3 and 4 Scrivener.)	St. Petersburg.	Frag. 3: Matt. xvii. 22—xviii. 3; xviii. 11—19; xix. 5—14; Luke xviii. 14—25; John iv. 52—v. 8; xx. 17—26. Frag. 4. Luke vii. 39—49; xxiv. 10—19.	Tischendorf, M. S. I., vol. i., Leipsic, 1855.	See I., of 5th century, above. Frag. 3 is Muralt's XIII. (1) (2) (3) (4) (5) (6). Frag. 4 is Muralt's XIII. (7) (8). V. Tisch., 378.
	N	"Purpureus." (Scrivener.)	London (1) formerly ι. Rome (2) formerly ι'. Vienna (3). Patmos (4).	(1) Matt. xxvi. 57—65; xxvii. 26—34; John xiv. 2—10; xv. 15—22. (2) Matt. xix. 6—13; xx. 6—22; xx. 29—xxi. 19. (3) Luke xxiv. 13—21, 39—49. (4) Mark vi. 53—xv. 23, with lacuna.	Tisch., M. S. I., 1846. The Patmos fragments were published by Duchesne in Archives des Missions Scientifiques, Paris, 1876, p. 386 ff	Forty-five leaves, 4 of which are in the British Museum (Cotton, Titus, c. 15), 6 in the Vatican (No. 3875), 2 at Vienna (Lambec. 2), and 33 in the Monastery of St. John at Patmos, used by Tisch. in his 8th critical edition. F—S. in Scr., p. 98. See Tisch., p. 382.
	Nᵃ	Cairensis.	Lib. of Patriarch. Alexr.	Mark ix. 14, 15, 16, 17, 18, 20, 21, 22; x. 23, 24, 29.	Described by Abp. Porfiri in a book entitled, Iter per Aegyptum et in Mon. Sanct., etc., St. Petersburg, 1856.	Two purple fragments written in gold, the letters very similar to those in Cod. N. Facsimiles may be found in Oriens Christianus Aegyptus et Sinai, St. Petersburg, 1857. See Tisch., p. 384.
	Oᵖ	Petropolitanus.	St. Petersburg, Imp. Lib., Muralt, ix.	2 Cor. i. 20—ii. 12.	Tisch., Notitio ad cod. bib. Sinait., Leipsic, 1860, p. 50.	A double leaf. Two columns; 18 lines to each page. Text, optimæ notæ. V. Tisch., p. 433.
	Oᵖ_b	Moscuensis.	Moscow.	Eph. iv. 1—18, with lacunæ.		Examined by Tischendorf at Moscow. V. Tisch., p. 434.
	Oᶜ	Veronensis.	Verona.	Luke i. 46—55.	Blanchini, Rome, 1740.	A Graeco-Latin Psalter. V. Tisch., p. 385.

Century.	Sign.	Title of Codices.	Present Place of Deposit.	Contents.	Editor, with Place and Date of Publication.	Remarks.
VI (Continued.)	P	**Guelpherbytanus.**	Weissenburg, 64.	Thirty-one fragments of 518 verses taken from the four Evangelists.	Knittel, Brunswick, 1762. Tischendorf, *M. S. I.*, vol. vi., Leipsic, 1869.	Palimpsest, 43 leaves, containing Matt. i. 11—21; iii. 13—iv. 19; x. 7—19; x. 42—xi. 11; xiii. 40—50; xiv. 15 - xv. 3; xv. 29—39; Mark i. 2—11; iii. 5—17; xiv. 13—24, 48—61; xv. 12—37; Luke i. 1—13; ii. 9—20; vi. 21—42; vii. 32 - viii. 2; viii. 31—50; ix. 26—36; x. 36—xi. 4; xii. 34—45; xiv. 14—25, xv. 13—xvi 22; xviii. 13—39; xx. 21—xxi. 3; xxii. 3—16; xxiii. 20—33; xxiii. 45—56; xxiv. 1, 14—37; John i. 29—41; ii. 13—25; xxi. 1—11. See Tisch., p. 386.
	R	**Nitriensis.**	Brit. Museum Library, Add. MSS. 17,211.	Twenty-five fragments of Luke, containing about 546 verses. (Three additional leaves, discovered by Dr. William Wright, contain Luke vi. 31—36, 38, 39; vii. 44, 46, 47.)	Tischendorf, *M S I.*, vol. ii., Leipsic, 1857. (See also Dr. William Wright in *Journal of Sac. Lit.*, Jan., 1864, p. 466.)	Palimpsest brought from the Syrian Convent in the Nitrian Desert. The letter R was formerly assigned by Griesbach and Scholz to an Evangelistarium containing John i. 38—50; and afterwards, by Tisch., to a palimpsest now marked W^y, q, v. F—S. in Scr., p. 145. See Tisch., p. 388.
	T^b	**Petropolitanus.**	St. Petersburg, Mural, x.	John i. 25—42; ii. 9—iv. 14; iv. 34—50.	See Tisch. *Notitia ad cod. bib. Sinait.*, p. 50.	T^b of John is on 6 8vo leaves. See Tisch., p. 392.
	T^c	**Porfirianus Chiovensis.**	St. Petersburg.	Matt. xiv. 19—xv. 8.		T^c of Matthew belongs to the collection of Abp. Porfiri. It agrees remarkably with א and B. See Tisch., p. 392.
	T^e	**Cantabrigiensis.**	Cambridge (Eng.) Univ. Lib., Add. 1875.	Matt. iii. 13—16.		Brought from Upper Egypt to Cambridge by G. I. Chester. See Tisch., p. 392.
	T^k	**Cairensis.**	In possession of A. Papadopulus Kerameus (?)	Matt. xx. 3—32; xxii. 4—16.		Three leaves. Letters resemble the Coptic. "Without doubt written in a Coptic monastery." Greg. See Tisch., p. 450.
	Z	**Dublinensis.**	Trinity College, Dublin.	Twenty-two fragments of Matthew, containing 311 verses.	Barrett, Dublin, 1801. (Supplement by Dr. Tregelles, London, 1863.) New ed. by T. K. Abbott, Dublin, 1880.	Palimpsest discovered by Dr. John Barrett in 1787. Thirty-two leaves. *Textus est optimae nota et facit cum* א *et B et D, praesertim cum* א. (Gregory.) F—S. in Scr., p. 153. See Tisch., p. 399.

157

Century.	Sign.	Title of Codices.	Present Place of Deposit.	Contents.	Editor, with Place and Date of Publication.	Remarks.
VI (Continued.)	Θᶜ	Petropolitanus, fol. 1. Porfirianus, fol. 1.	St. Petersburg. Muralt xii.	Θᵉ Matt. xxi. 19—24; John xviii. 29—35.		The *Matthew* fragments of Θᶜ belong to the Imperial Library of St. Petersburg; the *John* fragments of Θᶜ are from the MSS. of Abp. Porfiri. Tischendorf brought the former from the East in 1859. See *notitia editionis codicis bibliorum Sinaitici*, Leipsic, 1860. See Tisch., p. 404.
	{ Θᵉ Θᶠ Θᵍ	Porfirianus.	St. Petersburg, Library of the archbishop.	Θᵉ Matt. xxvi. 2—4, 7—9. Θᶠ Matt. xxvi. 59—70; xxvii. 44—56; Mark i. 34—ii. 12, with lacuna. Θᵍ John vi. 13, 14, 22—24.		Θᵉ *Textus est bonæ notæ.* Θᶠ *Textus est primæ notæ.* See Tisch., pp. 404, 405.
	Σ	Rossanensis.	Rossano in Calabria, Apb's Palace.	Matt. and Mark, excepting Mark xvi. 14—20.	Oscar L. von Gebhardt, Leipsic, 1883.	Written upon purple vellum. The text agrees often with ΑΑΠ, very often with N. See Wm. Sanday, *Studia Biblica.* Oxford, 1885, p. 103. See facsimile, Table VII. See Tisch., p. 408.
	Φ	Beratinus.	Berat (Belgrade) ch. of St. George.	Matt. vi. 3—vii. 26; viii. 7—xviii. 24; xix. 3—xxiii. 4; xxiii. 13—xxvii. 20; Mark i. 1—xiv. 62.	Peter Batiffol, Paris, 1886.	Contains 190 leaves of purple vellum, written in silver letters. "It often agrees in its pre-Syrian readings, with N and Σ, as well as with cursives 13, 69, 124, 346." (Gregory.) F—S. in Scr. p. 166. See Tisch., p. 444.
	ℶ	(?)		Gospels. Many leaves missing.	J. Rendel Harris, Lond. 1890, *Bib. Frag.*, No. 11.	"Thin purple parchment, written in silver and gold letters." See Tisch., p. 1307.
	ℸ¹¹	Sinaiticus.	Convent of St. Catharine, Mt. Sinai (?)	Matt. xxvi. 4—7, 10—12; Mark xii. 32—37.		See Tisch., p. 1308.
VII	Fᵃ	Parisiensis. Coislinianus I.	National Lib. Paris.	Matt. v. 48; xii. 48; xxvii. 25; Luke i. 42; ii. 24; xxiii. 21; John v. 35; vi. 53, 55; Acts iv. 33, 34; ix. 24, 25; x. 13, 15; xxii. 22; 1 Cor. vii. 39; xi. 29; 2 Cor. iii. 13; ix. 7; xi. 33; Gal. iv. 21, 22; Col. ii. 16, 17; Heb. x. 26.	Tisch., *M. S. I.*, 1846.	"The great copy of the Septuagint Octateuch, the glory of the Coislin Library." (Scrivener.) It consists of 227 leaves in double columns. It contains the Octateuch and the books of Kings. See Tisch., p. 375.

Century.	Sign.	Title of Codices.	Present Place of Deposit.	Contents.	Editor, with Place and Date of Publication.	Remarks.
	G^A	**Petropolitanus.**	St. Petersburg, Muralt xvii.	Acts ii. 45—iii. 8.	Tisch., *N. S.*, 1860.	One octavo leaf torn from the cover of a Syriac book. Found by Tischendorf, 1859. See Tisch., p. 413.
	I^act	**Petropolitanus.** *Fragments,* 6 and 7 (Scr.).	St. Petersburg, Muralt xix. (5) Muralt xviii. (6) Muralt xviii.	*Frag.* 6. Acts ii. 6—17; xxvi. 7—18. *Frag.* 7. Acts xiii. 39—46.	Tisch., *M. S. I.*, 1855.	Tisch. (5) and (6)=Scr. 6 and 7. See I. of 5th century. See Tisch., p. 415.
	O^d	**Turicensis.**		Luke i. 46—55, 68—79; ii. 29—31.	Tisch., *M. S. I.*, Leipsic, 1869, vol. iv.	From the Zurich Psalter. See Tisch., p. 385.
	T^d	**Rome. Borgianus II.**	Library of the Propaganda, Rome.	Matt. xvi. 13—20. Mark i. 3—8; xii. 35—37. John xix. 23—27; xx. 30, 31.		Fragment of an Evangelium, Greek, and Sahidic, found by Tisch. among the Borgian MSS. at Rome in 1866. See Tisch., p. 392.
	Θ^a	**Petropolitanus.**	One leaf at St. Petersburg, Muralt xvi. Four at Leipsic Un. Lib.	Matt. xii. 17—19, 23—25. Leipsic. xiii. 46—55; xiv. 8—29; xv. 4—14.	Tisch. *M. S. I.*, 1846, and *N. S.*, vol. ii, 1857.	Brought from the East in 1845. It consists of 5 leaves, 4to, of very thin vellum, besides a few fragments of Matt. xii. (once "Tischendorfianus I."). See Tisch., p. 403.
	Θ^b	**Petropolitanus.**	St. Petersburg, Muralt xi.	Θ^b Matt. xxii. 16—xxiii. 13; Mark iv. 24—35, v. 14—23.	Tisch., *N. S.*, 1860, p. 50.	See Tisch., p. 403.
VII. (Continued.)	R^p	**Cryptoferratensis.**	Monastery of Grotta Ferrata (A δ 24, or Z α 24.) Z. β. 1.	2 Cor. xi. 9—19, ῥήμα—ἀρρύνων.	Jos. Cozza, *Sacrorum Bibliorum vetustiss. fragmenta, pars secunda.* Rome, 1867. (?) pp. 332—335.	Palimpsest leaf of about the 7th century. No accents or breathings. Text good. Cited by Tisch. in his 8th critical edition (1872). See Tisch., p. 435.
	W^l	**Parisiensis.**	Paris, Nat. Lib.	Luke iv. 3—5, 6—8,10—13, 14—16, 18, 19, 21, 22, 23—25, 26—29.		Once the property of E. Miller. See Tisch., p. 442.
	W^l	**Parisiensis.**	Paris, Nat. Lib.	Mark xiii. 34—xiv. 29.		See Tisch., p. 443.
	W^m	**Parisiensis.**	Paris, Nat. Lib., Supp. Gr. 726 leaves 1—5 and 8—10.	Mark i. 27—41.		Four leaves of palimpsest—large uncial letters. Found by Gregory, 1885. See Tisch., p. 443.
	W^n	**Vindobonensis.**	Vienna, Imperial Lib.	John vi. 71—vii. 46.		John vii. 2 has ενγόr. See Tisch., p. 443.
ℵ^12	ℵ^12	**Sinaiticus.**	Convent of St. Catharine, Sinai.	Matt. xiv. 29—45; xv. 27—43; 45—xvi. 5.	J. R. Harris, Lond., 1890. *Bib. Frag.*, No. 12.	No. 13 (century VII.) *papyrus.* Luke I., 68, 78, 79 "*videtur de scriptori aliquo manure.*" See Tisch., p. 1308.

159

CENTURY.	SIGN.	TITLE OF CODICES.	PRESENT PLACE OF DEPOSIT.	CONTENTS.	EDITOR, WITH PLACE AND DATE OF PUBLICATION.	REMARKS.
VIII	B^R	Vaticanus.	Library of the Vatican, Rome, No. 2066.	The Revelation of St. John entire.	Tisch., *App. Nov. Test. Vaticani*, 1869. pp. iii.—vi., and 1—20.	Formerly Basil. 105. An octavo. Of some importance as confirming the codices ℵ A. C. See Tisch., p. 435.
	E	Basileensis.	Public Library at Basle. A.N. III. 12.	The four Gospels except Luke iii. 4—15; xxiv. 47—53. (Luke i. 69—ii. 4; xii. 58—xiii. 12; xv. 8—20, are supplied by a later hand.)		"One of the best second-rate uncials." (Scr.) Brought to Basle by Cardinal J. de Ragusio in 1431, probably from Constantinople. Collated by Wetstein, Tischendorf, and Tregelles. See Tisch., p. 372. See also cursive Rev. 15.
	L	Parisiensis.	National Lib., Paris, 62.	The four Gospels except Matt. iv. 22—v. 14; xxviii. 17—20; Mark x. 16—30; xv. 2—20; John xxi. 15—25.	Tisch., *M. S. L*, 1846.	"By far the most remarkable document of its age and class." (Scr.) It agrees remarkably with Cod. B., the quotations of Origen, and the margin of the Philoxenian Syriac Version. F—S. in Scr., p. 137. See Tisch., p. 381
	O^h	Taurinensis.	Turin, Royal Lib. B. VII. 30.	Luke i. 46—55, 68—79; ii. 29—31.		*Psalterium et Cantica cum glossis.* See Tisch., p. 441.
	S^AP	Athous Lauræ.	The Monastery Laura, Mt. Athos.	Acts, Cath. Epp., Rom., 1 Cor. i. 1—v. 8; xiii. 8—xvi. 24 ; 2 Cor. i. 1—xi. 23. Eph. iv. 20—vi. 20.		See Tisch., p. 447.
	W^a	Parisiensis.	National Lib., Paris, No. 314.	Luke ix. 35—47; x. 12—22.	Tisch., *M. S. L*, 1846.	A fragment brought to light by Scholz. consisting of two leaves at the end of another book. See Tisch., p. 394.
	W^b	Neapolitanus Borbonicus.	Naples, Royal Library.	Matt. xix. 14—28; xx. 23—xxi. 2; xxvi. 52—xxvii. 1; Mark xiii. 21—xiv. 67; Luke iii. 1—iv. 20.	Unpublished, except Mark xiv. 32—39 in the Vienna *Jahrb. d. Lit.*, 1847.	A palimpsest of 14 leaves, in the Royal Library of Naples (Borbon. II. C. 15), formerly called R. Deciphered by Tisch., 1866. As signed to the 8th or 9th century. Valuable Text. See Tisch., p. 394.
	W^k	Parisiensis.	Paris, Nat. Lib.	Luke xx. 19—23, 36—43; xxiii. 31—35, 36—41, 42—48, 49—54.		Once Emanuel Miller's. See Tisch., p. 442.

CENTURY.	SIGN.	TITLE OF CODICES.	PRESENT PLACE OF DEPOSIT.	CONTENTS.	EDITOR, WITH PLACE AND DATE OF PUBLICATION.	REMARKS.
VIII (*Continued.*)	Y	**Romanus Barberinus.**	Barberini Lib., Rome, 225.	John xvi. 3—xix. 41.	Tisch., *M. S. I.*, 1846.	Six leaves, containing 137 verses, prefixed to cursive G. 392. The text is mixed, and lies about midway between Cod. A. and Cod. B. See Tisch., 398.
	Θ^d	**Petropolitanus.**	St. Petersburg Imperial Lib., Murat, xxii.	Luke xi. 37—41, 42—45, with lacunae.	Tisch., *Notitia . . . Sinai.* Leipsic, 1860.	Half a leaf, in two columns, with accents and breathings by a later hand. See Tisch., p. 404.
	Ξ	**Zacynthius.**	Brit. and For. Bible Society, 24, London.	Luke i. 1—9, 19—23, 27, 28, 30—32, 36—66, 77—ii. 19, 21, 22, 33—39; iii. 5—8, 11—20; iv. 1, 2, 6—20; 32—43; v. 17—36; vi. 21—vii. 6, 11—37, 39—47; viii. 4—21, 25—35, 43—50; ix. 1—28, 32, 33, 35, 41—x. 18, 21—40; xi. 1, 2, 3, 4, 24—30, 31, 32, 33.	Tregelles, London, 1861.	Palimpsest brought from Zante by General Macaulay, and presented to the Bible Society in 1821. The text is surrounded with a commentary compiled from the writings of the Fathers. It is of high critical value, having a wonderful correspondence with the oldest MSS. See Scrivener's *Plain Introduction,* 4th ed., 1894. See Tisch., p. 406.
	Ψ	**Athous Laurae.**	The Monastery Laura, Mt. Athos.	Mark ix. 5 to the end. Luke, John, Acts; 1, 2 Peter; 1, 2, 3 John, Jude, Rom., Philem. Heb. i. 1—viii. 11; ix. 19 to the subscription.		John vii. 53—viii. 11 and 1 John v. 7, 8 are wanting. 1 Tim. iii. 16 has $\theta\epsilon\grave{o}\varsigma$ ἐφανερώθη. Mark xvi. 8 has τέλος after ἐφοβοῦντο γάρ, followed by the "shorter" and then the "longer conclusion," as in Cod. L. See Tisch., p. 445. W—H. App., p. 30.
	Ω	**Athous Dionysii.**	Mt. Athos, Monastery of St. Dionysius, 10.	The four Gospels entire. Matt., Mark, Luke, John.		Matt. x, 37, Lu. xxii. 43, 44 and John vii. 53—viii. 11 are obelized in the margin. See Tisch., p. 446.
	Γ^6	**Sinaiticus.**	Mt. Sinai.	Matt. xi, 27, 28.	J. R. Harris, London, 1890. *Bib. Frag.*, 6.	"Large letters inclining to the right." See Tisch., p. 1307.
	Γ^8	**Sinaiticus.**	Mt. Sinai.	Matt. xiii, 37—46; xiii. 55—xiv. 8; xiv. 29—xv. 3, 15—26.	J. R. Harris, London, 1890. *Bib. Frag.*, 8.	See Tisch., p. 1308.

Century.	Sign.	Title of Codices.	Present Place of Deposit.	Contents.	Editor, with Place and Date of Publication.	Remarks.
IX	ך	Athous Andreæ *B*.	Monastery of St. Andrew, Athos.	The four Gospels, with the following lacunae: Matt. ii. 15—iii. 11; Mark v. 41—vi. 18; viii. 35—ix. 19; John xviii. 34—xxi. 25; also Matt. xvi. 2—3.		Matt. i. 1—10 letters faint; 10—12 *mut.*; John v. 3, 4 is obelized in the margin. John vii. 53—viii. 11 is retained without comment. See Tisch., p. 446.
	E^p	Petropoli-tanus.	St. Petersburg. Muralt xx.	The Pauline Epistles, with defects. Its defects are in Rom. viii. 21—33; xi. 15—25, 1 Tim. i. 1—vi. 15; Heb. xii. 8—xiii. 25.		Formerly at the Abbey St. Germain, near Paris. A mere transcript of Cod. Claromon-tanus, after that MS. had been altered by later hands. It is accompanied with a Latin ver-sion, which Tisch. (p. 968) now catalogues as *d* of Paul's Epistles. See Tisch., p. 423.
	F	Rheno-Tra-jectinus (formerly Boreeli).	Public Library at Utrecht.	Matt. i. 9—John xiii. 33, with many mutila-tions. Wetstein's coll. began with Matt. vii. 6.	H. E. Vinke, Utrecht, 1843.	Collated and described by Heringa. 204 leaves remain. F—S. in Scr., p. 131. See Tisch., p. 374.
	F^p	Augiensis.	Trinity College, Cambridge. B. 17, 1.	Pauline Epistles, except Rom. i. 1—iii. 19; 1 Cor. iii. 8—16; vi. 7—14; Col. ii. 1—8; Philemon 21—25, and Hebrews.	Scrivener, Cambridge, 1859.	Originally from the Monastery of Augia Dives (Reichenau), in Lake Constance. Cors-sen regards F and G as copies of a common archetype. Accompanied with a Latin ver-sion. See Tisch., p. 424.
	G^b	Vaticanus Romanus.	Vatican Library at Rome, Gr. 2302 (formerly Latin 9671).	Acts xvi. 30—xvii. 17; 27—29, 31—34; xviii. (8 ενον και—) 11 εν αυτοις—ασωλοσ και προκιλλα 18, 26 "but letters and words are missing everywhere."	Joseph Cozza, Rome, 1877.	Palimpsest fragments once at Grotta Ferrata. The sixth leaf was discovered by Dr. Gregory in April, 1886. It contained Acts xvi. 30—40. See Tisch., pp. 414 and 446.
	G^p	Boerneri-anus.	Royal Library at Dresden. A. 145^b.	Pauline Epistles, ex-cept Rom. i. 1—5; ii. 16—25; 1 Cor. iii. 8—16; vi. 7—14; Col. ii. 1—8; Phile-mon 21—25, and Heb.	Matthæi, Meissen, 1791. With numerous errors (see Tisch., *Pro-leg.*, p. 1307) discovered by J. L. Marquis.	Purchased in 1705 by Prof. C. F. Boerner, at Leipsic. With an interlinear Latin version. It is part of the same volume as Cod. Δ below, and has a striking affinity to Cod. Augiensis (F of the Pauline Epistles). See Tisch., p. 426.

162

Century.	Sign.	Title of Codices.	Present Place of Deposit.	Contents.	Editor, with Place and Date of Publication.	Remarks.
IX (Continued.)	H^A	Mutinensis.	Grand Ducal Library at Modena [cxxvi.], ii. G. 3.	The Acts, with defects. (xxvii. 4—xxviii. 31 supplied by a XIth cent. hand.)		Collated by Scholz, Tischendorf (1843), and Tregelles (1846). The defects are Acts i. 1—v. 28; ix. 39—x. 19; xiii. 36—xiv. 3; xxvii. 4—xxviii. 31. See Tisch., p. 415.
	K	Cyprius.	National Lib., Paris, No. 63.	Four Gospels, entire.		Brought from Cyprus in 1673. Collated by Scholz, Tisch., and Tregelles. "Text of an unusual and interesting character." (Scriv.) F—S. in Scr., p. 153. See Tisch., p. 380.
	K^CP	Moscuensis.	Library of Holy Synod, Moscow, xcviii.	Catholic Epistles entire, and Pauline Epistles, except Rom. x. 18—1 Cor. vi. 13; viii. 7—11.		This is Matthaei's g. from Mt. Athos. Collated by Matthaei. Formerly called I in the Acts and Cath. Epp. ; in Scholz, No. 102 (Acts), 117 (Pauline Epp). See Tisch., p. 415.
	L^AP	Angelicus.	Angelica Lib. of Augustinian monks at Rome. A. 2, 15.	Acts from ch. viii. 10 μὲς τοῦ θεοῦ; the Catholic and Pauline Epistles down to Heb. xiii. 10 οὐκ ἔχουσιν.		Collated by Scholz, Fleck, Tisch. (1843), and Tregelles (1845). Formerly "Passionei," and designated by the letter G. See Tisch., p. 416.
	M	Parisiensis.	National Lib., Paris, No. 48.	Four Gospels, entire.	Facsim. by Silvestre Paleog. Univ. 1841. vol. ii.	Presented to Louis XIV., Jan. 1, 1707, by the Abbé François De Camps. Collated by Wetstein, Scholz, and Tregelles; transcribed in 1841 by Tischendorf. F—S. in Scr, p. 134. See Tisch., p. 381.
	M^P	"Codex Ruber," (Scrivener.)	Two leaves in the Public Lib. at Hamburg, Gr. 50, and two in the Brit. Mus. (London), Harl. 5613.*	*Hamburg.* Heb. i. 1—iv. 3; xii. 20—xiii. 25. *London.* 1 Cor. xv. 52—2 Cor. i. 15; x. 13—xii. 5.	Tischendorf, *Aneed. Sac. et prof.*, 1855, and more correctly, 1861.	Peculiar for the bright red color of the ink, as well as for the excellence of the text. Collated by Griesbach, Tregelles, and Tischendorf. The latter assigned it to the 9th century, but Scrivener to the 10th. F—S. in Scr, p. 134. See Tisch., p. 431.
	N^P	Petropolitanus.	St. Petersburg, Imp. Lib., Muralt xxxii., Dobrowskii 258 (Cat. v.1).	Gal. v. 12, καὶ ἀποκ—καταχημα vi. 4; Heb. v. 8—vi. 10.		Two leaves discovered by Tisch. in the covering of a manuscript book, containing the works of Manuel Cretensis (A.D. 1424). See Tisch., p. 433.
	O	Moscuensis.	Library of Holy Synod, Moscow, cxx. (Mt. 15).	John i. 1—4; xx. 10—13, 15—17, 20—24.	C. F. Matthaei, Riga, 1785, *Epp. Pauli ad Thess.* etc. Tregelles, App. to *Cod. Zacynth. vias*, 1861.	The eight leaves of this MS. were used for binding a copy of Chrysostom's Homilies, brought from Mt. Athos. It is accompanied with scholia. See We below, and Tisch., p. 384.

Century.	Sign.	Title of Codices.	Present Place of Deposit.	Contents.	Editor, with Place and Date of Publication.	Remarks.
IX (Continued.)	O[a]	Guelpher-bytanus.	Wolfenbüttel.	Luke i. 46—55, 68—79.	Tisch., Anecd., Leipsic, 1855.	The two hymns of Mary and Zacharias. See Tisch., p. 385.
	O[e]	Sangal-lensis.	St. Gall, 17.	Luke i. 46—55, 68—'0; ii. 20—31.		See Tisch., p. 386.
	O[f]	Moscuen-sis.	Moscow Museum.	Luke i. 46—55, 68—79 (i. 29—31 9).		See Tisch., p. 386.
	O[g]	Parisiis Arsenalis.	Paris, library of the Arsenal 8407 (or MS. Gr. 2).			Contains Psalms and Canticles from the O. T. and the Benedictus and Nunc Dimittis of the N. T. See Tisch., pp. 386, 438.
	P[APR]	Porfiri-anus.	St. Petersburg.	Acts, Epistles, and Revelation, with some defects, besides many illegible words in Acts xxviii. 21—23; James ii. 13—21, and a few in 2 Peter ii. 3—5.	Tischendorf, M. S. L., vol. v., 1865, and vol. vi., 1869.	A palimpsest found in possession of Abp. Porfiri at St. Petersburg. Its defects are Acts i. 1—ii. 13; 1 John iii. 20—v. 1; Jude 4—15; Rom. ii. 16—iii. 5; viii. 33—ix. 11; xi. 22—xii. 39; 2 Cor. ii. 14, 16; Col. iii. 16—iv. 8; 1 Thess. iii. 5—iv. 17; Rev. xvi. 12—xvii. 1; xix. 21—xx. 9; xxii. 6—21. The text in Acts and 1 Peter is inferior; elsewhere it often agrees with ℵ or A C. See Tisch., pp. 417, 434, 437.
	T[f]	Meliss. Horneri.	Bodleian Lib., Oxford.	Matt. iv. 2—11.	"A Græco Sahidic Lectionary." Scr.	Brought from Upper Egypt, 1873, by Rev. Geo. Horner, and presented by him to the Bodl. (Scr., vol. ii., p. 133.) See Tisch., p. 439.
	V	Moscu-ensis.	Library of Holy Synod, Moscow, 399 fol. 164.	Four Gospels to John vii. 39 οὔπω γὰρ ἦν, except Matt. v. 44—vi.12; ix. 18—x. 1; xxii. 44—xxiii. 35; John xxi. 10—25.		Collated by Matthaei. The remainder of the Gospels is in cursive character and = G. 260. See Tisch., pp. 393 and 516.
	W[c]	Sangallen-sis.	St. Gall, Cod. 18 and 45.	Mark ii. 8—16. Luke i. 20—32, 64—79.	Tisch., M. S. L., Leipsic, 1860.	Three palimpsest leaves, written in uncial letters, similar to those used in Δ⁹, Fᵃ, and Gᵖ. See Tisch., p. 395.
	W[d]	Cantabri-giensis.	Trinity College Library, Cambridge. (B. VIII. 5).	Mark vii. 34, 6—8, 30—36 ; 36—viii. 4, 4—10, 11—16; ix. 2, 7—9.	J. Rendel Harris, The Diatessaron of Tatian, London, 1890. Scrivener, Adversaria, Critica Sacer. Cambridge, 1893.	Discovered in 1857 in the binding of a volume of Gregory Nazianzen. The leaves are now arranged on glass. The text resembles Codd. ℵ, B, D, L, Δ. For photograph, see G. E. Merrill, The Parchments of the Faith, Phil., 1894, p. 214. See Tisch., p. 396.

Century.	Sign.	Title of Codices.	Present Place of Deposit.	Contents.	Editor, with Place and Date of Publication.	Remarks.
	W e	Athenensis.	Monastery of St. Dionysius at Athos, 7 leaves; 3 at Christ. Ch. Coll. Lib. (Wake. 2); 2 in the Nat. Lib. at Athens.	At Oxford: John iv. 9—14; at Athos: John ii. 17—iii. 8; at Athens: John iii. 12, 13, 20, 21, 22.		The two Athens leaves were discovered by Dr. Gregory in 1886. These and the Oxf. leaves are parts of the same MS. as Frag. Aθa. above. The same is true of Alford's Frag. Aθa. at the Monastery of St. Dionysius at Mt. Athos, collated by P. E. Pusey, which contains John ii. 17—iii. 8. See Tisch., pp. 396, 441.
	W f	Oxoniensis.	Oxford Christ. Ch., Wake., 37 (Cod. Act 192).	Mark v. 16—40, with lacuna.		Partly palimpsest. "*Textus non bonæ notæ est.*" Tisch., p. 397.
IX (*Continued.*)	W g	Londinius.	Brit. Mus. Add. 31919.	Matt. i. 1—14; v. 3—19; xii. 27—41; xxiii. 9—xxv. 30; xxv. 43—xxvi. 26; xxvi. 50—xxvii. 17. Mark i.1—42; ii. 21—v. 1; v. 29—vi. 22. (From another MS. vi. 14—20); x. 51—xi.13. Luke xvi. 21—xvii. 3; xvii. 19—37; xix. 15—31. John ii. 18—iii. 5; iv. 23—37; v. 35—vi. 2.	J. P. Mahaffy, *The Athenaeum*, Lond.,1881. See T. K. Abbott, art. in *Hermathena* (Dublin, 1884), No. 10, pp. 146–150, with facsimile and various readings.	Palimpsest (34 leaves) discovered in Trin. Coll., Dublin, by T. K. Abbott, and J. P. Mahaffy, 1881. Two other leaves found by Dr. Gregory in 1883. The MS. was purchased by the Brit. Museum in 1882. This is Scrivener's Cod. Y b (Blenheimius), 4th ed., p. 165. The MS. also contains a fragment of an evangelium, v. Evl. *334.* See Tisch., p. 439, and Scr. Evst. *282.*
	W h	Oxonii Bodl.	Oxford Bodleian Lib., Arch. Selden supra 2.	Mark iii. 15—32; v. 16—31.		A palimpsest. This is Evangelium 26. See Lectionaries. See Tisch., p. 440.
	W o	Mediolani Ambrosianus.	Ambrosian Lib., Milan. Q 6 sup.	Matt. xxv. 35—xxvi. 2; xxvii.3—17. Mark i. 12—24; ii. 26—iii. 10. Luke i. 24—37. i. 68—ii. (4?); iv. 28—40; vi. 22—35; viii. 22—30; ix. 42—53; xvii. 2—(14?); xvii. 7—(19?); xxii. 11—25, 52—66; xxiii. 35—(49?); xxiv. 32—46.		A palimpsest. The leaves resemble those of Cod. W b, above. See Tisch., p. 443.

CENTURY.	SIGN.	TITLE OF CODICES.	PRESENT PLACE OF DEPOSIT.	CONTENTS.	EDITOR, WITH PLACE AND DATE OF PUBLICATION.	REMARKS.
IX (Continued.)	X^b	Monacensis.	Munich Royal Lib., 208.	Luke i. 1—ii. 40.		This Codex has been reckoned among cursives as G. 429. See Tisch., p. 449.
	Γ	"Tischendorfianus IV." (Scrivener.)	Bodleian Lib. at Oxford and St. Petersburg.	The four Gospels, except 115 verses of Matt. and 105 verses (viz., iii. 35—vi. 20) of Mark.	Vid. Tisch., Anecdota, Leipsic, 1855, pp. 5, 6, and Notitia, Leipsic, 1860, p. 53.	Collated by Tisch. and Tregelles. See Cod. A (Tischendorfianus III.) below. The date inferred from the subscription is A.D. 844. F—S. in Scr., p. 134. See Tisch., p. 400.
	Δ	Sangallensis.	Library of the Monastery of St. Gall, No. 48.	Four Gospels, except John xix. 17—35.	H. Ch. M. Rettig, in lithographed facsimile, Zurich. 1836. J. Rendel Harris, The Codex Sangallensis, London, 1894.	Part of the same book as Cod. BOERNERIANUS (G of the Pauline Epistles), which see above. With an interlinear Latin version, written by Irish monks. See Tisch., p. 402.
	Λ	Oxoniensis. (Scrivener "Tischendorfianus III.")	Bodleian Lib., Oxford, misc. 310 (Auct. T., Infra I. I.).	Luke and John entire, and the subscription to Mark. For Matt. and Mark see G. 566.		Collated by Tischendorf and Tregelles. "The history of this MS. curiously coincides with that of Γ." (Scr.) The Gospels of Matt. and Mark in cursive characters, forming part of the same MS., were procured by Tisch. in 1859, and are now at St. Petersburg. F—S. in Scr., p. 131. See Tisch., p. 405.
	Π	Petropolitanus.	St. Petersburg. Mural xxxiv.	Four Gospels, except Matt. iii. 12—iv. 17; xix. 12—xx. 2; John viii. 6—39; Lu. i. 76—ii. 18. Also Mark xvi. 18—20; Lu. iv. 9—11,16,17,and John xxi. 22—25, in a later hand.		Presented by Parodus, a noble Greek of Smyrna, to the Emperor of Russia in 1859. Described in Tischendorf's Notitia et cod. Biblior. Sinait. (1860), p. 51 ff. See Tisch., p. 408.
	ℸ^9	Sinaiticus.	Convent of St. Catharine.	Matt. xiii. 46—52.	J. R. Harris, London, 1890, Bib. Frag., 9.	"Estne Ev.?" Gregory, p. 1308.

Century.	Sign.	Title of Codices.	Present Place of Deposit.	Contents.	Editor, with Place and Date of Publication.	Remarks.
IX	G	Harleianus. (Scrivener.)	Brit. Museum (Harl. 5684). (A frag. in the Lib. of Trin. College, Cam., B. 17, 20, No. 21.)	The Four Gospels, with defects. The Cambridge fragm. is a divided leaf, having some of Matt. v. 29—31, 39—43.	Facsimile in Scr, 4th ed., vol. i., p. 131.	The defects are Matt. i. 1—vi. 6; vii. 25—viii. 9; viii. 23—ix. 2; xxviii. 18—Mark i. 13; xiv. 19—25. Luke i. 1—13; v. 4—vii. 3; viii. 46—ix. 5; xii. 27—41; xxiv. 41—53; John xviii. 5—19; xix. 4—27. Collated by Tisch. and Tregelles. See H below. See Tisch., p. 375.
	H	Hamburgensis. Cantabrigiensis.	Public Library of Hamburg, No. 91. Trin. College, Camb. B. 17, 20, No. 21.	The Four Gospels, with some defects. The Cambridge frag. contains parts of Luke i. 3—6, 13—15.	F—S. in Scr, p. 134.	Formerly owned by J. C. Wolf (together with Cod. G, which was therefore called WOLFII A, see Cod. G above). The defects are Matt. i. 1—xv. 30; xxv. 33—xxvi. 3; Mark i. 32—ii. 4; xv. 44 xvi. 14; Luke v. 18—32; vi. 8—22; x. 2—19; John ix. 30—x. 25; xviii. 2—18; xx. 12—25. See Tisch., p. 376.
	Oᵇ	Bodleianus.	Oxford, Bodl. Misc. gr. 5.	Luke i. 46—55, 68—79; ii. 29—32.	Tisch., Anecdota Sac. et Prof., Leipsic, 1855, pp. 206–208.	In a Psalter. See Tisch., p. 385.
	S	Vaticanus.	Rome, Vatican Lib., 354.	Four Gospels entire.		Dated A.D. 949. Among the earliest dated MSS. of the Greek Testament. Collated by Birch, but more thoroughly by Tischendorf in 1866. See Tisch., p. 390.
	U	Venetus Marcianus.	Library of St. Mark (I. viii.), Venice.	Four Gospels entire.		Collated by Tisch. (1843), and Tregelles (1846). Elegantly written. Formerly Nanianus. "The text is plainly Constantinopolitan." F—S. in Scr., p. 137. See Tisch., p. 393.
	X	Monacensis.	University Lib at Munich, fol. 30.	The four Gospels, "with serious defects."		A valuable folio. Collated by Scholz, Tischendorf, and Tregelles. F—S. in Scr., p. 383. See Tisch., pp. 397 and 442.
	Θʰ	Porfirianus.	St. Petersburg.	Matt. xiv. 6—13; xxv. 9—16, 41—xxvi. 1.		Three leaves, in Greek and Arabic, of the 9th or 10th century, belonging to the library of Abp. Porfiri. See Tisch., p. 405.

NOTE.—Scrivener (4th ed., vol. i., p. 377) reports three "Additional Uncials," viz. (ℵ) Ἁγία Μονή, 124 [z.] ff. 339, containing Gosp., Ac., Cath., Rev., Paul. (in that order), and (Ⴀ) Ἁγία Μονή, 375 [ἰz.—x.], ff. 301, containing the Gospels (wanting Matt. i. 1—ix. 1), and one (Ⴀ) from Mt. Athos [x̄.], consisting of four fragments: a (Πρᾶτον 13), 4to, ff. 2, appended to homilies of Chrysostom; b (Πρᾶτον 14) ff. 3, with fragments of St. John appended to the lives of saints; c (Πρᾶτον 20) ff. (?); and d (Πρᾶτον 56) ff. 10, containing fragments of the Evangelists.

167

GOSPELS (Continued).

SIGN	TITLE	DATE	PAGE
Ξ	Zacynthius.	VIII.	161
Π	Petropolitanus.	IX.	166
Σ	Rossanensis.	VI.	158
Φ	Beratinus.	VI.	158
Ψ	Athous Lauræ.	VIII.	161
Ω	Athous Dionysii.	VIII.	161
	Athous Andreæ B'.	IX.	162
Γ10	(?)	V.	154
Γ11	Sinaiticus.	VI.	158
Γ12	Sinaiticus.	VII.	159
Γ8	Sinaiticus.	VIII.	161
Γ9	Sinaiticus.	IX.	166

ACTS AND CATHOLIC EPISTLES.

SIGN	TITLE	DATE	PAGE
ℵ	A, B, C, D. *See* Gospels.		
	Vatican, Gr 2061.	V.	153
E	Laudianus.	VI.	155
Fa	Coislinianus I.	VII.	158
G	Petropolitanus.	VII.	159
Gb	Vaticanus.	IX.	162
H	Mutinensis.	IX.	163
I	Petropolitanus (fragm. 5).	V.	153
I	Petropolitanus (fragm. 6, 7).	VII.	159
K	Moscuensis, S. S. xcviii.	IX.	163
L	Angelicus.	IX.	163
P	Porfirianus.	IX.	164
S	Athous Lauræ.	VIII.	160
Ψ	Athous Lauræ.	VIII.	161

PAULINE EPISTLES.

SIGN	TITLE	DATE	PAGE
ℵ	A, B, C. *See* Gospels.		
D	Claromontanus.	VI.	155
E	Petropolitanus (Mos. xx.).	IX.	162
F	Augiensis.	IX.	162
Fa	Coislinianus I. (Paris).	VII.	158
G	Boernerianus.	IX.	162
H	Coislinianus (Mosc, etc.).	VI.	155
I	Petropolitanus (fragm. 5).	V.	153
K	Moscuensis, xcviii.	IX.	163
L	Angelicus.	IX.	163
M	Ruber.	IX.	163
N	Petropolitanus (Mur. xxxiii).	VI.	156
O	Petropolitanus (Mur. ix.).	IX.	156
Ob	Moscuensis.	VI.	164
P	Porfirianus.	IX.	154
Q	Porfirianus.	V.	159
R	Cryptoferratensis.	VII.	160
S	Athous Lauræ.	VIII.	152
Tg	Parisiensis.	IV.	161
Ψ	Athous Lauræ.	VIII.	154
Γ14	Sinaiticus.	V.	

REVELATION.

SIGN	TITLE	DATE	PAGE
ℵ	A, C. *See* Gospels.		
B	Vaticanus.	VIII.	160
P	Porfirianus.	IX.	164

TABLE IX

CURSIVE MANUSCRIPTS

In the following lists the utmost care has been taken to secure perfect accuracy. The dates represent the judgment of Gregory (Tisch. Proleg.). To save space, certain *omissions* (sometimes) occur, *e. g.*, (1) *full* descriptions which are already given in other accounts of the same MS. (see MSS. Paul 270–289 comp. w. Acts 214–245). (2) References to Scrivener when his account adds nothing to our own. (3) Terms common to library designations of N. T. Greek MSS., *viz.:* Gr. [Greek], Theol., Lib., Univ., Nat., Imp., Royal (*e. g.* Vat. always = "Rome, Vatican Greek;" *Vienna* always = "The Imperial Library of Vienna;" *Paris* always = "The National Library of Paris;" *Athens* always = "The National Library of Athens;" *Munich* always = "Munich Reg. Gr." [Royal Lib., Greek Dept.]). (4) In a few instances, the *later* of two alternative dates. All dates are matters of judgment, and these lists show the *earliest* probable date in the judgment of Gregory. (5) All *Latin* comments are quoted from Gregory. All MSS. are presumed to be of parchment, unless marked *p* (*paper*).

The term "cursive," which is still used by Scrivener (Miller), and by Westcott and Hort, is retained here as being more familiar to English readers. "Minuscule" would on some accounts be a preferable designation, since it indicates more accurately the kind of letter commonly used in these manuscripts.

TABLE IX

CURSIVE MANUSCRIPTS: THEIR NUMBER, DESIGNATION, AND DATE [1]

A.—CONDENSED LIST OF THE CURSIVE MANUSCRIPTS OF THE GOSPELS

1[2]. Basle Univ. Lib.   A. N. IV.   2.
    X.   v. Table VII.   (A1P1).

2. B. U. L.   A. N. IV. 1.   **XII.**

3[3]. Vienna Imp. Sup. 52. **XII.** (A3P3.)

4. Paris Nat. Lib.   Gr. 84.   **XIII.**

5. P. N. 106.   **XIV.**   (A5P5.)

6. P. N. 112.   **XIII.**   (A6P6.)

7. P. N. 71.   **XII.**

8. P. N. 49.   **XI.**

9. P. N. 83.   **1167.**

9[2]. Oxf. Bodl.   (*Paper*) = **9. XV.**

10. P. N. 91.   **XIII.**

11. P. N. 121–2.   **XII.**

12. P. N. 230.   **XI.**

13. P. N. 50.   **XIII.**   v. p. 109.

14. P. N. 70.   **X.**

15. P. N. 64.   **XII.**

16. P. N. 54.   **XIV.**

17. P. N. 55.   **XV.**

18. P. N. 47. **1364.** (A113P132R51.)

19. P. N. 189.   **XII.**

20. P. N. 188.   **XI.**

21. P. N. 68.   **XII.**

22. P. N. 72.   **XII.**   v. p. 109.

23. P. N. 77.   **XI.** or **XII.**

24. P. N. 178.   **X.**

25. P. N. 191.   **XI.**

26. P. N. 78.   **XI.**

27. P. N. 115.   **X.**

28. P. N. 379.   **XI.**

29. P. N. 89.   **X.**

30. P. N. 100.   **XV.**

30[a]. Camb. Univ. (*Paper*) = 30. **XV.**

31. P. N. 94.   **XIII. XII.?**

32. P. N. 116.   **XII.**

33. P. N. 14.   **IX.** or **X.**   (A13P17.)

34[4]. P. N. Coislin.   195.   **X.**

35. P. N. C. 199.   **XI.** or **XII.**
    (A14P18R17.)

36. P. N.   C. 20.   **X.**

37. P. N.   C. 21.   **XI.** or **XII.**

38. P. N.   C. 200.   **XIII.**   (A19P377.)

39. P. N.   C. 23.   **XI.**

40. P. N.   C. 22.   **XI.** or **XII.**

41. P. N.   C. 24.   **XI.**

42. Medicæus.   Missing.

43. Paris, Arsenal Lib.   8409, 8410.
    XII.   (A54P130.)

44. Brit. Mus.   Add. 4949.   **XII.**

45. Oxf. Bodl. Baroc. 31.   **XIV.**

46. Oxf. Bodl. B. 29.   **XII.** or **XIII.**

47. Oxf. Bodl. Misc. 9.   **XV.**

48. Oxf. Bodl. Misc. 1.   **XII.**

49. Oxf. Bodl. Roe. 1.   **XI. XII.?**

50. Oxf. Bodl. Laud. 33.   **XI.** or **XII.**

51. Oxf. Bodl. L. 31.   **XIII.**   (A32P38.)

52. Oxf. Bodl. L. 3.   **1286.**

53. Oxf. Bodl. Seld. sup. 28.   **XIV.**

54. Oxf. Bodl. S. sup. 29.   **1338.**

55. Oxf. Bodl. S. 6.   **XIII.**

56. Oxf. Lincoln Coll. *II*. 18. *pap.* **XV.**

57. Oxf. Mag. Coll. 9.   **XII.** (A35P41.)

58. Oxf. New Coll. 68.   **XV.**

59. Camb. Caius Coll. 403.   **XII.**

60. Camb. Un. Dd. 9. 69.   **1297.**   (R10.)

61[5]. Dublin.   Trin.   Coll.   A.   4.   21.
    XVI.   (A34P40R92.)

62. Locality unknown.

63. Dublin. Trin. Coll. A. 1. 8. **X.**, **XI.**

64. Marq. of Bute.   **XII.** or **XIII.**

65. Brit. Mus. Harl. 5776.   **XI.**

66. Cam. Trin. O. 8. 3.   *p.*   **XI., XIII.**

67. Oxf. Bodl. Misc. 76.   **XI.**

68. Oxf. Lincoln Coll. *II*. 17.   **XII.**

69. Leicester 20.   **XV.**   (A31P37R14.)

70. Camb. Univ. Ll. 2. 13.   **XV.**

71. London, Lambeth, 528.   **XII.**

72. Brit. Mus. Harl. 5647.   **XI.**

73. Oxf. Christ-Ch. Wake. 26.   **XII.**

74. Oxf. Christ-Ch. Wake. 20.   **XIII.**

---

[1] The designation usually indicates *locality*. The dates are in *heavy-faced* Roman numbers (**X**) or figures (**1364**). The parentheses at the end of titles contain references to other parts of the N. T. contained in the same MSS. In these references G stands for Gospels, A for Acts, and Cath. Epp., P for Pauline Epp., R for Revelation, Evl. for Evangelistary, and Apl. for Apostolos. For abbreviations not explained in foot-notes, see Glossary.

[2] Cod. Basiliensis, v. p. 108 in this hand-book.

[3] Formerly in the convent at Corsendonck, now at Vienna.

[4] Once in the library of Bp. Coislin of Metz. Likewise the 7 MSS. which follow.

[5] Cod. Montfortianus, v. p. 111.

75. Geneva City Lib. Gr. 19. **XI.**
76. Vienna I. N. 300. **XII. or XIII.** (A43P49.)
77. Vienna Imp. N. 154. **XI.**
78. Pesth Nat. Mus. 2 4to Gr. **XII.**
79. Leyden Univ. Lib. 74. **XV.**
80. Paris, Lib. of M. Lesoeuf. **XII.**
81. Wanting, W.–H. = [1]G. 565.
82. W.–H. = G. 597.
83. Munich Roy. Lib. 518. **XI.**
84. Munich Roy. Lib. 568. **XII.**
85. Munich Roy. Lib. 569. **XIII.**
86. Presburg Lyceum Lib. **X.**
87. (?) Once at Treves. **XII.**
88. (?) " *Olim Camerarii.*"
89. Gottingen Theol. 53. **1006.**
90. Amstd. 186. *p.* **XVI.** (A47P14.)
91. Once "Perron."= G. 299 (?). **X.**
92. Basle Univ. Lib. O.II.27. **X.**
93. Once "Graevii." "Perh. = 80."
94. Basle Univ. Lib. O.II.23. *p.* **XV.**
95. Oxf. Lincoln Coll. *II.* 16. **XII.**
96. Oxf. Bodl. Misc. 8. *paper.* **XV.**
97. *Missing.* Once Hirschau, Bav.
98. Oxf. Bodl. E. D. Clarke. 5. **XII.**
99. Leipsic Univ. 35. **XV.** or **XVI.**
100. Pesth Univ. Lib. V. Gr. 1. **X.**
101. "*Delendus est.*"
102. Readings of Cod. B. (W–H.=489.)
103. (?) " Perh. = G. 14 or 278."
104. Once " Vignerii." **X.** (G. 885.?)
105. Ox. Bodl. Misc. 136. **XII.** (A48-P24.)
106. Once Winchelsea. **X.** Missing.
107. Oxf. Bodl. E. D. Clarke, 6. **XIII.**
108. Vienna Imp. Suppl. Gr. 6. **XI.**
109. Brit. Mus. Add. 5117. **1326.**
110. Berlin Ravianus. " *Del.*" **XVI.**
111. Oxf. Bodl. E. D. Clarke, 7. **XII.**
112. Oxf. Bodl. E. D. Clarke, 10. **XI.**
113. Brit. Mus. Harl. 1810. **XI.**
114. B. M. Harl. 5540. **XI.** (X ?)
115. B. M. Harl. 5559. **X.** or **XI.**
116. B. M. Harl. 5567. **XII.**
117. B. M. Harl. 5731. *p.* **XV.** (R6.)
118. Oxf. Bodl. Misc. 13. **XIII.**
119. Paris Gr. 85. **XII. or XIII.**
120. P. N. Sup. 185. **XII.** (Evl312.)

121. Paris, St. Genev. A.O.34. **1284.**
122. Leyden, 74. A. **XII.** (A177P219.)
123. Vienna Imp. Nessel. 240. **XI.**
124. Vienna Imp. Nessel. 188. **XII.**
125. Vienna Imp. Suppl. Gr. 50. **X.**
126. Wolfenbüttel, XVI. 6. **XI.**
127. Vatican Gr. 349. **XI.**
128. Vat. Gr. 356. **XIII.** or **XIV.**
129. Vat. Gr. 358. **XII.**
130. Vat. Gr. 359. *pap.* **XV.** or **XVI.**
131. Vat. Gr. 360. **XIV.** (A70P77.)
132. Vat. Gr. 361. **XII.** or **XIII.**
133. Vat. Gr. 363. **XI.** (A71P78.)
134. Vat. Gr. 364. **XII.**
135. Vat. Gr. 365. **X.**
136. Vat. Gr. 665. *paper.* **XIII.**
137. Vat. Gr. 756. **XI.** or **XII.**
138. Vat. Gr. 757. **XII.**
139. Vat. Gr. 758. **XII.**
140. Vat. Gr. 1158. **XII.**
141. Vat. Gr. 1160. **XIII.** or **XIV.** (A75P86R40.)
142. Vat. Gr. 1210. **XI.** (A76P87.)
143. Vat. Gr. 1229. **XI.**
144. Vat. Gr. 1254. **X.** or **XI.**
145. Vat. Gr. 1548. **XI.**
146[2]. Vat. Pal. 5. **XII.**
147. Vat. Pal. 89. **XIV.**
148. Vat. Pal. 136. **XI.**
149. Vat. Pal. 171. **XV.** (A77P88R25.)
150. Vat. Pal. 189. **XI.**
151. Vat. Pal. 220. **X.**
152. Vat. Pal. 227. **XIII.**
153. Vat. Pal. 229. **XIV.**
154. Vat. Reg. 28. *paper.* **XIII.**
155. Vat. Reg. 79. **XIV.**
156. Vat. Reg. 189. **XII.**
157. Urbino-Vat. Gr. 2. **XII.** v.p.112.
158. Vat. Reg. Pii II. 55. **XI.**
159. Rome, Barberini IV. 64. **XI.**
160. Rome, Barb. IV. 27. **1123.**
161. Rome, Barb. III. 71. **X.** or **XI.**
162. Rome, Barb. IV. 31. **1153.**
163. Rome, Barb. V. 16. **XI.**
164. Rome, Barb. III. 38. **1039.**
165. Rome, Barb. V. 37. **1291.**
166. Rome, Barb. III. 131. **XIII.**
167. Rome, Barb. III. 6. **XIII.**

---

[1] For special use of the sign =, see Glossary: W–H. =.
[2] From a collection once belonging to Palatine, Elector of Bohemia.

168. Rome, Barb. VI. 9. **XIII.**
169. Rome, Vallicellianus B. 133. **XI.**
170. Rome, Val. C. 61. **XIII., XIV.**
171. Rome, Val. C. 73. 2d. **XIV.**
172. *Missing.*
173[1]. Vaticanus. 1983. **XII. or XIII.**
174. Vat. 2002. **1052.**
175. Vat. 2080. **XI.** (A41P194R20.)
176. Vat. 2113. **XIII.**
177. Vat. ?. **XI.** (G. 871 ?).
178. Rome, Angelicus, A.1.3. **XII.**
179. Rome, Angelicus, A.4.11. **XII.**
180. Rome Propag. L. VI. 19. **XIV.**
   (A82P92R44.)
181. *"Hodie latet."*
182. Florence, Laurent. VI. 11. **XIV.**
183. Flo. Lau. VI. 14. **XII.**
184. Flo. Lau. VI. 15. **XIII.**
185. Flo. Lau. VI. 16. **XIV.**
186. Flo. Lau. VI. 18. **XI.**
187. Flo. Lau. VI. 23. **XII.**
188. Flo. Lau. VI. 25. **XII.**
189. F. L. VI. 27. **XIV.** (A141P239.)
190. Flo. Lau. VI. 28. **XIV.**
191. Flo. Lau. VI. 29. **XII.**
192. Flo. Lau. VI. 30. **XIII.**
193. Flo. Lau. VI. 32. **XII. or XIII.**
194. Flo. Lau. VI. 33. **XI.**
195. Flo. Lau. VI. 34. **XI.**
196. Flo. Lau. VIII. 12. **XII.**
197. F. Lau. VIII. 14. **XI.** (A90.)
198. Flo. Lau. Ædil. 221. **XIII.**
199. Flo. Lau. Conv. S. 160. **XII.**
200. Flo. Lau. Conv. S. 159. **XI.**
201. B. M. Add. 11837. (A91P104R94.)
   1357.
202. Brit. Mus. Add. 14774. **XII.**
203. Florence. " Not worthy of a No."
204. Bologna 2775. **XIII.** (A92P105.)
205. Venice, M. 5. **XV.** (A93P106R88.)
205[a]. Ven. M. 6. **XV.** (A94P107R109.)
206. Duplicate of 205. **XV.**
207. Venice, Mark 8. **XI.**
208. Venice, Mark 9. **XI.**
209. Ven. M. 10. **XIV.** (A95P108R46.)
210. Venice, Mark 27. **XI. or XII.**
211. Venice, Mark 539. **XII.**
212. Venice, Mark 540. **XI.**
213. Venice, Mark 542. **XI.**

214. Venice, Mark 543. *paper.* **XIV.**
215. Venice, Mark, 544. **X. or XI.**
216. Perh. = G. 523 (?). *Missing.*
217. Venice, Mark I. 3. **XII.**
218. Vienna Imp. Nes. 23. **XIII.**
   (A65P57R33.)
219. Vienna Imp. Nes. 321. **XIII.**
220. Vienna I. N. 337. **XIV.**
221. Vienna. **X.**
222. Vienna I. N. 180. *paper.* **XIV.**
223. Vienna. **X.** " No value."
224. Vienna I. Sup. Gr. 97. **XII.**
225. Vienna I. Sup. Gr. 102. **1192.**
226. Esc. χ. IV. 17. **XI.** (A108P228)
227. Escurial. χ. III. 15. **XIII.**
228. Esc. χ. IV. 12. *p.* (A109P229.)
   XIV.
229. Esc. χ. IV. 21. **1140.**
230. Esc. ψ. III. 5. **1013.**
231. Esc. ψ. III. 6. **XII.**
232. Esc. ψ. III. 7. **1302.**
233. Esc. Υ. II. 8. **XIII.**
234. Copenh. 1322. **1278.** (A57P72.)
235. Copenhagen. 1323. *pap.* **1314.**
236. *Vacat.* (Readings from No. 440.)
237. Moscow Holy Synod. 42. **X.**
238. Mosc. H. S. 48. **XI.**
239. Mosc. H. S. 47. **XI.**
240. Mosc. H. S. 49. **XI.**
241. Dresden. A. 172. (A104P120R47.)
   XI.
242. M. H. S. 380. **XII.** (A105P121R48.)
243. Moscow Typ. S. 13. *pap.* **XIV.**
244. Moscow Typogr. S. 1. **XII.**
245. Mosc. H. S. 278. **1199.**
246. Mosc. H. S. 261. *paper.* **XIV.**
247. Mosc. H. S. 373. **XII. or XI.**
248. Mosc. H. S. 277. **1275.**
249. Mosc. H. S. 94. **XI.**
250. Mosc. H. S. **XIII.** v. unc. cod. V.
251. Mosc. " Tabularii Cæsarii." **XI.**
252. Dresden. Roy. A. 145. **XI.**
253. Once " Mosc. Nicephori." **X., XI.**
254. Dresden. Roy. A. 100. **X. or XI.**
255. Mosc. H. S. 139. **XII. or XIII·**
256. Mosc. H. S. 138. (Typog. 3.). **IX.**
257. Mosc. H. S. 120. = unc. O., q. v.
258. Dresden. Roy. A. 123. **XIII.**
259. Mosc. H. S. 45. **XI. or X.**

---

[1] Brought from the library of the Basilian monks.

260. Paris N. Gr. 51. **XIII.**
261. Paris N. 52. **XII.**
262. Paris N. 53. **X.**
263. P. N. 61. **XIII.** (A117P137.)
264. Paris N. 65. **XII.**
265. Paris N. 66. **XII.**
266. Paris N. 67. **XIII. or XIV.**
267. Paris N. 69. **XII. or XIII.**
268. Paris N. 73. **XII.**
269. Paris N. 74. **XII.**
270. Paris N. 75. **XII.**
271. Paris N. Sup. Gr. 75. **XI.**
272. B. M. Add. 15581. **XI. or XII.**
273. Paris N. 79. **XIII.**
274. Paris N. Sup. Gr. 79. **X.**
275. Paris N. 80. **XII.**
276. Paris N. 81. **1092.**
277. Paris N. 81.A. **XI.**
278. Paris N. 82. **1072.**
279. Paris N. 86. **XI.**
280. Paris N. 87. **XII.**
281. Paris N. 88. **XII.**
282. Paris N. 90. **1176.**
283. Paris N. 92. **XIII.**
284. Paris N. 93. **XIII.**
285. Paris N. 95. **XV.**
286. Paris N. 96. *paper.* **1432.**
287. Paris N. 98. *paper.* **1478.**
288. (Ox. Bod. Can. 33: *Matt.*(Scr. 487).
     (Paris N. Gr. 99: *Luke.* (**XV.**)
     (Paris Ins. 3, 4to: *John* (Scr. 471).
289. Paris N. 100. A. *paper.* **1625.**
290. Paris N. Sup. 108. *p.* **XIII., XIV.**
291. Paris N. 113. **XIII.**
292. Paris N. 114. **XIII.**
293. Paris N. 117. *Pal.* **1262.**
294. Paris N. 118. **1291.**
295. Paris N. 120. **XIII.**
296. P. N. G. 123, 124. (A124P149R57.)
     XVI.
297. Paris N. Sup. Gr. 140. **XII.**
298. Paris N. Sup. Gr. 175. **XII.**
299. Paris N. 177. **X. or XI.**
300. Paris N. 186. **XI.**
301. Paris N. 187. **XI. or XII.**
302. Paris N. 193. *paper.* **XVI.**
303. Pons N. 194. A. *paper.* **1255.**
304. Paris N. 194. **XII.**
305. Paris N. 195. *paper.* **XIII.**
306. Paris N. 197. **XII.**

307. Paris N. 199. **X. or XI.**
308. Paris N. 200. **X. or XI.**
309. Paris N. 201. **X. or XI.**
310. Paris N. 202. **XII.**
311. Paris N. 203. **XII.**
312. Paris N. 206. **1307.**
313. Paris N. 208. *paper.* **XV.**
314. Paris N. 209. **X.**
315. Paris N. 210. **XIII.?**
316. Paris N. 211. *paper.* **XIV.**
317. Paris N. 212. **XII.**
318. Paris N. 213. **XIV. or XV.**
319. Paris N. 231. **XII.**
320. Paris N. 232. **XII.**
321. Paris N. 303. **XIV.** is Evl. **101.**
322. Paris N. 315. **XVI.** is Evl. **14.**
323. Paris N. S. 118. *pap.* **XIV., XV.**
324. P. N. 376. **XIV.** (Evl97Apl32.)
325. Paris N. 377. **XV.** is Evl. **98.**
326. Paris N. 378. *paper.* **XIV.**
327. Paris N. 380. is Evl. **99.**
328. Paris N. 381. is Evl. **100.**
329. Paris N. Coislin. 19. **XII.**
330. 8^pe. St. Petersburg Muralt. 101.
     XII. (A132P131.)
331. P. N. Coislin. Gr. 197. **X. or XI.**
332. Turin Univ. C. II. 4. 20. **XII.**
333. Tur. B. I. 9. 4. *paper.* **1214.**
334. Tur. B. III. 8. 43. **XII. or XIII.**
335. Tur. B. III. 2. 44. *paper.* **XVI.**
336. Tur. B. II. 17. 101. *pap.* **XVI.**
337. Tur. B. III. 25. 52. **XII.**
338. Tur. B. VII. 33. 335. **X.**
339. T.B.V.8. **XIII.** (A135P170R83)
340. Tur. B. VII. 16. 344. **XIV.**
341. Tur. B. VII. 14. 350. **1296.**
342. Tur. B. V. 24. 149. **XIII.**
343. Milan. Ambrosian. H. 13. sup. **XI.**
344. Milan. Ambr. G. 16. sup. **X.**
345. Milan. Ambr. F. 17. sup. **XI.**
346. Milan. Ambr. S. 23. sup. **XII.**
347. Milan. Ambr. R. 35. sup. **XII.**
348. Milan. Ambr. B. 56. sup. **1022.**
349. Milan. Am. F. 61. sup. *p.* **1322.**
350. Milan. Ambr. B. 62. sup. **XI.**
351. Milan. Ambr. B. 70. sup. **XII.**
352. Milan. Ambr. B. 93. sup. **XI.**
353. Milan. Ambr. M. 93. sup. **XII.**
354. Venice. Mark. 29. **XI.**
355. Ven. Mar. 541. **XII.**

356. Ven. Mar. 545. *paper.* **XVI.**
357. Ven. Mar. 28. **XI.**
358. Modena. Estensis. II. A. 9. **XIV.**
359. Mod. Es. III. B. 16. *pap.* **XIII.**
360. Parma, Roy. Lib. 2319. **X.** or **XI.**
361. Parma, Roy. Lib. 1821. **XIII.**
362. Florence, L. Conv. S. 176. **XIII.**
363. Fl. L. VI. 13. (A144P180). **XIV.**
364. Fl. Lau. VI. 24. **X.**
365. F. L. VI. 36. (A145P181). **XIII.**
366. Fl. Lau. Conv. Sopp. 171. **XII.**
367. Fl. Lau. S. 53. *p.* (A146P182R23). **1331.**
368. F. Ric. Lib. 84. *pap.* (A150R84). **XV.**
369. Fl. Riccardi Lib. 90. **XIV.**
370. Fl. Ricc. 5. *paper.* **XIV.**
371. Vatican. Gr. 1159. **X.**
372. Vat. 1161. **XVI.**
373. Vat. 1423. *paper.* **XV.**
374. Vat. 1445. **XII.**
375. Vat. 1533. **XI.** or **XII.**
376. Vat. 1539. **XI.**
377. Vat. 1618. *paper.* **XV.**
378. Vat. 1658. **XIV.**
379. Vat. 1769. *p.* **XV.**
380. Vat. 2139. **1499.**
381. Palatino-Vat. 20. *paper.* **XIV.**
382. Vat. 2070. **XIII.**
383-4-5. Once Coll. Romani. **XVI.**
386. Vat. Ott. 66. (A151P199R70.) **XIV.**
387. Vat. Ott. 204. **XII.**
388. Vat. Ott. 212. **XIII.**
389. Vat. Ott. 297. **XI.**
390. Vat. Ott. 381. (A164P203.) **1282.**
391. Vat. Ott. 432. **XI.**
392. Rome Barberin, V. 17. **XII.**
393. Rome Val. E. 22. (A167P185). *paper.* **XIV.**
394. Rome Vall. F. 17. (A170P186.) **1330.**
395. Rome, Casanat. G. IV. 1. **XII.**
396. Rome, Chisianus, R. IV. 6. **XII.**
397. Rome, Vall. E. 40. **X.**
398. Turin Univ. C. II. 5. *pap.* **XVI.**
399. Turin Univ. C. II. 14. *pap.* **XVI.**
400. Ber. Roy. Lib. **XV.** (A181P220).
401. Naples Nat. Lib. II. A. a. 3. **XII.**

402. Naples Nat. Lib. II. A. a. 5 **XIV.**
403. Naples Lib. II. A. a. 4. *pap.* **XIII.**
404. Naples "Abbatis Scotti." **XI.**
405. Lost.
        Venice, Mark I. 10. **X.**
406. V. M., I. 11. **XI.**
407. V. M. I. 12. **XII.** or **XIII.**
408. V. M. I. 14. **XII.**
409. V. M. I. 15. **XIV.**
410. V. M. I. 17. **XIII.** or **XIV.**
411. V. M. I. 18. **X.**
412. V. M. I. 19. **1301.**
413. V. M. I. 20. **1302.**
414. V. M. I. 21. **XIV.**
415. V. M. I. 22. **1356.**
416. V. M. I. 24. **XIV.**
417. V. M. I. 25. **XIV.**
418. V. M. I. 28. **XV.**
419. V. M. I. 60. **XII.**
420. Messina Univ. Lib. 18. **X.**
421. Syracuse. **XII.** (A176P218).
422. Munich Roy. Lib. 210. **XI.**
423. Mun. Roy. Lib. 36 & 37. **1556.**
424. Mun. Roy. Lib. 83. *p.* **XVI.**
425. Mun. Roy. Lib. 37 is G. 423, vol. ii.
426. Mun. Roy. Lib. 473. *p.* **XIV.**
427. Mun. Roy. Lib. 465. **XIII.**
428. Mun. Roy. Lib. 381. *p.* **XIII.**
429. *Un.* No., v. Unc. X[b].
430. Mun. Roy. Lib. 437. **XI.**
431. Strasburg Presby. Sem. **XII.** (A180P238.)
432. "Unworthy a No."
433. Berlin Roy. MS. 4to. 12. **XI.**
434. Vienna Imp. Ness. 71. **XIV.**
435. Leyden Gronov. 137. **X.**
436. Once Meermann 117. **XI.** "*Latet.*"
437. St. Petersburg. **XI.**
438. Brit. Mus. Add. 5111–12 (bef. A.D. **1189.**)
439. B. M. Add. 5107. **1159.**
440. Camb. Mm. 69. **XII.** (A111P221.)
441. (Printed book.) "*Delendus.*"
442. (Printed book.) "*Delendus.*"
443. Camb. Nn. 2. 36. **XII.**
444. B. M. H. 5796. **XV.** (A153P240.)
445. B. M. Harl. 5736. *p.* **1506.**
446. B. M. Harl. 5777. **XV.**
447. B. M. Harl. 5784. **XV.**
443. B. M. Harl. 5790. **1478.**

12

449. B. M. Add. 4950–51. **XIII.**
450. Jer. Holy Sepulchre 1. **1043.**
451. Jer. H. S. 2. **XI.**
452. Jer. H. S. 3. **XIV.**
453. Jer. H. S. 4. **XIV.**
454. Jer. H. S. 5. **XIV.**
455. Jer. H. S. 6. **XIV.**
456. Jer. H. S. 7. **XIII.**
457. St. Saba, 2. **XIII.** (A186P234.)
458. St. Saba, 3. **1272.**
459. St. Saba, 7. **XII.**
460. St. Saba, 8. **XII.**
461. St. Petersburg. **835.**
462. St. Sa. 10. **XIV.** (A187P235R86.)
463. St. Saba, 11. *p.* **XIV.**
464. St. Saba, 12. *p.* **XI.**
465. St. Saba, 19. **XIII.**
466. St. Sa. 20. **XIII.** (A189P237R89.)
467. Patmos. **XI.**
468. Patmos. **XII.**
469. Patmos. **XIV.**
470[a] Scr. Lambeth 1175. **XI.** Scr. 509.
471[b] Scr. Lamb. 1176. **XII.** Scr. 510.
472[c] Scr. Lamb. 1177. **XIII., XIV., XV.** Scr. 511. *"optimæ notæ."*
473[d] Scr. Lamb. 1178. **XIII.** Scr. 512.
474[e] Scr. Lamb. 1179. **XI.** Scr. 513.
475[f] Scr. Lamb. 1192. **XI.** Scr. 515.
     [g] Scr. = Gospels 71
476[h] Scr. B. M. Arun. 524. **XI.** Scr. 566.
477[i] Scr. Camb. Trin. B. 10 17. **XIII.** Scr. 508.
     [j] Scr. = Uncial N., v. Table VIII.
478[k] Scr. B. M. Add. 11300. **X.** Scr. 575.
479[l] Scr. Wordsworth, **XIII.** Scr. 542. (A193P249.)
     [m] Scr. = Gospels, 201.
480[n] Scr. B. M. Bur. 18. **1366.** Scr. 568. (A247P250.)
481[o] Scr. B. M. Bur. 19. **X.** Scr. 569.
482[p] Scr. B.M. Bur. 20. **1285.** Scr. 570.
483[q] Scr. Once Pickering. **1295.** Scr. 543. *Latet.* (A194P251.)
484[r] Scr. B.M. Bur. 21. **1292.** Scr. 571.
485[s] Scr. B. M. Bur. 23. **XII.** Scr. 572.
486[t] Scr. Lambeth, 1350. **XV.** Scr. 517.
487[u] Scr. Const'ple Lib. of Patr. of Jer. (?) Scr. 516.
488[v] Scr. Const'ple. *p.* **XIV.** Scr. 514.

489[w] Scr. Camb. Trin. B. 10, 16. *p.* **1316.** Scr. 507. (A195P252.)
490. B. M. Add. 7141. **XI.** Scr. 574.
491. B. M. Add. 11836. **XI.** Scr. 576. (A196P253.)
492. B.M. Add. 11838. **1326.** Scr. 577.
493. B.M. Add. 11839. *p.* **XV.** Scr. 578.
494. B.M. Add. 32341. **XIV.** Scr. 325.
495. B. M. Add. 16183. **XII.** Scr. 581.
496. B. M. Add. 16184. **XIII.** Scr. 582. (A197P254.)
497. B. M. Add. 16943. **XI.** Scr. 583.
498. B. M. Add. 17469. **XIV.** Scr. 584. (A198P255R97.)
499. B. M. Add. 17741. **XII.** Scr. 586.
500. B.M. Add. 17982. **XIII.** Scr. 587.
501. B.M. Add. 18211. **XIII.** Scr. 588.
502. B. M. Add. 19387. **XII.** Scr. 589.
503. B.M. Add. 19389. **XIII.** Scr. 590.
504. B. M. Add. 17470. **1033.** Scr. 585.
505. B. M. Harl. 5538. **XII.** Scr. 567.
506. Oxf. Ch. Ch. Wake, 12. **XI.** Scr. 492. (A199P256R26.)
507. Oxf. C. C. W. 21. **XI.** Scr. 493.
508. Oxf. C. C. W. 22. **XIII.** Scr. 494.
509. Oxf. C. C. W. 24. **XII.** Scr. 495.
510. Oxf. C. C. W. 25. **XII.** Scr. 496.
511. Oxf. C. C. W. 27. **XIII.** Scr. 497.
512. Oxf. C. C W. 28. **XIV.** Scr. 498.
513. Oxf. C.C. W. 29. **1130.** Scr. 499.
514. Oxf. C. C. W. 30. **XII.** Scr. 500.
515. Oxf. C. C. W. 31. **XI.** Scr. 501.
516. Oxf. C. C. W. 32. **XI.** Scr. 502.
517. Oxf. Ch. Ch. Wake 34. **XI.** Scr. 503. (A190P244R27.)
518. Oxf. C. C. W. 36. **XII.** Scr. 504.
519. Oxf. C. C. W. 39. **XIII.** Scr. 505.
520. Oxf. C. C. W. 40. **XII.** Scr. 506.
521. Oxf. Bodl. d. 1. **XIV.** Scr. 562.
522. Oxf. Bodl. Canon. Gr. 34. **1515.** (A200P257R98.) Scr. 488.
523. Oxf. B. C. Gr. 36. **XI.** Scr. 489.
524. Oxf. B.C. Gr. 112. **XII.** Scr. 490.
525. Oxf. B.C. Gr. 122. **XV.** Scr. 491.
526. Oxf. B. Barocc 59. **XI.** Scr. 610.
527. Oxf. B. Crom. 15. **XI.** Scr. 482.
528. Oxf. B. Crom. 16. **XI.** Scr. 483.
529. Oxf. Bodl. Misc. 17. **XI.** Scr. 484.
530. Oxf. Bodl. Misc. 141. **XI.** Scr. 485.
531. Lond. Braithwaite 1. **XII.** Scr. 327.

532. Lond. B–C. Highgate, I. 3. **XII.** Scr. 545.

533. Lond. B–C. H. I. 4. **XII.** Scr. 546.

534. Lond. B–C. H. I. 7. **XIII.** Scr. 547.

535. Lond. B–C. H. I. 9. **XI.** Scr. 548.

536. Lond. B–C. H. II. 7. **XII.** (A201.) Scr. 549.

537. Lond. B–C. H. II. 13. **XIII.** Scr. 550.

538. Lond. B–C. H. II. 18. **XIII.** Scr. 552.

539. Lond. B–C. H. II. 23. **XI.** Scr. 551.

540. Lond. B–C. H. II. 26. 1. **XIV.** Scr. 553.

541. Lond. B–C. H. II. 26. 2. **XIV.** Scr. 554.

542. Lond. B–C. III. 4. **XIII.** Scr. 555.

543. Lond. B–C. III. 5. **XII.** Scr. 556.

544. Lond. B–C. III. 9. **XIII.** Scr. 557.

545. L. B–C. III. 10. **1430.** Scr. 558.

546. Lond. B–C. III. 41. **XIV.** Scr. 559.

547. Parham (Curzon) 71. 6. **XI.** (A.202P.258). Scr. 534.

548. Parham Cur. 72. 7. **X.** Scr. 535.

549. Parham Cur. 73. 8. **XI.** Scr. 536.

550. Parham Cur. 74. 9. **XII.** Scr. 537.

551. Parham Cur. 75. 10. **XII.** Scr. 538.

552. Parham Cur. 76. 11. **XII.** Scr. 539.

553. Par. Cur. 77. 12. **XIII.** Scr. 540.

554. Par. Cur. 78. 13. **1272.** Scr. 541.

555. Camb. U. Hh. 6. 12. *p.* **XV.** Scr. 609.

556. Cheltenham, 13975. **XII.** Scr. 526.

557. Holkham, Eng 3. **XIII.** Scr. 524.

558. Holkham, Eng. 4. **XIII.** Scr. 525.

559. Sion Coll. Lond. Arc. 1. 3. **XI.** Scr. 518.

560. Hunterian Museum, Glasgow Un. V. 7. 2. **XII.** Scr. 520.

561. H. M. G. U. V. 7. 3. **XIII.** Scr. 521.

562. Hunt. Mus. Glas. Un. T. 8. 2. **XVI.** Scr. 522.

563. Edin. Un. A. C. c. 25. **XI.** Scr. 519.

564. Leipsic Tisch. IV. **X.** Scr. 478.

565. [2 Pe.] St. Petersburg Muralt, 53, VI. 470, **IX.** Scr. 473.

566. [tisch 2.] (?) St. Pet. Muralt, 54. **IX.**

567. = Evl. **251.**

568. St. Pet. Muralt, 67. **X.** Scr. 879.

569. [7 Pe.] St. Pet. Mur. 72. **IX.** 3.471 **1062.** Scr. 475.

569. [8 Pe.] = Gospels, 330.

570. [tisch 4.] ? St. P. Muralt, 97. **XII.** Scr. 479.

571. [4 Pe.] St. P. M. 98. **XII.** Scr. 474.

572. St. Pet. Mur. 99. **XII.** Scr. 480.

573. Braithwaite, 2. **XIII.** Scr. 328.

574. St. Pet. Mur. 105. **XII.** Scr. 880.

575. [11 Pe.] St. Pet. Mur., 118. (Q. V. I. 15). **XV.** Scr. 477.

576. Lord Herries. **XIII.** Scr. 580.

577. Montepelier, France (Med. Sch.) H. 446. **1346.** Scr. 871.

578. Arras, Fr. 970. **1361.** Scr. 872.

579. Paris, 97. **XIII.** Scr. 743.

580. Paris, 119. **XII.** Scr. 744.

581. Ferrara Univ. 119 NA. 4. **XIV.** Scr. 450.

582. Ferrara 187, 188 NA. 7. **1334.** Scr. 451. (A206P262R103.)

583. Parma Roy. 5. **XI.** Scr. 452.

584. Parma Roy. 65. **X.** Scr. 453.

585. Modena Est. II. A. 1. **XI.** Scr. 454.

586. Mod. Est. II. A. 5. **XIV.** Scr. 455.

587. Milan, Amb. M. 48. **XII.** Scr. 456.

588. Milan, Amb. Lib. E. 63 sup. **1321.** Scr. 457.

589. Milan, Amb. Lib. A. 178 sup. **XIV.** Scr. 830.

590. Parma, Roy. 15. **XIII.** Scr. 831.

591. Rome, Corsin. 41. G. 16. **XIII.** Scr. 883.

592. Milan Amb. Lib. Z. 34 sup. **XV.** Scr. 461. (A207P263.)

593. Venice Mark, I. 58. **XIII.** Scr. 462.

594. Ven. S. Laz. 1531. **XIV.** Scr. 470.

595. Ven. Mark. I. 56. *p.* **XVI.** Scr. 468.

596. Ven. Mark. I. 57. **XI.** Scr. 465.

597. Ven. Mark. I. 59. **XIII.** Scr. 464.

598. Ven. Mark. 494. *p.* **XIII.** Scr. 466.

599. Ven. Mark. 495. *p.* **XV.** Scr. 467.

600. Ven. Mark. II. 7. *p.* **XIV.** Scr. 463.

601. Cairo Patr. Alex. 2. **XIII.** Scr. 643.

602. Cairo Patr. Alex. 15. **XI.** Scr. 644.

603. Cairo Patr. Alex. 16. **XI.** Scr. 645.

604. Cairo Patr. Alex. 17. **XI.** Scr. 646.

605. Cairo Patr. Alex. 68. **X.** Scr. 647.

606. Cairo Mon. S. 100. *p.* **XVI.** Scr. 648.

607. Jerusalem H. S. 2. **X.** Scr. 649.

608. Jerus. H. S. 5. **X.** Scr. 650.

609. Paris Sup. 911. **1043.** Scr. 634.

610. Jerus.H.Sepul.14. **XII.** Scr.652.
611. Jerus.H.Sepul.17. **XI.** Scr.653.
612. Jerus.H.Sepul.31. **XI.** Scr.654.
613. Jerus.H.Sepul.32. **XI.** Scr.655.
614. Jerus.H.Sepul.33. **XII.** Scr.656.
615. Jerus.H.Sepul.40. **XII.** Scr.657.
616. Jerus.H.Sepul.41. **XI.** Scr.658.
617. Jerus.H.Sepul.43. **XI.** Scr.659.
618. Jerus. H. S. 44. **XIV.** Scr. 660.
619. Jerus. H. Sepul.45. **XII.** Scr.661.
620. Jerus. H.Sepul.46. **XI.** Scr.662.
621. Jer.Col.Ho.Cross,3. **XI.** Scr.663.
622. St. Saba, 27. **XII.** Scr. 664.
623. St. Saba, 52. **XI.** Scr. 665.
624. St. Saba, 53. **XI.** Scr. 667.
625. St. Saba, 54. **XII.** Scr. 673.
626. St. Saba, 56. **X.** Scr. 677.
627. St. Saba, 57. **X.** Scr. 678.
628. St. Saba, 58. **X.** Scr. 679.
629. St. Saba, 59. **X.** Scr. 681.
630. St. Saba, 60. **X.** Scr. 682.
631. St. Saba, 61. **XI.** Scr. 685.
632. St. Saba, 61. **XI.** Scr. 686.
633. St. Saba, 61. **XI.** Scr. 688.
634. St. Saba, 61. **XI.** Scr. 695.
635. St. Saba, 61. **XI.** Scr. 700.
636-640. St. Saba, 62. **XII.** Scr.
    701–702–706–710–711.
641. St. Saba,Tower,45. **XI.** Scr.712.
642. St. Saba,Tower,46. **XI.** Scr.715.
643. St.Saba,Tower,47. **XI.** Scr.716.
644. Larnaka (Cyp.) **XII.** Scr. 720.
645. B.M.Add.22506. **1305.** Scr.591.
646. Const. H. S. 436. **XVI.** Scr. 721.
647. Const. H. S. 520. **XIII.** Scr.722.
648. Const. H. S.'574. **XIV.** Scr. 724·
649. Const.Ph.So.1. **1303.** Scr. 725.
650. Const. Ph.So.5. **XIII.** Scr.726.
651. Dessau Ducal Lib. **XI.** Scr. 874.
652. Munich roy. 594. **X.** Scr. 875.
653. Berlin, 8vo 3. **1077.** Scr. 640.
654. Berlin 8vo 4. **XII.** Scr. 641.
655. Berlin 4to 39. **XI.** Scr. 635.
656. Berlin 8vo 9. **XIV.** Scr. 642.
    (A213P269.)
657. Berlin 8vo 12. **XI.** Scr. 876.
658. Berlin 4to 47. **XII.** Scr. 636.
659. Berlin 4to 55. **XII.** Scr. 637.
660. Berlin 4to 66. **XI.** Scr. 638.
661. Berlin 4to 67. **XI.** Scr. 639.

662. Lond. Butler. **XII.** Scr. 632.
663. (Stras.) Reuss. **XIII.** Scr. 877.
664. Zittau, City Lib. A.I. **XV.**
    Scr. 605. (A253P303R106).
665. Cheltenh. 6899. **XVI.** Scr. 895.
666. Camb.U.S.A. **XII.** See Table XI.
667. Madison, N. J. Drew Sem. MS. 3.
    XI. Scr. 900. See Table XI.
668. Syracuse Univ. N. York. **XII.**
    Scr. 1144. See Table XI.
669. Sewanee, Tenn. A. A. Benton. 3.
    X. Scr. 902. See Table XI.
670. Sewanee, Tenn. A. A. Benton. 2.
    XI. Scr. 901. See Table XI.
671. Ashburnham, Eng. 204. **XII.**
    Scr. 544.
672. Camb. Add. 720. **XI.** Scr. 618.
673. Camb.U.A.1837. **XII.** Scr. 619.
674. C. U. A. 1879, 11. **XII.** Scr. 620.
675. C. U. A. 1879, 24. **XIII.** Scr. 621.
676. Cheltenham, 1284. **XII.** Scr.
    527. (A254P304).
677. Chelt. 2387. **XIII.** Scr. 528.
678. Chelt. 3886. **XII.** Scr. 529.
679. Chelt. 3887. **XIII.** Scr. 530.
680. Chelt. 7682. **XI.** Scr. 531.
    (A255P305R107).
681. Chelt. 7712. **XIII.** Scr. 532.
682. Chelt. 7757. **XI.** Scr. 533.
683. Holkham, Norfolk, 5. **XIII.**
684. Holkham, Norfolk, 104. **1228.**
685. Lond. Huthii, 354. **XIII.**
686. B.M. Add. 5468. **1338.** Scr. 573.
687. B. M. Add. 11868. **XI.** Scr. 579.
688. B.M.Add.22736. **1179.** Scr.592.
689. B.M.Add. 22737. **XIII.** Scr.593.
690. B.M.Add.22738. **XIV.** Scr.594.
691. B.M.Add.22739. **XIII.** Scr.595.
692. B.M.Add.22740. **XII.** Scr.596.
693. B.M.Add.22741. **XIII.** Scr.597.
694. B.M.Add.24112. **XV.** Scr.598.
695. B.M.Add.24373. **XIII.** Scr.599.
696. B.M.Add.24376. **XIII.** Scr.600.
697. B.M.Add.26103. **XIII.** Scr.601.
698. B.M.Add.27861. **XIV.** Scr.602.
699. B.M.Add. 28815. B–C.H. Lond.
    II. 4 Eph-Apoc. **XI.** Scr. 603.
    (A256P306R108).
700. B.M.Egerton,2610. **XI.** Scr.604.
701. Lond.Mr.White(?) **XIV.** Scr.523.

702. Lond. Mr. White. **XII.** Scr. 884.
703. Lond. Quaritch. **1251.** Scr. 885.
704. Manchester, Ryland's Lib. **XIII.**
Scr. 886.
705. Hack. Amherst. Scr. 887. **XIII.**
706. Oxf. Bo. Mis. 293. **XIII.** Scr. 486.
707. Oxf. Bodl. Misc. 305. **XI.** Scr. 606.
708. Oxf. Bodl. Misc. 306. **XI.** Scr. 607.
709. Oxf. Bodl. Misc. 314. **XI.** Scr. 737.
710. Oxf. Bo. Mis. 323. **XIII.** Scr. 81.
711. Oxf. Oriel. MS. 81. **XI.** Scr. 617.
712. Wisbech. Camb.'shire. **XI.** Scr.
560. (A257P307).
713. Wisbech, **XI.** Scr. 561. (Apl90).
714. Br. Mus. Egerton, 2783 (once W.
F. Rose). **XIII.** Scr. 563.
715. B. M. Egert. 2785. **XIII.** Scr. 564.
716. B. M. Egert. 2784. **XIV.** Scr. 565.
717. Coniston, Eng. (John Ruskin). **XI.**
718. Ashdon, Essex, Eng. (H. B. Swet).
XIV. Scr. 736.
719. Vienna Th. 19. *pap.* **1196.** Scr.
824.
720. Vienna Th. 79, 80. *pap.* **1138.**
Scr. 825. (A258P308).
721. Vienna Theol. 90. **XII.** Scr. 826.
722. Vienna Theol. 95. *pap.* **XV.** Scr.
827.
723. Vienna Theol. 122. *pap.* **XV.**
724. Vienna Imp. Priv. Lib. 7972.
parch. & pap. **XV.** Scr. 829.
725. Brussels. 11358. **XIII.** Scr. 881.
726. Brussels, 11375. **XIII.** Scr. 882.
727. Paris N. Gr. 179. **XIV.** Scr. 745.
728. Paris N. Gr. 181. **XIV.** Scr. 746.
729. Paris N. 182. **XIII.** Scr. 747.
(Evl61.)
730. P. N. Gr. 183. *p.* **XIV.** Scr. 748.
731. P. N. Gr. 184. *p.* **XIV.** Scr. 749.
732. Paris N. Gr. 185. **XIII.** Scr. 750.
733. Paris N. Gr. 190. **XII.** Scr. 751.
734. Paris N. Gr. 192. **XIV.** Scr. 752.
735. Paris N. Gr. 196. **XV.** Scr. 753.
736. Paris N. Gr. 198. **XII.** Scr. 754.
737. Paris N. Gr. 204. **XIII.** Scr. 755.
738. P. N. Gr. 205. *p.* **1327.** Scr. 756.
739. Paris N. Gr. 207. **XV.** Scr. 757.
740. Paris N. Gr. 234. **XIV.** Scr. 761.
741. Paris N. Gr. 235. **XIV.** Scr. 763.
742. P. N. Gr. 1775. *p.* **XV.** Scr. 764.

743. Paris N. Sup. 159. **XIV.** Scr.
738. (A259R123.)
744. Paris N. Sup. 219. **XIII.** Scr. 759.
745. P. N. Sup. 227. *p.* **XVI.** Scr. 633.
746. Paris N. Sup. 611. **XI.** Scr. 740.
747. Paris N. Sup. 612. **XII.** Scr. 741.
748. Paris N. Sup. 903. **XII.** Scr. 758.
749. Paris N. Sup. 904. **XIII.** Scr. 773.
750. Paris N. Sup. 914. **XII.** Scr. 742.
751. Paris N. Sup. 919. **XIII.** Scr. 739.
752. Paris N. Sup. 927. **XII.** Scr. 774.
753. Paris N. Sup. 1035. **XI.** Scr. 760.
754. Paris N. Sup. 1076. **XI.** Scr. 763.
755. P. N. S. 1080. *p.* **XVI.** Scr. 771.
756. Paris Sup. 1083. **XI.** Scr. 772.
757. Athens Theol. 12. *paper.* **XIII.**
Scr. 846. (A260P309R110.)
758. Athens T. 13. **XIV.** Scr. 847.
759. Athens T. 14. **XIII.** Scr. 848.
760. Athens T. 15. **XII.** Scr. 849.
761. Athens T. 16. **XIV.** Scr. 850.
762. Athens T. 17. **XIV.** Scr. 852.
763. Athens T. 18. **XIV.** Scr. 854.
764. Athens T. 19. **XIV.** Scr. 855.
765. Athens T. 20. **XII.** Scr. 856.
766. Athens T. 21. **XIV.** Scr. 857.
767. Athens Theol. 22 cent. ? Scr.
858. (A261P310.)
768. Athens T. 23. **XII.** Scr. 859.
769. Athens T. 24. *p.* **XIV.** Scr. 861.
770. Athens T. 66. **XII.** Scr. 862.
771. Athens T. 67. **XII.** Scr. 863.
772. Athens T. 216. **XIV.** Scr. 867.
773. Ath. Sakkelion, 1. **XI.** Scr. 868.
774. Athens Sak. 2. **XII.** Scr. 869.
775. Athens Sak. 3. **XIII.**
776. Ath. Sak. 5. **XI.**
777. Ath. Sak. 6. **XII.**
778. Ath. Sak. 7. **XII.**
779. Ath. 1. **XII.**
780. Ath. 5. **XI.**
781. Ath. 14. *paper.* **XIV.**
782. Ath. 16. **XII.**
783. Ath. 17. **XIV.**
784. Ath. 20. *paper.* **XIV.**
785. Ath. 21. **XI.**
786. Ath. 22. **XIV.**
787. Ath. 23. **XII.**
788. Ath. 26. **XI.**
789. Ath. 27. **XIV.**

790. Ath. 39.   *paper.*   **XIV.**
791. Ath. 60.   **XII.**
792. Ath. 67m.   **XIII.**   (R111.)
793. Ath. 71.   **XII.**
794. Ath. 118.   *p.* **XIV.** (A262P311.)
795. Ath. 150.   *paper.*   **XIV.**   (?)
796. Ath. 767.   **XI.**   (A263P312.)
797. Ath.   *paper.*   **XIV.**
798. Ath.   (?)
799. Ath.   **XII.**
800. Ath.   **XII.**
801. Ath. Nat. *p.*   **XV.** (A264P313.)
802. Ath.   **XIV.**
803. Ath.   *paper.*   **XVI.**
804. Ath.   τῆς βουλῆς.   **XII.**
805. Ath.   τῆς βουλῆς.   **XIII.**
806. Ath.   τῆς βουλῆς.   **XIV.**
807. Ath.   τῆς βουλῆς.   **XIV.**
808. Ath.   Dom Mamoukae.   **XII.**
   (A265P314R112.)
809. Ath. Dom Mamoukae.   **XI.**
810. Ath.   Οἰκονόμου 6.   **XI.**
811. Ath. Chn. Archeol. Soc.
812. Corfu. Abp. Eustathius.   **XII.**
813. Corfu. Abp. Eust.   **XII.**
814. Corfu. Abp. Eust.   *paper.*   **XIII.**
815. Corfu. Count Gonemus.   **XIV.**
816. Corfu.   **XII.**
817. Basil A. N. III. 15.   *paper.*   **XV.**
818. Escurial ψ III. 13.   *paper.*   **XIV.**
819. Escurial ψ III. 14.   *paper.*   **XIV.**
820. Escurial Ω I. 16.   *paper.*   **XIII.**
821. Madrid Royal Lib. O.10.   *p.* **XVI.**
822. Madrid Royal Lib. O. 62.   **XII.**
823. Berlin Royal Lib. 8vo 13.   **XIII.**
   (A266P315.)
824. Grotta Ferrata A′. *a′*. 1. *pap.* **XIV.**
   Scr. 622.   (A267P316R113.)
825. Grotta Fer. A′. *a′*. 2. **XIII.** Scr. 623.
826. Grotta Fer. A′. *a′*. 3.   **XII.** Scr. 624.
827. Grotta Fer. A′. *a′*. 4. **XIII.** Scr. 625.
828. Grotta Fer. A′. *a′*. 5.   **XII.** Scr. 626.
829. Grotta Fer. A′. *a′*. 6.   **XII.** Scr. 627.
830. Grotta Fer. A′. *a′*. 8. **XIII.** Scr. 628.
831. Grotta Fer. A′. *a′*. 17.   **XI.** Scr. 629.
832. Florence Laur. VI. 5.   **X.**   (A143.)
833. Flor. Laur. VI. 26.   *paper.*   **XIV.**
834. Flor. Laur. XI. 6.   **XIV.**
835. Flor. Laur. XI. 8.   **1284.**
836. Flor. Laur. XI. 18.   *pap.* **XIV.**

837. Milan Amb. E.S. IV.14 Fol. 38–
   66.   **XIV.**
838. Once Milan Hoeplii.   **X.** or **XI.**
839. Messina Univ. 88.   **XIV.** Scr. 630.
840. Mess. U. 100.   *p.* **XIII.** Scr. 631.
841. Modena III. F. 13.   *paper.*   **XV.**
842. Modena III. G. 9.   **XIV.**
843. Naples II. A.A. 37.   **XII.**
844. Padua Univ. 695.   **XV.**
845. Pistoja. Fabron. Lib. 307.   **1330.**
846. Rome Bib. Angelica B.I.4.   **XIV.**
847. Rome B. A. B.I.5.   **XII.** Scr. 723.
848. Rome B. A. D.3.8.   **XIV.** Scr. 611.
849. Rome Barb. IV. 77.   *pap.* **XVII.**
   Scr. 730.
850. Rome B. IV. 86.   **XII.** Scr. 729.
851. Rome Coll. Prop. L. VI. 9.   **XIV.**
852. Rome C. Prop. L. VI. 10.   **1300.**
   S. 732.
853. Rome Casan. G. II. 9.   *pap.* **XV.**
854. Vatican 641. *p.*   **1287.** Scr. 666.
855. Vat. Gr. 643.   **XII.** Scr. 668.
856. Vat. Gr. 644. *p.*   **1280.** Scr. 669.
857. Vat. Gr. 645.   **XII.** Scr. 670.
858. Vat. Gr. 647. *paper.*   **XIV.** Scr.
   671.   (P400.)
859. Vat. Gr. 759. *p.*   **XVI.** Scr. 672.
860. Vat. Gr. 774.   **XII.**
861. Vat. G. 1090. *p.*   **XVI.** Scr. 674.
862. Vat. Gr. 1191.   **XII.** Scr. 675.
863. Vat. Gr. 1221.   **XIII.** Scr. 676.
864. Vat. Gr. 1253.   *paper.*   **XIV.**
865. Vat. Gr. 1472.   *paper.*   **XV.**
866. Vat. Gr. 1882.   **XIV.**   (R114.)
867. Vat. Gr. 1895.   **XIV.** Scr. 680.
868. Vat. Gr. 1933. *p.*   **XVII.** Scr. 683.
869. Vat. Gr. 1996.   **XII.** Scr. 684.
870. Vat. Gr. 2115.   **XI.**
871. Vat. Gr. 2117.   **XI.** Scr. 687.
872. Vat. Gr. 2160.   **XII.** Scr. 690.
873. Vat. Gr. 2165.   **XI.** Scr. 689.
874. Vat. 2187.   **XIII.** Scr. 691.
875. Vat. 2247 (?)   Scr. 692.
876. Vat. 2275. *pap.*   **XVI.** Scr. 693.
877. Vat. 2290.   **1197.** Scr. 694.
878. Vat. Ottob. 37.   **XII.** Scr. 703.
879. Vat. Ott. 100.   *p.* **XVI.** Scr. 704.
880. Vat. Ott. 208.   *p.* **XV.** Scr. 705.
881. Vat. Ottob. 453, 454, 455.   *pap.*
   XV. Scr. 707–9.

882. Vat. Palat. 32.   **X.**   Scr. 713.
883. Vat. Pal. 208. *p.* **XV.** Scr. 714.
884. Vat. Reg. Gr. 3.   **XI.**   Scr. 696.
885. Vat. Reg. Gr. 5. *p.* **XV.** Scr. 697.
886. V. R. 6. *pap.* **1454.** Scr. 698.
    (A268P317R115.)
887. Vat. Reg. Gr. 9.   **XI.**   Scr. 699.
888. Ven. Mark. 26. *pap.* **XIV. XV.**
889. Ven. Mark. 30.   **XIV.**
890. Ven. Mark. 31. *paper.* **XIV.**
891. Ven. Mark. 32. *p.* **XIV.** (P318.)
892. B. M. Add. 33277.   **IX.** or **X.**
893. Ven. Mark. I. 61.   **XII.**
894. Ven. Mark. II. 144.   **XI.**
895. (?) [Once Lond. Quaritch.]   **XI.**
896. Edinburg, Makellar, 311.   **XII.**
897. Edinburg, David Laing, 6.   **XIII.**
898. Edinburg, Laing, 667.   **XIII.**
899. Upsal Univ. 4.   Sparvenfield 45.
    XI.   Scr. 613.
900. Up. Un. 9. Sturtzenbecker. **XIII.**
    Scr. 614.
901. Up. Un. 12. Bjornsthal 2.   **XI.**
    Scr. 615.   (A269P319.)
902. Up. Un. 13. Bjor. 3. **XII.** Scr. 616.
903. Cairo Patri. Alex. 421. **1382.**
904. Cairo Patri. Alex. 952. **1360.**
905. Athos St. Andrew *A'.*   **XII.**
906. Athos St. A. *E'.*   **XII.**
907. Athos St. A. *H'. paper.*   **XIV.**
908. Athos St. A. *Θ'.*   **XIII.**
909. Athos Batopedios 206.
910. Athos Bat. 207.
911. Athos Bat. 211.
912. Athos Bat. 212.
913. Athos Bat. 213.
914. Athos Bat. 214.
915. Athos Bat. 215.
916. Athos Bat. 216.
917. Athos Bat. 217.
918. Athos Bat. 218.
919. Athos Bat. 219.
920. Athos Bat. 220.
921. Athos Bat. 414.
922. Ath. Gregory 3. (A270P320R116.)
    1116.
923. Athos St. Greg. *τοῦ ἡγουμένου.*
    XII.
924. Athos St. Dionysius 4.   **XII.**
925. Athos St. Dion. 5.   **XIV.**

926. Athos St. Dion. 7.   **XIII.**
927. Athos St. Dion.   8.   **1133.**
    (A271P321.)
928. Athos St. Dion. 9.   **1305.**
929. Athos St. Dion. 12.   **XIII.**
930. Athos St. Dion. 22.   **XII.**
931. Ath. St. D. 23.   **XIII.** (Evl400.)
932. Athos St. Dion. 24.   **XIII.**
933. Athos St. Dion. 25.   **XII.**
934. Athos St. Dion. 26.   **XII.**
935. Ath. St. D. 27. **XIII.** (A272P322.)
936. Athos Dion. 28.   **XII.**
937. Athos Dion. 29.   **XI.**
938. Athos Dion. 30.   **1319.**
939. Athos Dion. 31.   **XIII.**
940. Athos Dion. 32.   **XIII.**
941. Ath. D. 33.   **XIII.** (A273P323.)
942. Athos Dion. 34.   **XIII.**
943. Athos Dion. 35.   **XIII.**
944. Athos Dion. 36.   **XIII.**
945. Ath. D. 37.   **XIII.** (A274P324.)
946. Athos Dion. 38.   **XIII.**
947. Athos Dion. 39.   **XIII.**
948. Athos Dion. 40.   **X.**
949. Athos Dion. 64.   **XIII.**
950. Athos Dion. 67.   **XII. ?**
951. Athos Dion. 80.   **XIV.**
952. Athos Dion. 310.   **XIV.**
953. Athos Dion. 311.   **XIV.**
954. Athos Dion. 312.   **XIV.**
955. Athos Dion. 313.   **XV.**
956. Athos Dion. 314. **XVII.** (A275.)
957. Athos Dion. 315.   **XVI.**
958. Athos Dion. 316.   **XV.**
959. Ath. D. 317. **1331.** (A276P325.)
960. Athos Dion. 318.   **XIV.**
961. Athos Dion. 319.   **XV.**
962. Athos Dion. 320.   **1498.**
963. Athos Dion. 321.   **1636.**
964. Athos Docheiar. 7.   **XIII.**
965. Athos Doch. 21.   **XII.**
966. Athos Doch. 22.   **XIV.**
967. Athos Doch. 30.   **XIII.**
968. Athos Doch. 35.   **XIII.**
969. Athos Doch. 39.   **XIV.**
970. Athos Doch. 42.   **XIII.**
971. Athos Doch. 46.   **XIII.**
972. Athos Doch. 49.   **XIII.**
973. Athos Doch. 51.   **XII.**
974. Athos Doch. 52.   **XII.**

975. Athos Doch. 55. **XIII.**
976. Athos Doch. 56. **XII.**
977. Athos Doch. 59. **XIV.**
978. Athos Doch. 76. *p.* **1361.**
979. Athos Doch. 142. *p.* **XVII.**
980. Athos Esphigmen. 25. **XII.**
981. Athos Esphig. 26. **XIV.**
982. Athos Esphig. 27. *Pal.* **1311.**
983. Athos Esphig. 29. **XIII.**
984. Athos Esphig. 30. **XIV.**
985. Athos Esphig. 31. **XII.**
986. Athos Esphig. 186. *p.* **XIV.**
   (A277P326R117.)
987. Athos Zograph. 4. **XII.**
988. Athos Zograph. 14. *p.* **1674.**
989. Athos Iberon. 2. **XII.**
990. Athos Iber. 5. **XIV.**
991. Athos Iber. 7. **XI.**
992. Athos Iber. 9. **XIII.**
993. Athos Iber. 18. **XII.**
994. Athos Iber. 19. **X.**
995. Athos Iber. 21. **XIV.**
996. Ath. Ib. 28. **XIV.** (A278P327.)
997. Ath. Ib. 29. **XIII.** (A279P328.)
998. Athos Iber. 30. **XII.**
999. Ath. Ib. 31. **XIV.** (A280P329.)
1000. Athos Iber. 32. **XIII.**
1001. Athos Iber. 33. **XIII.**
1002. Athos Iber. 51. **XIV.**
1003. Athos Iber. 52. **XII.**
1004. Athos Iber. 53. *Pal.* **1291.**
1005. Athos Iber. 55. **XIV·**
1006. Athos Iber. 56. **XI.**
1007. Athos Iber. 59. **XII.**
1008. Athos Iber. 61. **XIII.**
1009. Athos Iber. 63. **XIII.**
1010. Athos Iber. 66. **XII.**
1011. Athos Iber. 67. **1263.**
1012. Athos Iber. 68. **XI.**
1013. Athos Iber. 69. **XII.**
1014. Athos Iber. 72. **XI.**
1015. Athos Iber. 75. **XIII.**
1016. Athos Iber. 371. **XIII.**
1017. Athos Iber. 548. *pap.* **XV.**
1018. Athos Iber. 549. *pap.* **XV.**
1019. Athos Iber. 550. *pap.* **XIV.**
1020. Athos Iber. 562. *pap.* **XIV.**
1021. Athos Iber. 599. **XIII.**
1022. Athos Iber. 607. *pap.* **1263.**
1023. Athos Iber. 608. *pap.* **1336.**

1024. Athos Iber. 610. *pap.* **XVII.**
1025. Athos Iber. 636. **XIII.**
1026. Athos Iber. 641. **XIV.**
1027. Athos Iber. 647. *pap.* **1492.**
1028. Athos Iber. 665. **XI.**
1029. Athos Iber. 671. *pap.* **XIV.**
1030. Athos Iber. 809. *pap.* **1518.**
1031. Athos Iber. 871. **XIII.**
1032. Athos Caracalla, 19. **XIV.**
1033. Athos Carac. 20. **XIV.**
1034. Athos Carac. 31. **XIII.**
1035. Athos Carac. 34. **XIII.**
1036. Athos Carac. 35. **XIV.**
1037. Athos Carac. 36. **XIV.**
1038. Athos Carac. 37. **XIV.**
1039. Athos Carac. 111. *pap.* **XIV.**
1040. A. C. 121. *p.* **XIV.** (A282P331.)
1041. Athos Carac. 128. *pap.* **1293.**
1042. Athos Carac. 198. *pap.* **XIV.**
1043. Athos Constam. 1. *pap.* **XIV.**
1044. Athos Constam. 61. *pap.* **XVI.**
1045. Athos Constam. 106. **XIII.**
1046. Athos Cutlum. 67. **XII.**
1047. Athos Cutl. 68. **XIII.**
1048. Athos Cutl. 69. **XII.**
1049. Athos Cutl. 70. **XII.**
1050. Athos Cutl. 71. **1268.**
1051. Athos Cutl. 72. **XI.**
1052. Athos Cutl. 73. **XIII.**
1053. Athos Cutl. 74. **XIV.**
1054. Athos Cutl. 75. **XII.**
1055. Athos Cutl. 76. **XI.**
1056. Athos Cutl. 77. **XI.**
1057. Athos Cutl. 78. **XIII.**
1058. Ath. C. 90a. **XI.** (A283P332.)
1059. Athos Cutl. 278. *pap.* **XIV.**
1060. Athos Cutl. 281. *pap.* **XV.**
1061. Athos Cutl. 283. *pap.* **1362.**
1062. Athos Cutl. 284. *pap.* **XIV.**
1063. Athos Cutl. 285. *pap.* **1674.**
1064. Athos Cutl. 286. *pap.* **XVIII.**
1065. Athos Cutl. 287. *pap.* **XVI.**
1066. Athos Cutl. 288. *pap.* **1583.**
1067. Athos Cutl. 289. *pap.* **1562.**
1068. Athos Cutl. 290. *pap.* **1562.**
1069. Athos Cutl. 291. *pap.* **1576.**
1070. Athos Cutl. 293. *pap.* **1597.**
1071. Athos Laura. **XII.**
1072. Ath. Laura. (A284P333R118.)
   XIV.

1073. Athos Laura. **X.** (A285.)
1074. Athos Laura. **XI.**
1075. Ath. Lau. *p.* (A286P334R119.) **XIV.**
1076. Athos Laura. **X.**
1077. Athos Laura. **X.**
1078. Athos Laura. **X.**
1079. Athos Laura. **X.**
1080. Athos Laura. **IX.** or **X.**
1081. Athos Xerop. 103. **XII.**
1082. Athos Xerop. 105. **XIV.**
1083. Athos Xerop. 107. **XII.**
1084. Athos Xerop. 108. **XIV.**
1085. Athos Xerop. 115. **XII.**
1086. Athos Xerop. 123. *p.* **1648.**
1087. Athos Xerop. 200. **XIII.**
1088. Athos Xerop. 205. *p.* **XVI.**
1089. Athos Xerop. 221. *p.* **XIV.**
1090. Ath. Xer. in ecclesia. **XII.** (?)
1091. Athos Pantel. XXV. **XIII.**
1092. Athos Pantel. XXVI. **XIV.**
1093. Athos Pantel. XXVIII. **1302.**
1094. Athos Pantel. XXIX. **XIV.**
       (A287P335R120.)
1095. Athos Paul. 4. **XIV.**
1096. Athos Paul. 5. **XIII.**
1097. Athos Protat. 41. **X.**
1098. Athos Simop. 25. **XII.**
1099. Athos Simop. 26. **XII.**
1100. Athos Simop. 29. **X.**
1101. Athos Simop. 34. (?) **1276.**
1102. Athos Simop. 38. **XIII.**
1103. Athos Simop. 39. **XI.**
1104. Athos Simop. 40. **XIV.**
1105. Athos Simop. 41. **XIII.**
1106. Athos Simop. 63. *pap.* **1321.**
1107. Athos Simop. 145. *pap.* **1571.**
1108. Athos Simop. 146. *pap* **XIV.**
1109. Athos Simop. 147. *pap* **XIV.**
1110. Athos Stauron. 43. **XI.**
1111. Athos Staur. 53. **XIV.**
1112. Athos Staur. 54. **XIII.**
1113. Athos Staur. 56. **XIII.**
1114. Athos Staur. 70. *paper* **XIV.**
1115. Athos Staur. 97. *paper.* **1596.**
1116. Athos Staur. 127. *pap.* **XV**
1117. Athos Philotheus, 5. **XIV.**
1118. Athos Philo. 21. **XII.**
1119. Athos Philo. 22. **XIV.**
1120. Athos Philo. 33. **X.**

1121. Athos Philo. 39. **1304.**
1122. Athos Philo. 41. **XIII.**
1123. Athos Philo. 44. **XI.**
1124. Athos Philo. 45. **XII.**
1125. Athos Philo. 46. **XII.**
1126. Athos Philo. 47. **XIII.**
1127. Athos Philo. 48. **XII.**
1128. Athos Philo. 51. **XII.**
1129. Athos Philo. 53. **XIII.**
1130. Athos Philo. 68. *paper.* **XV.**
1131. Athos Philo. 71. *paper.* **XV.**
1132. Athos Philo. 72. *paper.* **XV.**
1133. Athos Philo. 74. *paper.* **XIV.**
1134. Athos Philo. 77. *paper.* **1671.**
1135. Athos Philo. 78. *paper.* **XV.**
1136. Athos Philo. 80. *paper.* **1337.**
1137. Athos Philo. 86. *paper.* **XIII.**
1138. Athos Chilian. 5. **XII.**
1139. Athos Chilian. 19. *p.* **XVIII.**
1140. is Evl. No. 938, q. v.
1141. Berat, Abp. Pal. **XI.**
1142. Berat, Mangal. Ch. **XII.**
1143. Berat, ch. τοῦ εὐαγγελισμοῦ. **X.**
1144. Chalcis Mon. Trin. 11. Scr. 727.
1145. Chalcis Mon. Trin. 12. Scr. 728.
1146. Chalcis Sch. 8. Scr. 731.
1147. Chalcis Sch. 27. **1370.** Scr. 733.
1148. Chalcis Sch. 95. **XIII.** Scr. 734.
1149. Chalcis Sch. 133. **XIII.** Scr.
       735. (A288P336.)
1150. Const'le (Holy Sep.) 227.
1151. Const'le (Holy Sep.) 417. *pap.*
1152. Const'le(HolySep.)419. **1133.**
1153. Const'le (Holy Sep.) 435. **XIII.**
1154. Const'le (Holy Sep.) 439. **XII.**
1155. Const'le (Holy Sep.) 441. **XII.**
1156. Lesbos Mon. τοῦ λείμωνος, 35.
       1322.
1157. Lesbos Mon. 67. τοῦ λείμ. **XI.**
1158. Lesbos M. τ. λείμ. 97. *pap.* **XV.**
1159. Lesbos M. τ. λείμ. 99. *pap.* **XIV.**
1160. Patmos, 58. **XII.**
1161. Patmos, 59. **IX.** or **X.**
1162. Patmos, 60. **XI.**
1163. Patmos, 76. **1038.**
1164. Patmos, 80. **XI.** or **XII.**
1165. Patmos, 81. **1335.**
1166. Patmos, 82. **X.**
1167. Patmos, 83. **XI.**
1168. Patmos, 84. **XI.**

1169.	Patmos, 90.	XII.
1170.	Patmos, 92.	XII.
1171.	Patmos, 94.	XIII.
1172.	Patmos, 95.	X.
1173.	Patmos, 96.	XIII.
1174.	Patmos, 97.	XIII.
1175.	Patmos, 98.	XIV.
1176.	Patmos, 100.	XII.
1177.	Patmos, 117.	XIII.
1178.	Patmos, 203.	XIII.
1179.	Patmos, 275.	1082.
1180.	Patmos, 333.	*p.* XV.
1181.	Patmos, 334.	*p.* 1368.
1182.	Saloniki Gr. Gym. 6.	*p.* XIV.
1183.	Salon. Gr. Gymn. 11.	*p.* XIV.
1184.	Salon. Σπυρίου.	XIII.
1185.	Sinai, 148.	
1186.	Sinai, 149.	XII.
1187.	Sinai, 150.	X. or XI.
1188.	Sinai, 151.	XI.
1189.	Sinai, 152.	1346.
1190.	Sinai, 153.	XI. or XII.
1191.	Sinai, 154.	X. or XI.
1192.	Sinai, 155.	XI.
1193.	Sinai, 156.	XIV (?)
1194.	Sinai, 157.	X. or XI.
1195.	Sinai, 158.	
1196.	Sinai, 159.	Partly *paper*. XIV.
1197.	Sinai, 160.	(?)
1198.	Sinai, 161.	XII. or XIII.
1199.	Sinai, 162.	XI. or XII.
1200.	Sinai, 163.	XII.
1201.	Sinai, 164.	
1202.	Sinai, 165.	XV.
1203.	Sinai, 166.	X.
1204.	Sinai, 167.	XII.
1205.	Sinai, 168.	XIII.
1206.	Sinai, 169.	XIV.
1207.	Sinai, 170.	X. or XI.
1208.	Sinai, 171.	XIII. or XIV.
1209.	Sinai, 172.	
1210.	Sinai, 173.	XI. or XII.
1211.	Sinai, 174.	X. or XI.
1112.	Sinai, 175.	XI.
1213.	Sinai, 176.	1286.
1214.	Sinai, 177.	XI.
1215.	Sinai, 178.	XIII.
1216.	Sinai, 179.	X.
1217.	Sinai, 180.	1186.
1218.	Sinai, 181.	XII. or XIII.

1219.	Sinai, 182.	XI.
1220.	Sinai, 183.	X.
1221.	Sinai, 184.	XI.
1222.	Sinai, 185.	X. or XI.
1223.	Sinai, 186.	X. or XI.
1224.	Sinai, 187.	XI.
1225.	Sinai, 188.	X.
1226.	Sinai, 189.	XIII.
1227.	Sinai, 190.	XIV.
1228.	Sinai, 191.	XII.
1229.	Sinai, 192.	XIII.
1230.	Sinai, 193.	1124.
1231.	Sinai, 194.	
1232.	Sinai, 195.	*paper.* XV. (?)
1233.	Sinai, 196.	*paper.* XV.
1234.	Sinai, 197.	*paper.* XIV.
1235.	Sinai, 198.	*paper.* XIV.
1236.	Sinai, 199.	*paper.* XIV.
1237.	Sinai, 200.	*pap.* XV. or XVI.
1238.	Sinai, 201.	*paper.* 1244.
1239.	Sinai, 203.	XVI.
1240.	Sinai, 259.	(A289P337.)
1241.	Sinai, 260.	(A290P338.)
1242.	Sinai, 261.	XIV. (A291P339.)
1243.	Sinai, 262.	(A292P340.)
1244.	Sinai, 263.	(A293P341.)
1245.	Sinai, 264.	(A294P342.)
1246.	Sinai, 265.	(A295P343.)
1247.	Sinai, 266.	XV. (A296P344.)
1248.	Sinai, 267.	(A297P345.)
1249.	Sinai, 268.	*p.* XV. (A298P346.)
1250.	Sinai, 269.	*p.* XV. (A299P347.)
1251.	Sinai, 270.	*p.* (?). (A300P348.)
1252.	Sinai, 302.	1306.
1253.	Sinai, 303.	*paper.* XVI. (?)
1254.	Sinai, 304.	
1255.	Sinai, 305.	
1256.	Sinai, 306.	
1257.	Smyrna Evang. sch. Γ´ 1.	XI.
1258.	Smyrna Evang. sch. Γ´ 2.	XIII.
1259.	Smyrna Evang. sch. Γ´ 5.	XV.
1260.	Cortona (communal library), 201. *paper.*	1460.
1261.	Paris Cois. 128.	XIII. Scr. 765.
1262.	Paris Cois. 129.	XIV. Scr. 766.
1263.	Paris Cois. 198.	*paper.* XIV. Scr. 767.
1264.	P. N. Coislin. 201.	*paper.* XV.
1265.	P. N. Cois. 203.	XIII. Scr. 768.
1266.	P.N.Cois.206.	X.or XI. Scr.769.

1267. P. N. Cois. 207. *paper*. **XIV.**
    Scr. 770. (P428.)
1268. B. M. Add. 19386. **XIII.** or
    XIV. Scr. 110.
1269. R. Vat. Urb. 4. *paper*. **XIV.**
1270. Cairo. Patr. Alex. 82. *p.* **XIV.**
1271. Cairo. Pat. Alex. 87. **XI.**
1272. Athens. Nat. (111). **XV.**
1273. Aukland City(New Zealand).(?)
1274. B. M. Add. 11859,11860. *Palimp.*
    XI. Scr. 608. (A417.)
1275. Madison, N. J. Drew Sem. **XI.**
1276. Madison, N. J. Drew Sem. **XI.**
    v. Table XI. for both MSS.

1277. Camb. Univ. **XI.** or **XII.**
    (A418P484R185.)
1278. Hayes,Kent. H. C. Hoskier. **XII.**
1279. B. M. Add. 34107. (?)
1280. B. M. Add. 34108. (?)
1281. London, B. Quaritch. **X.**
1282. London, B. Quaritch. **XI.**
1283. Berne, Bongarsian Lib. *pap.*
    XIII. or **XIV.**
1284. Leipsic, Univ. Tisch. XII.ᶜ **XIV.**
1285. Gotting. Un. Theol. 534. **XIII.**
1286. Const'ple in " old Serai," 34. (?)
1287. "Adhuc sine loco" *Gregory.*
    XIII. or **XIV.** (A419P485.)

Scrivener (4th ed.) has the following additions to the list of MSS. of the Gospels. The numbers are Scrivener's. See Scr. vol. i. pp. 279–283.

[1145.] Athens, 13. ff. 299. [XV.]
[1146.] Ath. 139. ff. 444. (2 *Palimp.*
    leaves.) [XV.]
[1147.] Ath. 347. ff. 131. *Pal.* [IX.–X.]
[1148.] Jerus. Patr.[1] Lib. 25. ff. 273.
    mut. [XI.]
[1149.] Jer. Pat. Lib. 28. ff. 212. [XI.]
    (P53. Scr.)
[1261.] Jer. Pat. Lib. 31. ff. 295.[XI.]
[1262.] Jer. Pat. Lib. 37. ff. 355. [XI.]
    (A417P57Apoc153. Scr.)
[1263.] Jer. Pat. Lib. 41. ff. 298. [XI.]
[1265.] Jer. Pat. Lib. 42. ff. 248. [XI.]
[1266.] Jer. Pat. Lib. 46. ff. 278. [XII.]
[1267.] Jer. Pat. Lib. 47. ff. 216. [XI.
    and XIII.] (A329P38. Scr.)
[1268.] Jer. Pat. Lib. 48. ff. 258. [XI.]
[1274.] Jer. Pat. Lib. 49. ff. 306. [XI.]
[1275.] Jer. Pat. Lib. 56. ff. 218. [XI.]
[1276.] Jer. Pat. Lib. 59. ff. 299. [XI.]
[1277.] Jer. Pat. Lib. 60. ff. 299. [XI.]
[1278.] Jer. Pat. Lib. 62. ff. 385. *pap.*
    [1721.]
[1279.] Jer. Pat. Lib. 139. ff. 124. *pap.*
    [XIV.]
[1280.] Lesbos τ. Λείμωνος μονης, 141.
    pap. [XV.]
[1281.] Lesbos τ. Λ. μ. 145. *pap.* [XV.]
[1282.] Lesbos τ. Λ. μ. 227. ff. 136. *mut.*
    [XII.]

[1283.] Lesbos Μανταμάδου, Ταξίαρχοι
    ΚΑ. ff. 288. [XIII.]
[1284.] Mitylene, Gym. 9. ff. 292. [XII.,
    XIII.]
[1285.] Mit. Gym. 41. ff. 258. [X.]
[1286.] Andros Μονή ἀγία 1. ff. 342.
    [1156.]
[1287.] And. M. ἀγ. 33. [XII., XIII.]
[1288.] And. M. ἀγ. 34. [1523.]
[1289.] And. M. ἀγ. 35.
[1290.] And. M. ἀγ. 37. [XII.]
[1291.] And. M. ἀγ. 38. *paper.*
[1292.] And. M. ἀγ. 48. [1709.]
[1293.] And. M. ἀγ. 49. [1234.]
[1294.] And. M. ἀγ. 50. [XII.–XIII.]
[1295.] Cosinitsa Mon. Lib. 219. [1285.]
[1296.] Cosin. Mon. Lib. 58. ff. 288.
    [IX., X.]
[1297.] C.M.L.216[?] (A416P377. Scr.)
[1298.] Cosin. Mon. Lib. 217.
[1299.] Cosin. Mon. Lib. 218.
[1300.] Cosin. Mon. Lib. 219.
[1301.] Cosin. Mon. Lib. 220.
[1302.] Cosin. Mon. Lib. 222.
[1303.] C. M. L. 223. ff. 201. [1471.]
[1304.] Cosin. Mon. Lib. 198.
[1305.] Athos Protaton, 15. [XI.]
[1306.] Athos Protaton, 44. *p.* [XIV.]
[1307.] Athos Paul. 1.4ᵗᵒ ff. 50. [XIV.]
[1308.] Athos Chiliandari, 6. [XIII.]

---

[1] The MSS. of the Jerusalem Patriarchal library in this list are catalogued by Papadopulos Kerameos (St. Petersburg, 1891). See Tisch. Prolg. p. 637.

[1309.] Athos Constamon. 99. [XIV.]
    Palimp.
[1310.] Athos Xenophon, 1. 4to. [1181.]
[1311.] Athos Xenoph. 3. 8°. [XIII]
[1312.] Athos Xenoph. 58. 8vo. *p.* [XVI.]
[1313.] Athens Nat. Lib. 72. ff. 191.
    [1181.]
[1314.] Ath. Nat. Lib. 92. ff. 277. [XIV.]

[1315.] Ath. Nat. Lib. 113. ff. 232. [XI.]
[1316.] Ath. Nat. Lib. 123. ff. 189. [1145.]
[1317.] Ath. Nat. Lib. 128. ff. 181. [XII.]
[1318.] Ath. Nat. Lib. 132. ff. 210. [X.]
[1319.] Ath. Nat. Lib. 135. ff. 150. [XV.]
[1320.] Earl of Crawford, 1. ff. 239.
    [XI.]
[1321.] E. of Craw. 2. ff. 240. [XI., XII.]

B.—THE ACTS AND CATHOLIC EPISTLES

1. =Basileensis. (G1P1.) v. p. 108.
2. Basle. A. N. IV. 4. **XII.** (P2.)
3. Vienna, 52. **XII.** (G3P3.)
4. Basle. A. N. IV. 5. **XV., XVI.** (P4.)
5. Paris Nat. 106. **XIV.** (G5P5.)
6. Paris N. 112. **XIII.** (G6P6.)
7. Paris N. 102. **XI.** (P9.)
8. *Missing.*
9. Camb. Kk. 6. 4. **XI., XII.** (P11.)
10. Paris N. 237. **X.** (P12R12.)
11. Paris N. 103. **XI.** (P140.)
12. Paris N. 219. **XI.** (P16R4.)
13. Paris N. 14. **X.** or **XI.** (G33P17.)
14. P. N. 199. **XI., XII.** (G35P18R17.)
15. Paris N. Coislin. 25. **X.** or **XI.**
16. Paris N. C. 26. **X.** (P19.)
17. Paris N. C. 205. **X.** (P21R19.)
18. P. N. C. 202. (2.) *p.* **XIII.** (P22R18.)
19. Paris N. C. 200. **XIII.** (G38P377.)
20. B. M. Royal MS. I. B. I. *paper.* **XIV.** (P25.)
21. Camb. Univ. Dd. XI. 90. **XIII.** (P26.)
22. B. M. Add. 5115, 5116. **XI.** or **XII.** (P75.)
23. Ox. Bodl. Baroc. 3. **XI.** (P28R6.)
24. Camb. Chr. Coll. F. 1. 13. **XII.** (P29.)
25. B. M. Harl. 5537. **1087.** (P31R7.)
26. B. M. Harl. 5557. **XII.** (P32.)
27. B. M. Harl. 5620. *p.* **XV.** (P33.)
28. B. M. Harl. 5778. **XII.** (P34R8.)
29. Geneva City Lib. 20. **XI.** (P35.)
30. Ox. Bodl. Misc. 74. **XI.** (P36R9.)
31. Leicester City Lib. 20. **XV.** v. p. 112. (G69P37R14.)
32. Oxf. Bo. La. 31. **XIII.** (G51P38.)
33. Oxf. Lin. Coll. ω. 25. **XII.** (P39.)
34. Dubl. Trin. A. 4. 21. (G61P40R92.) **XVI.**
35. Oxf. Magd. 9. **XII.** (G57P41.)

36. Oxf. New Coll. 58. **XII.**
37. Oxf. New Coll. 59. **XIII.** (P43.)
38. Leyden Acad. Lib., Voss. Q. 77. **XIII.** (P44.)
39. *Missing.* *Paper.* (P45R11.)
40. Vat. Reg. 179. **XI.** (P46R12.)
41. Vat. 2080. **X., XI.** (G175P194R20.)
42. Frankfort - on - the - Oder. **XI.** (P48R13Evl923Apl56.)
43. Vienna, 300. **XII., XIII.** (G76P49.)
44. *Vacat.* W – H. = Acts 224. (G82P51R5.)
45. Hamburg City Lib. 1252. *paper.* **XV.** (P52R16.)
46. Munich, 375. **X.** (P55.)
47. Amsterdam, 186. **XVI.** (G90P14.)
48. Oxf. Bodl. Misc. 136. (G105P24.)
49. Basle, O. II. 27. *"Unworthy No."*
50. *Missing.* (P8.)
51. Par. Nat. 56. **XII.** (P133R52.)
52. Rhodiensis, *missing.* (P50.)
53. Camb. Em. Coll. *I.* 4. 35. **XII.** (P30.)
54. Paris Ars. 8410. **XII.** (G43P130.)
55. 2d Copy of Jude in Acts 47.
56. Oxf. Bodl. Clarke 4. **XII.** (P227.)
57. Copen. 1322. **1278.** (G234P72.)
58. Oxf. Bodl. Clarke 9. **XIII.** (P224Evl922.)
59. B. M. Harl. 5588. *p.* **XIII.** (P62.)
60. B. M. Harl. 5613. *paper.* **1407.** (P63R29.)
61. Br. Mu. Add. 20003 (1oti. see p. 111). **1044.**
62. Par. Nat. 60. *paper.* **XIV.** (P65.)
63. Vienna Imp. Lib. 313. **XIV.** (P68.)
64. Vienna Imp. Lib. 303. **XII.** (P69.)
65. Vienna, 23. **XIII.** (G218P57R33.)
66. Vienna, 302. **XI.** (P67R34.)
67. Vienna, 221. **1330.** (P70.)

68. Upsal, 2 MSS. **XII.** and **XI.** (P73.)
69. Wolfenbüttel, 16.7. *pap.* **XIII.,** **XIV.** (P74R30.)
70. Vat.360. **XIV.** or **XV.** (G131P77.)
71. Vat. 363. **XI.** (G133P78.)
72. Vat. 366. *pap.* **XV.** (P79R37.)
73. Vat. 367. **XI.** (P80.)
74. Vat. 760. **XI.**
75. Vat. 1160. **XIII.** (G141P86R40.)
76. Vat. 1210. **XI.** (G.142P87.)
77. Vat.Pal.171. **XV.** (G149P88R25.)
78. Vat. Reg. 29. **X.** (P89.)
79. Vat. Urbino, 3. **XI.** (P90.)
80. Vat. Pii. II. 50. **XII.** (P91R42.)
81. Rome, Barberini VI. 21. **XIV.**
82. Ro. Prop. L. 6.19. (G180P92R44.)
83. Naples, II. Aa. 7. **XII.** (P93R99.)
84. Florence Lau. IV. 1. **X.** (P94.)
85. Flor. Lau. IV. 5. *pap.* **XIII.** (P95.)
86. Flor. Lau. IV. 30. **X.** (P96R75.)
87. Flor. Lau. IV. 29. **X.** (P97.)
88. Flor. Lau. IV. 31. **XI.** (P98.)
89. Fl. Lau. IV. 32. **1092.** (P99R45.)
90. Flor. Lau. VIII. 14. **XI.** (G197.)
91. B. M. Add. 11837. (G201P104R94.)
92. Bologna.2775. **XIII.** (G204P105.)
93. Venice, Mar. 5. (G205P106R88.)
94. Venice, 6. **XV.** (G206P107R109.)
95. Ven. 10. **XIV.** (G209P108R46.)
96. Ven. 11. **XIII.** or **XIV.** (P109.)
97. Wolfenbüttel, 104. 2. **XII.** (P241.)
98. Dresden, A.104. **XI.** (P113Apl82.)
99. Moscow Synod, 5. *p.* **1345.** (P114.)
100. Mosc. S. 334. **XI.** (P115.)
101. Mosc. S. 333. *p.* **XIII.** (P116.)
102. Mosc. S. 98. (cf. Cod. K. Tab. VIII.) **IX.** [W-H.=G489.] (P117.)
103. Mosc. S. 193. **XII.** (P118.)
104. Dresden, A.172. (G241P120R47.)
105. Mosc. S. 380. (G242P121R48.)
106. Mosc. S. 328. **XI.** (P122.)
107. = Acts. 98 above.
108. Escur. χ. IV. 17. **XI.** (G226P228.)
109. Escur. χ. IV. 12. **XIV.** (G228P229.)
110. Wanting.
111. Camb. Mm. 6.9. **XII.** (G440P221.)
112[1]. Modena II. G. 3. **IX.** or **X.** (P179.)
113. Paris N. 47. (G18P132R51.)

114. Paris N. 57. **XI.** (P134.)
115. Paris N. 58. **XI.** (P135.)
116. Paris N. 59. *p.* **XV.** (P136R53.)
117. Paris N. 61. (G263P137.)
118. Paris N. 101. *p.* **XIII.** (P138R55)
119. Paris N. 102 A. **XIII.** (P139R56.)
120. Paris N. 103 A. **XIII.** (P141.)
121. Paris N. 104. *p.* **XIII.** (P142.)
122. Paris N. 105. **X.** (P143.)
123. Paris N. 106 A. *p.* **XIV.** (P144)
124. Paris N.123,124. (G296P149R57.)
125. Paris N. 125. **XIV.** (P150.)
126. Paris N. 216. **X.** (P153.)
127. Paris N. 217. **XI.** (P154)
128. Paris N. 218. **XI.** (P155)
129. Paris N. 220. **XIV.** (P156.)
130. Paris N. 221. **XII.**
131. Paris N. 223. **1045.** (P158.)
132. St. Petersburg Muralt, 101. **XII.** (G330P131.)
133. Turin C. VI. 19. **XII.** (P166.)
134. Turin B. V. 19. **XII.** (P167.)
135. Tur. B. V. 8 (302). (G339P170R83.)
136. Tur. C. V. 1. **XII., XIII.** (P169.)
137. Milan Ambr. E. 97 Sup. **XIII.** (P176.) cf. W-H. § 212.
138. Milan Ambr. E. 102 Sup. *paper.* **XV.** (P173.)
139. Milan Ambr. H. 104 Sup. *paper.* **1434.** (P174R156.)
140. Venice, Mark. 546. **XI.** (P215R74.)
141. Flor. Laur. VI. 27. (G189P239.)
142. Modena Est. III. B. 17. **XI.** (P178.)
143. Flor. Lau. VI. 5. **X.** (G832.)
144. Flor. Lau. VI. 13. (G363P180.)
145. Fl. L. VI. 36. **XIII.** (G365P181.)
146. Flor. Lau. Conv. Soppr. 53. **1331.** (G367P182R23.)
147. Wanting.
148. Flor. L. C. Sop. 191. **984.** (P184.)
149. Fl. L. C. S. 150. **XII.** (P349R180.)
150. Florence Ric. 84. (G368P230R84.)
151. Vatican Ott. 66. (G386P199R70.)
152. Printed Edition. (G442P223.)
153. B. M. Harl. 5796. (G444P240.)
154. Vatican, 1270. **XIV.** (P187.)
155. Vat. 1430. *Cath. epp.* **XII.** (P188.)
156. Vat. 1650. **1037.** (P190.)

---

¹ Cod. 112 is part of UNC. H. of the Acts, q. v.

157. Vat. 1714. **XI.** (P191.)
158. Vat. 1761. **XI.** (P192.)
159. Vat. 1968. **X.**
160. Vat. 2062. **X.** (P193R24.)
161. Vat.Ot.258. *p.* **XIV.** (P198R69.)
162. Vat. Ottob. 298. **XIV.** (P200.)
163. Vat. Ottob. 325. *p.* **XIV.** (P201.)
164. Vat. Ott. 381. (G390P203R71.)
165. Vat. Ottob. 417. **XVI.**
166. Rome Vall. B. 86. **XII.–XIV.**
(P204R22.)
167. Rome Vall. E. 22. (G293P185.)
168. Rome Vall.F.13. *p.* **XIV.** (P205.)
169. Ro. Chis. R.V 29. **1394.** (P206.)
170. Rome Vall. F. 17. (G394P186.)
171. ⎰ " Missing 1886 " Gr. ⎰ (P209.)
172. ⎱   ⎱ **XVI.**
⎱ (P210.)
173. Naples, II. Aa. 8. **XI.** (P211.)
174. Naples, II. Aa. 9. **XV.** (P212.)
175. Messina Univ. 104. **XII.** (P216.)
176. *Missing.* (G421P218.)
177. Leyden Pub. 74 A. (G122P219.)
178. Berlin, Phillips, 1461. **XIV.** or
XV. (P242R87.)
179. Munich, 211. **XI.** (P128R82.)
180. Strasburg. **XII.** (G431P238.)
181. Berlin, A. 10. (G400P220.)
182. Patmos, **XII.** (P243.)
183. Jerus. Ch. of H. S. 8. [Scr. 7.]
XIV. (P231.)
184. Jer. H. S. 9. [Scr. 15.] **XIII.**
(P232R85.)
185. St. Saba, 1. **XI.** (P233.)
186. St. Saba, 2. **XIII.** (G457P234.)
187. St. Saba, 10. (G462P235R86.)
188. St. Saba, 15. **XII.** (P236.)
189. St. Saba, 20. (G466P237R89.)
190. Oxf. Chr. Ch. Wake, 34. **XI.**
(G517P244R27.)
191. Oxf. C. C. Wake, 38. **XI.** (P245.)
192. Oxf. C. C. Wake, 37. **XI.** (P246.)
193ᵍ ˢᶜʳ· Wordsworth. (G479P249.)
194. "Pickering." Scr.187.(G483P251.)
195. Camb. Trin. B. 10. 16. Scr. 224.
(G489P252.)
196. B. M. Add. 11836. Scr. 226.
(G491P253.)
197. B. M. Add. 16184. Scr. 227.
(G496P254.)

198. B. M. A. 17469. Scr. 228.
(G498P255R97.)
199. Oxf. Chr. Coll. Wake, 12. Scr.
193. (G506P256R26.)
200. Oxf. Bodl. Canon Gr. 34. Scr.
211. (G522P257R98.)
201. Lond. H.B. Coutts. II. 7. Scr.
219. (G536.)
202. Parham (Curzon), 71, 6. Scr.
215. (G547P258.)
203. B. M. Add. 19392a. Scr. 230. **XI.**
204. B. M. Add. 22734. **XI.** Scr. 107.
205. B. M. Add. 28816. **1111.** Scr.
232. (P477R181.)
206. Ferrara Univ. 187, 188 NA. **7.**
Scr. 194. (G582P262R103.)
207. Milan Ambros. Z. 34. Sup. Scr.
197. (G592P263.)
208. Jer.II.S.40. Scr.259. (G615P264.)
209. Jer.H.S.45. Scr.260. (G619P265.)
210. S.Saba,52. Scr.328. (G623P266.)
211. S.Saba,53. Scr.317. (G624P267.)
212. S.Saba,54. Scr.318. (G625P268.)
213. Berlin Gr. 8vo. 9. Scr. 252.
(G656P269.)
214ᵃ ˢᶜʳ· Lond. Lambeth. 1182. *p.*
XIII. Scr. 182. (P270.)
215ᵇ ˢᶜʳ· Lond. Lambeth. 1183. *p.*
1358. Scr. 183. (P271.)
216ᶜ ˢᶜʳ· Const'ple Patr. Jeru. *p.* **XV.**
Scr. 184. (P272.)
217ᵈ ˢᶜʳ· Lond. Lambeth. 1185. *paper.*
XV. Scr. 185. (P273.)
218ᵉ ˢᶜʳ· Const'ple Patr. Jeru. *paper.*
XIV. Scr. 186. (P274.)
f Scr. ɪѕ G483A194P251.
g Scr. ɪѕ G479A193P249.
h Scr. ɪѕ G201A91R94.
219ʲ ˢᶜʳ· B. M. Burney, 48. *pap.* **XIV.**
Scr. 225.
k Scr. ɪѕ G489A195P252.
l Scr. ɪѕ A24P29.
m Scr. ɪѕ A178P242R87.
n Scr. ɪѕ A53P30.
o Scr. ɪѕ G440A211P221.
p Scr. ɪѕ A61.
220. B. M. Add. 19388. **XIV.** Scr.
229. (P275.)
221. Oxf. Bodl. Canon Gr. 110. **X.**
Scr. 212. (P276.)

222. Ox. Bodl. Misc. 118. **XIII.** Scr. 213. (P277.)
223. Lond. H-B-C. III. 1. **XI.** Scr. 220. (P278.)
224. Lond. B-C. III. 37. **XIII.** Scr. 221. (P279.)
225. Cheltenham, 7681. **1108.** Scr. 198. (P280.)
226. Curzon, 79. 14. **1009.** Scr. 216. (P281.)
227. Curzon, 80. 15. **XII.** Scr. 217. (P282.)
228. Curzon, 81, 16. **XIII.** Scr. 218. (P283.)
229. B. M. Egerton, 2787. [Formerly Worle.] **XIV.** Scr. 223. (P248.)
230. Escurial *P.* III. 4. **XIII.** Scr. 202.
231. Esc. τ. III. 12. **XIII.** Scr. 203.
232. Esc. χ. III. 3 **XII.** Scr. 204.
233. Esc. χ. III. 10. **XII.** Scr. 205. (P473.)
234. Esc. σ. I. 5. *pap.* **XVI.** Scr. 206.
235. Esc.ψ.III.6. **XI.** Scr.207. (R125.)
236. Esc.ψ.III.18. **X.** Scr.208. (R126.)
237. Esc. ω. IV. 22. *p.* **XV.** Scr. 209. (P475.)
238. Modena Bibl. Este. II.A.13. **XV.** Scr. 195. (P479.)
239. Modena Bibl. Este. II.C.4 **XI.** Scr. 196. (P476.)
240. Cairo Patr. Alex. 8. *paper.* **XIV.** Scr. 253. (P284.)
241. Cairo Patr. Alexand. 59. **XI.** Scr. 254. (P285.)
242. Cairo Patr. Alexand. 88. **XI.** Scr. 255. (P286.)
243. S. Saba, 20. **XI.** Scr. 301. (P287R102.)
244. S.Saba,35. **XI.** Scr.302. (P288.)
245. Vienna Gr. Theol. 141. *p.* **XII.** Scr. 335. (P289.)
246. Vienna Gr. Theol. 150. *p.* **XIV.** Scr. 415. (P297.)
247. Metz, 4. Scr. 110. (G480P250.)
248. Berlin Gr. 4° 57. *p.* **XIII.** Scr. 251. (P298.)
249. Paris Sup. 906. **XII.** Scr. 263.
250. P. N. Coislin, 224. **XI.** Scr. 264. (P299R121.)

251. Athens Th. 217. *paper.* **XIV.** (P301R122.)
252. Berlin Gr. 4° 40. **XI.** Scr. 249. (P302.)
253. Zittau City Lib. A. 1. **XV.** Scr. 233. (G664P303R106.)
254. Cheltenham, 1284. **XII.** Scr. 200. (G676P304.)
255. Cheltenham, 7682. **XI.** Scr. 199. (G680P305R107.)
256. B. M. Add. 28815. **XI.** Scr. 251. (G699P306R108.)
257. Wisbech, Camb'shire, Peck. 20. **XI.** Scr. 222. (G712P307.)
258. Vienna Gr. Theol. 79, 80. **1138.** Scr. 289. (G720P308.)
259. Paris Sup. Gr. 159. (1, 2. 3, Joh.) **XIV.** Scr. 260. (G743R109.)
260. Athens Theol. 12. **XIII.** Scr. 209. (G757P309R110.)
261. Athens Theol. 22 (?) Scr. 267. (G767P310.)
262. Athens, 118. **XIV.** Scr. 269. (G794P311.)
263. Athens, 767 **XI.** Scr. 321. (G796P312.)
264. Athens. Scr. 326. (G801P313.)
265. Ath. Mamouk. (G808P314R112.)
266. Berlin Gr. 8° 13. (G823P315.)
267. Grotta Ferrata A'. a'. 1. **XIV.** Scr. 242. (G824P316R113.)
268. Vat. Reg. Gr. 6. **1454.** Scr. 334. (G886P317R115.)
269. Upsal,12. Scr. 337. (G901P319.)
270. Athos St. Gregory. 3. **1116.** (G922P320R116.)
271. Athos Dion. 8. (G927P321.)
272. Athos D. 27. **XIII.** (G935P322.)
273. Athos D. 33. **XIII.** (G941P323.)
274. Athos D. 37. **XIII.** (G945P324.)
275. Athos D. 314. **XVII.** (G956.)
276. AthosD.317. **1331.**(G959P325.)
277. Athos Esphigmen. 186. **XII.** (G986P326R117.)
278. Athos Iber. 28. (G996P327.)
279. Athos Iber. 29. (G997P328.)
280. Athos Iber. 31. (G999P329.)
281. Athos Iber. 52. (G1003P330.)
282. Athos Carac. 121. (G1040P331.)
283. Athos Cutl. 90a. (G1058P332.)

284. Athos Laura. (G1072P333R118.)
285. Athos Laura. **X.** (G1073.)
286. Athos Laura. (G1075P334R119.)
287. Athos Pantel. XXIX. **XIV.**
    (G1094P335R120.)
288. Chalcis sch. 133. (G1149P336.)
289. Sinai, 259. **XV.** (G1240P337.)
290. Sinai, 260. (G1241P338.)
291. Sinai, 261. **XIV.** (G1242P339.)
292. Sinai, 262. (G1243P340.)
293. Sinai, 263. (G1244P341.)
294. Sinai, 264. (G1245P342.)
295. Sinai, 265. (G1246P343.)
296. Sinai, 266. (G1247P344)
297. Sinai, 267. (G1248P345.)
298. Sinai, 268. (G1249P346.)
299. Sinai, 269. (G1250P347.)
300. Sinai, 270. (G1251P348.)
301. Paris Arsenal 9. **XI.** Scr. 240.
    (P259R102.)
302. Berlin. Gr. 4to 43. **XIV.** Scr.
    250. (P260.)
303. Berlin. Hamilton. 244. (625.)
    1090.(?) Scr. 248. (P261.)
304. Athens Nat. Th. 70. **XI.** (P292.)
305. Ath. Nat. Th. 71. **XV.** (P295.)
306. Ath.Nat.Th.72. *p.* **1364.** (P296.)
307. Ath. (43.) **XII.** (P469R105.)
308. Ath. Nat. (45.) *p.* **1295.** (P420.)
309. Ath. N. (64.) **XII.** (P300R124.)
310. Ath. Nat. (66.) **XI.**
311. Ath. Nat. (221.) **XV.** (P419.)
312. Ath. Nat. *pap.* **XIV.** (P421.)
313. Ath. Nat. **XIV.** (P422.)
314. Zante (island of). **1580.**
315. St. Pet. Porfiri. **1301.** (P474.)
316. Madrid. Reg. O. 78. **XI.**
317. Grotta Ferrata. *A'. B'.* 1. **X.**
    Scr. 243. (P423.)
318. Grotta Ferrata. *A'. B'.* 3. **XI.**
    Scr. 244. (P424.)
319. Grotta Ferrata. *A'. B'.* 6. **XI.**
    Scr. 245. (P425.)
320. Messina Univ. 40. *paper.* **XIII.**
    Scr. 241. (P426.)
321. Rome Casanatensis. G. II. 6.
    pap. **XV.** Scr. 261. (P427.)
322. Athos Iberon. 639. *p.* **XV.**
323. Lesbos mon. τοῦ Λείμωνος 55.
    IX. (P429R127.)

324. Jerusalem Holy Cross 1. **X.**
325. Vat. 652. *p.* **XIV.** Scr. 239.
326. Vat.1208. **XII.** Scr.246. (P430.)
327. Vat. 1227. *paper.* **XV.**
328. Vat. 1971. **X.** Scr. 334. (P431.)
329. Vat. 2099. **XI.** Scr. 256. (P432.)
330. Vat. Palat. 38. **XI.** or **XII.** Scr.
    247. (P433.)
331. { Vat. Reg. Gr. 76. Jas. 1. 2 Pet.
    XV. (P145.)
    Par. Nat. 109–111, *Paul.* **XV.**
332. Venice, St. Mark. II. 114. **1069.**
    (P434R128.)
333. Edinburg, Makel. **XIII.** (P435.)
334. Linköping, Benzel. 35. **X.** Scr.
    238. (P436.)
335. Upsal Un. Gr. 11. **XI.** Scr. 236.
    (P437R129.)
336. Athos Batoped. 41.
337. Athos Bat. 201.
338. Athos Bat. 203.
339. Athos Bat. 210.
340. Athos Bat. 259.
341. Athos Bat. 328.
342. Athos Bat. 380.
343. Athos Bat. 419.
344. Athos Dion. 68. **XIII.** (P438.)
345. Athos Dion. 75 **1376.**
346. Ath. Dion.382. *p.* **1660.** (P439.)
347. Ath. Docheiar,38. **XIV.** (P440.)
348. Athos Doch. 48. **XIV.** (P441.)
849. Ath.Doch.136. *p.* **1702.** (P442.)
350. Athos Doch. 139. *p.* **XV.** (P443.)
351. Ath.Doch.147. *p.* **XIV.** (P444.)
352. Athos Esph. 63. **XIII.** (P445.)
353. Athos Esph. 64. **XIII.** (P446.)
354. Athos Esph. 65. **XIV.** (P447.)
355. Athos Esph. 66. **XII.** (P448.)
356. Athos Esph. 67. **XIII.** (P449.)
357. Athos Esph. 68. **XII.** (P450.)
358. Athos Iber. 24. **XIV.** (P451.)
359. Athos Iber. 25. **XI.** (P452R130.)
360. Athos Ib. 37. **XIII.** (P453.)
361. Athos Ib. 57. **XIII.** (P454.)
362. Athos Ib. 60. **XIII.** (P455R131.)
363. Athos Ib. 642. *paper.* **XV.**
364. Athos Ib. 643. *paper.* **1520.**
365. Athos Ib. 648. *paper.* **XIV.**
366. Athos Const. 108. **XIII.** (P456.)
367. Athos Cutlumus, 16. **XII.**

368. Athos Cutl. 57. **XIV.** (P457.)
369. Athos Cutl. 80. **1262.** (P458.)
370. Athos Cutl. 81. **XIII.** (P459.)
371. Athos Cutl. 82. **XIV.** (P460.)
372. Athos Cutl. 83. **XIII.** (P461.)
373. Athos Cutl. 275. **XVI.** (P462.)
374. Athos Paul. 2. **IX.** (P463R132.)
375. Athos Protat. 32. **XIV.** (P464.)
376. Athos Simop. 42. **XIII.** (P465.)
377. Athos Stauron. 52. **XIII.** (P466.)
378. Athos Philoth. 38. **XIII.** (P467.)
379. Ath. Phil. 76. *p.* **1577.** (P468.)
380. Berat. Abp. **1158.**
381. Cairo Pat. Alex. 942. **XI.** (P352.)
382. Chalcis Mon. Trin. 16 (?) (P353.)
383. Chalcis School 9 (?) (P354.)
384. Chalcis Sch. 26. **X.** (P355R133.)
385. Chalcis Sch. 33. **XI.** (P356.)
386. Chalcis Sch. 96. **XII.** (P357R134.)
387. Patmos, St. John, 14. **1215.** (P358.)
388. Pat. St. John, 15. **XI.** (P359.)
389. Patmos, St. John, 16. **X.** (P360.)
390. Patmos, St. John, 263. **X.** (P361.)
391. Saloniki Gymn. 12. **XII.** (P362.)
392. Saloniki Gymn. 15. **XIV.** (P363.)
393. Saloniki Gymn. 16. **XI.** (P364.)
394. Sinai, 274. **X.** (P365.)
395. Sinai, 275. **XI.** (P366.)
396. Sinai, 276.
397. Sinai, 277.
398. Sinai, 278.
399. Sinai, 279. *p.* **XV.** (P367R135.)
400. Sinai, 280. *p.* **XIV.** (?) (P368.)
401. Sinai, 281.
402. Sinai, 282.
403. Sinai, 283. **X.** (P369.)

404. Sinai, 284. *Acts.*
405. Sinai, 285. *Acts.*
406. Sinai, 287. ⎫
407. Sinai, 288. ⎪
408. Sinai, 289. ⎪
409. Sinai, 290. ⎬ Acts (?)
410. Sinai, 291. ⎪
411. Sinai, 292. ⎪
412. Sinai, 293. ⎭
413. Sinai, 300. *p.* **XVI.** (P370.)
414. Sinai, 301. *Acts* (?)
415. Paris, St. Genevieve, A.o.35. **XV.** Scr. 210. (P247.)
416. Venice, St. Mark, II.61. *paper.* **XVI.** Scr. 147.
417. B. M. add. 11860. *Palimp.* **XIII.** [James, iv. 1–16; Jude, 4–15.] (G1274.)
418. Camb. Un. (G1277.)
419. "*Sine loco*" Greg. (G1287P485.)
420. Gotha Ducal Lib. Ch. B. 1767. *p.* **XVI.** [*Acts:* wanting, xxvi. 29–xxviii. 27.]
Scrivener [4th ed.] *adds the following, pp.* 305–6 :
[416.] Jerus. Patr. lib. 38, 280 leaves. [Acts, i. 1–11.] *cent.* **XI.** and **XIII.** (P58R181. Scr.)
[417.] J. P. lib. 43, 138 leaves. [Acts, i. 1–xii. 9.] **XII.** (P64 [?].)
[418.] Cosinitsa, 54. **1344.** [Acts, Cath. Epp.] (P492[?].)
[419.] Athos, St. Paul 2 = Gregory **374.**
[420.] Athens, Nat. Lib. 222, 246 leaves. [Acts, Cath. Paul.] **XVII.** (P494. [?])

C.—THE PAULINE EPISTLES

1. Basle Un. A. N. IV. 2. [Philemon. Hebrews.] (G1A1.)
2. Basle U. A. N. IV. 4. [Phm. Heb.] (A2.)
3. Vien. Sup. Gr. 52. [P.H.] (G3A3.)
4. Basle U. A. N. IV. 5. [P. H.] (A4.)
5. Paris, 106. (G5A5.)
6. Paris, 112. [P. H.] (G6A6.)
7. Basle A. N. III. 11. **XI.**
8. *Missing.* (A50.)
9. Paris Gr. 102. [Heb. Tim.] (A7.)

10. *Missing.* (A8.)
11. Camb. Univ. Kk. 6. 4. [P.H.] (A9.)
12. Paris, 237. [P. H.] (A10R2.)
13. Readings quot. by d'Étaples. **1512.**
14. Amst'dam Ref. ch. 186. (G90A47.)
15. MS. cited by Erasmus.
16. Paris, 219. [Heb. Tim.] (A12R4.)
17. Paris, 14. [H. T.] (G33A13.)
18. Par. Cois. 199. [P.H.] (G35A14R17.)
19. Paris, Cois. 26. [P. H.] (A16.)
20. Paris, Cois. 27. (Athos.) **X.** [P.H.]

21. Paris Cois. 205. [P.H.] (A17R19.)
22. Par.Cois.202.(2.) [H.T.] (A18R18.)
23. Paris Cois. 28. [P.H.] **1056.**
24. Ox. Bo. M.136. [P.H.] (G105A48.)
25. B.M.Royal MS. I.B.I. [P.H.] (A20.)
26. Camb. Univ. Dd. 11. 90. (A21.)
27. { Oxf. Magd. Coll. Gr. 7 and
     { Camb. Un. Ff. I. 30. **XI.**
28. Oxf.Bodl.Bar.3. [P.H.] (A23R6.)
29. Camb. Ch. Coll. [P. H.] (A24.)
30. Camb. Em. Coll. [P. H.] (A53.)
31. B. M. Harl. 5537. [P.H.] (A25R7.)
32. B. M. Harl. 5557. [P. H.] (A26.)
33. B. M. Harl. 5620. [P. H.] (A27.)
34. B. M. Harl. 5778. [P.H.] (A28R8.)
35. Geneva City Lib. 20. [P.H.] (A29.)
36. Ox.Bodl.Misc.74. [P.H.] (A30R9.)
37. Leicester, 20. [P.H] (G69A31R14.)
38. Oxf.Bodl.Laud.31.[P.H.](G51A32.)
39. Oxf. Lincoln ω. 25. [P.H.] (A33.)
40. Dublin, Trin. Coll. A. 4. 21. [P.H.]
    (G61A34R92.)
41. Oxf.Mag.Coll.9. [P.H.] (G57A35.)
42. *Vacat.*
43. Oxf. New Coll. 59. [P. H.] (A37.)
44. Leyden Voss. Q. 77. [P. H.] (A38.)
45. *Missing.* (A39R11.)
46. Vat. Reg. 179. [H.T.] (A40R12.)
47. Oxf. Bodl. Roe 16. **XI.** [H. T.]
    "*Bonæ notæ*," *Tisch.* v. p. 110.
48. Fr'ft-on-O. (A42R13Evl923Apl56.)
49. Vienna, 300. [P. H.] (G76A43.)
50. *Missing.* (A52.)
51. *Vacat.*
52. Hamburg, 1252. [P.H.] (A45R16.)
53. *Vacat.*
54. Munich Gr. 412. **XII.** or **XIII.**
54ª. Munich Gr. 110. *p.* **XVI., XVII.**
55. Munich, 375. [P.H.] (A46.)
56. *Vacat.*
57. Vienna, 23. [H.T.] (G218A66R33.)
58. *Vacat.*
59. Paris Cois. 204. **X.** or **XI.**
60. *Vacat.*
61. *Vacat.*
62. B. M. Harl. 5588. [P.H.] (A59.)
63. B. M. Harl. 5613. [P.H.] (A60.)
64. *Vacat.*
65. Paris, 60. [H.T.] (A62.)
66. B. M. Harl. 5552. **XVI.** "*un No.*"

67. Vienna, 302. [P.H.] (A66R34.)
68. Vienna, 313. [P.H.] (A63.)
69. Vienna, 303. [P.H.] (A64.)
70. Vienna, 221. [P.H.] (A67.)
71. Vien.Sup.G.61. **X.** or **XI.** [H.T.]
72. Copen. 1322. [P.H.] (G234A67.)
73. Upsal.Univ.Gr.1. [H.T.] (A68.)
74. Wolfenb. 16.7. [P.H.] (A69R30.)
75. B. M. Add. 5116. [P.H.] (A22.)
76. Leipsic Univ.361. *Palimp.* **XIII.**
77. Vat.Gr.360. [H.T.] (G131A70.)
78. Vat.Gr.363. [P.H.] (G133A71.)
79. Vat. Gr. 366. [P.H.] (A72R37.)
80. Vat. Gr. 367. [H.T.] (A73.)
81. Vat. Gr. 761. **XII.** [P.H.]
82. Vat. Gr. 762. **XII.**
83. Vat. Gr. 765. **XI.** [P.H.]
84. Vat. Gr. 766. **XII.** [P.H.]
85. Vat. Gr. 1136. **XIV.** (A39.)
86. V.G.1160.[P.H.](G141A75R40.)
87. Vat.Gr.1210. [P.H.] (G142A76.)
88. V.P.171. [P.H.] (G149A77R25.)
89. Vat. Reg. Gr. 29. (A78.)
90. Vat. Urbino, 3. [P. H.] (A79.)
91. V. Pius II. 50. [P.H.] (A80R42.)
92. Rome Propag. L. VI. 19. [P.H.]
    (G180A82R44.)
93. Naples II. Aa. 7. [H.T.] (A83.)
94. Flor. Lau. IV. I. [P.H.] (A84.)
95. Flor. Lau. IV. 5. (A85.)
96. Fl.Lau.IV.30. [P.H.] (A86R75.)
97. Flor. Lau. IV. 29. [P.H.] (A87.)
98. Flor. Lau. IV. 31. [P. H.] (A88.)
99. Flor. Lau. IV. 32. [P.H.] (A89.)
100. Fl. Lau. X. 4. **XI.** or **XII.** [P.H.]
101. Flor. Lau. X. 6. **X.** [P.H.]
102. Flor. Lau. X. 7. **XI.** [P. H.]
103. Flor. Lau. X. 19. **XIII.** [P. H.]
104. B.M.Add.11837. (G201A91R94.)
105. Bolog. 2775. [P.H.] (G204A92.)
106. Venice, 5. [P.H.] (G205A93R88.)
107. Ven. 6. [P.H.] (G206A94R109.)
108. Ven. 10. [P. H.] (G209A95R46.)
109. Venice, Mark. 11. [H.T.] (A96.)
110. Venice, Mark. 33. **XI.** [P. H.]
111. Ven. M. 34. **XI.** or **XII.** [P. H.]
112. Ven. M. 35. **XI.** [P.H.]
113. Dresd. A. 104. [P.H.] (A98R77.)
114. Moscow Synod, 5. [P. H.] (A99.)
115. Moscow Synod, 334. (A100.)

116. Mos. Synod, 333. [P. H.] (A101.)
117. UNC. cod. K. q. v. (A102.)
118. Mos. Synod, 193. [P. H.] (A103.)
119. Moscow Synod, 292. **XI.** or **XII.**
120. Dresden. [P.H.] (G241A104R47.)
121. M.S.380. [P.H.] (G242A105R48.)
122. Moscow Syn. 328. [P.H.] (A106.)
123. Mos. Syn. 99. **X.** or **XI.** [P. H.]
124. Mos. S. 350. [? 250. Scr.] *p.* **XIV.**
125. Munich, 504. *paper.* **1387.**
125ᵃ Munich, 455.
126. =125.*p.* **1389.** (?) "*un* new *No.*"
127. *Vacat.*
128. Munich, 211. [P.H] (A179R82.)
129. Munich Roy. Gr. 35. *pap.* **XVI.**
130. Paris Ar. 8410. [P.H.] (G43A54.)
131. St. Pet.Muralt. 101. (G330A132.)
132. P. N. 47. [P.H.] (G18A113R51.)
133. Paris, 56. [P. H.] (A51R52.)
134. Paris, 57. [P. H.] (A114.)
135. Paris, 58. [P. H.] (A115.)
136. Paris, 59. [P. H.] (A116R53.)
137. Paris, 61. [H.T.] (G263A117.)
138. Paris, 101. [P.H.] (A118R55.)
139. Paris, 102 A. [P.H.] (A119R56.)
140. Paris, 103. [H.T.] (A11.)
141. Paris, 103 A. [P.H.] (A120.)
142. Paris, 104. [P. H.] (A121.)
143. Paris, 105. (A122.)
144. Paris, 106 A. [P. H.] (A123.)
145. Paris, 108–111. [P. H.] (A331.)
146.)
147. } All included in 145 above.
148.)
149. Paris, 123, 124. (G296A124R57.) [P. H.]
150. Paris, 125. [P.H.] (A125.)
151. Paris, 126. **XVI.** [P. H.]
152. "*Delendus.*"
153. Paris, 216. [P. H.] (A126.)
154. Paris, 217. [Eph.H.Ph.] (A127.)
155. Paris, 218. [P. H.] (A128.)
156. Paris, 220. [P. H.] (A129.)
157. Paris, 222. **XI.** [P. H.]
158. Paris, 223. **1045.** [P.H.] (A131.)
159. Paris, 224. **XI.** [P.H.] (R64.)
160. Paris, 225. *paper.* **XVI.**
161. Paris, 226. *paper.* **XVI.**
162. Paris, 227. *paper.* **XVI.**
163. Paris, 238. **XIII.**

164. Paris, 849. *pap.* **XVI.** [H.T.]
165. Turin Univ. C. VI. 29. *p.* **XVI.**
166. Turin C.VI. 19. [H.T.] (A133.)
167. Turin B. V. 19. [P. H.] (A134.)
168. Turin C. V. 10. **X.** [P. H.]
169. Turin C. V. 1. [P. H.] (A136.)
170. Turin B.V.8. [P.H.] (G339A135.)
171. Milan Amb. B. 6. **XIII.** [P. H.]
172. Milan Am.A.51 Sup. **XII.** [H.T.]
173. Milan Am.E.102 S. [P.H.] (A138.)
174. Milan Ambr. H. 104 Sup. [P. H.] (A139R156.)
175. Milan Am. F. 125 Sup. *p.* **XIV.**, **XV.** [P. H.]
176. Milan A. E. 97 S. [P. H.] (A137.)
177. Modena Est. II. A. 14. **XV.**
178. Milan III.B.17. [P.H.] (A142.)
179. Modena, Est. II. G. 3 (v. Cod. H.) **XII.** [P. H.] (A112·)
180. Fl. L. VI. 13. [P.H.] (G363A144.)
181. Fl. L. VI. 36. [P.H.] (G365A145.)
182. Fl.L.C.Sop. 53. (G367A146R23.)
183. *Vacat.*
184. Flor.L.C.Sop. 191. [P.H.] (A148.)
185. Ro.Val.E.22. [P.H.] (G393A167.)
186. Ro.Vall.F.17. [P.H.] (G394A170.)
187. Vat. Gr. 1270. [H. T.] (A154.)
188. Vat. 1430. [P. H.] (A155.)
189. Vat. 1649. **XIII.** [H. T.]
190. Vat. Gr. 1650. [H. T.] (A156.)
191. Vat. Gr. 1714. (A157.)
192. Vat. Gr. 1761. [P. H.] (A158.)
193. Vat. Gr. 2062. [P.H.] (A160R24.)
194. V.G.2080. [P.H.] (G175A41R20.)
195. Vat. Ottob 31. **XI.** [P. H.]
196. Vat. Ottob. 61. *pap.* **XV.** [H.T.]
197. Vat.O.176. *p.* **XV.** [P.H.] (R78.)
198. Vat. Ott. 258. [P.H.] (A161R69.)
199. Vat.O.66.(G886A151R70.)[P.H.]
200. Vat. Ott. 298. [P. H.] (A162.)
201. Vat. Ott. 325. [P. H.] (A163.)
202. Vat. Ott. 356. *paper.* **XV.**
203. V.O.381. [P.H.] (G390A164R71.)
204. Ro.Val. B. 86. [H.T.] (A166R22.)
205. Rome Vall. F. 13. [P. H.] (A168)
206. Ro. Chi. R. V. 29. [P.H.] (A169.)
207. Rome C.R.V.32. *p.* **1394.** [P.H.]
208. Rome Chis. VIII. 55. **XI.** [P.H.]
209. *Missing.* (A171.)
210. *Missing.* (A172.)

211. Naples II. Aa. 8. [P. H.] (A173.)
212. Naples II. Aa. 9. [P.H.] (A174.)
213. Rome Barb.IV.85. **1330.** [P.H.]
214. Vienna Th.166. *p.* **XIV.**
215. Venice, 546. [P. H.] (A140R74.)
216. Messina Univ. 104. (A175.)
217. Palermo I. E. II. **X.**
218. *Missing.* (G421A176.)
219. Leyden,74A. [H.T.] (G122A177.)
220. BerlinA.XII.10.[P.H.](G400A181.)
221. Camb.Mm.6,9.[P.H.](G400A111.)
222. "*Delendus.*" (G441A110.)
223. "*Delendus.*" (G442A152.)
224. Oxf. Bodl. Clark 9. [P.H.] (A58.)
225. *Vacat.* (A9P11.)
226. "*Delendus.*" (P27.)
227. Oxf.Bodl.Clark 4. [P. H.] (A56.)
228. Escurial χ. IV. 17. (G226A108.)
229. Escurial χ. IV. 12. (G228A109.)
230. *Vacat.*
231. Jerus. Holy Sep. 8. (A183.)
232. Jeru. H. Sep. 9. (A184.)
233. St. Saba 1. (A185.)
234. St. Saba 2. (G457A186.)
235. St. Saba 10. (G462A187R86.)
236. St. Saba 15. (A188.)
237. St. Saba 20. (G466A189R89.)
238. *Lost.* (G431A180.)
239. Flor. Laur. VI. 27. (G189A141.)
240. B.M.H.5796.[P.H.](G444A153.)
241. Wolfenb. Gud. Gr. 104, 2. (A97.)
242. Chelten. 1461. [P.H.] (A178R87.)
243. Patmos. (A182.)
244. Oxf. Chr. Ch. Wake. 34. [P. H.] (G517A190R27.)
245. Oxf. C. C. W. 38. [P.H.] (A191.)
246. Ox. C. C. Wa. 37. [P. H.] (A192.)
247. Par. St. Genevieve A.O.35.[P.H.] (A415.)
248. B.M.Egerton,2787.[P.H.](A229.)
249ᵍ ˢᶜʳ· Wordsw. [P.H.] (G479A193.)
250. Metz 4. [P. H.] (G480.)
251. *Latet.* (G483A194.)
252. Camb. [P. H.] (G489A195.)
253. B. M. Add. [P.H.] (G491A196.)
254. B. M. Add. [P. H.] (G496A197.)
255. B. M. Add. [P. H.] (G498A198.)
256. Oxford. [P. H.] (G506A199.)
257. Ox.Bodl.[P.H.](G522A200R98.)
258. Curzon. [P. H.] (G547A202.)

259. Paris Ar. [H. T.] (A301R102.)
260. Berlin. [P. H.] (A302.)
261. Berlin. (Tit. H. P.] (A303.)
262. Ferrara. [P.H.](G582A206R103.)
263. Milan. [P. H.] (G592A207.)
264. Jer. Scr. 152. (G615A208.)
265. Jer. Scr. 304. (G619A209.)
266. S. Sab. Scr. 230. (G623A210.)
267. S. Sab. Scr. 316. (G624A211.)
268. S. Sab. Scr. 317. (G625A212.)
269. Berlin. [— Heb.] (G656A213.)
270. Lond. Scr. 252. [P. H.] (A214.)
271. Lond. Scr. 253. [P. H.] (A215.)
272ᵉ ˢᶜʳ· Const'ple. Scr. 254. (A216.)
273ᵈ ˢᶜʳ· Lond. Scr. 255. [P.H.] (A217.)
274ᵉ ˢᶜʳ· Const'ple. Scr. 321. (A218.)
275. London. Scr. 270. [P.H.] (A220.)
276. Oxford. Scr. 250. [P.H.] (A221.)
277. Oxford. Scr. 251. [P.H.] (A222.)
278. London. Scr. 264. [P.H.] (A223.)
279. Lond. Scr. 265. [P. H.] (A224.)
280. Chelten. Scr. 280. [P.H.] (A225.)
281. Curzon. Scr. 234. [P.H.] (A226.)
282. Curzon. Scr. 235. [P.H.] (A227.)
283. Curzon. Scr. 236. [P.H.] (A228.)
284. Cairo. Scr. 248. (A240.)
285. Cairo. Scr. 275. (A241.)
286. Cairo. Scr. 296. (A242.)
287. S. Saba. Scr. 334. (A243R104.)
288. S. Saba. Scr. 313. (A244.)
289. Vien. Scr. 329. [—Heb.] (A245.)
290ᵉ ˢᶜʳ· Lond. Lambeth. 1186. **XI.**   Scr. 256. [P. H.] (R93.)
291. B. M. Add. 7142. **XIII.** Scr. 267. [P. H.]
292. Athens Th. 70. [P. H.] (A304.)
293. Vatican,Gr. 1209. **XV.** Scr. 263. [Heb. ix. 14–xiii. 25.] (R91.)
294. Flo.Ric. 85. *p.* **XV.** S. 226. [P.H.]
295. Athens Th. 71. [P. H.] (A305.)
296. Athens Th. 72. [P. H.] (A306.)
297. Vienna. Scr. 335. [P. H.] (A246.)
298. Berlin. Scr. 301. [P. H.] (A248.)
299. Paris Cois. [P. H.] (A250R121.)
300. Athens (64). [H.T.] (A309R124.)
301. Athens Th. [P.H.] (A251R122.)
302. Athens Scr. 299. [H.T.] (A252.)
303. Zittau. [P. H.] (G664A253R106.)
304. Cheltenham. [P.H.] (G676A254)
305. Chel. [H. T.] (G680A255R107.)

306. London H. B. C. Scr. 266. [H.T.] (G699A256R108.)
307. Wisbech. [P. H.] (G712A257.)
308. Vienna. Scr. 398. (G720A258.) [Gal. P. Heb. Rom. 1, 2, Cor.]
309. Athens.[P.H.](G757A260R110.)
310. Athens. [P. H.] (G767A261.)
311. Athens. [H. T.] (G794A262.)
312. Athens. [P. H.] (G796A263.)
313. Athens. [P. H.] (G801A264.)
314. Athens. [P.H.](G808A265R112.)
315. Berlin S.404. [P.H.] (G823A266.)
316. Grot.-F.[P.H.](G824A267R113.)
317. Vat.Reg.[P.H.](G886A268R115.)
318. Ven.Scr.406. (P.H.want.)(G891.)
319. Upsal. 312. Scr. 274. (G901A269.)
320. At.S.407.[P.H.](G922A270R116.)
321. AthosDion.Scr.423. (G927A271.)
322. AthosDion.Scr.424. (G935A272.)
323. AthosDion.Scr.425.(G941A273.)
324. Athos Dion. (G945A274.)
325. Athos Dion. (G959A276.)
326. Ath. Esp. (G986A277R117.)
327. Ath. Iber. [P. H.] (G996A278.)
328. Ath. Iber. [P. H.] (G997A279.)
329. Ath. Iber. [P. H.] (G999A280.)
330. Ath. Iber. (G1003A281.)
331. Ath. Carac. (G1040A282.)
332. Ath. Cutlum. (G1058A283.)
333. At. L. [P.H.] (G1072A284R118.)
334. Ath. L.(G1075A286R119.)[P.H.]
335. Ath. Pantel. (G1094A287R120.) [P.H.]
336. Chalcis Sch.[P.H.] (G1149A288.)
337. Sinai, 259. (G1240A289.)
338. Sinai, 260. (G1241A290.)
339. Sinai, 261. (G1242A291.)
340. Sinai, 262. (G1243A292.)
341. Sinai, 263. (G1244A293.)
342. Sinai, 264. (G1245A294.)
343. Sinai, 265. (G1246A295.)
344. Sinai, 266. (G1247A296.)
345. Sinai, 267. (G1248A297.)
346. Sinai, 268. (G1249A298.)
347. Sinai, 269. (G1250A299.)
348. Sinai, 270. [P.H.] (G1251A300.)
349. Flor. Lau. [P. H.] (A149R180.)
350. Leyden, 66. pap. XV. [P.H.]
351. Athens. [P. H.] (A307R105.)
352. Cairo. [P. H.] (A381.)

353. Chalcis Mon. [H. T.] (A382.)
354. Chalcis Sch. (A383.)
355. Chalcis Sch. [P. H.] (A384.)
356. Chalcis Sch. [P. H.] (A385.)
357. Chalcis Sch. [P. H.] (A386.)
358. Patmos. (A387.)
359. Patmos. (A388.)
360. Patmos. (A389.)
361. Patmos. (A390.)
362. Saloniki. [H. T.] (A391.)
363. Saloniki. [P. H.] (A392.)
364. Saloniki. [H. T.] (A393.)
365. Sinai. [P. H. ?] (A394.)
366. Sinai. [P. H.] (A395.)
367. Sinai. (A399R135.)
368. Sinai. [H. T. ?] (A400.)
369. Sinai. [P. H.] (A403.)
370. Sinai. [H.T. ?] (A413.)
371. Madison, N. J. (Drew Sem. Lib.) [P.H.] **1366, 1369.**
372. B. M. Arundel, 534. *paper.* **XIV.**
373. Vienna Theol. 157. **1088.** [H.T.]
374. Besancon, 200. *pap.* **XV.** [H. T.]
375. Paris Nat. 224 A. *paper.* **XV.**
376ᵃ. Paris Sup. 1001. **XIV.** Scr. 338.
    ᵇ. Paris N. Suppl. 1035. (13 frag.)
    ᶜ. Escurial ω. II. 20.
    ᵈ. Vat. Ottob. 74. *p.* **XV.** Scr. 326.
    ᵉ. Vat. Pal. Gr. 423. **XII.** Scr. 330.
377. Paris Cois. Gr. 200. Scr. 341. [H. T.] (G38A19.)
378. Paris Cois. 29. **XIII.**
379. Paris Cois. 30. **XII.** [P. H.]
380. Paris C. 95. **XI.** Scr. 339. [P. H.]
381. Paris C.217.**XIII.**Scr.340.[P.H.]
382. Athens Nat. 69. **X.** [P. H.]
383. Athens Nat. 100. *p.* [P.H.] **XIII.**
384. Escurial χ. IV. 15. **XII.**
385. Bologna 2378. **XIV.**
386. Flor. Lau.VI. 8. *p.* **XIII.** [P.H.]
387. Flor. Lau. X. '9. *paper.* **XIV.**
388. Flor. Lau. XI. 7. *paper.* **XV.**
389. Flor. Lau. Conv. Sop. 21. *p.* **XVI.**
390. Milan. Am A. 62 inf. **XI.** [P.H. ?]
391. MilanAm.C.(E ?)295. **XI.** [P.H.]
392. Milan Ambr. D. 541 inf. **XI.** Scr. 288. [P. H.]
393. Mil. Am.E. 2 inf. *p.* **XIII.** Scr. 286.
393ᵃ. Milan Ambr. A. 241 inf. *paper.* **XVI.** Scr. 287.

394. Naples II. B. 23. *p.* **XIV.** [P.H.]
395. Naples II. B. 24. *p.* **XV.** [P.H.]
396. Rome Barberin VI. 13. **XII.**
Scr. 297. [P. H.]
397. Rome Casa.G.V.7.*p.***XIV.**[P.H.]
398. Vat. Gr. 549. **XII.** Scr. 305.
399. Vat. Gr. 646. *p.* **XIII.** Scr. 310.
400. Vat. Gr. 647. *pap.* **XIV.** (G858.)
401. Vat. Gr. 648. **1232.** Scr. 312.
402. Vat. Gr. 692. **XI.** Scr. 314.
403. Vat. Gr. 1222. *p.* **XVI.** Scr. 315.
404. Vat. 2180.*p.***XV.** Scr. 323. [P.H.]
405. Vat. Ottob. 17. *p.* **XV.** [H. T.]
406. Vat. Pal. 10. **X.** Scr. 327. [P. H.]
407. Vat.Pal.204. **X.** Scr.328. [P. H.]
408. Venice Mark, 36. **XVI.** [H. T.]
409. Athos Cutlumus, 90 b. **XII.**
410. Athos Cutl. 129. *paper.* **XIV.**
411. Constantinople Holy Sep. 2.
412. Constantinople Holy Sep. 3.
413. Patmos, S. John, 61. **X.**
414. Patmos, S. John, 62. **XII.** [H.T.]
415. Patmos, S. John, 63. **XI.** or **XII.**
416. Patmos, S. John, 116. **XIII.**
417. S. Saba (in Tower), 41. **XIV.**
418. GroningenUniv.A.C.1.**XV.**[P.H.]
419. Athens (221). [P.H.] (A311.)
420. Athens (419). [H. T.] (A308.)
421. Athens. [P. H.] (A312.)
422. Athens. [P. H.] (A313.)
423. Grotta-Ferrata, A. B. 1. Scr. 291.
[H. T.] (A317.)
424. G.-F.A.B.3.Scr.292.[P.H.](A318.)
425. G.-F.A.B.6.Scr.293.[H.T.](A319.)
426. Messina, 40. S. 283. [P.H.](A320.)
427. Casan. G. II. 6. Scr. 336. [H. T.]
(A321.)
428. Coislin, Gr. 207. (G1267.)
429. Lesbos, 55. [P.H.] (A323R127.)
430. Vat.1208.Scr.294.[H.T.](A326.)
431. Vat.1971.Scr.319.[H.T.](A328.)
432. Vat. Gr. 2099. Scr. 322. (A329.)
433. Vat. Pal. 38. [P.H.] (A330)
434. Ven. II. 114. [P.H.](A332R128.)
435. Edin. Makel. [P. H.] (A333.)
436. Linköping, Benzel, 35. Scr. 272.
[H. T.] (A334R129.)
437. Upsal. 11. Scr. 273. (A335.)
438. Athos Dion. 68. (A344.)
439. Athos Dion. 382. (A346.)

440. Athos Docheiar. 38. (A347.)
441. Athos Docheiar. 48. (A348.)
442. Athos Docheiar. 136. (A349.)
443. Athos Docheiar. 139. (A350.)
444. Athos Docheiar. 147. (A351.)
445. Athos Esphigmen. 63. (A352.)
446. Athos Esphigmen. 64. (A353.)
447. Athos Esphigmen. 65. (A354.)
448. Athos Esphigmen. 66. (A355.)
449. Athos Esphigmen. 67. (A356.)
450. Athos Esphigmen. 68. (A357.)
451. Athos Iber. 24. (A358.)
452. Athos Iber. 25. (A359R130.)
453. Athos Iber. 37. (A360.)
454. Athos Iber. 57. (A361.)
455. Athos Iber. 60. (A362R131.)
456. Athos Constamon. 108. (A366.)
457. Athos Cutlum. 57. (A368.)
458. Athos Cutlum. 80. (A369.)
459. Athos Cutlum. 81. (A370.)
460. Athos Cutlum. 82. (A371.)
461. Athos Cutlum. 83. (A372.)
462. Athos Cutlum. 275. (A373.)
463. Ath.S.Paul,2.[P.H.](A374R132.)
464. Athos Protat. 32. (A375.)
465. Athos Simopet. 42. (A376.)
466. Athos Stauron. 52. (A377.)
467. Athos Philoth. 38. (A378.)
468. Athos Philoth. 76. (A379.)
469. Athens, 43. [P.H.] (A307R105.)
470. Escurial, *T.* III. 17. **XII.** (R142.)
471. Athens (259). **XV.** or **XVI.**
472. Escurial,ψ.III.2.*p.* **XIV.** Scr.232.
473. Escurial, χ. III. 10. (A233.)
474. St. Petersburg Porfiri. (A315.)
475. Escurial, Ω IV. 22. (A237.)
476. Modena,Estensis II.C.4. (A239.)
477. B. M. Add. 28816. (A205R181.)
[P.H.]
478. Milan,N.272Sup.*p.***XVI.**Scr.225.
479. Modena,Estensis II. A.13. (A238.)
480. Vat. Reg. Gr. 4. **X.** Scr. 324.
481. Flor.Lau.IX.10.**XI.**or**XII.**[P.H.]
482. Vat. Gr. 636. *p.* **XIII.** or **XIV.**
483. Copen. Thott. 14. *p.* **XVI.** [P.H.]
484. Camb. **XI.** (G1277A418R?185.)
485. "*Sine loco.*" (G1287A419.)
486. *Vacat.*
487. Berlin, Henry Brugsch. (?). *pa-pyrus.* [2d Thess. i. 1–2, 2.]

D. —THE BOOK OF REVELATION

1. Mayhingen, Bav.   (ff. 65–90. *pap.*)
    XII. *bonæ notæ,* c f. W-H p. 263.
2. Paris 237. Stephens' *ι έ.* (A10P12.)
3[1] *Missing.*
4. Paris N. Gr. 219.   (A12P16.)
5. *Missing.*   (W–H = G597.)
6. Ox. Bodl. Bar. 3.   (A23P28.)
7. B. M. Harl. 5537.   "*bon. not.*"
    (A25P31.)
8. B. M. Harl. 5778.   (A28P34.)
9. Ox. Bodl. Misc. 74.   (A30P36.)
10. Camb. Un. Dd. 9. 69.   **XV.** (G60.)
11. *Missing.*   (A39P45.)
12. Vat. Reg. Gr. 179. **XV.** (A40P46.)
13. Frankfort. (A42P48Evl.923Apl56.)
14. Leicester. (G69A31P37.) (v.p.112.)
15[2] Basil, A. N. III. 12.   (R.iii, 3–iv.8.)
16. Hamburg, 1252.   (A45P52.)
17. Paris N. Cois. 199.   (G35A14P18.)
18. Paris N. Cois. 202. XII.   (A18P22.)
19. Paris N. Cois. 205.   (A17P21.)
20. Vat. Gr. 2080.   (G175A41P194.)
21. Rome Vallicell. D. 20. *paper.* **XV.**
22. Rome Val. B. 86.   (A166P204.)
23. Flor. L. C. S. 53. (G367A146P182.)
24. Vatican Gr. 2062.   (A160P193.)
25. Vat. Pal. Gr. 171. (G149A77P88.)
26. Oxf. Ch. C. W. 12. (G506A199P256.)
27. O. C. C. W. 34. **XI.** (G517A190P244.)
28. Oxf. Bodl. Baroc. 48. *paper.* **XV.**
29. B. M. Harl. 5613. (A60P63.)
30. Wolfenbüt. 16. 7. **XIV.** (A69P74.)
31. B. M. Harl. 5678.   *paper.* **XV.**
32. Dresden A. 124.   **XV.**
33. Vien. The. 23. *mut.* (G218A65P57.)
34. Vienna Theol. 302.   (A66P67.)
35. Vienna Theol. 307.   **XIV.**
36. Vienna Sup. Gr. 93.   **XIII.**
37. Vat. Gr. 366.   (A72P79.)
38. Vatican 579. *p.* **XV.** (v. p. 110.)
39. Vat. Gr. 1136. [w. *lacunæ.*] (P85.)
40. Vat. Gr. 1160.   (G141A75P86.)
41. Vat. Reg. Gr. 68.   *paper.* **XV.**
42. Vat. Pii II. Gr. 50.   (G80P91.)
43. Rome Barb. IV. 56.   **XIV.**
44. Ro. Prop. L. VI. 19. (G180A82P92.)

45. Flor. Lau. IV. 32.   (A89P99.)
46. Venice, 10. **XV.** (G209A95P108.)
    (v. p. 112.)
47. Dresden A. 172. (G241A104P120.)
48. Moscow Syn. 380. (G242A105P121.)
49. Mos. S. 67. *p.* **XV.** "*bonæ notæ.*"
50. Moscow Syn. 206.   *paper.* **XV.**
51. Paris Nat. Gr. 47. (G18A113P132.)
52. Paris Nat. Gr. 56.   (A51P133.)
53. Paris Nat. Gr. 59.   (A116P136.)
54. *Vacat.*
55. Paris N. Gr. 101.   (A118P138.)
56. Paris N. Gr. 102 A.   (A119P139.)
57. P. N. Gr. 123,124. (G296A124P149.)
58. Paris Nat. 19. *p.* **XV.** or **XVI.**
59. Paris Sup. 99. *pap.* **XV.** or **XVI.**
60. "*Delendus.*"   (P152.)
61. Paris Nat. 491. *p.* **XIII.** or **XIV.**
62. Paris, 239.   *paper.* **1422.**
63. Paris, 241.   *paper.* **XVI.**
64. Paris Nat. 224.   (P159.)
65. Moscow Univ. Lib. 25.   **XII.**
66. *Vacat.*
67. Vatican, 1743.   **1301.**
68. Vatican, 1904.   **XI.** or **XII.**
69. Vatican Ottob. 258.   (A161P198.)
70. Vat. Ott. 66.   (G386A151P199.)
71. *Vacat.*
72. Rome Chisianus, R. IV. 8.   **XVI.**
73. Rome Corsin. 41. E. 37.   **XV.**
74. Venice Mark, 546.   (A140P215.)
75. Florence Lau. IV. 30.   (A86P96.)
76. *Vacat.*   (= R75.)
77. Flor. Laurent. VII. 9.   *pap.* **XVI.**
78. Vatican Ottob. Gr. 176.   (P197.)
79. Vatican Gr. 656.   *paper.* **XIV.**
79[2] Munich, 248.   *paper.* **XVI.**
80. Munich, 544.   *paper.* **XIV.**
81. Munich, 23.   *paper.* **XVI.**
82. Munich, 211.   (A179P128.)
83. Turin B. V. 8.   (G339A135P170.)
84. Flor. Riccardi 84.   (G368A150.)
85. Jerusalem H. S. 9.   (A184P232.)
86. S. Saba 10.   (G462A187P235.)
87. Cheltenham, 1461.   (A178P242)
88. Venice Mark, 5. (G205A93P106.)

---

[1] Cited in Revelation seventy-seven times by Stephens.
[2] A cursive addition to uncial E. q. v.

89. S. Saba, 20. (G466A189P267.)
90. Dresden A. 95. **XII.**
91. Vat. 1209. "*bonæ notæ.*" (P293.)
92. Dublin Trin. Col. A 4. 21. **XVI.**
  (G61A34P40.)
93. Lond. Lamb. 1186. *Mut.* (P290.)
94. B.M.Add.11837.(G201A91P104.)
95. Parham (Curzon), 82. 17. **XI.** or
  XII. "*eximiæ notæ.*"
96. Parham (Curzon), 93. 2. *p.* **XIV.**
97. B.M.Add.17469.(G498A198P255.)
98. Ox. Bodl. Canon. Gr. 34 (text like
  R30). (G522A200P257.)
99. Naples II. Aa. 7 (?). (A83P93.)
100. Naples II. Aa. 10 (?). **XIV.**
101. St. Pet. Mur. 129. *p.* **XV.**Scr.103.
102. Paris Arsenal, 9. (A301P259.)
103. Ferrara, 187, 188. NA. 7. Scr.
  102. (G582A206P262)
104. S.Saba,20. Scr.205. (A243P287.)
105. Athens(43).Scr.111.(A307P469.)
106. Zittau. A. 1. (G664A253P303.)
107. Chelten. 7682. (G680A255P305.)
108. Lon.H.B-C.ii.4.(G699A256P306.)
109. Venice, 6. (G206A94P107.)
110. Athens,Th.12. (G757A260P309.)
111. Athens, 67ᴹ· Scr. 149. (G792.)
112. Ath. Mam. (G808A265P314.)
113. Grot.F.A′.a′.1.(G824A267P316.)
114. Vat. Gr. 1882. Scr. 115. (G866.)
115. Vat. Reg. 6. (G886A268P317.)
116. Athos Greg. 3. (G922A270P320.)
117. Athos Esp.186.(G986A272P326.)
118. Athos Laur. (G1072A284P333.)
119. Athos Laur. (G1075A286P334.)
120. AthosPan.29.(G1094A287P335.)
121. Paris Coisl. 224. (A250P299.)
122. Athens Nat. 217. (A251P301.)
123. Paris Sup. Gr. 159. (G743A259.)
124. Athens Nat. (64). (A309P300.)
125. Escurial, ψ. III. 6. (A235.)
126. Escurial, ψ. III. 18. (A236.)
127. Lesbos, τ. λειμ. 55. (A323P429.)
128. Venice,Mark II.114. (A332P434.)
129. Linköp. Benzel. 35. (A334P436.)
130. Athos Iber. 25. (A359P452.)
131. Athos Iber. 60. (A362P455.)
132. Athos S. Paul, 2. (A374P463.)
133. Chalcis Sch. 26. (A384P355.)
134. Chalcis Sch. 96. (A386P357.)
135. Sinai, 279. (A399P367.)

136. Vienna Theol. 69. *pap.* **1507.**
137. Vienna Theol. 163. *pap.* **XV.**
138. Vienna Theol. 220. *pap.* **XV.**
139. Paris, 240. *paper.* **1543.**
140. Paris Coislin. 256. **XI.** or **XII.**
141. Athens, τῆς βουλῆς. *p.* **XVI.**
142. Escurial, *T.* iii. 17. **X.** (P479.)
143. Escurial, Χ. iii. 6. **1107.**
144. Madrid, O. 19, No 7. *p.*(?) **XVI.**
145. Florence Lau. vii. 29. *p.* **XVI.**
146. Messina Un. 99. **XIII.** Scr. 113.
147. Modena Est. III.E.1. *pap.* **XV.**
148. Modena Est. III.F.12. *pap.* **XV.**
149. Rome, Ang. A.4.1. *p.* **XIV.**S.120.
150. Rome, Ang. B.5.15.*p.***XV.** S.121.
151. Ro. Chis. R. V.33. *p.* **XIV.** S. 122.
152. Vat. Gr. 370. **XI.**
153. Vat. 542. **1331.** Scr. 114.
154. Vat. Gr. 1190. *p.* **XV.** or **XVI.**
155. Vat. Gr. 1426. *p.* **XIII.**
156. Milan A. H. 104 sup.(A139P174.)
157. Vat. Gr. 1976. *p.* **XVI.** Scr. 116.
158. Vat.Gr.2129. *p.* **XVI.** (Evl.561.)
159. Vat. Ottob. Gr. 154. *pap.* **XV.**
160. Vat. Ottob. Gr. 283. *pap.* **1574.**
161. Vat. Palat. Gr. 346. *paper.* **XV.**
162. Venice, Mark, I.40. *pap.* **XVI.**
163. Ven. M. II.54. *p.* **XV.** or **XVI.**
164. Athos St. Anna 11. *p.* **XV.**
165. Athos Batopedion, 90.
166. Athos Batopedion, 90 bis.
167. Athos Diony. 163. *pap.* **1622.**
  (Evl642Apl170.)
168. Athos Docheiar. 81. *p.* **1798.**
169. Athos Iber. 34. **XIV.**
170. Athos Iber. 379. **X.**
171. Athos Iber. 546. *paper.* **XIV.**
172. Athos Iber. 594. *paper.* **XVII.**
173. Athos Iber. 605. *paper.* **1601.**
174. Athos Iber. 644. *paper.* **1685.**
175. Athos Iber. 661. *paper.* **1562.**
176. Athos Constamon. 29. *p.* **XVI.**
177. Athos Constamon. 107. **XIII.**
178. Patmos, 12. **XIV.** (Apl161.)
179. Patmos mon. St. John. 64. **XII.**
180. Flor. L. C. Sop. 150. (A149P349.)
181. B. M. Add. 28816. (A205P477.)
182. Dresden Reg. 187. **XVI.** Scr. 112.
183. Saloniki, 10. **X.** (Apl163.)
184. Leyden(IsaacVoss),48. *p.* **1560.**
185. (G1277A418P484) (?)

LECTIONARIES

(1.) THE EVANGELIUM

The practice of using formal tables of Scripture lessons seems to have been regarded as ancient even in the IVth century. "·Chrysostom devotes a whole homily to explain why the Acts of the Apostles are publicly read throughout the festal season, between Easter-day and Whitsun-day, and elsewhere states that the rule of the Fathers (τῶν πατέρων ὁ νόμος) directs that book to be laid aside after Pentecost" (Scr. in *Smith's Dict. of Ch. Antiq.*). The earliest known Synaxaria, or table of lessons for the whole year, are found in two uncial MSS. at Paris (Codd. **K**. [Cyprius] and **M**. [Campianus]), both of the IXth century. On the margins of those MSS.—and of Cod. L. (VIIIth century), of the same library—are found marginal notes, usually in red ink, indicating the beginning ('ΑΡΧΗ' [ἀρχή]) and end (ΤΕΛΟΣ [τέλος]) of each lesson, with the day appointed for it, and sometimes the initial words by which the lesson is to be introduced.

The earliest known of the *Evangelia*, or Gospel lesson books proper, most of which are uncials (marked by the letter *U*), seem to belong to the **IX.** or **X.** centuries, as will appear from the following table. The Greek ecclesiastical year began with Easter-day (τῇ ἁγίᾳ καὶ μεγάλῃ κυριακῇ τοῦ πάσχα), and daily continuous lessons are prescribed (with some interruptions) from John and Acts till Whitsun-day (κυριακῇ τῆς πεντηκοστῆς); but, after that, the Saturday (σαββάτῳ) and Sunday (κυριακῇ) lessons are often given alone, without those of the five ordinary week days (see table in Scrivener, Intr. pp. 80–86). They are denominated σαββατοκυριακαί (σαβ. κυρ.), whereas a daily reading for every week is called ἑβδομάς (εβδ.). In the following table of the *Evangelia* the MSS. marked with an asterisk [*] (John, εβδ. Mt. Luc. σαβ. κυρ.) are those which have the daily lessons throughout the seven Johannean weeks (Easter to Pentecost), and afterwards lessons from Matt. and Luke for Saturday and Sunday during the rest of the year. Those marked with an obelisk [†] (John, Matt. Lu. εβδ.) have daily lessons from the three Gospels throughout the year. Those which have (Matt. Lu. σαβ. κυρ.), *without* (John, εβδ.), are marked *-J. The sign †-J. indicates daily lessons for Matt. and Lu., *without* John. The abbreviation εωθ. stands for ἑωθινά, a morning lesson, for eleven successive Sundays, beginning with All Saints.

For other peculiarities the reader is referred to Gregory (Prol.) and Scrivener, and to the article *Lectionary*, by Scrivener, in *Smith's Dict. of Ch. Antiquities.* Prof. Gregory informs us that a few—viz.: Evl. 1. 6. 30, 117, 131, 132, 142, 204, 206, 300—have only select readings; also, that Evl. 10, 305, 398 are wanting in σαββατοκυριακῶν, while Evl. 438 has only the σαβ. κυρ. *in* John, and that Evl. 114, 306, 836, present only the κυριακάς, or Lord's day, lessons. A few, such as Evl. 60, 104, 133, 241, 250(?), 421, have, also, readings from the Acts and Epp., and are, therefore, denominated ἀποστολοευαγγέλια.

(2.) THE APOSTOLOS

"The Apostle" ('Ο 'Απόστολος) was the most ancient designation of a lectionary containing the Epistles. The practice of copying out these lessons was not so general as of the Gospels, and the MSS. are for the most part of later date.

E.—LECTIONARIES: (1) THE EVANGELIUM

1. Paris, 278. **X.** (?) *U.*
2. Paris, 280. **X.** *U.*
3. Oxf. Lin. Coll. *II.* 15. **XI.** *U.**
4. Camb. Univ. Dd. 8.49. **XI.**
5. Ox. Bodl. Baroc. 202. **X.** *U.**
6. Leyden (Scaliger) 243. *p.* **XI.**? *U.*
7. Paris, 301. **1204.**
8. Paris, 312. **XIV.**†
9. Paris, 307. **XIII.**†
10. Paris, 287. **XIII.**
11. Paris, 309. **XIII.**†
12. Paris, 310. **XIII.**†
13. Paris Cois. 31. **XI.** *U.**
14. Paris, 315. *paper.* **XVI.**†
15. Paris, 302. **XIII.**†
16. Paris, 297. **XII.**
17. Paris, 279. **IX.** *U.*
18. Oxf.Bodl.Laud.32. **XII.** or **XIII.**†
19. Oxf. Bodl. Misc. 10. **XIII.**†
20. Oxf. Bodl. Laud. 34. **1047.** *
21. Oxf. Bo. Ar. Sel. B. 56. **XII.** *-J.
22. Oxf.Bodl.Arch.Selden. B.54. **XIV.**
23. *Missing.* Unc.
24. Munich, 383. **X.** *U.*
25. Brit. Mus. Harl. 5650. **XIII.** *
26. Oxf. B. Ar. Sel. Sup. 2. **XIII.** *
    (Apl28.)
27. Oxf. Bodl. Seld. Sup. 3. **XIV.** and
    IX. *-J.fragm.(partly *U.&Pal.*)
28. Ox. Bodl. Misc. 11. **XIII.** *
29. Oxf. Bodl. Misc. 12. **XII.** or **XIII.**
30. Oxf.Bo.Crom.11. **1225.** (Apl265.)
31. [(?) "*Olim* Nuremb." *missing.*] **XII.**
32. Gotha, Ducal Lib. MS. 78. **XI.**
33. Rome "Card Alex. Albani." **XI.** *U.*
34. Munich, 329. **IX.** † *U.*
35. Vatican, 351. **X.** *U.*
36. Vatican, 1067. **VIII.** or **IX.**† *U.*
37. Rom. Pro. Borg. L. VI. 6. **XII.** *
    (Apl.7.)
38. = 117 below. (W–H. = 183.)
39. = 118 below. (W–H. = 184.)
40. Escurial I. **X.** *U.*
41. Escurial χ. III. 12. **X.** or **XI.** *U.*
42. Escurial χ. III. 13. **X.** or **XI.** *U.*
43. Escurial χ. III. 16. **XI.** or **XII.**
44. Copenhagen 1324. **XII.** (Apl8.)
45. Vienna Law Lib. Gr. 5. **X.** *U.*

46. Vienna Sup. Gr. 12. **IX.** or **X.** *U.*
47. Moscow H. Synod 42. **X.** *U.*
48. Moscow H. Synod 43. **1055.**
49. Moscow Typ. Syn. 11. **X.** and **XI.**
50. Moscow Typ. Syn. 226. **XIV.** *U.*
51. Moscow Typ. Syn. 9. *paper.* **XIV.**
52. Mos. H. Syn. 266. **XIV.** (Apl16)
53. Mos.H.Syn.267. *p.* **XV.** (Apl17.)
54. Mos. H.Syn.268. *p.* **1470.** (Apl18.)
55. Typog. Syn. 47. *p.* **1602.** (Apl19.)
56. Typog. Syn. 9. *pap.* **XV.** (Apl20.)
57. Dresden A. 151. *paper.* **XV.**
58. Paris Sup. Gr. 50. *paper.* **XVII.**
59. *Vacat.* (W–H. = Evl.185.)
60. Paris, 375. **1021.** * (Apl12.)
61. Paris, 182. (G729.)
62. = G. 303.
63. Paris, 277. **IX.** * *U.*
64. Paris, 281. **IX.** * *U.*
65. Paris, 282. *Palimp.* **IX.** *U.*
66. Paris, 283. *Palimp.* **IX.** *U.*
67. Paris, 284. **XII.** *U* (?)
68. Paris, 285. **XII.**†
69. Paris, 286. **XII.**†
70. Paris, 288. **XII.**†
71. Paris, 289. **1066.** *
72. Paris, 290. [**1257** (Scr.)].*
72.² Three uncial leaves in 72. **IX.**
73. Paris, 291. **XII.**
74. Paris, 292. **XII.** *
75. Paris, 293. **XII.**†(?)
76. Paris, 295. **XII.**†
77. Paris, 296. **XII.** *
78. Paris, 298. **XII.**
79. Paris, 299. **XIV.**†
80. Paris, 300. **XII.**†
81. Paris, 305. **XIV.** *
82. Paris, 276. *pap.* **XIV.** * (Apl31.)
83. Paris, 294. **XII.**† (Apl21.)
84. Paris Sup. 32. **XIII.** (Apl9.)
85. Pa.Sup.33. **XII.** or **XIII.** (Apl10.)
86. Paris, 311. **1336.**†
87. Paris, 313. **XIV.** *
88. Paris, 314. **XIV.** *
89. Paris, 316. *paper.* **XIV.** *
90. Paris, 317. *paper.* **1533.** *
91. Paris, 318. **XIV.** *
92. Paris, 324. *pap.* **XIV.** (Apl35.)

93. Paris, 326. *pap.* **XVI.** (Apl36.)
94. Paris, 330. **XII.** (Apl29.)
95. Paris, 374. **XIV.***
96. Par.Sup.115.ἑωθ. **XVI.**(Apl262.)
97. Paris, 376. **XIV.** (G324Apl32.)
98. Paris, 377. *Pal.(part. bis).* **XV.***
99. Paris, 380. *paper.* **XVI.***
100. Paris, 381. *paper.* **1550.***
101. Paris, 303. **XIV.**†
102. Milan Amb. S. 62 Sup. *p.* **1370.**
103. Milan Amb. D. 67 Sup. **XIII.***
104. Mil.Am.D.72 Sup. **XII.** (Apl47.)
105. Milan Amb. M. 81 Sup. **XIII.***
106. Milan Amb. C. 91 Sup. **XIII.***
107. Venice, 548. **XII.***
108. Venice, 549. **XI.** or **XII.**†
109. Venice, 550. **XIV.**†
110. Venice, 551. **XIII.***
111. Modena Est. II. C. 6. **X.*** *U.*
112. Flor. Laur. Conv. Sop. 24. (Apl4.)
113. Flor. Lau. VI. 2. **XIII.** †
114. Flor. Lau. VI. 7. **XIV.**
115. Flor. Lau. VI. 21. **X.*** *U.*
116. Flor. Lau. VI. 31. **X.*** *U.*
117. Flor. Lau. Med. Pal. 244. **XII.**
118. Flor. Lau. Med. Pal. 243. **XIV.**†
119. Vatican 1155. **XIII.**†
120. Vat. 1156. **XII.** or **XIII.***
121. Vat. 1157. **XI.**†
122. Vat. 1068. (Scr. 1168.) **1175.***
123. Vat. 1522. **X.** *U.*
124. Vat. 1988. **XII.***
125. Vat. 2017. **XI.** or **XII.***
126. Vat. 2041. **XII.**†
127. Vat. 2063. **IX.*** *U.*
128. Vat. 2133. **XIV.***
129. Vat. Reg. 12. **XII.**†
130. Vat. Ottob. 2. **IX.*** *U.*
131. Vat. Ottob. 175. **XIV.**
132. Vat. Ottob. 326. **XIV.**
133. Vat.Ottob.416.*p.* **XIV.**† (Apl39.)
134. Rome Barb. VI. 4. **XIII.**†
135. Rome Barb.IV.54. *Pal.* **VIII.** *U.*
136. Rome Barb. IV. 54. **XII.***
137. Rome Vall. D. 63. **XI.** or **XII.***
138. Naples,II.A.a.6.*p.* **XV.**or**XVI.***
139. Venice, 12. **X.*** *U.*
140. Venice, 626. *paper.* **XIII.**
141. Venice, I. IX. **XI.***
142. Venice, I. XXIII. **XIV.** or **XV.**

143. *Vacat.* = G. 595.
144. Rome [?] (once Malatest. Cesena).
      U. XXVII. 4. **XII.**
145. Rome [?] (M. C.) XXIX. 2. **XII.**
146. Camb. Dd. VIII. 23. **XII.**†
147. B. M. Harl. 2970. ⎫ Latin MSS.
148. B. M. Harl. 2994. ⎭
149. *Vacat.* = G. 505.
150. B. M. Harl. 5598. **995.**† *U.*
151. B. M. Harl. 5785. **XII.***
152. B. M. Harl. 5787. **IX.** or **X.*** *U.*
153. = G. 436. (Evl. ?)
154. Munich, 326. **XIII.**
155. Vienna, 209. **X.*** *U.Pal.*Scr.180.
156. Rome, Vall. D. 4. 1. **XI.** *latet.*
157. Ox. Bodl. Clarke 8. **1253.***
158. Jerus. H. Sep. 10. **XIV.**
159. Monasterii virginum. **XIII.**
160. S. Saba, 4. **XIV.**
161. S. Saba, 5. *paper.* **XV.**
162. S. Saba, 6. *paper.* **XV.**
163. S. Saba, 13. *paper.* **XIII.**
164. S. Saba, 14. **XIV.**
165. S. Saba, 17. *paper.* **XV.**
166. S. Saba, 21. **XIII.**
167. S. Saba, 22. **XIV.**
168. S. Saba, 23. **XIII.**
169. S. Saba, 24. **XIII.**
170. S. Saba, 25. **XIII.** Scr. 326.
171.S.S.?**1059.**[*"menæum?"*](Apl52.)
172.Patmos,Mon.St John.**IV.**(**IX?**)*U.*
173. Patmos, M. St. J. **IX.** *U.*
174. Patmos, M. St. J. **X.** *U.*
175. Patmos, M. St. J. **X.** *U.*
176. Patmos, M. St. J. **XII.**
177. Patmos, M. St. J. **XIII.**
178. Patmos, M. St. J. **XIV.**
179. Treves.143.F. **X.**, **XI.** *U.* (Apl55.)
180. Andover Theol.Sem.(v.Table XI.)
      MS. i. **XIV.*** Scr. 463.
181 pa Scr. Curzon.83,18.**980.***Scr.234.
182. Curzon. 1, 1. **IX.** Scr. 233.
183 x Scr. B. M. Ar. 547. **X.*** *U.* S. 257.
184 y Scr. B. M. Bur. 22. **1319.**† S. 259.
185 z Scr. Cambr. Chr. C. 13, 4, 6.† **XI.**
      Scr. 222. (Apl59.)
186. Cambr. Trin. Coll. O. IV. 22.
      XII.* Scr. 221.
187. B. M. Arun. 536. **XIII.*** Scr. 256.
188. B. M. A. 5153. **1033.*** Scr. 260.

189. B. M. Add. 11840. **XII.*** Scr. 261.
(Apl175.)
190. B. M. A. 17370. **XI., XII.** S. 262.
190ª B. M. A. 19392b. **XIII.** Scr. 262.
191. B. M. Add. 18212. **XII.†** Scr.263.
192. B.M.Add.19460. **XIII.*** Scr.264.
193. B. M. A. 19993. **1335.*** p. S. 266.
194. Oxf.Bo.Can.85. **IX.*** Scr. 202. U.
195. Oxf. Bodl. Can. 92. **X.*** Scr. 203.
196. Oxf. B. C. 119. p. **XV.†** Scr. 204.
197. Oxf. B. C. 126. p. **XV.** Scr. 205.
198. Oxf. B. Clark. 45. **XII.†** Scr. 206.
199. Oxf. B. C. 46. **XIII.*** Scr. 207.
200. Oxf. B. C. 47. **XII.†** Scr. 208.
201. Oxf. B. C. 48. **XIII.*** Scr. 209.
202. Oxf.Bo.Crom.27. **XII.†** Scr.210.
203. Ox. B. Misc. 119. **XIII.†** Scr. 211.
204. Oxf. B. Misc. 140. **XI.** Scr. 212.
205. Oxf. B. Baroc. 197. **X.** Scr. 201.
206. Oxf. Ch. Ch. Wake. 13. **XI.**
206ª Oxf. Ch. Ch. Wake. 13. (Leaves
i–iv.of **206.**) U. **IX.** Scr.213.
207. Oxf. C. C. W. 14. **XII.*** Scr. 214.
208. Oxf. C. C. W. 15. **1068.*** S. 215.
209. Oxf. Ch. Ch. W. 16. **XII.*** S. 216.
210. Oxf. C. C.W. 17. **XII.*** Scr. 217.
211. Oxf. Ch. Ch. Wake. 18. **XII.** or
XIII.† Palimp. Scr. 218.
212. Oxf. C. C. W. 19. **XI.*** Scr. 219.
213. Oxf. C. C. W. 23. **XIII.†** S. 220.
214. Lond. H. B–Coutts I.2. **XII.** or
XIII.* Scr. 239.
215. Lond. H. B–Coutts I.8. **XIII.***
U. (Apl176.) Scr. 240.
216. Lond. H. B–C. I.10. **XII.** Scr. 251.
217. Lond. H. B–C. I.23. **XIII.*** S. 241.
218. L.H.B–C. I.23. [24 Scr.] 2. **XIV.***
219. Lond.H. B–C. II.5. **XII.†** Scr.243.
220. Lond. H. B–C. II.16. Pal. **XIV.***
Scr. 244.
221. L. H. B–C. II.30. p. **XIII.†** S. 245.
222. Lond. H.B–C.III.21. **XIII.** S.246.
223. Lon.H.B–C.III.29. p. **XIV.** S.252.
224. Lon. H.B–C.III.34. **XIV.*** S.247.
225. Lond. H. B–Coutts III.43. pap.
1437.* Scr. 248.
226. Lon.H.B–C. III.46. **XIV.†** S. 249.
227. Lon.H.B–C.III.52. **XIV.*** S. 250.
228. Lond. H. B–Coutts III.53. [Scr.
253².] paper. **XV.** (Apl263.)

229. Lond. Lamb. 1187. **XIII.*** S.223.
230. Lond. Lamb. 1188. **XIII.†** S. 224.
231. Lond. Lamb. 1189. **XIII.*** S.225.
232. Lond. Lamb. 1193. **XII.*** S. 226.
233. Parham, Cur. 84.19. **XI.†** S. 235.
234. London, Sion Coll. Arc. 1.1.
XIII.* Scr. 227.
235. Lon. S. C. A. 1.2. **XIII.*** Scr. 228.
236. Lon. S. C. Arc. 1.4. **XIII.*** S. 229.
237. Ashburnh. 205. **XII.*** Scr. 237.
237ª Ashburn. 208 fasc. B. Leaves 6,
7. Palimp. **IX.** U. Scr. 238.
238. Coniston. (Ruskin). Scr. 254. **XI.**
239. Glasgow Hunt. Mus. V.5.10.
1259.* Scr. 230.
240. Glasg. H. M. V. 3.3. **XII.*** S. 231.
241. Glasgow Hunt. Mus. V.4.3.
1199.† Scr. 232. (Apl44.)
242. Mosc. Synod, 313. **VIII.** U.
243. St. Pet. Muralt. 21. **VII.** U.
244. St. Pet. Muralt. 35. **IX.** or **X.** U.
245ª St. Pet. Muralt. 36. **X.** or **XI.** U.
245ᵇ St. Pet. Muralt. 37. Pal. **IX.** U.
246¹ ᵖᵉ· St. Pet. Muralt.39 (IV.13). **IX.**
U. Scr. 194.
247. St. Pet. Muralt. 40 (IV.). **IX.**
248ª and ᵇ· St. Pet. Mur. 43. **IX., X.** U.
249 ᵖᵉᵗʳᵒᵖ ᵉᵛ· St. Petersb. Muralt. 44.
IX. U. Scr. 191. (Apl178.)
250. St. Pet. M. 55. **IX.** (Apl179.)
251³ ᵖᵉ· St. Pet. Muralt. 56. (VII.179.)
X. Scr. 195.
252. St. Pet. Muralt. 69. **X.** or **XI.**
253⁶ ᵖᵉ· St. Pet. Muralt. 71. (X.180.)
1020. Scr. 196.
254. St. Pet. Muralt. 80. **XI.** Scr. 474.
255. St. Pet. Muralt. 84. **XI.** or **XII.**
256 ᵖᵉᵗʳᵒᵖ ᵉᵛ· ²· St. Pet. Muralt. 90. **XII.**
Scr. 192. (Apl180.)
257. St. Pet. Muralt. 37a. **XIII.**
258⁹ ᵖᵉ· St. Pet. Muralt. 111. (XI.3.181.
[101 ?]) **XIII.** Scr. 197.
259. St. P. Mur. 112. Pal. **XIII.** S. 477.
260¹⁰ ᵖᵉ· Panticap. Palaeol. Scr. 198.
261. Paris Sup. 27. **XII.*** Scr. 158.
262. Paris Sup. 242. **XVII.†** Scr. 159.
263. Besançon, 44. **XIII.*** Scr. 193.
264. Venice, I.4. p. **1381.** Scr. 170.
265. Venice, I.45. **X.** U. Scr. 171.
266. Venice, I.46. **XII.** (?) * Scr. 172.

267. Venice, I.47. **1046.**† Scr. 173.
268. Venice, I.48. **XII.*** Scr. 174.
269. Venice, I.49. **VII.** *U.* Scr. 175.
270. Venice, I.50. *p.* **XIV.***? Scr. 176.
271. Venice, I.51. *p.* **XVII.** Scr. 177.
272. Venice, I.52. *p.* **XVI.**† Scr. 178.
273. Venice, II. 17. **XIII.** Scr. 478.
274. Venice, II. 143. *paper.* **1580.***
275. Venice, I. 53. **XII.** Scr. 181.
276. Venice, I.54. **XIII.**†–J. Scr. 182.
277. Venice, I.55. *p.* **1439.**† Scr. 183.
278. Venice, St. Georgio B′. **XIII.**
    or **XIV.*** Scr. 186.
279. Venice, St. Geo. A′. **XII.**† Scr. 184.
280. Venice, St. Geo. Γ′. **XIV.**† Scr. 185.
281. Bologna, 3638. **XIV.**† Scr. 160.
282. Parma, 14. **XIV.**† Scr. 161.
283. Siena. Univ. X. IV. 1. **XI.** or
    XII.† Scr. 162.
284. Milan, Q. 79. Sup. **X.** Scr. 163.
285ª. Milan, E. S. V. 14. **XII.*** Scr. 164.
285ᵇ. Milan, E. S. V. 14. **XIV.** Scr. 165.
286. Milan, E. 101. Sup. *Pal.* **IX.** *U.*
287. Milan, Ambr. D. 108. Sup. **XIII.**†
    Scr. 166. (Apl181.)
288. Milan, A. 150. Sup. **XIII.*** S. 167.
289. Milan, A. C. 160. Inf. **XIV.**†–J.
290. Milan, Ambr. P. 274. Sup. *paper.*
    XIV. or **XV.***Scr. 169. (Apl182.)
291. Flor. Lau. St. Mark, 706. **XI.** or
    XII.* Scr. 187.
292 ᶜᵃʳᵖ· ᵉᵛ· Carpentras (City Lib.), 11.
    X. *U.* Scr. 189.
293 ᵗⁱˢᶜʰ· ᵉᵛ· Leipsic, Tisch. V. *Palimp.*
    VIII. or **IX.**† *U.* Scr. 190.
294 ᵗᵘᵇⁱⁿᵍ· ᵉᵛ· Tubingen, Un. 2. **XI.**
    (cf. *Unc.* R. Table VIII.)
295 ᵇᵃⁿᵈᵘʳ· ᵉᵛ· [Mosc. ?] **X.** (cf. Unc. O.)
296. Harvard Univ. Dr. 69. **IX.** or **X.**
    U. (v. Table XI.) Scr. 483.
297. Harvard Univ. A.R.g 3.10. **XII.**
    (v. Table XI.) Scr. 484.
298. Harvard Univ. A.R.g1.3. **XIII.**
    (v. Table XI.) Scr. 485.
299. Lond. B. F. Bib. Soc. (24.) *Pali.*
    XIII.† Scr. 200.
300. Sinai, 204. ("Golden Evangelist-
    ary.") **X.** or **XI.** *U.* Scr. 286.
301. Madison, N. J., Drew Sem. MS. 2.
    XII. (v. Table XI.) Scr. 486.

302ª. Sewickley, Pa. (R. A. Benton's.)
    XII. or **XIII.** (v. Table XI.)
302ᵇ. Sewickley, Pa. (R. A. Benton's,
    fragment.) **XII.** (v. Table XI.)
302ᶜ. Sewanee, Tenn. (A. A. Benton's.)
    p. **XV.** (cf. G. 669. v. Table XI.)
303. Princeton, N. J., Theol. Sem. **XII.**
304. Woolwich [?] (Ch. C. G. Bate's.)
    p. **XIV.** or **XV.**† Scr. 492.
305. Camb. Univ. Add. 679. 2. **XII.**
    Scr. 291. (cf. Apl77.)
306. Camb. Univ. Add. 1836. **XIII.**
    Scr. 292. (Apl183.)
307. Camb. U. A. 1839. **XII.** S. 293.
308. Camb. U. A. 1840. **XI.** Scr. 294.
309. Camb. U. A. 1879, 2. **X.** Scr. 295.
310. Camb. U. A. 1879, 12. **XI.** S. 296.
311. Camb. U. A. 1879, 13. **XII.** S. 297.
312. Sinai, (cf. Unc. *Λ*. Table VIII.) **IX.**
313. Lond. H. B–C. (II. 5.) **XIV.**†
314. Lond. H. B–C. (II. 14.) **XII.**
315. Lond. H. B–C. (III. 42.) **XIV.**
    Scr. 253. (Apl184.)
316. Lond. B. M. Add. 14637. *Pal.*
    (J.M.L.σαβ.κυρ.) **VII.** *U.* S. 496.
317. Lond. B. M. Add. 14638. *Pal.* fragm.
    (J.M.L.σαβ.κυρ.) **IX.** *U.* Scr. 497.
318. Lond. B. M. Add. 19737. *mut.*
    XII. or **XIII.**† Scr. 265.
319. Lond. B. M. Add. 21260. **XII.**
    or **XIII.**† Scr. 267.
320. Lond. B. M. Add. 21261. **XIV.***
    Scr. 268.
321. Lond. B. M. Add. 22735. **XII.**
    or **XIII.**† Scr. 269.
322. Lond. B. M. Add. 22742. fragm.
    (J. Mt. ἑβδ.) **XI.**† Scr. 270.
323. Lond. B. M. A. 22743. **XIII.**† S. 271.
324. Lond. B. M. Add. 22744. **XIII.**†
    Scr. 272. (Apl258.)
325. Lond. B. M. A. 24374. **XIII.** S. 273.
326. L. B. M. A. 24377. **XIII.*** Scr. 274.
327. L. B. M. A. 24379. **XIV.**† Scr. 276.
328. L. B. M. A. 24380. **XIV.*** Scr. 277.
328ª. L. B. M. A. 25881. **XIV.** Scr. 33.
329. L. B. M. A. 27860. **XI.*** Scr. 278.
330. L. B. M. A. 28817. **1185.*** Scr. 279.
331. L. B. M. A. 28818. **1272.*** Scr. 280.
332. L. B. M. A. 29713. **XIV.**† Scr. 62.

333. L.B.M.A.31208. **XIII.**† Scr.281.
334. L. B. M. A. 31919. *Palimp.* **XI.**
   [Mt.*ἐβδ.*] (cf. Unc.W^g.) Scr.282.
335. L. B. M. A. 31920. **XI.*** Scr. 283.
336. L.B.M.A.31921.**XIV.**[Mt.L.*ἐβδ.*]
   Scr. 284.
337. L. B. M. A. 31949. **XII.*** Scr.285.
338. L.B.M.Bur.408.*Pal.***X.***U.*Scr.499.
339. L. B. M. Egerton, 2163. **XIII.** or
   XIV.† Scr. 59.
340. L. B. M. Harl. 5561. **XIII.** or
   XIV. Scr. 258. (Apl186.)
341. Oxf.Bodl.Misc.307. **XI.**† Scr.288.
342. O.B.M.308.**XII.**or**XIII.***Scr.289.
343. Oxf. Keble Coll. **XIII.*** Scr. 298.
344. Parham Cur.85.20.**XII.**†Scr.236.
345. Wisbech(Peckover's,70). **XIII.***
346. B.M.Egerton,2786.**XIV.***Scr.255.
347. Vienna, 160. **XIII.** Scr. 501.
348. Vien. Ar'd. Rainer's. *p'yrus.* **VI.**
349. Vien. Archduke Rainer's. **VI.**
350. Montpelier Med.Sc.H.405. *p.* **XV.**
351. Paris,once Henry Bordier's. **XII.**†
352. Paris, E. Miller,4. **VIII.**or**IX.** *U.*
353. Paris, E. M. 5. **IX.** *U.* Scr. 507.
354. Paris, E. M. 6. **VII.** *U.* Scr. 508.
355. Paris, E. M. 7. **VII.** *U.* Scr. 509.
356. Paris, E. M. 8. **X.** *U.* Scr. 512.
357. Paris, E. M. 9. **X.** *U.* Scr. 513.
358. Paris, E. M. 10. **X.** *U.* Scr. 514.
359. Paris, E. M. 11. **X.** *U.* Scr. 515.
360. Paris,E.M.12. **VIII.** *U.* Scr.516.
361. Paris, Gr. 256. **XII.**† Scr. 426.
362. Paris,928. *Pal.* **IX.** *U.* Scr.427.
363. Paris,975.B. *Pal.* **X.** *U.* Scr.299.
364. Paris Sup. 24. **XII.**† Scr. 416.
365. Paris Sup. 29. **XII.*** Scr. 417.
366. Paris Sup. 74. **XII.**
367. Paris Sup. 567. **XIV.** *U.*
368. Paris Sup.686. **IX.** *U.* Scr.421.
369. Paris Sup. 758. **XII.*** Scr. 423.
370. Par.Sup.805.*Pal.***IX.***U.*(Apl187.)
371. Paris Sup. 834. **XIII.** Scr. 424.
372. Paris Sup.905. **1055.**?* Scr.425.
373. Paris Sup.1081.**X.**or**XI.** *U.*S.517.
374. Paris Sup.Gr.1096. **1070.** S.419.
375. Berlin Gr.fol.51. **XII.**† Scr.370,
376. Berlin, fol. 52. **XII.**† Scr.371.
377. Berlin, fol. 53. **XI.*** Scr. 372.
378. Berlin, 4to, 44. **XII.** Scr. 373.

379. Berlin,4to,61. **XII.***–J. Scr.374.
380. Berlin,4to,64. **XII.,XIII.*** S.375.
381. Berlin (once "Hamilton, 245 ").
   XII.† Scr. 368.
382. Berlin,"Ham.246." **XIII.**†S.369.
383. Athens Theol. 25. **XII.*** S. 518.
   (Apl259.)
384. Athens T. 26. **XII.**† Scr. 519.
385. Athens T. 27. **XII.*** Scr. 520.
386. Athens T. 28. **XII.**† Scr. 521.
387. Athens T. 29. **XI.**† Scr. 522.
388. Athens T. 30. **1527.*** Scr. 523.
389. Athens T.31.**XI.**or**XII.***Scr.524.
390. Athens T. 32. **X.** or **XI.*** Scr. 528.
391. Athens T. 33. **XVI.**† Scr. 529.
392. Athens T. 34. **XII.*** Scr. 530.
393. Athens T. 35. **XII.*** Scr. 531.
394. Athens T. 36. **XII.*** Scr. 532.
395. Athens T. 37. **XIV.*** Scr. 534.
396. Athens T. 38. *p.* **1328.**† Scr. 535.
397. Athens T. 39. (?)†–J. Scr. 536.
398^a. Athens T.40.*Pal.***XIV.**†-J.S.537.
398^b. Athens T. 40. **X.***–J.
399^a. AthensT.41(ff.1-6,132-178.)**XIII.**
   [Scr.A.D.1311,Unc.(?)]Scr.538.
399^b. Athens T.41 (ff.7-131). *p.* **XIV.***
400. Athos, St.Dion.23. **VI.?** (G931.)
401. Athens T. 42. **1048.*** Scr. 541.
402. Athens T. 43. **1089.**† Scr. 542.
403. Athens T. 44. **XIV.*** Scr. 543.
404. Athens T. 45. **XII.***–J. Scr. 544.
405. Athens T. 46. **1274.**† Scr. 546.
406. Athens T. 47. *paper.* **XIV.***–J.
407. Athens T. 48. **XIII.*** Scr. 550.
408. Athens T. 49. **XII.**† Scr. 552.
409. Athens T. 50. **XI.*** Scr. 553.
410. Athens T. 51. **XIII.*** Scr. 556.
411. Athens T. 52. **XII.**† Scr. 560.
412. Athens T. 53. **XII.*** Scr. 561.
413. Athens T. 54. **XIV.**† Scr. 563.
414. AthensT.55. *Pal.* **XIV.*** Scr.564.
415. Athens T. 56. **XIV.*** Scr. 565.
416. Athens T.57. *pap.* **XV.**† Scr. 566.
417. AthensT.58.*pap.***1534.***Scr.567.
418. Athens T. 59. *pap.* **XV.*** Scr. 568.
419. Athens T. 60. *p.* **XVI.*** Scr. 569.
420. Ath. T. 61.*p.***XV.,XVI.***Scr.570.
421. Ath. T. 62. **XII.***S.571.(Apl188.)
422. A.T.63.*p.* **XIV.**†S.572.(Apl189.)
423. Athens T. 64. *p.* **1732.** (Apl190.)

424ᵃ. Athens Theol. 65 pp. 1–4. *frag.* **XII.** Scr. 574.
424ᵇ. Ath. Th. 65 pp. 5–8. *frag.* **XIII.**
424ᶜ. Ath. Th. 65 pp. 9–52. *frag.* **XIII.**
424ᵈ. At. T. 65 pp. 53–134. *frag.* **XIII.***
425. Athens Sakkelion 4. **X.*** *U.*
426. Ath. (3). **XII.** S. 804. (Apl191.)
427. Ath. (5). **XIII.†–J?** (Apl192.)
428. Athens (10). **XII.*** Scr. 829
429. Athens (12). **XII.***
430. Athens (13). **XII.†**
431. Ath. (13) [14 ?]. *p.* **XV., XVI.†**
432. Athens (15). **XII.***
433. Athens (17). **XII.***
434. Athens (18). **XII.***
435. Athens (19). **XIV.***
436. Athens (19) [?]. *paper.* **1545.†**
437. Athens (24). **XII.†**
438. Athens (25). **XIII.†** (v. page 29.)
439. Athens (66). **XIV.** (Apl193.)
440. Ath. (112). *p.* **1504.*** (Apl194.)
441. Athens. **XI.***
442. Athens. **XII.***
443. Athens (86). **XIII.** (Apl195.)
444ᵃ. Athens. *Palimp.* **X.** *U.*
444ᵇ. Athens. **XIV.**
445. Athens. *paper.* **XIV.***
446. Athens. **XII. or XIII.** (Apl196.)
447. Athens. **XI. or XII.†**
448. Athens. **XIII.***
449. Athens. **XII.***
450. Athens. τῆς βουλῆς. **XII.***
451. Athens (Bournias). **1052.***
452ᵃ. Athens (Bournias). **X.** *U.*
452ᵇ. Athens (Bournias). **XII.**
453. Athens (Varouccas). **XI.***
454. Dublin A.1.8: fol.1. **IX.** (cf.G63.)
455. Toledo armar 31, num. 31. **X.**
456. Corfu. Abp. Eustathius. **XIII.***
457. Corfu. Abp. Eust. *paper.* **XIV.***
458. Corfu. Abp. Eustathius. *p.* **XV.†**
459. Corfu. Elutherius Joh. filii. **XII.***
460. Corfu. Eluth. Johan. filii. **XII.†**
461. Corfu. Elu. Joh. filii. *p.* **1413.†**
462. Corfu. Aristides S. Varouccas. *p.* **XVII. or XVIII.†**
463. Grotta Ferrata *A'. a'.* 7. **XII.*–J.** Scr. 313.
464. Grot. Ferra. *A.'a'.* 9. **XII.†** S. 314.
465. Grot. Fer. *A'. a'.* 10. **XI.*** Scr. 315.

466. Grot. Fer. *A'. a'.* 11. *Palimp.* **XIV.*–J.** Scr. 316.
467. Grotta Ferrata *A'. a'.* 12. **X.** or **XI.*–J.** Scr. 317.
468. Grotta Fer. *A'. a'.* 13. partly *Palimp.* **XIV.** or **XV.** Scr. 318.
469. Grot. Fer. *A'. a'.* 14. **XII.** S. 319.
470. G. F. *A'. a'.* 15. **XI.** or **XII.** S. 320.
471. Grot. Fer. *A'. a'.* 16. **XI.** S. 321.
472ᵃ. Grot. Fer. *A'. δ'.* 11. **XI.** Scr. 330.
472ᵇ. Grot. Fer. *A'. δ'.* 11. **XII.** S. 330.
472ᶜ. Grot. Fer *A'. δ'.* 11. **XIII.** S. 330.
473. G. F. *A'. δ'.* 2. **X.** S. 323. (Apl197.)
474. Auck. N. Z. City Lib. **?** (v. G.1273.)
475. Grotta Ferrata *A'. δ'.* 4. *Palimp.* **XIII.** Scr. 325. (Apl198.)
476. Lon B.C. III. 44. *p.* **XV.** (Apl199.)
477. Lon. Lam. 1194. **XI.** S. 363. (Apl62.)
478. G. F. *A'. β'.* 2 S. 322. **XI.** (Apl102.)
479. Athos Sim. 148. *p.* **XVII.** (Apl147.)
480. G. F. *A'. δ'.* 16. *Palimp.* **X.** S. 331.
481. G. F. *A'. δ'.* 17. *Pal.* **X.** S. 332.
482. G. F. *A'. δ'.* 19. *Pal.* **X.** *U.* S. 333.
483. Grotta Ferrata, *A'. δ'.* 20 (or Δ δ 6 *frag.*³ *Pal.* **X.** or **XI.** S. 334.
484. Gr. Fe. *A'. δ'.* 21. *Pal.* **X.** S. 335.
485. Gr. Fe. *A'. δ'.* 22. *Pal.* **X.** S. 336.
486ᵃ ᵇ ᶜ ᵈ. Grotta Ferrata, *A' δ'.* 24, four frag. viz : (*a.*) frag. 1 (numb. also Z'. a'. 2). **XIII.—**(*b.*) fr. 2 (num. also β'. a'. 23.) *Palimp.* **VIII. or IX.** Unc.—(*c.*) frag. 4 (num. also Z'. a'. 24, formerly Z'. β'. 1.) = R. Paul.—(*d.*) frag. 9 (num. also Γ'. β'. 3.) *Pal.* **XI.**
487. G. F. Γ'. a'. 18. ἑωθ. pap. **XVII.** S. 338.
488. G. F. Γ'. β'. 2. **XI.** Scr. 339. (Apl201.)
489. G. F. Γ'. β'. 6. **XIII.** S. 341. (Apl202.)
490. G. F. Γ'. β'. 7. **IX.** or **X.** S. 342.
491. G. F. Γ'. β'. 8. **XIII.** *Pal.* S. 343.
492. G. F. Γ'. β'. 9. **XVI.** S. 344. (Apl203.)
493. Grot. Fer. Γ'. β'. 11. **XII.** S. 345.
494. G. F. Γ'. β'. 12. **XIV.** (Apl204.)
495. G. F. Γ'. β'. 13. **XIII.** S. 347. (Apl205.)
496. Grot. Fer. Γ'. β'. 14. **XIII.** S. 348
497. Grotta Ferrata, Γ'. β'. 15. **XI.– XIII.** Scr. 349. (Apl206.)
498. Grotta Ferrata, Γ'. β'. 17. *paper.* **1565.** Scr. 350. (Apl207.)

499. Paris Sup. Gr. 687. **XIII.** S. 422.
500. Grotta Ferrata, Γ′. β′. 19. *paper.*
　　XVI. Scr. 352. (Apl208.)
501. Grotta Ferrata, Γ′. β′. 23. *paper.*
　　1641. Scr. 353. (Apl209.)
502. Grotta Ferrata, Γ′. β′. 24. *paper.*
　　XVI. Scr. 354. (Apl210.)
503. G. F. Γ′. β′. 35. **XIII.** Scr. 355.
504. Grotta Ferrata, Γ′. β′. 38. *paper.*
　　XVII. Scr. 356. (Apl211.)
505. Grotta Ferrata, Γ′. β′. 42. *paper.*
　　XVI. Scr. 357. (Apl212.)
506. Grotta Ferrata, Δ′. β′. 22. *paper.*
　　XVIII. Scr. 358. (Apl213.)
507. Grotta Ferrata,Δ′.γ′.7. ἑωθ. **XIV.**
508. Grotta Ferrata, Δ′. γ′. 26. *paper.*
　　ἑωθινά. **XVIII.** Scr. 359.
509. Grot.Fer.Δ′.δ′.6 frag.3. *Pal.* **VIII.**
　　and **X.** S. 360. (cf. Evl483.)
510. Flor. Laur. Gad. 124. **XII.***
511. Flor. Ric. 69. *Palimp.* **IX.** Unc.
512. Messina University, 58. *paper.*
　　XV. or **XVI.*** Scr. 306.
513. Mes. Un. 65. **XII.†** Scr. 300.
514. Mes. Un. 66. **IX.†** *U.* Scr. 301.
515. Mes. Univ. 73. **XII.†** Scr. 305.
516. Mes. Un. 75. **XIII.*** Scr. 302.
517. Mes. Un. 94. **XII.*** Scr. 307.
518. Mes. Un. 95. **XIII.*** Scr. 311.
519. Mes. Un. 96. **XII.†** Scr. 303.
520. Mes. Un. 98. **1148.†** Scr. 304.
521. Mes. Un. 111. *Pal.* **XII.*** S. 308.
522. Mes. Un. 112. **XII.*** Scr. 309.
523. M.U.150. **XII.** S. 312(?)(Apl214.)
524. Mes. Univ. 175. **XII.*** Scr.4310.
525. Messina Univ. 175. **VIII.** or **IX.**
526. Pistoja, Fabronian Lib. **X.**
527. Rome, Angel. D. 2. 27 : (*a.*) fol. 4,
　　5, 6. **X.** Unc.—(*b.*) fol. 7. **X.**
　　Unc.—(*c.*) fol. 8. *mut.*
528. RomeBarb.III.22.*p.***XV.**(Apl215.)
529. RomeBar.III.129.**XIV.**(Apl216.)
530. Rome Bar.IV.1. *p.* **XV.** (Apl217.)
531. Rome Bar. IV. 13. **XI.** or **XII.**
532. Rome Bar. IV. 25. **XI.** (Apl218.)
533. Rome Bar.IV.28. **XII.** (Apl219.)
534. Rome Bar.IV 30. **XII.*** Scr.404.
535. R.B.IV.43. **XIII.** or **XIV.*** S.403.
536. R.B.IV.53. **XI.** or **XII.*** Scr.405.
537. R. B. VI. 18. **XII.†**–J. Scr.411.

538. Rom.Chis.R.VII.52. **X.** *U.* S.414.
539. Vatican Gr. 350. **XI.†**
540. Vat. Gr. 352. **XIII.*** Scr. 376.
541. Vat. Gr. 353. **IX.*** Scr. 377. *U.*
542. Vat. Gr. 355. **IX.*** Scr. 378. *U.*
543. Vat. Gr. 357. **IX.*** Scr. 379. *U.*
544. Vat. Gr. 362. **XI.*** Scr. 380.
545. Vat.Gr.540. *fragm.* **X.** Scr.381.
546. Vat. Gr. 781. **X.*** Scr. 382.
547. Vat. Gr. 1217. **XIII.***
548. Vat. G. 1228. *p.* **XIV.** (Apl220.)
549. Vat. G. 1534 B. **XIII.*** Scr. 383.
550. Vat. G. 1601. **XII.*** Scr. 384.
551. Vat. Gr. 1625. **XIII.†**
552. Vat. G. 1813. **XIV.** Scr. 385.
553. Vat.G.1886. **XIII.†**[–J?] S.386.
554. Vat. G. 1973.*Pal.***XIV.**(Apl221.)
555. Vat.G.1978. *pap.* **XV.** (Apl222.)
556. Vat.G.2012.**XV.**S.387.(Apl223.)
557. Vatican, 2051. *p.* **XV.** (Apl224.)
558. Vat. 2052. *p.* **1561.** (Apl225.)
559. Vat. 2061. *Palimp.* (*a.*) **VIII.** (*b.*),
　　VII. or **VIII.** *U.* (cf. unc. ⅂)
560. Vatican, 2100. **XIV.** Scr. 388.
561. Vatican, 2129. *p.* **XVI.** Scr. 389.
562. Vatican, 2138. **991.**
563. Vatican, 2144. **VIII.*** *U.* S. 390.
564. Vatican, 2167. **XIII.†.** Scr. 392.
565. Vat. 2251. **VIII.** (?) *U.* Scr. 393.
566. V. Ot. 444. fol. A. B. **IX.** *U.* S. 396.
567. Vat. Palat. 1.fol.A. **IX.** *U.* S.397.
568. Vat. Palat, 221. *pap.* **XV.** S. 398.
569. Vat. Palat. 239. *p.* **XVI.** S. 399.
570. Vat. Pius II. 33. **X.*** Scr. 188.
571. Vat.Reg.44. *pap.* **XVII.** Scr.394.
572. Vat. Reg. 49. *p.* **XIV.** (Apl226.)
573. V. R. 59. **XII.** S. 395. (Apl227.)
574. Syracuse Sem. 3. **1125.†** S. 362.
575. Syra. Sem. 4. *pap.* **XV.** (Apl228.)
576. Venice, St. Lazarus 1631. **XII.***
577. Athos Diony. 378. *paper.* **XVII.**
578. Edin. Univ. Laing. 9. **XI.†**
579. Athos S. Andrew Γ′. **XIII.***
580. Athos S. Andrew Δ′. **IX.*** [–J.]
581. Athos S. Andrew ϛ′. *pap.* **XVI.†**
582. Athos S. Andrew Ζ′. **XIV.***
583. Athos Batopedion, 48.
584. Athos Batopedion, 192.
585. Athos Batopedion, 193.
586. Athos Batopedion, 194.

587. Athos Batopedion, 195.
588. Athos Batopedion, 196.
589. Athos Batopedion, 197.
590. Athos Batopedion, 198.
591. Athos Batopedion, 200.
592. Athos Batopedion, 202.
593. Athos Batopedion, 204.
594. Athos Batopedion, 205.
595. Athos Batopedion, 208.
596. Athos Batopedion, 209.
597. Athos Batopedion, 220.
598. Athos Batopedion, 221.
599. Athos Batopedion, 223.
600. Athos Batopedion, 224.
601. Athos Batopedion (225).
602. Athos Batopedion (226).
603. Athos Batopedion (227).
604. Athos Batopedion, 228.
605. Athos Batopedion, 229.
606. Athos Batopedion, 230.
607. Athos Batopedion, 231.
608. Athos Batopedion, 232.
609. Athos Batopedion, 233.
610. Athos Batopedion, 234.
611. Athos Batopedion, 235.
612. Athos Batopedion, 236.
613. Athos Batopedion, 237.
614. Athos Batopedion, 238.
615. Athos Batopedion, 239.
616. Athos Batopedion, 240.
617. Athos Batopedion, 241.
618. Athos Batopedion, 242.
619. Athos Batopedion, 243.
620. Athos Batopedion, 253.
621. Athos Batopedion, 254.
622. Athos Batopedion, 255.
623. Athos Batopedion, 256.
624. Athos Batopedion, 257.
625. Athos Batopedion, 271.
626. Athos Batopedion, 291.
627. Athos S. Dion. 1. **VIII.**, **IX.*** *U.*
628. Athos S. Dionysios, 2. **XII.**
629. Athos S. Dionysios, 3. **XII.**
630. Athos S. Dionysios, 6. **XIII.**
631. Athos S. Dionysios, 11. **XIII.**
632. Athos S. Dionysios, 13. **XIII.**
633. Athos S. Dionysios, 14. **XI.**
634. Athos S. Dionysios, 15. **XII.**
635. Athos S. Dionysios, 16. **XII.**
636. Athos S. Dionysios, 17. **XII.**

637. Athos S. Dionysios, 18. **X.**
638. Athos S. Dionysios, 19. **XI.**
639. Athos S. Dionysios, 20. **XII.**
640. Athos S. Dionysios, 21. **IX.** *U.*
641. Athos S. Dionysios, 85. **XII.**
642. Ath. S. Dion. 163. (R167Apl170.)
643. Athos S. Dion. 302. *pap.* **1655.**
644. Athos S. Dion. 303. *pap.* **1559.**
645. Athos S. Dion. 304. *pap.* **XVII.**
646. Athos S. Dion. 305. *pap.* **XVII.**
647. Athos S. Dion. 306. *pap.* **XVII.**
648. Athos S. Dion. 307. *pap.* **XVII.**
649. Athos S. Dion. 308. *paper.* **XV.**
650. Athos S. Dion. 309. *pap.* **1395.**
651. Athos Docheiarios, 1. **XII.**
652. Athos Docheiarios, 10. **1247.**
653. Athos Docheiar. 13. **1276.** *U.*
654. Athos Docheiar. 14. **XII.**
655. Athos Docheiar. 15. **XIV.**
656. Athos Docheiar. 19. **XIII.**
657. Athos Docheiar. 23. **XIII.**
658. Athos Docheiar. 24. **XII.**
659. Athos Docheiar. 36. **XI.**
660. Athos Docheiar. 58. **XIV.**
661. Athos Docheiar. 137. *pap.* **XV.**
662. Athos Esphig. 19. **XI.**
663. Athos Esphig. 20. **XI.**
664. Athos Esphig. 21. **XII.**
665. Athos Esphig. 22. **XII.**
666. Athos Esphig. 23. **XI.**
667. Athos Esphig. 24. **XII.**
668. Athos Esphig. 27. *Pal.* **IX.** or **X.**
669. Athos Esphig. 28. **XIV.**
670. Athos Esphig. 35. **XIV.**
671. Athos Esphig. 60. **XIII.**
672. Athos Iber. 1. **IX.** or **X.*** *U.*
673. Athos Iber. 3. **XII.** or **XIII.**†
674. Athos Iber. 4. **XIV.***
675. Athos Iber. 6. **XII.**
676. Athos Iber. 20. **XIII.***
677. Athos Iber. 23. **1205.**
678. Athos Iber. 35. **XIV.***
679. Athos Iber. 36. **1201.***
680. Athos Iber. 39. **XIII.** (Apl229.)
681. Athos Iber. 635. *paper.* **XIV.**
682. Athos Iber. 637. **XIV.**
683. Athos Iber. 638. *paper.* **XV.**
684. Athos Iber.639.*p.***XV.**(Acts,322.)
685. Athos Iber. 640. *paper.* **XIV.**
686. Athos Iber.825. *p.* **XV.** (Apl230.)

687. Athos Iber.884. *p.* **XV.** (Apl231.)
688. Athos Carac. 3. **XIV.**
689. Athos Carac. 11. **IX.?** *U.*
690. Athos Carac. 15. **XIII.**
691. Athos Carac. 16. **XIII.**
692. Athos Carac. 17. **1232.**
693. At.Constam.6.*p.***1560.**(Apl232.)
694. Athos Constam. 98. **XIV.**
695. Athos Constam. 99. *Pal.* **XIV**
696. Athos Cutlum. 60. **1169.**
697. Athos Cutlum. 61. **XII.**
698. Athos Cutlum. 62. **XII.**
699. Athos Cutlum. 63. **XII.**
700. Athos Cutlum. 64. **XI.**
701. Athos Cutlum. 65. **XI.**
702. Athos Cutlumus. 66. **XI.**
703. Athos Cutlum. 86. **IX.** *U. Pal.*
704. Athos Cutlum. 90. **X.?** Unc.
705. Athos Cutlum. 279. *pap.* **XIV.**
706. Athos Cutlum. 280. *pap.* **XVI.**
707. Ath. Cut. 282. *p.* **XVI.** (Apl233.)
708. Athos Cut. 292. *paper.* **XVI.**
709. At. Cut. 356. *p.* **XVII.** (Apl234.)
710. Athos Xenophon. 1. **XII.**
711. Athos Xenophon. 58. *p.* **XVI.**
712. Athos X.59.$\dot{\epsilon}\omega\theta.p.$**XVI.**(Apl235.)
713ᵃ. Athos Xeno. 68.$\dot{\epsilon}\omega\theta.$ *p.* **XVIII.**
713ᵇ. Athos Gregorius,71.$\dot{\epsilon}\omega\theta.p.$**XVII.**
714. Athos Xeropotamos, 110. **XIII.**
715. Athos Xeropotamos, 112. **XII.**
716. Athos Xerop.118.*p.* **XIII.,XIV.**
717. Athos Xeropotam. 122.*p.* **1560.**
718. Athos Xeropotam. 125. *p.* **1654.**
719. Athos Xeropotam. 126. *p.* **1586.**
720. Athos Xeropotam. 234. **IX.** *U.*
721. A. X.247.$\dot{\epsilon}\omega\theta.p.$ **XVII.** (Apl236.)
722. Athos Pantel. L. **X.** Unc.
723. Athos Pantel. IV.6.4. **XIV.**
724. Athos Pantel. IX.5.3. **XI.†**
725. Athos P.XXVII.6.2. **XII.,XIII.**
726. Athos Pantel. XXVII. 6. 3. **XI.†**
727. Ath.P.XXVIII.1.1. **XIII.,XIV.***
728. Athos Παυλος, 1. **XIII.**
729. Athos Protat. 11. **XII.**
730. Athos Prot.14.**IX.**(?)(Lamb.VII.)
731. Athos Protat. 15. **XI.**
732. Athos Protat. 44. *paper.* **XIV.**
733. Athos Prot.56. **IX.** (Lamb.VII.)
734. Athos Simopetra, 17. **XIV.**
735. Ath.Simop.19. **XII.** (Lamb.XIV.)

736. Athos Simopetra, 20. **XII.**
737. Athos Simopetra, 21. **XII.**
738. Athos Simopetra, 24. **XI.**
739. Athos Simopetra, 27. **XIII.**
740. Athos Simopetra, 28. **XIV.**
741. Athos Sim. 30. **XIII.** (Apl237.)
742. Athos Simopetra, 33. **XII.**
743. At. Sim. 70. *p.* **XIV.** and **XVII.** (Apl238.)
744. Athos Stauroniceta, 1. **XII.**
745. Athos Stauroniceta, 27. **XIII.**
746. Athos Stauroniceta, 42. **XIV.**
747. Athos Stauron, 102. *p.* **1319.**
748. Athos Philotheus, 1. **XII.**
749. Athos Philotheus, 2. **VIII.** (?)
750. Athos Philoth. 3. **XIII.**
751. Athos Philoth. 6. **XI.** (Apl239.)
752. Athos Philoth. 18. **XII.**
753. Athos Philoth. 25. **XIV.**
754. Athos Philoth.61. *paper.* **1583.**
755. Ath.Philo.213. *p.* **XVI.** (Apl240.)
756. Athos Chilian. 6. **XIII.**
757. Athos Chilian.15.*p.***XV.**(Apl241.)
758. Berat. (in ch.). **XI.** or **XII.**
759. Cairo Pat. Al. Coxe, 18. *paper.* **XV.** (Apl242.)
760. Cairo Pat.Al.C.927. **XIV.**or**XV.**
761. Cairo Pat. Al. Coxe, 929. **1338.**
762. Cairo Pat. Al. Coxe, 943. **XIII.**
763. Cairo Pat. Al. Coxe, 944. **XIV.**
764. Cairo Pat.Al.C.945. **XI.**or**XII.**
765. Cairo Pat. Al. Coxe, 946. **XII.**
766. Cairo Pat. Al. Coxe, 948. **XI.**
767. Cairo Pat. Al. Coxe, 950. **XII.**
768. Cairo Pat. Al. Coxe, 951. **XI.**
769. Cairo Pat. Al. C. 953. **XI.**or**XII.**
770. Chalcis [Chalké] (Trin. Mon.), 1.
771. Chalcis (Trin. Mon.), 2.
772. Chalcis (Trin. Mon.), 3.
773. Chalcis (Trin. Mon.), 4.
774. Chalcis (Trin. Mon.), 5.
775. Chalcis (Trin. Mon.), 6.
776. Chalcis (Trin. Mon.), 7.
777. Chalcis (Trin. Mon.), 8.
778. Chalcis (Trin. Mon.), 9.
779. Chalcis (Trin. Mon.), 10.
780. Chalcis (sch.), 1.
781. Chalcis (sch.), 2.
782. Chalcis (sch.), 3.
783. Chalcis (sch.), 4.

784. Chalcis (sch.), 5.
785. Chalcis (sch.), 6.
786. Chalcis (sch.), 7.
787. Chalcis (sch.), 12. **XII.**
788. Chalcis (sch.), 74 (75?). **XIV.**
789. Chalcis (sch.), 84. *paper.* **1338.**
790. Constant'ple.(ch.St.Geo.). **XIII.***
791. Const.(ch.St.Geo.). **XIII., XIV.**†
792. Constant. Ἅγιος τάφος. **XIII.**†
793. Constant. Ἅγιος τάφος. **XII.***
794. Constant. Ἅγιος τάφος, 426. **XII.** or **XIII.**†
795. Constant. Ἅγιος τάφος, 432. **XIII.** or **XIV.**†
796. Const. Gr. Phil. Soc. 48. *p.* **XV.***
797. Jerus.col.H.Cross,6.**XI.**(Apl243.)
798. Lesbos, mon. Λείμ. 1. **X.***
799. Lesbos Λείμ. 37. **X.** or **XI.**
800. Lesbos Λείμ. 38. **XI.**
801. Lesbos Λείμ. 40. *paper.* **XIV.**
802. Les. Λείμ. 41. *p.* **XII.** or **XIII.**
803. Lesbos Λείμ. 66. **XII.** or **XIII.**
804. Island of Milo. **XII.** Scr. 412.
805. Patmos, 68. **IX.**
806. Patmos, 69. **IX.**
807. Patmos, 70. **IX.**
808. Patmos, 71. **IX.**
809. Patmos, 72. **XII.**
810. Patmos, 73. **XII.**
811. Patmos, 74. **XII.**
812. Patmos, 75. **XII.**
813. Patmos, 77. **1069.**
814. Patmos, 78. **XII.**
815. Patmos, 79. **XI.**
816. Patmos, 85. **XI.**
817. Patmos, 86. **XI.**
818. Patmos, 87. **XIII.**
819. Patmos, 88. **XIII.**
820. Patmos, 89. **XIII.**
821. Patmos, 91. **XIII.**
822. Patmos, 93. **1205.**
823. Patmos, 99. **XI.**
824. Patmos, 101. **XIV.**
825. Patmos, 330. *paper.* **1427.**
826. Patmos, 331. *paper.* **XV.**
827. Patmos, 332. *paper.* **1444.**
828. S. Saba, Coxe, 40. **XII.**
829. S. Saba [Tower] Coxe. 16. **XII.** (Apl244.)
830. Saloniki Gym. Α΄. **IX.** or **X.*** *U.*

831. Saloniki Β΄. *paper.* **XIV.**†
832. Saloniki Γ΄. *p.* **XV.** or **XVI.**†
833. Saloniki Δ΄. **XIV.** or **XV.**†
834. Saloniki Ε΄. **XII.** or **XIII.***
835. Saloniki Ζ΄. **1072.**
836. Saloniki Θ΄. *p.* [1340? **XVI.**?]
837. Saloniki ΙΔ΄. *p.* **XV.** (Apl245)
838. Saloniki Μ. Σπυρίου. **1186.**†
839. Sinai, 205.
840. Sinai, 206.
841. Sinai, 207.
842. Sinai, 208.
843. Sinai, 209.
844. Sinai, 210. **X.** (?) *U.*
845. Sinai, 211. **IX.** *U.*
846. Sinai, 212.
847. Sinai, 213. **967.** *U.*
848. Sinai, 214. **XI.** *U.*
849. Sinai, 215. **X.** *U.*
850. Sinai, 216. **XII.**
851. Sinai, 217. **XI.**
852. Sinai, 218. **XI.**
853. Sinai, 219. **XI.**
854. Sinai, 220. **1167.**
855. Sinai, 221. **XII.**
856. Sinai, 222. **XI.**
857. Sinai, 223. **1039.**
858. Sinai, 224. **XI.**
859. Sinai, 225. **XI.** or **XII.**
860. Sinai, 226. **XII.**
861. Sinai, 227. **XI.**
862. Sinai, 228. **XV.**
863. Sinai, 229. **XI.**
864. Sinai, 230. **XI.**
865. Sinai, 231. **1033.**
866. Sinai, 232. **1174.**
867. Sinai, 233. **XII.**
868. Sinai, 234. **1119.**
869. Sinai, 235. **XI.** or **XII.**
870. Sinai, 236. **XI.**
871. Sinai, 237. **XI.**
872. Sinai, 238. **XI.**
873. Sinai, 239. **1373.**
874. Sinai, 240. **XV.** or **XVI.**
875. Sinai, 241. **XI.**
876. Sinai, 242. **XI.** or **XII.**
877. Sinai, 243. **XI.**
878. Sinai, 244.
879. Sinai, 245.
880. Sinai, 246.

881. Sinai, 247.
882. Sinai, 248.
883. Sinai, 249.
884. Sinai, 250.
885. Sinai, 251. *paper.* **XIV.**
886. Sinai, 252. *paper.* **XVI.**
887. Sinai, 253. *paper.* **XIV.**
888. Sinai, 254. *paper.* **XIV.**
889. Sinai, 255. **pap. XIII.** or **XIV.**
890. Sinai, 256. **1420.**
891. Sinai, 257. **XIV.** (?)
892. Sinai, 258. *paper.* **XV.**
893. Si.271.*p.***XV.** or **XVI.** (Apl246.)
894. Sinai, 272. *p.* **XV.** (?) (Apl260.)
895. Sinai, 273. (Apl261.)
896. Sinai, 550. **XIII.**
897. Sinai, 659. *paper.* **XV.**
898. Sinai, 720. *paper.* **XVII.**
899. Sinai, 738. **XIV.**
900. Sinai,748.*p.***XV.,XVI.** (Apl247)
901. Sinai, 754. partly *paper.* **1177.**
902. Sinai, 756. **1205.**
903. Sinai, 775. **XIII.**
904. Sinai, 796. **XIII.**
905. Sinai, 797. **XV.**
906. Sinai, 800. *paper.* **XIV.** or **XV.**
907. Sinai, 929. *Palimp.* **IX.** or **X.**
908. Sinai, 943. *p.* **1697.** (Apl248.)
909. Sinai, 957. **X.**
910. Sinai, 960. *Pal.* **XIII.** or **XIV.**
911. Sinai, 961. **XIII.** (Apl249.)
912. Sinai, 962. **XI.** or **XII.**
913. Sinai, 965. **XIV.**
914. Sinai, 968. **1426.**
915. Sinai,972. *paper.* **XV.** (Apl250.)
916. Sinai,973. *pap.* **1153.** (Apl251.)
917. Sinai, 977. *paper.* **XV.** (Apl252.)
918. Sinai,981.*paper.***XIV.**and**XVI.**
919. Sinai, 982. *paper.* **XIV.**
920. Sinai, 986. *paper.* **XV.**
921. Sinai, 1042. *paper.* **XIV.**
922. Oxf. Bodl. Clark, 9. (A58P224.)

923. Frankfort-on-the-Oder. (A42P48R13Apl56.)
924. Vat. Reg. 54. **XIII.** (Apl253.)
925. Venice, II. 188. *paper.* **XVII.**
926. B. M. Add. 10068. **XII.?**
927. B. M. Add. 24378. **XIV.** Scr. 275. (Apl185.)
928. Paris Sup. 179. 180. *pap.* **XIII.**
929. New York, Union Th. Sem. **XIII.** [v. Table XI.] (Apl254.)
930. B. M. Add. 19459. **XIII.†**
931. Venice,II.130. *pap.* **XV.**or**XVI.** (Apl126.)
932. Lond.H.B–C.I.1.**XIII.**Scr.G.612.
933. Rome,Vall.C.7. **1292.** Scr.G.733.
934. [5 Pe.] St.Pet'g.Mur.64 (IX.1). **994.**
935. Paris,13. **XII.**or**XIII.** (Apl256.)
936. Paris, 263. **XIII.** Scr. 428. (Apl257.)
937. Vienna.*p.***XIII.**or**XIV.**(Apl266.)
938. Athos Chilian.ch.Treas.105. **XII.**
939. Brit. Mus. Add. 34059. (?)
940. Brit. Mus. Egerton, 2743. **XIII.**
941. Brit. Mus. Egerton, 2745. **XIV.**
942. Const'le, "Old Serai," 21. **XII.**
943. Paris(?)Fr.V.Scheil.*p'yrus.***VI.** *U.*
944. Strasb'g Un. L.1.**X.,XI.**,&**XIII.***
944ᵃ.Strasb'g Un. L. 7. *init.* **XIV.**
945. Berlin,4ᵗᵒ,17. *pap.* **XV.**or**XVI.** (Apl268.)
946. Berlin, Fol. 29. *paper.* **X.** *U.*
946ᵃ.Berlin, Fol. 45. **XII.**
947. Castelli Chattorum city lib. **XII.***
948. Leipsic Un.Acc.1892.4110.**XVII.**
949. ⎰ Upsal Univ. (2 copies, bought
950. ⎱   at Pergamos, in Asia, 1890.)
951. Madison, N. J., Drew Theol. Sem. **XI.** or **XII.** (v. Table XI.)
952. Madison, N. J., Drew Theol. Sem. **1148.** (v. Table XI.)
953. Constant. (A. L. Long). ἑωθινά. *p.* **XIV.** (v.Tab.XI.DrewS. MSS.)

Miller (Scrivener 4th ed.) also catalogues the following MSS. of *The Evangelium*, which appear to be additional to the above-mentioned. The numbers, as well as dates, are Miller's.

[329.] St. Saba 44 [xii], 4ᵗᵒ, Coxe.
[361.] St. Saba Tower, lib 12 [xi], 4ᵗᵒ, Coxe.
[365.] St. Saba Tower, 52 [xii], 4ᵗᵒ, *mus.* Coxe.
[391.] Patmos, 4 [xi], 4ᵗᵒ, Unc. Coxe.
[400.] Patmos, 10 [xi], Unc. Coxe.

[401.] Patmos, 22 [xi], fol. Unc. Coxe.

[402.] Patmos, 81 [viii], Unc. Coxe.

[413.] Constantinople, Patriarch of Jerusalem, 10 [xii], 4to., a *palimpsest*, written over a geometrical treatise.

[488.] Cambridge, Clare College [xiv], ff. 163 (21), *mut.* at end.   Brought from Constantinople, and presented by Mr. J. Rendel Harris, Fellow of the College.

[498.] (Apost. 288), Jerus. Patr. Libr. 105 [A.D. 1762, May 11], ff. 228 *pict. vers.* Written by Athanasius ἱερεὺς Σαρασίτος (Kerameus).

[923.] Jerus. Patriarchal Library, 33 [xi], ff. 335 (221–252=32) [xiii.] *mus.*, *rubr.*, *syn.*, *orn.* (Kerameus.)

[927.] Jerus. Patr. Lib. 161 [xvii], *chart.*, collections of bits of Evst. (Kerameus.)

[928.] Jerus. Patr. Lib. 526 [A.D. 1502], ff. 108, 2 cols. *syn.*, with many directions. (Kerameus.)

[932.] Jerus. Patr. Lib. 530, *chart.*   Turkish in Greek letters. (Kerameus.)

[934.] St. Saba, 55 [xii], 4to. Coxe.

[935.] Quaritch, 8 [about A.D. 1200], ff. 346 (26), 2 cols., *mut.*, letters in red, green, blue, yellow, bound in red morocco case. (Catalogue, Dec. 1893.)

[936.] Lesb. τ. Λείμ.μον. 100.   Ἀποστολοευαγγέλια in the midst of the four Liturgies and other matters. (Kerameus.)

[937.] Lesb. τ. Λείμ.μον. 146 [A.D. 1562–66].   Begins with St. Matt. (Kerameus.)

[938.] Lesb. ἐν μονῇ Ἁγίου Ἰωάννου τοῦ Θεολόγου 11 [xii], ff. 157 (2, 5, and 6 being *chart.* ; one is of the XIth century). (Keramus.)

[939.] Lesb. Ἁγ. Ἰωάνν. 12, ff. 110. (Kerameus.)

[940.] Lesb. Benjamin Library at Potamos ΛΛ [A.D. 1565], ff. 378. (Kerameus.)

[942.] Athos. Constam. 100.

[943.] Athens Nat. Libr. 60 [ix], ff. 87. Unc. *mus.*

[944.] Athens Nat. Libr. 78 [x], ff. 143.   *Palimpsest* under XVth century writing. *mus.*

[945.] Ath. Nat. Libr. 83 [xv], ff. 324, *chart.*, *mut.* at end.

[946.] Ath. Nat. Libr. 97 [xii], ff. 136, *mut.* at beg. and end, *mus.*

[947.] (Apost. 227.) Ath. Nat Libr. 126 [A.D. 1504], ff. 276.   Written by Euthymius.

[948.] Ath. Nat. Libr. 143 [A.D. 1522], ff. 242.   A few leaves wanting at beginning.

[949.] Ath. Nat. Libr. 147 [xii beg.], ff. 255—first eight injured. *mus.*

[950.] Ath. Nat. Libr. 148 [xv end], ff. 104, *mut.* at beginning and end.

To this list Mr. Miller (Scr.) adds an enumeration of "thirteen MSS. in the National Library at Athens, containing portions of Apostoloeuaggelia;" to which he assigns numbers from 951–963 inclusive.   The Athens Lib. numbers are 668, 685, 700, 707, 750, 757, 759, 760, 766, 769, 784, 786, and 795.

LECTIONARIES: (2) THE APOSTOLOS

In this table the asterisk [*] signifies that the lectionary contains daily readings (ἐβδ) of the Acts and Epistles from Easter to Pentecost, and Saturday and Sunday readings (σαβ. κυὲρ.) for the rest of the year. The obelisk [†] signifies daily readings (ἐβδ) throughout the year.

1. Leyden Un. Scaliger 243. (Evl6.)
2. B. M. Cot. Vespas. B. XVIII. **XI.***
3. *Missing.*
4. Flor. Laur. 24. **XI.** (Evl112.)
5. Gottingen Univ. Theol. 54. **XV.**
6. B. M. Harl. 5731. (G. 117.)
7. Rome Coll. Propag. (Evl37.)
8. Copenhagen, 1324. **XII.** (Evl44.)
9. Paris Sup. 32. (Evl84.)
10. Paris Sup. 33. (Evl85.)
11. Paris Sup. 104. **XIII.***
12. Paris Nat. 375. (Evl60.)
13. Moscow Syn. 4. **IX. or X.**
14. Moscow Syn. 291. **XI. or XII.**
15. Moscow Typ. 31. **1116.**
16. Moscow Syn. 266. (Evl52.)
17. Moscow Syn. 267. (Evl53
18. Moscow Syn. 268. (Evl54.)
19. Moscow Typ. Syn. 47. (Evl55.)
20. Moscow Typ. Syn. 9. (Evl56.)
21. Paris, 294. (Evl83.)
22. Paris, 304. **XIV.**
23. Paris, 306. **XII.**
24. Paris, 308. **XIII.**
25. Paris, 319. **XII.**
26. Paris, 320. **XII.†**
27. Paris, 321. **XIV.**
28. Ox. Bo. Seld. S. 2. **XIII.** (Evl26.)
29. Paris, 330. (Evl94.)
30. Paris, 373. **XIV.***
31. Paris, 276. (Evl82.)
32. Paris, 376. (G324Evl97.)
33. Paris, 382. ff. 1–10. *paper.* **X.†**
34. Paris, 383. *paper.* **XVI.†**
35. Paris, 324. (Evl92.)
36. Paris, 326. (Evl93.)
37. *Vacat.*
38. Vatican Gr. 1528. *paper.* **XV.†**
39. Vatican Ottob. Gr. 416. (Evl133).
40. Rome, Barberini, 18. *Palimp.* **X.**
41. Rome, Barberini, (?) **XI.**
42. Rome, Vallicell. C. 46. *pap.* **XVI.**
43. *Vacat.* (?)
44. Glas. Hunt. Mus. V.4.3. (Evl241.)
45. Glasgow, Hunt. Mus. V.3.4. **XII.**

46. Milan. Ambros. C. 63 Sup. **XIV.**
47. Milan. Amb. D. 72 Sup. (Evl104.)
48. *Vacat.*
49. S. Saba, 16. *paper.* **XIV.**
50. S. Saba, 18. **XV.**
51. S. Saba, 26. **XIV.**
52. S. Saba. (Evl171)
53. S. Saba, 4. (Evl160.)
54. S. Saba. **XV.**
55. Treves Cath. **X.** (Evl179.)
56. F-on-the-Od. (A42P48R13Evl923).
57. *Vacat*
58. Oxf. C. C. Wake, 33. **1172.** (?)†
59. Camb. Ch. Coll. 13, 4, 6. (Evl185.)
60. Lond. Lamb. 1190. **XI.†** Scr. 57.
61. Lo. La. 1191. **XIII.*** Scr. 59.
62. Lond. Lamb, 1194. S. 60. (Evl477.)
63. Lond. Lamb. 1195. *p.* **XV.** Scr. 61.
64. Lond. Lamb. 1196. **XII.*** Scr. 62.
65. B. M. Add. 32051. **XIII.*** Scr. 52.
66. Lond. H. B–C. I.10..S.64. (Evl216.)
67. Lon. H.B–C. III.29. S. 66. (Evl223.)
68. Lond. H. B–C. III.24. **XIV.†** S. 65.
69. St. Pet. Mur. 44. S. 178. (Evl249.)
70ᵃ· St. Pet. Mur. 38. *Pal.* **IX.** Scr. 72.
70ᵇ· St. Pet. Muralt. 49. **IX.** Scr. 172.
71. St. Pet. Mur. 40a. *Pal.* **XI.** S. 173.
72. St. Pet. Muralt. 45a. **XIII.** S. 183.
73ᵖᵉ· St. P. Mu. 57. VIII.80. **IX. or X.**
74. St. P. Mur. 110. *Pal.* **XIII.** S. 197.
75. Camb. U. S. A. Harv. Lib. A. R. g3.10. **XII.** Scr. 70. v. Tab. XI.
76. New York, Astor Lib. **XIII.** (?) v. Table XI.
77. Camb. Univ. Lib. 679. 1. **XII.†** Scr. 79.
78. Lond. B–C. III.44. (Evl476.)
79. B. M. Add. 11841. **XI.** Scr. 75.
80. Leipsic Univ. Lib. Tisch. VI. f. **IX. or X.** Scr. 71. *U.*
81. B. M. Add. 29714. **1306.** Scr. 69.
82. Dresden A. 104. S. 77. (A98P113.)
83. Oxf. Bodl. Misc. 319. **XIII.** Scr. 76.
84. Oxf. Bodl. Arch. Seld. Sup. 9. **IX.** *Pal.* Scr. 74. *U.*

85. Vienna Theol. 308. **XI.***
86. Besancon City Lib. 41. **XII.***
87ᵃ. Paris, 922 fol. A. **XIV.** S. 201.
87ᵇ. Paris S. Gr. 804. *p.* **XV.** S. 202.
88. Paris, 800. *p.* **XIV.** Scr. 130.
89. Modena, Est. II.D.3. *p.* **XV.** S.50.
90. Wisbeck. S. 203. (G713.) *U. Pal.*
91. Athens, 68. **XII., XIII.**† S. 204.
92. Athens, 69. *p.* **1485.**† S. 205.
93. Athens (35). *p.* **XV.** or **XVI.**†
94. Athens (63). **XI.** or **XII.**†
95. Athens (65). **XI.**† Scr. 208.
96. Athens (95). *p.* **1576.**† S. 209.
97. Athens. **XII.** or **XIII.** Scr. 210.
98. Athens. *p.* **XV., XVI.**† S. 211.
99. Athens. *p.* **XV., XVI.*** S. 212.
100. Esc. χ. IV. 9. *p.* **XIV.** S. 214.
101. Escurial. ψ. III.9. **XIII.** S. 213.
102. Gr. Fer. Aʹ. βʹ. 2. S. 90. (Evl478.)
103. Gr. Fer. Aʹ. βʹ. 4. **X.*** Scr. 83.
104. Grotta Fer. Aʹ. βʹ.ʹ 5. **XI.**† S. 84.
105. Grotta Fer. Aʹ. βʹ. 7. **XI.*** S. 85.
106. Gr. Fer. Aʹ. βʹ. 8. **XIV.** (?)* S. 86.
107. Gr. Fer. Aʹ. βʹ. 9. **XII.*** Scr. 87.
108. Gr. Fer. Aʹ. βʹ. 10. **XIII.** Scr. 88.
109. Gr. Fer. Aʹ. βʹ. 11. **XI.**† Scr. 89.
110. Grotta Ferrata, Aʹ. δʹ. 24. No. 3.
    (Also Γʹ βʹ 21.) *Pal.* **X.** S. 263.
111. Fl. La. Mark. 704. **XII.** S. 223.
112. Milan Amb. C.16 inf. **XIII.** S.81.
113. Messina 93. **XII.** or **XIII.**† S. 82.
114. Rome B. IV.11. *p.* **1556.*** S.125.
115. Rome Barb. IV.60. **XII.**† S. 126.
116. Rome Barb. IV.84. **XII.**† S. 127.
117. Sinai, 295. *p.* **XV.** Scr. 213.
118. Vatican, 368. **XIII.*** Scr. 116.
119. Vatican, 369. *paper.* **XIV.**
120. Vatican, 2068. **XII.**†
121. Vatican, 2116. **XIII.*** Scr. 119.
122. Vat. Pal. 241. *pap.* **XV.***
123. Vat. Reg. 11. **XII.**† Scr. 120.
124. Venice, II.115. **XI.** or **XII.**†
125. Venice, II.128. *p.* **XIV.**† S. 114.
126. Venice, II.130. (Evl931.) S. 115.
127. Athos Dion. 386.*p.***1542.** S. 169.
128. Athos Dion. 387. *p.* **XVII.**
129. Athos Dion. 392. *p.* **XVI.**
130. Athos Doch. 17. **XII.** Scr. 186.
131. Athos Doch. 20. **XIV.**
132. Athos Doch. 27. **XIII.**

133. Athos Doch. 141. *p.* **XVII.**
134. Athos Doch. 146. *p.* **1524.**
135. Athos Iber. 831. *p.* **XV.**
136. Athos Caraca. 10. **XI.**
137. Athos Caraca. 156. *p.* **XV.**
138. Athos Constam. 21. *p.* **XVII.**
139. Athos Constam. 22. *p.* **XIV.**
140. Athos Constam. 23. *p.* **XV.**
141. Athos Cutlum. 277. *p.* **XVI.**
142. Athos Cutlum. 354. *p.* **XV.**
143. Athos Cutlum. 355. *p.* **XVII.**
144. Athos Protat. 54. *p.* **XIV.**
145. Athos Simopet. 6. **1305.**
146. Athos Simopet. 10. **XII.**
147. Athos Simopet. 148. (Evl479.)
148. Athos Simop. 149. *pap.* **XVII.**
149. Athos Simop. 150. *paper.* **XVI.**
150. Athos Simop. 151. *paper.* **XVI.**
151. Athos Stauron. 129. *pap.* **1554.**
152. Athos Philoth. 17. **XII.**
153. Berat. Abp. **XIII.**
154. Chalcis S. Trin. Mon. 13.
155. Chalcis Trin. Mon. 14.
156. Chalcis Trin. Mon. 15.
157. Chalcis Sch. 59. **XIII.** or **XIV.**
158. Chalcis Sch. 74. **XII.** or **XIII.**
159. Chalcis Sch. 88. *paper.* **1564.**
160. Patmos S. John, 11. **XI.**
161. Patmos S. John, 12. (R178.)
162. Saloniki Gym. 8. *p.* **XVI.**†
163. Saloniki Gym. 10. **XI.** (R184.)†
164. Saloniki Gym 13. *pap.* **1474.**†
165. Sinai, 296. *paper.* **1454.**
166. Sinai, 297. *paper.* **1510.**
167. Sinai, 298. *paper.* **1551.**
168. Sinai, 299. *paper.* **XVI.**
169. Gro. Fer. Γʹ. βʹ. 18. **XIV.** S. 105.
170. Athos Dion. 163. (R167Evl642.)
171. Grotta Ferrata Aʹ. δʹ 5. **1072.**
172. Grotta Ferrata, Aʹ. δʹ. 6. **XIII.**
173. Grotta Ferrata, Aʹ. δʹ. 9. **XII.**
174. Sinai, 294. *paper.* **XIV.**
175. B. M. Add. 11840. (Evl189.)
176. Lond. High. B–C. I.8. (Evl215.)
177. Glasg. Hunt. Mus.V.4.3. (Evl241.)
178. *Vacat.* (see Scr. 178.)
179. St. Pet. Muralt. 55. (Evl250.)
180. St. Pet. Muralt. 90. (Evl256.)
181. Milan, Amb. D.108Sup. (Evl287.)
182. Milan, Amb. D.274Sup. (Evl290.)

183. Camb. Un. Add. 1836. (Evl306.)
184. Lond. B–C. III.42. S. 67. (Evl315.)
185. Lond. B.M. Add. 24378. (Evl927.)
186. B. M. Harl. 5561. S, 53. (Evl346.)
187. Paris Sup. 805. (Evl370.)
188. Athens Theol. 62. (Evl421.)
189. Athens Theol. 63. (Evl422.)
190. Athens Theol. 64. (Evl423.)
191. Athens (3). (Evl426.)
192. Athens (5). (Evl427.)
193. Athens (66). (Evl439.)
194. Athens (112). (Evl440.)
195. Athens (86). (Evl443.)
196. Athens. (Evl446.)
197. Gro. Fer. Α'.δ'. 2. S. 91. (Evl473.)
198. G. F. Α'. δ'. 4. Scr. 92. (Evl475.)
199. Lond. B–C. III.44. (Evl476.)
200. Gr. Fer. Α'. δ'. 24. (9). (Evl486d.)
201. Grotta Fer. Γ'. β'. 2. (Evl488.)
202. Grotta Fer. Γ'. β'. 6. (Evl489.)
203. Grotta Fer. Γ'. β'. 9. (Evl492.)
204. Grotta Fer. Γ'. β'. 12. (Evl494.)
205. Grotta Fer. Γ'. β'. 13. (Evl495.)
206. Grotta Fer. Γ'. β'. 15. (Evl497.)
207. Grotta Fer. Γ'. β'. 17. (Evl498.)
208. Grotta Fer. Γ'. β'. 19. (Evl500.)
209. Grotta Fer. Γ'. β'. 23. (Evl501.)
210. Grotta Fer. Γ'. β'. 24. (Evl502.)
211. Grotta Fer. Γ'. β'. 38. (Evl504.)
212. Grotta Fer. Γ'. β'. 42. (Evl505.)
213. Grotta Fer. Δ'. β'. 22. (Evl506.)
214. Messina Univ. 170. (Evl523.)
215. Rome, Barb. III.22. (Evl528.)
216. Rome, Barb. III.129. (Evl529.)
217. Rome, Barb. IV.1. (Evl530.)
218. Rome, Barb. IV.25. (Evl532.)
219. Rome, Barb. IV.28. (Evl533)
220. Vatican, 1228. (Evl548.)
221. Vatican, 1973. (Evl554.)
222. Vatican, 1978. (Evl555.)
223. Vatican, 2012. (Evl556.)
224. Vatican, 2051. (Evl557.)
225. Vatican, 2052. (Evl558.)

226. Vat. Reg. 49. (Evl572.)
227. Vat. Reg. 59. (Evl573.)
228. Syrac. Sem. 4. (Evl575.) Scr. 113.
229. Athos Iber. 39. (Evl680.)
230. Athos Iber. 825. (Evl686.)
231. Athos Iber. 884. (Evl687.)
232. Athos Constam. 6. (Evl693.)
233. Athos Cutlum. 282. (Evl707.)
234. Athos Cutlum. 356. (Evl709.)
235. Athos Zenoph. 59. (Evl712.)
236. Athos Xeropot. 247 (Evl721.)
237. Athos Simopet. 30. (Evl741.)
238. Athos Simopet. 70. (Evl743.)
239. Athos Philoth. 6. (Evl751.)
240. Athos Philoth. 213. (Evl755.)
241. Athos Chilian. 15. (Evl757.)
242. Cairo Pat. Al. Coxe. 18. (Evl759.)
243. Jerus. H. Cross. 6. (Evl797.)
244. S. Saba Tower, 16. (Evl829.)
245. Saloniki Gym. ΙΔ'. (Evl837)
246. Sinai. 271. (Evl893.)
247. Sinai. 748. (Evl900.)
248. Sinai. 943. (Evl908.)
249. Sinai. 961. (Evl911.)
250. Sinai. 972. (Evl915.)
251. Sinai. 973. (Evl916.)
252. Sinai. 974. (Evl917.)
253. Vat. Reg. 54. (Evl924.)
254. N. Y. Union Th. Sem. (Evl929.)
255. Vat. Reg. Gr. 70. **1544.** S. 122.
256. Paris, 13. Scr. 128. (Evl935.)
257. Paris, 263. (Evl936.)
258. B. M. Add. 22744. (Evl324.)
259. Athens Theol. 25. (Evl383.)
260. Sinai. 272. (Evl894.)
261. Sinai. 273. (Evl895.)
262. Paris Sup. 115. S. 129. (Evl196.)
263. Lon. B–C. III.53. S. 68. (Evl228.)
264. Vatican, 774. S. 117. (G860.)
265. Ox. Bod. Crom. 11. (Evl30.)
266. Theodore Graf. (Evl937.)
267. Athos Philoth. 25. (Evl753.)
268. Berlin Roy. Lib. 4to 17. (Evl945.)

Miller (Scr. 4th ed.) adds the following :

[227.] Lesbos τ. Λείμονος μονῆς 55, Act., Paul., Cath., Apoc., syn., men., proll., mus., rubr. (Kerameus.)

[228.] Lesbos, τ. Λείμ. μον. 137 [xv], chart. (Kerameus.)

[255.] Andros, Μονὴ Ἁγία 2, ff. 140. Injured, but well written. (Ἀντ. Μηλιαράκης.)

[256.] Andros, Μονὴ Ἁγία 3, *chart.*, moth-eaten. (Ἀντώνιος Μηλιαράκης.)

[262.] Athos. Protaton. 32, 4ᵗᵒ, amidst other matter, κεφ. τ., *syn.*, *men.* Σπ. Λαμπρός.

[267.] Kosinitsa Ἁγία Μονή Ἰωάννης ὁ Περευτέσης (?) 198 [A.D. 1503], written by the aforenamed.

[268.] Kos. Ἀγ. Μον., Νίκολλος 55 [xi], written by the aforenamed.

[269.] Kos. Ἀγ. Μον., Συμέων Λουτζέρες 195 [A.D. 1505], written by the aforenamed.

[270.] Ath. Nat. Libr. 101 [xiv], ff. 169, *mut.* at beginning and end.

[271.] Ath. Nat. Libr. 102 [xvii], ff. 229.

[272.] Ath. Nat. Libr. 106 [xiv–xv], ff. 243, *mut.* at beginning and end.

[273.] Ath. Nat. Libr. 133 [xiv], ff. 348, *pict.*

[274.] Ath. Nat. Libr. 144 [xv], ff. 76, *mut.* at beginning and end.

Mr. Miller also adds numbers 275–288 to correspond with his Evst. [Evangelia] 956–967 and 498, added on page 213 above.

TABLE X

THE ANCIENT VERSIONS OF THE NEW TESTAMENT

THE SECOND CENTURY

OLD LATIN VERSION.—Originated in North Africa in the second century. A revised text was current in Italy in the fourth century, and the existing MSS. vary greatly from each other. Whether there was originally only one or more than one independent version is still in dispute. The principal manuscripts are:

I. Of the Gospels, *a*. Cod. **Vercellensis**, at Vercelli, Italy (**IV.**); *a*². Cod. **Sangallensis** (**V.**), formerly designated *n* [including *Curiensia fragmenta* (small fragments of two leaves, containing verses from the 11th and 13th chapters of Luke, in the Reatisches Mus. at Chur.), and *o. p.* Cod. **Sangallensis**, MS. **1394**, vol. i. and ii. (small fragments at St. Gall) (**VII.** and **VIII.**)]; *b*. Cod. **Veronensis**, at Verona (**IV.** or **V.**); *c*. Cod. **Colbertinus**, Paris Nat. Lib. 254 (**XII.**); *d*. Cod. **Bezae Cantabrigiensis** [see uncial D] (**VI.**), conformed generally to the Greek text of the MS.; *e*. Cod. **Palatinus**, at Vienna (**V.**) (one leaf, Matt. xii. 13–23, at Dublin, Trin. Coll., N. 4, 18), cf. W–H. § 113, p. 81, and *The Academy*, Lond. Aug. 1880; *f*. Cod. **Brixianus**, at Brescia (**VI.**); *ff*¹. **Petropolitanus**, Imp. Lib. at St. Petersburg (**X.**), v. W–H. § 114; *ff*². Paris Nat. Lib. 17225 (**VII.**), both *ff*¹. and *ff*². were once at the Abbey of Corbie, in Picardy; *g*¹., *g*². Codd. Paris Nat. Lib. 11553 and 13169 (*g*.¹ **VIII.**, *g*.² **X.**), both formerly at St. Germain, Paris; *h*. **Vaticanus** [Matthew only] (**IV.** or **V.**); *i*. Cod. **Vindobonensis**, Vienna Imp. Lib., No. 1235 (**V.** or **VI.**); *k*. Cod. **Taurinensis**, Turin Lib., G. vii. 15, fragm. of Matt., text "*optimæ notæ*" (**V.**); *l*. **Vratislaviensis**, in Church of St. Elizabeth, Breslau (**VII.**); *m*. Cod. **Sessorianus** LVIII., a MS. of the "Speculum," ascribed to Augustine, containing extracts from Scripture, now in the monastery of Santa Croce, Rome (**VIII.–IX.**); *q*. Cod. **Monacensis** reg. Lat., 6224, at Munich (**VI.**); *r*. Cod. **Dublinii.**, Coll. Trin. A. 4, 15 (**VI.**); *s*. Cod. **Ambrosianus**, at Milan (**VI.**); *t*. Cod. **Bernae**, Berne Univ. Lib. (**VI.**); *v*. Cod. **Vindob.**, Vienna Imp. Lib. (**VII.**); *z*. (the *j* of W–H.) Cod. **Sarzannensis**, formerly in the church at Sarezzano, near Tortona (**V.**).

II. Of the Acts we have *d*. *m*., as in the Gospels; *e*. Cod. **Laudianus** (cf. UNC. E. **VI.**); *g*. (Apoc.) **Stockolm** "Gigas librorum" (**XIII.**); *g*². **Ambrosianus**, Milan (**X.** or **XI.**); *reg.* (Apoc.): **Paris** Nat. 6400 G., formerly in the Benedictine Monastery at Fleury (**VII.**); *s*. **Vindob.**, Vienna Imp. Lib., 16, *Palimp.* (**V.**); *x*¹. [Bentley's χ².] **Oxf. Bodl.** 3418 (**VII.** or **VIII.**); see Westcott, in Smith's *Bib. Dict.*, p. 3458ᵇ., and Berger, *Histoire de la Vulgate*, pp. 44, 398.

III. Of the Catholic Epistles, *ff*. **Petrop.**, **X.** contains the Ep. of James; *m*. as in the Gospels; *q*. Cod. **Monacensis**, Munich, Clm. (6220, 6230, 6277), 6436, once Frisingensis 236 (**VI.**); *s*. as in the Acts.

IV. Of the Pauline Epistles we have *m*. as in the Gospels; Codd. *d. e. f. g.* are the Latin versions of Dᴘ Eᴘ Fᴘ Gᴘ; *gue.* Cod. **Guelpherbytanus**, Weissenburg, 64 [*Palimpsest* fragments of the Ep. to Romans] (**VI.**); *r*. twenty-six leaves collected from the bindings of codices (the MS. marked *q*. in the Cath. Epistles, Monacensis reg. Clm. 6436), of which two were discovered in 1892 in the lib. of the Univ. of Munich (**VI.**); r^2. also from the Munich collection, containing Phil. iv. 11–23, and 1 Thess. i. 1–10, also numbered Clm. 6436 [Fris. 236] (**VI.**); r^3. **Gottvici**, Fragments of Romans and Galatians, from the Benedictine Abbey of Gottweig on the Danube, containing Rom. v. 16–vi. 4; vi. 6–19; Gal. iv. 6–19, iv. 22–v. 2; x^2. **Oxf. Bodl.** Laud. Lat. 108 (E. 67); St. Paul's Epp. in Saxon letters (**IX.**). See **X**^{1}. of the Acts.

V. Of the Apocalypse we have only g. of Acts, which alone gives the Apoc. entire, m. ("Speculum") of the Gospels, and $reg.$ of Acts, which is Westcott and Hort's h. of the African recension.

Of these MSS. e. and k. are substantially African, f. and q. are distinctly Italian, and the rest, though having African readings in some cases and Italian in others, are in general substantially European (v. W–H. § 113). In $ff. g^1. g^2.$ we find a mixed text, which leads Westcott and Hort to regard them as based upon the Vulgate. Most of the old Latin Gospels are of the **IV.**, **V.**, or **VI.** century. One, however, Cod. c. (Colbertinus) is as late as the **XII.** century.

PUBLICATION

Of these MSS., I. of the Gospels, $a. b. f.$ were *published* by Bianchini, *Evang. Quadruplex*, Rome, 1749; a. also by Irico, 1748; $a^2. n. o. p$. by Peter Batiffol, in *Revue Archerologique*, vol. iv., Paris, 1885, see also H. I. White, in *Old. Lat. Bib. Texts*, No. 2, Oxf., 1886; c. by Sabatier, *Bibl. Sac. Lat. Versiones Ant.*, vol. iii., 1749, and by John Belsheim, Christiania, 1888; d. by Kipling, 1793, and Scrivener, 1864; see also J. Rendel Harris, *A Study of Cod. Bezæ*, Camb., 1891, and F. H. Chase, *The Old Syriac Element in Bezæ*, Lond., 1893; e. by Tischendorf, *Evang. Pal. Ined.*, 1847; f. cf. Ranke, *Cur.* Marburg, 1872; ff. by Martianay, 1695, and ff^2. by Belsheim, 1881–87 (on $ff^2., g^1.$, and g^2. see Samuel Berger, *Histoire de la Vulgate*, etc., Paris, 1893, and the Art. by him in *Bulletin Critique*, Paris, 1891); h. by Card. Mai, in *Script. vet. nov. coll.*, vol. iii., 1828, and by Belsheim *Evangelium secundum Mattheum*, 1892; i. by Belsheim, *Codex Vindobonensis Membr. Purp. Antiq. Evang. Luc. et Marci Trans. Lat. Frag.*, Leipsic, 1885; k. by Tisch., in the Vienna *Jahrbücher*, 1847–49, and, very accurately, by Sanday & Wordsworth in *Old Latin Bible Texts*, Oxford, 1886; l. by F. Haase, Breslau, 1865–66; m. by Card. Mai, in *Nov. Patr. Biblioth.*, 1852, and by F. Weihrich in *Corp. Script. Eccles. Latinorum*, vol. xii., Vienna, 1887; q. by White, *Old Latin Bible Texts ;* cf. Hort, *Classical Review*, Lond., 1889, pp. 11–12; r. by T. K. Abbott, *Evangel. Versio Antehieronym.*, etc., Dublin, 1884, Part 2; also cf. Samuel Berger, *Revue Celtique*, vol. vi., pp. 348–357, Paris, 1883–1885; s. by Ceriani, in *Mon. Sac. et Profana*, Milan, 1861; t. by Prof. H. Hagen of Berne, in *Zeitschrift f. w. Theol.*, Leips., 1884, and in *Old. Lat. Bib. Texts*, Oxf., 1882, No. 2; v. by Wordsworth & White, *Old. Lat. Bib. Texts*, No. 3, Oxf., 1886, pp. 161–166; $z. = j$. described by Amelli, of the Ambrosian Library, in a monograph pub. in 1872. Scrivener (4th ed., 1894) says: "The MS. (j.) is now at Rome undergoing careful restoration, but no part of it has yet been published."

II. As to the Acts, e. was published by Hearne (not very accurately), in 1715, and by Tisch. in *Mon. Sac. Inedita*, vol. ix., in 1870, *with facsimile* (v. f–s in Table VII.); g. by Belsheim, Christiania, 1879, comp. Oscar L. Gebhardt, in *Theologische Literaturzeitung*, Leips., 1880, v. W–H. § 116; g^2. by Ceriani, *Mon. Sac. et prof.*, Milan, 1866; fragments of $reg.$ have been published by Ormont (two leaves from Apoc.), *Bibliotheque de l'Ecole des Chartes*, Paris, 1883, vol. xliv., also by Belsheim,

Christiania, 1887, and a valuable discussion of the subject by Samuel Berger in the *Revue de Theol. et de Philos.*, Lausanne, 1886, who subsequently published all the fragments accurately, under the title *Le Palimpseste de Fleury*, Paris, 1889 (comp. what Berger adds in *Bulletin Critique*, Paris, 1891, pp. 303, 304, note 1) ; s. by Tisch., in the Vienna *Jahrbücher, d. lit.*, 1847, and by Belsheim, in *Theol. Tidsskrift for den Evang. Luth. Kirke i Norge*, ser. 3, Christiania, 1886.

III. *q.* Of the CATHOLIC EPISTLES composed of fragm. of 1st and 2d Peter, and 1st John, were published by Ziegler, at Munich, in 1877. He discovered the words of 1st Peter, i. 8–19, and ii. 20–iii. 7, imprinted upon the paste which attached the leaves of a book to its binding. He deciphered the inscription by inverting the words with a mirror, and retracing them by the help of a microscope.

IV. PAULINE EPP. *gue.* was published by Tisch. in his *Anec. Sac.*, etc., Leips., 1855, p. 153, ff.; *r.* was published by Ziegler, in his *Itala-fragmente*, Marburg, 1876. Tisch. had already seen and used some of these leaves for his New Test. of 1859.

THE CURETONIAN SYRIAC.—This interesting relic of what is believed to represent the most ancient version of the Syriac New Testament (usually referred to by the sign *syr*ᶜᵘ), consists of eighty-two and a half leaves, containing portions of the Gospels, from the monastery of St. Mary Deipara, in the Nitrian desert; edited, London, 1858, with an English translation by Dr. Wm. Cureton. Three more leaves, containing John vii. 37–viii. 19 (but without the passage about the woman taken in adultery, vii. 53–viii. 12, which is not found in the Syriac versions); Luke xv. 22–xvi. 12, xvii. 1–23, were discovered by Brugsch in 1871, and are now in the Imperial Library in Berlin. For a Greek translation of the whole, see Frederick Bæthgen, *Evangelienfragmenta Der Griechische Text des Curetonschen Syrers Wiederhergestellt*, Leipsic, 1885. Compare also an article by Henry M. Harman, "Cureton's Fragments of Syriac Gospels," in the *Journal of the Soc. of Bib. Lit. and Exeg.*, Boston, 1885. In the opinion of Westcott and Hort the Curetonian Syriac fragments represent a text from which was derived the Peshitto or popular version of the Syriac N. T. In this view Tregelles, Tischendorf, and I. H. Hall concur.

In February, 1892, a manuscript was discovered in the Convent of St. Catharine, on Mt. Sinai, by Mrs. Agnes Smith Lewis, which upon examination proved to be a copy of the Syriac Gospels in a text resembling the Curetonian. There are 178 leaves, and only about eight pages are missing. It agrees with the Vatican and Sinaitic MSS. in omitting Mark xvi. 9–20. It is defective in Matt. vi., from the word "Come" in v. 10 to the end of the next leaf, and therefore gives no testimony on the doxology to the Lord's Prayer. In Matt. xxvii. 17, Pilate's question reads: "Which will ye that I release to you, Jesus Bar-Abba, or Jesus that is called Christ?" In Luke xxiv. 32 it reads: "Was not our heart heavy," etc., instead of: "Did not our heart burn," etc. In Matt. i. 16, the reading of the Syriac is: "Joseph, to whom the Virgin Mary was betrothed, begat Jesus." Matt. i. 25 omits "and knew her not." A good transcript of the Sinai Manuscript has appeared in England. The Four Gospels transcribed from the Syriac *Palimpsest*, etc., by R. L. Bensly, J. Rendel Harris, and F. C. Burkitt, with an introduction by Agnes Smith Lewis, Cambridge, at the University Press, 1894, 4to, pp. xlvi. 320. Mrs. Lewis has published an English translation of the Gospels.[1]

---

[1] *A Translation of the Four Gospels from the Syriac of the Sinaitic Palimpsest.* By Agnes Smith Lewis. 239 pp. Macmillan & Co. : London and New York.

THE SECOND AND THIRD CENTURY

EGYPTIAN VERSIONS

I. MEMPHITIC [or Coptic[1]] (cop.). A version in the dialect of Lower Egypt (called the Bohairic version by Rev. G. Horner, in Scrivener), contains all the books of our present canon except the Apocalypse, which is found, however, in some later MSS. The order of the books is: (1) Gospels; (2) Pauline Epp.; (3) Catholic Epp.; (4) Acts. Of the Gospels the order is Matthew, Mark, Luke, John. In vocabularies, however, John often comes first. The Pauline Epp. include Hebrews. "Of all the versions, the Memphitic is perhaps the most important for the textual critic" (Lightfoot in Scrivener). Gregory's list of Memphitic MSS. gives 64 of the Gospels, 27 of the Pauline Epp., Catholic Epp., and Acts, and 16 of the Apocalypse, which is for the most part written separately and evidently held in less esteem—a fact usually accounted for through the influence of Dionysius of Alexandria (A. D. 233–265). An edition of the Gospels was published at Berlin by M. G. Schwartze in 1846–48. The Acts and Epp. were afterwards published in 1852 at Halle, by P. Boetticher (*alias* P. A. de Lagarde), entitled *Acta Apostolorum Coptice*, and *Epistulæ Nov. Test. Coptice*. A new edition "based on a collation of all known manuscripts" is announced by Scrivener (vol. ii., p. 125), as in preparation by Rev. G. Horner.

II. THEBAIC or SAHIDIC (sah.). A version in the dialect of Upper Egypt. Fragments first collated by Woide in 1779. Believed by Lightfoot to belong to the second century. Fragments published by Mingarelli, 1785; Giorgi (a copy in Lenox Library), 1789; Munter, 1789; and by Mingarelli, 1790. Woide's edition appeared after his death; published by Prof. Ford in 1799. "Second only to the Memphitic in textual value" (Lightfoot, in Scrivener); contains the whole N. T., but, like the Memphitic, assigns an inferior place to the Apocalypse. Gregory catalogues ninety of these fragments: the first eleven groups of which are in England; three (**12–14**) are in Paris; one (**15**) in Naples; sixty-seven (**16–82**), which were formerly in the Borgian Library, are in the College of the Propaganda, at Rome; one (**83**) is at Turin; one (**84**) [the "Nanian fragments"], formerly at Venice, is now missing; four (**85–88**) are at St. Petersburg; and two (**89, 90**) are at Cairo.

The Biblical MSS. of the Borgian Collection, now in the Library of the Propaganda, have been published by M. Amelineau (1886–88) in the *Zeitschrift für Aegyptische Sprache*, and by Ciasca at Rome. A publication of the Paris fragments is begun.

III. BASHMURIC (basm.). Bashmuric is the designation still employed by Gregory (Tisch.) to represent a third dialect of Egypt, whose locality and history yet remain obscure. L. Stern (*Zeitschrift für Aegyptische Sprache*, 1878) regarded the dialect as "Middle Egyptian." Scrivener (4th ed., vol. ii. pp. 140–143) prefers the designation "Fayoum version" for one class of specimens, and still retains Middle Egyptian or Lower Sahidic for another. He says, however, "the lines between this dialect and version and that of the Fayoum are

---

1 Coptic (from the Greek Αιγύπτιος) is the general term for the Egyptian language as written or spoken by Christian people in Christian times. It, with the sign (*cop.*), is retained here because the Memphitic (or Bohairic [Scr.], or Bohiric [Tisch.]) is so referred to by Tischendorf and others.

not clearly defined, and further research may make it necessary to rearrange the specimens."

A few fragments are described by Gregory, two of which were brought from the Fayoum to England by W. M. Flinders Petrie, two are in the College of the Propaganda, at Rome, one is in the Paris library, and one in the Boulak museum at Cairo. Those in the Propaganda were originally in the Borgian Museum, and were published, in 1811, at Copenhagen by W. F. Engelbreth; the one in Paris (Matt. v. 46–vi. 19) was published in 1889 in the *Recueil de travaux relatifs à la philologie et à la archeologie egyptiennes et assyriennes*, by G. Maspero; the one in the museum, in *Mémoires de l'institut egyptien* (vol. ii., pp. 567–604. Cairo, 1889), by Urbanus Bouriant, and the two in England (Lond.[?]), by W. G. Crum (Lond. 1893).

THE FOURTH CENTURY

PESHITTO SYRIAC (syr[pesh])

The Syriac version, which was in common use among the Syrian sects throughout the flourishing period of Syrian history, and of which the largest collection of manuscripts remains to our day, is called Peshitto ("Simple "). The origin of the term has been variously accounted for. The following explanation is given by Prof. I. H. Hall: "The text of the Harclensian, like the text of the Old Testament Hexaplar, was interspersed with *obeli* and asterisks and with other marks; while the margins, also, were often occupied with various readings in Greek. The design of the whole being *text-critical*, or to mark passages where testimonies varied respecting the text or reading. But the Peshitto copies were free from all this apparatus—or 'simple.' . . . It was 'the clear text' edition, and simple in that sense." [1] It is evidently based upon the most ancient text originating in the second century, and, as evidently, it has been subjected to revisions from Greek manuscripts at a very early period. The great uniformity of the text in existing manuscripts leads some of our best critics (Westcott and Hort, Gregory, I. H. Hall) to believe that an authoritative revision of the text was made some time in the third or fourth century, and that the earlier copies were destroyed or lost. The Lenox Library contains several editions, among which is the Widmanstadt edition of 1556, reissued in 1562.

By the indefatigable labors of Dr. Caspar René Gregory, the *Prolegomena* of Tischendorf are now furnished with a description of about 246 Syriac MSS., of which 122 are Gospels, 58 Acts and Cath. Epp., and 66 of the Pauline Epp.

American scholars will be interested to know that the first two on the catalogue are Codices now in New York. No. **1.** (Acts 1., Paul 1.) is the property of the Syrian Protestant College at Beirût, Syria, but now deposited in the library of the Union Theol. Seminary. It is a parchment of the ninth century. A description will be found in Table XI. below. It has been collated by Prof. Isaac H. Hall, of the Metropolitan Museum of Art. See *Journal of the American Oriental Society*, New Haven, October, 1877, pp. xvi–xix.

Another manuscript, numbered **1**ª in the catalogue, containing Luke xxi. 30–

---

[1] See Appendix II. to the *sixth* edition of Murdock's translation of the Syriac N. T., published by Horace L Hastings. Boston, Mass.: 1894.

xxii. 17, once the property of Rev. A. L. Long, D.D., of Robert College, Constantinople, has also been described by Professor Hall in the *New York Independent*, August 20, 1885. See our Table XI., *The Hall Manuscripts ;* also, see an article by Dr. Hall on Syriac Literature in the *Schaff-Hertzog Encyclopedia of Rel. Knowledge.* New York: 1884.

GOTHIC (goth.)

A version made by Ulfilas (b. about A.D. 310, Bishop of the Goths about A.D. 341–381) from the Greek text, chiefly Antiochan, with many western readings and some ancient readings not western. The principal MSS. are three, viz.: (1) Cod. **Argenteus**, in the Univ. lib. at Upsal, ff. 187, containing fragments of the Gospels (the order of which is Matt. John, Lc. Mk.), of century **VI.**, in purple vellum, written with silver letters. (2) Codd. **Ambrosianus Vaticanus** and **Aug. Taurinorum**, consisting of *palimpsest* fragments of century **VI.**, discovered by Card. Mai in the Ambrosian Library at Milan, 1817, containing portions of Paul's Epistles, to which have been added some fragments of John in the Vatican, and of Galatians and Colossians in Vienna (formerly at Turin). (3) Cod. **Carolinus**, also a *palimpsest* of century **VI.**, containing about forty verses of the Ep. to Romans. These fragments, containing in all portions of all the New Test. books except the Acts, Cath. Epp., Heb., and Apoc., were collected and published by Gabelentz and Loebe, at Leipsic, in 1836–43. Several other editions have appeared, one (*The Gospel of Mark*) by W. W. Skeat, London, 1882, and by G. H. Balg, Milwaukee, Wis. (1890?). The title of the latter is: *The First Teutonic (Germanic) Bible translated chiefly from the Greek by the Gothic bishop Wulfila in the fourth century and the other remains of the Gothic language. Edited, with an introduction, a syntax, and a glossary.*

VULGATE (vg.)

Revised from the Old Latin by Jerome at the request of Pope Damasus in A.D. 383–385. Authorized edition published by Sixtus V. in 1590, and by Clement VIII. of Rome, 1592. Not less than 8000 MSS. of the Vulgate are believed to exist in the libraries of Europe. Some of the oldest MSS. are:

I. OF THE WHOLE NEW TESTAMENT. (1) Cod. **Amiatinus** (*am.*) [now in the Laurentian lib. at Florence] about A.D. 700, collated by Tischendorf, 1843, and Tregelles, 1846, published by Tischendorf, 1850, 2d ed. 1854. "Stands first among the authorities for the Hieronyman text" (Westcott). (2) Cod. **Fuldensis** (fuld.), sixth century, collated by Lachman and Buttmann, and published by Ranke, 1868. "Of nearly equal value with Cod. Amiatinus, and apparently derived from the same source" (Westcott). (3) Cod. **Toletanus** (*tol.*), once at Toledo, but now at Madrid, eighth century; the collation by Christopher Palomares, was published by Bianchini in his *Vindiciæ canon Script.*, Rome, 1740.

II. OF THE GOSPELS. (1) Cod. **Forojuliensis** (*for.*), Friuli, sixth or seventh century, published by Bianchini. Parts of the same MS. are at Prague, and were published by Dobrowsky, 1778 (Cod. Pragensis). (2) Cod. **Harleianus** (*harl.*), 1775 (British Museum), seventh century. Partial collation by Griesbach, *Symb. Crit.* vol. i. pp. 305–326. (3) Cod. **Aureus** (*aur.*), sixth or seventh century. Royal Library at Stockholm, edited by J. Belsheim, Christiana, 1878. Has a mixed text (v. Wordsworth, *Old Lat. Bib. Texts*, No. 1, Oxf. 1883.)

III. Acts, Epp., and Rev.   (1.) Codex **Demidovianus** (*demid.*), published by Matthaei, Nov. Testament.   Gr. et. Lat., 1782–88, twelfth century, but the text is valuable.

Our knowledge of the Vulgate manuscripts has now been greatly enlarged by Gregory (Tisch. *Prol.*, pp. 993–1108), who has catalogued 2228 MSS., as well as by Samuel Berger: *Histoire de la Vulgate Pendant les Premiers Siecles du Moyen Age*, Paris, 1893, and by the labors of the eminent Professor Wordsworth, Bishop of Salisbury, and his distinguished co-laborers in the issuance from the Clarendon press at Oxford of a new and critical edition of the Hieronymian text.   The first *fasciculus* appeared in 1889, containing the Gospel of Matthew; the second, containing Mark, in 1891; and the third, containing Luke, in 1893.

American scholars will be interested to know that the Lenox Library (Fifth Avenue, New York) contains not less than thirty editions of the Vulgate, printed anterior to 1481.

ÆTHIOPIC (æth.)

Attributed by Dillmann to the sixth century; but Gildermeister and other Orientalists assign it to the sixth or seventh century.   (Gregory publishes in the *Prolegomena* some arguments of Gildermeister in support of this view, in a letter written from Bonn in April, 1882, but prefers to follow the judgment of Dillmann.   Gildermeister died in 1890.)   The dialect is the one formerly spoken in Abyssinia, especially in the province of Axoum.   Published at Rome, 1548–1549, by three Abyssinians.   A copy in the Lenox Library, New York.   Reprinted in Walton's Polyglott.   In 1826–30 Thomas Pell Platt published an edition under the auspices of the British and Foreign Bible Society of London.   Dr. Gregory has catalogued 101 Æthiopic MSS., of which 6 belong to the B. and F. Bible Soc.; 38 (**7–44**) in the British Museum; 3 (**45–47**) to the Bodleian lib.; 2 (**48, 49**) are at Vienna; 10 (**50–59**) are found in the catalogue of Anton. d'Abbadie [Paris, 1859]; 19 (**60–78**) are in the Paris Lib.; 2 (**79, 80**) are at Berlin; 1 (**81**) at Dresden; 1 (**82**) at Frankfort; 1 (**83**) at Leipsic; 2 (**84, 85**) at Munich; 1 [locality unknown]; 1 (**87**) at Florence [Pal. Med. 16]; 9 (**88–96**) in the Vatican; and 5 (**97–101**) at St. Petersburg.   See Thos. Pell Platt's *Catalogue*, London, 1823; Zotenberg, *Cat. des MSS. ethiopens*, Paris [1877]; and for the Brit. Museum the *Catalogues* of Wright and Dillmann.

THE FIFTH CENTURY

ARMENIAN (arm.)

First printed by Bishop Uscan in 1666.   A copy in the Lenox Library, New York.   The best edition published at Venice by Zohrab in 1789.   Its Codices are all of modern date, and some show corruptions from the Latin Vulgate; but Westcott and Hort say: "The Armenian translators certainly followed Greek MSS., probably obtained from Cappadocia, the mother of Armenian Christianity."   Gregory (Tisch.) describes 64 (1 of which is in America, 17 in England, 2 in Vienna, 1 in Copenhagen, 5 in Paris, 18 in Berlin, 2 in Leipsic, 3 in Munich, and 17 in Italy), none of which are earlier than century **X.** or **XI.**, and only 8 are earlier than century **XIII.**   No. **1.**, a parchment Cod. of the Gospels, is in possession of S. Brainard Pratt, of Boston, Mass.   It is dated 1262. See Table XI.

JERUSALEM SYRIAC

A partial Lectionary of the Gospels, in the Vatican, dated A.D. 1030, was formerly the only manuscript of this version. Its grammatical forms resemble the Chaldee. An edition was published at Verona in 1861 – 64 by Count F. Miniscalchi-Erizzo. Later an edition has appeared in Göttingen (1891–92), by Paul de Lagarde (posthumous).

To this have now been added seven fragments, described by Gregory in Tisch. *Proleg.*, numbered as follows: (2) **London**, Gospels, *palimp.* Century **X.**, B. M. Add. 14664. (3) **London**, Matt. xxvi., 48–64, century **IX.**, B. M. Add. 14450. (4) **St. Petersburg**, Gosp. and Acts, *palimp.* century **VII.** and **VIII.**, (this one was described by Tisch. in 1855 in *Anecdota Sac et Profana*). (5) **Sinaiticus**, Conv. of St. Catharine, fragments of Galatians, century **VIII.**, published by J. Rendel Harris, *Biblical Fragments from Mt. Sinai*, Lond. 1890. (6 and 7) No. 6, discovered at Mt. Sinai by Agnes Smith Lewis; No. 7, discovered and collated by Harris in 1892. (8) **Oxford Bodl.** Syr. c. 4, century **VIII.** *palimp.* fragments of Col. I. Thess., 2 Tim., Titus. Four leaves brought from Egypt to Oxford in 1891. Published by G. H. Gwilliam, *Anecdota Oxoniensis*, Oxford, 1893.

THE SIXTH CENTURY

PHILOXENIAN or HARCLENSIAN SYRIAC (syrᴾ.)

Made under the direction of Philoxenus, Bishop of Mabug (Hierapolis), in Eastern Syria, A.D. 508. "Its characteristic feature is its excessive closeness to the original [which, however, does not always result in bad Syriac]. . . ; its very defects, however, as being servilely accurate, give it weight as a textual authority" (Scrivener). In A.D. 616 it was revised and compared with several Greek MSS. by Thomas of Harkel or Heraclea. This revision was published, under the name of the Philoxenian Syriac, by Joseph White, Oxford, 1778–1803. Though we have many MSS. of the Harclensian revision in the Gospels, till recently only one was known to contain the Acts and Epistles, and that was imperfect, ending with Hebrew xi. 27. But the Syriac MS., bought for the Library of the University of Cambridge, England (Add. MSS. 1700), at a sale of the library of the late M. Jules Mohl of Paris, which contains a Syriac translation of the two Epp. to the Corinthians ascribed to Clement of Rome, is found to supply the gap, containing the N. T. complete, with the exception of the Apocalypse. An edition of Heb. xi. 28–xiii. 25 has been published by Robt. L. Bensly (Cambridge, 1889) from this MS. See Lightfoot's *S. Clement of Rome*, London, 2d ed., 1890, vol. i., pp. 129–136. A critical edition of the Gospel of John in the Harclensian Syriac was published by C. H. Bernstein, Leipzig, 1853. Bernstein thinks that the Cod. Angelicus, belonging to the Angelica Library of the Augustinian monks at Rome, is a MS. of the unrevised form of this version —*i. e.* of the Philoxenian proper—but Prof. Hall has shown that this is incorrect (see *The Williams Manuscript*, mentioned below).

In 1627 Edward Pococke published at Leyden the Apocalypse, from a Leyden MS.— the *editio princeps* — and in 1630, from a Bodleian manuscript, the four Epp. (2 Peter, 2 and 3 John, and Jude).

In 1877 Dr. Isaac H. Hall, then Professor in the Syrian Protestant College at Beirût, Syria, discovered a manuscript containing portions of the Gospels in

15

a Pre-Harclensian version, in all probability the original Philoxenian. In 1886 Prof. Hall published *The Williams Manuscript: The Syrian Antilegomena Epistles (i.e.* 2 Peter, 2 and 3 John, and Jude), *written A.D. 1471 by Suleiman of Husn Keifa,* 8 leaves and 17 photo-facsimiles, Baltimore, 1886. The manuscript is a text-critical edition of the Acts and Epistles with textual notes.

By his extensive researches in this department of Oriental literature Dr. Hall has made himself an acknowledged authority in Syriac, and the hope is expressed by Dr. Gregory that his labors may in time afford us a solution of the vexed questions which yet attend the subject of Philoxenian-Heraclean, or, as Dr. Hall prefers to call them, Harclensian versions.

GEORGIAN or IBERIAN (georg.)

A version of the whole Bible in a language very little known, first published in Moscow, 1743. Of little value for critical purposes. The British and Foreign Bible Society has an edition, printed at Tiflis, containing the New Testament and the Psalms. There are said to be manuscripts in the Monastery of the Holy Cross at Jerusalem, and of Etchmiadzin at Mt. Ararat. Gregory catalogues (from Mai) three in the Vatican containing the Gospels.

THE NINTH CENTURY AND LATER

SLAVONIC (sl.)

Translated by two Greek brothers, Cyril and Methodius, from the best Greek Codices of the age, sometime after A.D. 863.

Gregory (Tisch.) has now published Dobrowsky's catalogue of 32 Slavonic MSS. [(*a.*) Gospels sl^1—sl^{10}; (*b.*) Acts and Epp. sl^1—sl^{11}; (*c.*) Apoc. sl^1—sl^{11}.] of the X. to the XVIII. century, besides a list of 136 uncollated Lectionaries and other MSS., which are mostly at Moscow (New Jerusalem Monast., No. **9–14**; Rumiantzov. Museum No. **15–42**; Synodal lib., No. **43–79**; Undolskov. lib., No. **81–92**; Public lib. at Wilna, No. **93–106**; and in Monastic libraries of Northern Russia, No. **107–136**), but Nos. **1** and **2** are at Leipsic, No. **3** at Munich, and Nos. **4–8** in the Vatican.

"The earliest dated complete manuscript of the Gospels is dated 1144; the earliest manuscript of the whole Bible A.D. 1499, and the earliest printed edition is the famous Ostrog Bible of 1581."—Scr. A copy of this last is in the Lenox Library, New York.

FRANKISH (fr.)

A version of the Gospel of Matthew in the Frankish dialect of the Teutonic, from Codex Sangallensis of Cent. **IX.**, was published by **J. A.** Schmeller in 18?7 at Stuttgart.

ANGLO-SAXON (sax.)

Numerous versions in the Anglo-Saxon exist, all of which are from the Vulgate, and therefore useful only for the criticism of that text. See Skeat, *The gospel acc. to St. Matt. in Anglo-Saxon,* etc., Camb. 1887.

PERSIAN (pers.)

Of these there are two; one of Walton's Polyglott (pers^p), from the Peshitto Syriac; and the other from the Greek, edited by Wheelock (pers^w).

Gregory has catalogued 27 Persic manuscripts, of which **1** and **2** are at

Cambridge; **3–8** at Oxford (Bodl.); **9** and **10** at Vienna; **11–13** at Leyden; **14–16** in Paris; **17** at Munich; **18–21** at Florence (Palat. Med. 17, 19, 23, 33); **22–26** in the Vatican; and No. **27** at St. Petersburg (Orient, 248). The dates indicated range from century **XIV.–XIX.** Thirteen are without decision of dates.

ARABIC (arab.)

Many versions, but of slight importance. For the list see Gregory's Tischendorf. The list describes 136 Codices, of which 35 are in England (**1, 2** in Camb.; **3, 4** in Gresham Coll. Lond.; **5–12** in Brit. Mus.; **13** in Marsden Lib. [?]; **14–35** in Oxford); 3 at Vienna (Nos. **36, 37, 38**); 14 in Holland (**39** at Amsterdam; **40** at Leuwardon; **41–53** at Leyden); 14 at Paris (**54–68**); 14 in Germany (**69, 70** at Berlin; **71** at Dresden; **72–74** at Gotha, **74ᵃ** Wolfenbüttel; **75–79** at Leipsic; **80–83** in Munich); 50 in Italy (**84** at Gubbio; **85–94** at Flor., Palat. Med.; **95**, Milan; **96–130ᵃ**, Vatican; **131**, Venice; **132, 133**, Upsal.; **134–136**, St. Petersburg).

A version of the Gospels was published at Rome in 1590–91 (referred to in early critical editions as arʳ or arʳᵒ), by J. Baptiste Raymundi, a copy of which is in the Lenox Library, New York; another at Leyden, in 1624, by Thomas Erpenius (arᵉ), containing the whole New Testament. Prof. J. Rendel Harris, in *Biblical Fragments from Sinai*, Camb. 1890, has given a facsimile of a fragment of an Arabic version (from a MS. of cent. **IX.**), which bears marks of great antiquity.

THEOTISCA (theot.)

We also find mention in Tisch.'s *Prolegomena* of a version denominated Theotisca, which Dr. Gregory regards as really a Franco-Bavarian version, quoted at Matt. xx. 28, derived from codex 3093 of the Vienna Imp. lib. (and from two leaves in the pub. lib. of Hanover), which codex was formerly in the Monsee monastery, and seems to have been written in the beginning of cent. **IX.** (see Geo. A. Hench, *The Monsee Fragments. Newly collated text with introductory notes and grammatical treatises* [glossary and photo. lith. facsimile], Strasburg, 1890, pp. 212, of which the first part [pp. 1–142] was delivered as a dissertation before the faculty of Philosophy at Johns Hopkins University, Baltimore, Md.).

BOHEMIAN (bohem.)

There are in the judgment of Joseph Dobrowsky two recensions of the Bohemian version. The oldest is represented by three manuscripts — one at Dresden (without date); the Leitmeritz, at Breslau (**1411**); and one at Olmutz, Lyceum lib. (**1417**). A later recension appears in two codices—one at Olmutz (without date); and one at Leitmeritz (**1429**).

Codex **Pragensis** (in the monastery of Emmaus at Prague), written in Glagolitic letters in 1416, holds an intermediate place between the two recensions. In the opinion of Dobrowsky that codex of the most ancient Dresden version, now in the royal library, formerly belonged to the Leskowetzian family somewhere between the years 1390 and 1410.

The Bohemian Bible seems to have been first printed at Prague in the year 1488 (two copies of this are in the Lenox Library, New York city). Some notice of Bohemian MSS. is given by Dr. Gregory, taken from Hanslik's catalogue of the University library at Prague and from Jos. Jungmann's *History of Bohemian Literature*, Prague, 1847. See Gregory (Tisch.), *Proleg.* pp. 1127, 1128.

TABLE XI

MANUSCRIPTS KNOWN TO BE IN AMERICA

The list of manuscripts here presented has been the result of a somewhat extended correspondence with individuals and institutions in the United States. Since college duties allowed the writer no time for personal inspection of many manuscripts, the descriptions here given are chiefly the kind contributions of their scholarly custodians or of personal friends. Though the search has been extensive, we may hope that its results have not been exhaustive, and that others may still come to light. If the publication of these shall awaken new desire for acquiring like precious witnesses to the sacred text, it will not be in vain.

America is now taking a foremost rank among the nations in her facilities for Biblical instruction. Her one hundred and fifty theological schools, with their eight hundred teachers, give promise of good work in all departments of sacred learning. Our weakest point as yet is in the fundamental realm of textual criticism. The materials for this have been somewhat difficult of access. The ocean separates us from most of the original sources, and time and means are wanting to most of us for that kind of patient investigation essential to the best results. It is a gratifying circumstance that the successor of Tischendorf, as one of the leading text editors, himself a recognized authority in criticism, is an American; but it is yet greatly to be desired that a larger number of American scholars should become practical critics of the text, and that, for this purpose, a larger number of original manuscripts should be placed within their reach.

It is a fact, perhaps not generally understood, that a great work yet remains to be done in the use of existing materials. Thousands of manuscripts are as yet uncollated, and hundreds of Christian scholars could find useful employment in bringing out from them gems to reflect light upon the pages of Divine Truth.

The work is not so difficult, nor is a preparation for it so formidable as may be supposed. Even a theological education is not indispensable. There are Christian laymen who have done excellent service in this department. Mr. H. C. Hoskier, to whom frequent allusion is made in these pages, the author of an exhaustive collation and analysis of the Egerton MS. 2610 in the British Museum (catalogued here and in Tisch. as Gospels **700**[1] [Scr. Cod. Ev. 604])—which W. Sanday (*The Academy*, Aug. 9, 1890) characterizes as "a piece of very honest, careful, and valuable work, which may be counted for the future among the really trustworthy materials for the criticism of the New Testament"—this Mr. Hoskier is a young and successful business man in New York city, who, though wrestling daily with the bulls and bears of Wall Street, yet finds time to recreate in the restful fields of Biblical scholarship.

Now if our Christian men of business who take their vacations in Europe could appreciate their opportunity to help the cause of Biblical learning, by se-

---

[1] The numbers as well as the dates, in *heavy-faced* type, are those assigned by Gregory; and the descriptions which accompany them are translated from his *Prolegomena* to Tischendorf's 8th edition. They occur, therefore, only in connection with those MSS. which are catalogued in the *Prolegomena*.

curing and transferring to American libraries some of the priceless legacies of the past, they would deserve and receive the gratitude of succeeding ages.[1]

It is noticeable that a goodly number of the manuscripts now in this country are here through the thoughtful generosity of intelligent laymen. Harvard College received hers chiefly from Edward Everett, Charles Sumner, and Lewis Cass. Several, which were formerly deposited in the library, were the private property of Mr. George Livermore, of Dana Hill, Cambridge. The Haverford collection came from Walter Wood and J. Rendel Harris. The Lenox Library MSS. were purchased and presented by Mr. Lenox, the founder of the library, and by Mr. Robert L. Stuart, of New York. Mr. S. Brainard Pratt, of Boston, and Mr. Robert S. Williams, of Utica, N.Y., are each possessors of manuscripts, one of Armenian and one of Syriac; while the famous Latin manuscript, sometimes called the "Golden Gospels of Henry the VIII.," is the property of Mr. Theodore Irwin, of the Second National Bank in Oswego. One lady, Mrs. Caroline S. Reid, has honored herself and the Syracuse University by presenting to its library cursive Codex No. **668** of the Gospels.

There are many consecrated souls among the Christian laymen of America who would delight, if they only knew how, to share in the sacred work of revealing the true Christ. This they may do, if they will, by helping to summon these venerable witnesses to the *ipsissima verba* of sacred writ.

AMERICAN MANUSCRIPTS[2] OF THE NEW TESTAMENT

THE AMERICAN BIBLE SOCIETY MANUSCRIPTS

The library of the American Bible Society has a very fine copy of the Bible in Latin, which is said to have once belonged to Charles I. of England. The manuscript is a very delicate parchment, and the writing is exceedingly fine. It has 365 leaves and 2 columns to the page. The page measures $6\frac{5}{8} \times 4\frac{5}{8}$ in. (17×11.3 cm.), and the text $4\frac{4}{5} \times 3\frac{1}{4}$ in. (12×8.5 cm.). Its date is supposed to be in the XIVth century. It is mutilated at the beginning and end, opening in the middle of the 14th chapter of the Book of Numbers, and ending at the 2d verse of the 18th chapter of Revelation. It has the Apocrypha. There is a prologue to the Book of Proverbs and two to the Book of Job. The Pauline Epp. precede the Acts and Cath. Epp. On the margin of the 9th chapter of 2 Esdras is this inscription: "*Richard Gwillim, Yeoman off the Stikkupp to Charles the ffirst off that name king off England 1652.*" It is illuminated throughout in blue and red, the headings of chapters being red and the running titles of the pages in alternate letters of red and blue. The numbers of chapters in the margins and ornamental scrolls are also of mingled colors.

---

[1] Just as this matter is going to press, the following note comes to the author from Dr. Gregory, who is delivering a course of lectures on Paleography and Textual criticism before the University of Chicago:

"CHICAGO, ILL., *September* 2, 1895.

"MY DEAR DR. MITCHELL:

"I am very glad that you have succeeded in finding so many Biblical MSS. in America, and that you intend to add them to your book, which is in itself a valuable token of American diligence in the department of New Testament criticism. May your list lead many Americans to turn from the early printed books and to buy MSS. of the Bible; they are far more unique, far more interesting, and far more useful to the cause of science and of religion.

"Believe me to be, with much respect, yours truly,

"CASPAR RENÉ GREGORY."

[2] The MSS. are written in Greek, unless otherwise stated.

It is bound in heavy boards and embossed leather, and the insides of the covers are of crimson morocco, stamped with the crown, and offset by heavy parchment fly-leaves, stamped, in gilt, with the royal coat of arms. The *outside* of the cover seems to have been repaired, or re-covered by a modern binder, and lettered on the back : " AN ILLUMINATED MANUSCRIPT OF THE 14 CEÑTURY."

The manuscript was presented to the American Bible Society by Mr. Charles J. Baker, of Baltimore, Md.

The library of the Bible Society also contains a Lectionary of the Gospels in Syriac. The four gospels are written in the Estrangelo character, arranged in lessons for the liturgy of the Jacobite Syrian Church ; probably of the XIIIth cent. It was given to Dr. Grant, missionary to the Nestorians, by a Syrian priest at Mosul, Mesopotamia, and in 1842 Dr. Grant presented it to the Bible Society. It is a 4to, 14½ × 9 in. (37 × 25 cm.). The text is 7½ × 10¾ in. (19 × 27¼ cm.), arranged in 2 columns. The letters are very large. The leaves are much worn, as if by frequent use, and the cover is broken and dilapidated.

The Bible Society has also a Slavic Gospel of Matthew on thick vellum, 24 leaves. It ends (chap. xxii. 21) with the words : *Render therefore unto Cæsar the things that are Cæsar's.* The "Ammonian" sections and Eusebian canons are noted, as also the titles and beginnings and endings of church lessons. Its orthography is old Bulgarian, and its readings present some interesting variations from the established Russian church text. There is no indication of date, but its dialectic peculiarities would point to a period before the XVth century. These points respecting the manuscripts were noted by Rev. Dr. A. L. Long, Feb. 20, 1886.

We are indebted to the Rev. Dr. E. W. Gilman, secretary of the American Bible Society, for the opportunity of examining these manuscripts.

THE ANDOVER MANUSCRIPT

Andover Theological Seminary, Massachusetts

Lectionary of the Gospels No. **180**[1] (numbered by Scrivener 463), cent. **XIV.**, size 20.3 × 15 centimeters (8 × 6 inches), parchment, containing 202 leaves, having 1 column each, of 24 lines. (Daily readings [εβδ.] in John from Easter to Pentecost ; Sabbath and Lord's Day readings [σαβ. κυρ.] in Matthew and Luke.)

Leaves 1–8 at the beginning, and pp. 317–356, are *paper.* Many of the parchment leaves are *palimpsest,* over a cursive liturgy. The manuscript was brought from Constantinople to America by Rev. W. G. Schauffler, D.D., missionary to the Jews. Examined by Dr. Gregory, July 4, 1886. See Gregory (Tisch.), *Prolegomena*, p. 713 ; see also H. C. Hoskier, *Collation of the Greek cursive Codex Evangelium* 604 (London, 1890), Appendix I., which describes a visit to Andover in 1887, and an examination of the manuscript. The following extract from his description of the MS. is, with his permission, quoted from page 2 of the appendix : "The MS. is contained in an *old* binding, with a kind of enamelled painting on the front cover ; the Saviour on the cross, with miniatures in all four corners ; a large cross-beam, on which the feet rest ; IC . . . XC on either side of the head, upon each arm of the cross ; above, the inscription. It measures 8¼ × 6 inches, and is in form a small quarto. There are 194 leaves as paged by Guy, including the 20 folios *chart.* (pp. 317–356), and 6 *leaves,* more or less intact, *chart.*, at the beginning, and 3 fragments, also *chart.* Guy has left in it a table of contents, with at the top, "Collated by Mr. Edward A. Guy, 1873.""

Mr. Hoskier gives an exact list by number of each of the leaves which are *palimpsest*, from which it appears that 84 of the 174 *parchment* leaves are *palimpsest*. Guys collations were never published.

THE ASTOR LIBRARY MANUSCRIPTS

New York City

(1.) *Lectionary of the Apostolos* No. **76**, cent. **XV.** or **XVI.**, size 24 × 17 cm. (9½ × 6⅞ in.) on paper, 225 leaves, with 2 columns and 25 lines to the page [the writing measures 6½ × 4¾ in.]. It was formerly the property of Baron Meerman, then of Rev. T. Williams, and then of the Duke of Sussex, who purchased it for £36, 15s. It is elegantly bound in morocco, with gilt-edged leaves, and lettered *Epistolæ Apostolicæ Græce*.

(2.) *An Evangelistary in Latin.* A richly illuminated 4to "Carlovingian manuscript" on vellum, having 197 leaves, and dated A.D. 870 (?) ; size (text) 6½ × 4 in. ; leaf 10 × 7½ in.

(3.) *Biblia Sacra Latina*, a large folio, No. **4** of "Vulgate Versions" (Tisch.), 5½ × 11 in. [the writing 10½ × 7½ in.], written on vellum, with illuminations (a choice copy), dated A.D. 1350. It has 447 leaves, 2 columns, 45 lines, with the prologues of St. Jerome and a list of proper names with interpretations. It is in perfect condition, beautifully written, with numerous superb miniatures in gold and colors. It contains the New Testament entire (including the Apocalypse). See Gregory (Tisch.), *Proleg.* p. 994.

THE BENTON MANUSCRIPTS

A.—MS. belonging to A. A. Benton, DD., of Sewanee, Tenn.

(1.) *Lectionary of the Gospels* No. **302**c (Scrivener, 490), cent. **XV.** ; size, 30 × 21.7 cm. [folio 12 in. high × about 8¼ broad ; J. R. Harris in *S. S. Times*, June 4, 1887], on paper ; imperfect at the beginning and end. At the end are portions of a menology (or saints day calender). It was brought, with the other Benton MSS., by Dr. Benton's father, from Chanea, in Crete, something over fifty years ago. Prof. J. Rendel Harris, who examined the Benton MSS. in 1887, says of it : "The manuscript is of no critical importance ; its chief paleographical value consists in the fact that it is written upon paper, which must, I think, have been imported from Venice (for Chanea is a Venetian colony) ; and the three curious water-marks which are found in the paper are thus shown to be of Italian manufacture."

(2.) *Cursive of the Gospels* No. **670** (Scrivener, 901), cent. **XII.** or **XIII.**, "consisting of a single sheet of thick, coarse parchment of a brown color, containing Luke viii. 3–24, and ix. 13–34."—J. R. Harris.

(3.) *Cursive of the Gospels* No. **699** (Scrivener, 902), ["The Gem of the whole collection," Harris], cent. **X.** ; size, 19.6 × 16.6 cm. [6¾ × 5½ in.], 290 leaves, having 1 column and 17 lines to the page, 22–25 letters to the line. It begins with Matt. xxvii. 59, Ἰωσὴφ, and is mutilated at the commencement of Luke and John. It has chapters, titles, sections, canons. (The chapter-tables, and the συναξαριον, or table of lessons for the whole year, are by a later hand.) It was illuminated by ornamental designs, some of which have been taken out, but one, at the head of the Gospel of Mark, remains. Some of the initial letters have been done in [now faded] colors. The initial A in ΑΡΧΗ [ἀρχή], of St. Mark is in gold and blue.

The first pages of Luke are missing as far as ii. 16, Μαριάμ. John's gospel begins at i. 14, [εθεα] σάμεθα τὴν δόξαν. Chap. xii. is mutilated from v. 26, καὶ ὅπου εἰμ[ὶ], to v. 28, ἦλθεν οὖν, and from κἀγὼ αν ὑψω[θῶ], in verse 32, to υἱὸν τοῦ ανθρώπου, in v. 34. Its exact contents may be thus stated: Matt. xxvii. 59 to the end; Mark complete; Luke ii. 16 to the end; John i. 14–xii. 26, 28–32, 34 to the end. Like Evl. **302**ᶜ and cursive **670** of the Gospels, it was formerly the property of the Rev. George Benton, who was a missionary of the Protestant Episcopal Church in Crete, between the years 1837 and 1844. Dr. A. A. Benton, son of the above, the present possessor, intimates a purpose to prepare a collation of Gospel cursive **670**, "as a praxis in textual criticism, as it has some points which make it a good elementary example." Such a work could not fail to be useful to American students. Some years ago Dr. Benton, with the help of two students, collated the Gospel of Mark, in Cod. **699** of the Gospels, with Westcott and Hort and the *Textus Receptus*, discovering some signs which seem to him to indicate an earlier origin than the date (cent. **X.**) assigned by Prof. Harris. He would place it before A.D. 850. It has, in Mark xiv. 41, the curious interpolation of τέλος after ἀπέχει, which is found in Uncial Cod. D (Bezæ), and some later MSS. (an error found also in the Pesh. Syr., and in some forms of the old Latin), thought to have "come into the text from the margin of verse 42, where it indicates the close of the Gospel for the third day of the carnival week" (Burgon), or to have been borrowed from Lev. xxii. 37 (W–H.).

B.—*MSS. belonging to Rev. R. A. Benton, of Sewickley, Penn.*

(1.) *Lectionary of the Gospels* No. **302**ᵃ (Scrivener, 487), cent. **XII.** or **XIII.**, has 15 leaves, of 2 columns and 22 lines each. Red ink headings. It is a parchment folio 13 × 9½ inches. Prof. Harris says it "must once have been a fine volume." The leaves are mostly loose and separate. Mr. Benton has had excellent photographs taken of two pages of this MS., which show the text to be in a very legible condition. One of them, containing a page from one [No. 9] of the "Twelve Gospels of the Passions" (Εὐαγγέλια τῶν ἁγίων πάθων ῑυ χυ), taken from John xix. 29–36, will be found in Table VII.

(2.) *Lectionary of the Gospels* No. **302**ᵇ (Scrivener, 488), cent. **XII.**, is a fragment in 2 columns, of 28 lines each, size 8 × 6½ inches; most of the leaves of which are stuck together, and the vellum is brittle, so that it is difficult, if not impossible to separate them. It has ornamented headings and capitals. Mr. Benton says: "Thirty-three leaves measure ⅜ of an inch in thickness, while the whole book is 2½ inches thick, from which you can easily calculate some 220 leaves."

THE BOSTON ATHENÆUM MANUSCRIPT
Boston, Mass.

A Latin manuscript, apparently made up of extracts from the Old and New Testaments, about one-third being from the latter. It is written upon white vellum, octavo, 10½ × 6½ cm. (text 7½ × 4½), dated 1563? On the fly-leaf is written, *Liber Richardi Kettell vicary La Stephani London*. Kettell died in 1563. It has colored ornamentation. It is written in black ink, but difficult to decipher.[1]

---

[1] This account of the MS. is furnished by courtesy of Wm. C. Lane, Librarian.

THE BROWN UNIVERSITY MANUSCRIPT
Providence, R. I.

A Greek Lectionary of the Gospels, written on parchment, cent. **XII.** or **XIII.**, 4to, size 10$\frac{1}{4}$ × 8$\frac{1}{2}$ inches, 4 inches thick, 238 leaves, 2 columns, 24 lines. The capital letters and musical signs are red throughout. It is written in dark-brown ink; letters handsome, and very distinct. It came from a Greek convent. In 1845 it was found in the library of the Greek Mission at Athens by the Baptist Missionaries, Rev. Dr. A. N. Arnold and Rev. Horace T. Love. It was presented to the Library in 1863 by Rev. Dr. Arnold. It is in good order, bound in oak boards. No clasp.

The above memoranda are furnished through the kindness of R. A. Guild, LL.D., for many years librarian of the University.

THE COLGATE UNIVERSITY MANUSCRIPT
Hamilton, N. Y.

A Lectionary of the Gospels, in Syriac, written by Dencha, a presbyter of Armudagaj, completed Aug. 16, A.D. 1526 (Ab. 16, 1837 of the Seleucidan era). It has 151 leaves of cotton paper, 30.5 × 20.3 cm. (12 × 8 inches), and two columns, of 21 lines to each page, including the colophon, which occupies 6 columns. The MS. was brought to America by Baba Yosep, of Urumiah, who obtained it in Tyari; it was secured for the library by Prof. Nathaniel Schmidt.

Professor Schmidt writes: "The lectionary contains texts from the Gospels for reading during the ecclesiastical year. Provision is made for 56 Sundays. Each selection was originally preceded by a statement in red ink of the gospel whence it was taken; but this is now, in many places, illegible. I have compared the text with the Peshitto and the Sinaitic Codex, and also, where possible, with the Curetonian fragments and the Jerusalem lectionary. There are a number of deviations from the Peshitto, but most of them are orthographical. A few variants agree with the Sinaitic against the Peshitto, but none of these seem at present important. In the colophon, the date is given as Thursday, Ab 16, 1437 of the Seleucidan era. This, however, has evidently been obtained by skilful retouching of the original letters, which are still faintly visible; for the 16th Ab did not fall on a Thursday in 1437 (A.D. 1126), as it did in 1837 (A.D. 1526). Simeon, the patriarch, mentioned immediately after the date, is probably Simeon VII. (A.D. 1510–30); the patriarch in 1126 being Eliah. Armudagaj, according to local tradition, once an episcopal seat, bears what seems to me a Turkish name (pear-orchard), which would be highly improbable in 1126. The name Armudagaj has been partially erased, possibly to give the impression that 'the holy city' preceding it refers to Edessa; but it can still be read. From Dencha's account we learn that this city, 20 miles northwest of Urumiah, was the centre of the district of Dasan, according to Assemani, part of the ecclesiastical province of Mosul. The name of the 'malik' is scarcely legible; it seems to be neither Suleiman nor Tamasp, but Chobyar, probably a local ruler. The curse of the 318 bishops of Nicœa and the leprosy of Gehazi are invoked upon the man that shall remove or deface the lectionary."

THE CORNELL UNIVERSITY MANUSCRIPT

The President White Library, Ithaca, N. Y.

A Latin manuscript of the Pauline Epistles, cent. XI. or XII., on pure white vellum, 4to, containing 59 leaves, with 1 column and 15 lines to the page. The manuscript has serious *lacunæ.* It begins at Romans xiv. 6, *Domino non manducat,* and ends at Heb. vi. 16, *Homines enim per majorem.* There are also wanting Romans xvi. 11–19, 1 Cor. vii. 5–15, and all the leaves from 1 Cor. vii. 27, to Colossians iii. 14, including the whole of 2 Corinthians, Galatians, Ephesians, and Philippians. Besides this, there are wanting 1 Thess. iv. 11–2 Thess. iii. 8 ; 1 Tim. i. 1–11 (the title to 1 Tim. is on the preceding leaf), and Heb. iii. 7–iv. 1.

Prof. Geo. L. Burr, Librarian of the University, through whose courtesy the above data are furnished, adds the following particulars: "I need hardly say that I have only for convenience indicated these gaps by chapter and verse. The MS. is, of course, neither chaptered nor versed, and neither the beginnings nor the endings of the *lacunæ* coincide with our verses.

"The manuscript, as you saw, is on pure white vellum, in a uniform hand, and has both interlinear and marginal glosses of a date not much later than the text. A later gloss in a XVth century hand has been carefully erased, but its traces are still abundant, especially on the later pages. The manuscript was bought by President White in Naples in 1877. So far as I know it has never been collated by any scholar."

THE DREW THEOLOGICAL SEMINARY MANUSCRIPTS

Madison, N. J.

(1.) *Cursive of the Gospels* No. **667** (Scrivener, 900) cent. **XI.** or **XII.**, size 10 × 9 cm., parchment of 178 leaves, with 1 column and 25–27 lines on a page, in minute letters, with chapter-tables, chapters, titles, and metrical verses. Leaves 163 and 170 are of the XVIth century. It was purchased at Constantinople, and sent to America in 1888 by the Rev. Dr. Albert L. Long. Library designation, *MS.* 3. See Gregory (Tisch.), *Proleg.* p. 565.

(2.) *Cursive of the Gospels* No. **1275**, cent. **XI.**, 21 × 15.5, parchment, 39 leaves, 1 column (15.2 × 9), with 19 lines to the page. It has chapters, titles [the so-called Ammonian], sections, and Eusebian canons. It contains Luke xxi. 28–xxiii. 7; xxxiii. 17–xxiv. 4; John ii. 5–iii. 18, iv. 5–v. 44, vi. 9–46, vi. 57–viii. 42. A later hand has inserted leaf 36, which gives John vii. 53–viii. 12. The leaves were found in an old temple in the city of "Stamboul," Constantinople. Sent to America by Dr. Long. See Gregory (Tisch.), *Proleg.* p. 1309.

(3.) *Cursive of the Gospels* No. **1276**, cent. **XI.**, 21.5 × 15.5, parchment, 79 leaves, 1 column, 24 lines, silver letters, chapter-tables, chapters, titles, reading lessons, subscriptions. It has ἐξέδετο in Mark xii. 1, Luke xx. 9 ; verses in heroic metre. It contains Mark i. 1–xii. 11 ; xiii. 15—*ad finem ;* Luke i. 1–xxi. 18. See Gregory (Tisch.), *Proleg.* p. 1309.

(4.) *Cursive of the Pauline Epistles* No. **371**, dated **1366** and **1369**, 28.4 × 20, parchment, 103 leaves, 1 column, 23 lines. It has the prologues (or ὑπόθεσεις), reading-lesson marks (ἀναγνώσματα), the beginnings of which are indicated in the margin, subscriptions (ὑπογραφαί) at the ends of the books, and στίχοι. The Epistle to the Hebrews follows the pastoral epistles. There are wanting : Rom.

i. 1–16, 18; 1 Cor. x. 24–xi. 27; 1 Cor. xv. 22–40; Philemon; Heb. i. 1–vii. 2. Written by one Joasaph, who also wrote No. **480** of the Gospels (Scr. 568), and **169** and **345** of the Acts. Library designation, *MS*. 1. Purchased in 1885 by Dr. Long. See *The Independent*, New York, Jan. 28, 1886.

(5.) *Lectionary of the Gospels* No. **301**, cent. **XII.**, 32 × 22, parchment, 334 leaves, 2 columns, 19 lines, red musical notes; mutilated. Sent to America by Dr. Albert Long in 1888.

(6.) *Lectionary of the Gospels* No. **951**, cent. **XI.** or **XII.**, 31 × 25 cm., parchment, 247 leaves, 2 columns, 27 lines, red musical notation.

(7.) *Lectionary of the Gospels* No. **952**, A.D. **1148**, 25 × 21, parchment, 175 leaves. The fourth *fasciculus* is cut out.

(8.) *Lectionary of the Gospels* No. **953**, cent. **XIV.**, 29 × 21, paper, 12 leaves, 2 columns, 19 lines. Written by the monk and presbyter Joasaph. This MS. is still in Constantinople in the hands of Dr. Long, who procured it for the Seminary, as he did the other three lectionaries mentioned above.

(9.) *Greek Lectionary.* Sæc. XII. vel. XIII.; size 23 × 30 cm.; membr. foll. 334, coll. 2, ll. 19. Synaxarion of Greek Ch., with two full-page illuminations, one of St. John, and one of St. Luke. Purchased by Dr. A. L. Long in Constantinople, 1893, and originally brought from Iconium, in Asia Minor.

(10.) *Service-Book for Perpetual Adoration of the Virgin Mary.* Sæc. XIII., paper, 12mo.; ff. 220; size 14 × 20.5 cm.

(11.) *Sticherarion, i. e.*, Hymnal of Greek Church, with musical notation. Sæc. XVI., paper, 12mo.; ff. 424; 15.2 × 21.5.

(12.) *Three Liturgical Rolls in Greek.*

    (1) Dated 6884 = 1376 A.D. *Membr.* 18 ft. 3 in. long × 10⅝ in. wide, containing liturgy of Chrysostom and Basil. Procured by Dr. A. L. Long from Lemnos, 1890.

    (2) Middle of XIIth century. *Membr.* 17 ft. long × 10¾ in. wide; illuminated with 18 initials, and bordered in gold; written on both sides. Probably the property of John Cautacuzenus. Procured by Dr. A. L. Long from Lemnos, 1890.

    (3) Early XI. Sæc. Fine white vellum, 14 ft. 6 in. long × 7¾ in. wide; written on both sides; has 8 large illuminated initials; begins, τοῦτο ποιεῖτε εἰς τὴν ἐμὴν ἀνάμνησιν. Procured by Dr. A. L. Long, in Constantinople, 1890. [1]

THE HALL MANUSCRIPTS

In possession of Dr. I. H. Hall, of the Metropolitan Museum of Art, New York

(1.) *A MS. of the Peshitto Syriac of the New Testament,* containing 304 leaves, of cotton paper; size 18 × 13¼ cm. (7 × 5¼ inches), written portion of page about 5½ × 3½ inches; 1 column and 26 lines to the page. The larger sections numbered doubly through the whole; some minor divisions marked, but not numbered. The quires are usually in 6 or 7 folios, or 12 or 14 sheets each.

"It is written in a small, fine Estrangelo, probably of the Xth century, though the hand-writing looks older. The first original quire is wanting, but a

---

[1] For the above data, so far as they add to the information already contained in Gregory's *Prolegomena*, the author is indebted to the courtesy of Prof. Charles T. Sitterly, of Drew Seminary.

portion of it is supplied by a Nestorian hand much later, perhaps of the XVth or XVIth century. [The leaves thus supplied are not counted above.]

"The MS. begins with quire 2, at Matt. ix. 31, and ends with Heb. xiii. 6 ; probably 6 leaves wanting at the end, with colophon, etc.

"The order of the books is : Gospels, Acts, Catholic Epp., Pauline Epp., and Hebrews.

"By reason of some disorder (or re-binding) 2 Cor., Galatians, and Ephesians are disarranged. The binding is of the XVIth century. ↲ The first quire is mutilated at the lower outer corner ; the 5 later leaves also mutilated at the lower outer corner. It begins Matt. vii. 15, and ends Matt. ix. 37. It has no note of lessons. The text is good, so far as examined."—I. H. H.

(Dr. Hall has also kindly furnished a description of a manuscript belonging in Chicago, which he has examined.)

(2.) *A MS. of the Peshitto New Testament*, on thickish parchment [owned by a Syrian (Oroomia) student in the Divinity School of the University of Chicago]. Date, the year of Alexander, 1575, which corresponds to A.D. 1204. It is of 4to size, containing 268 leaves (536 pp.), with 1 column, and usually 29 lines to the page. It is written in the Estrangelo character. The larger Syriac sections noted, doubly numbered, each portion by itself, and one set through each group of portions. The size of the written page is 18×12.2 cm. $(7 \times 4\frac{3}{4}$ inches); sheets in quiniones (bunches of five).

It begins with Matt. vi. 1—preceding parts gone. The first few leaves are mutilated ; *e. g.*, one leaf, containing Matt. vi. 10–viii. 6, is gone. Twenty leaves, Matt. xxi. 45–Mark vi. 31, are missing ; also the leaf containing John xxi. 23–Acts i. 16.

The following leaves are misplaced : John xii. 48–xiii. 10 is misplaced after xv. 6 ; John xvi. 33–xviii. 1 is misplaced after xviii. 38 ; Acts xix. 20–39 is misplaced after xx. 18 ; Gal. iii. 10–19 is misplaced after 1 Pet. v. 3. There are a number of minor mutilations.

The order of the books is : Gospels (in the usual order), Acts, Catholic Epp., Pauline Epp., ending with the Hebrews. It has a good text. There is no note of lessons. Of course, the *pericope*, John vii. 53–viii. 11, the epistles 2 Pet., 2 and 3 John, and Jude, and the Apocalypse, with other passages not usually found in the Peshitto, are absent.—I. H. H.

(3.) No. **1**^{a}, *of the Peshitto Syriac MSS. of the Gospels*, sent to America by A. L. Long, D.D., of Robert College, Constantinople. Cent. **X.** ; size 36.8×25 cm. $(14\frac{3}{4} \times 10$ in.); vellum, one leaf containing 2 columns and 26 lines to the page, having the [so-called Ammonian] sections, the (Eusebian) canons, and, presumably, the lessons. The text is the Harclensian version, but with a slight variation or two from White's edition. It contains Luke xxi. 30–xxii. 17. See article by Prof. I. H. Hall, in *N. Y. Independent*, Aug. 20, 1885 : pp. 1068, 1069. See Gregory (Tisch.), *Proleg.* p. 829.

(4.) There is also, in the Library of the Metropolitan Museum of Art, a very fine copy of the entire Bible, in Latin, on very thin vellum ; probable date, cent. XIII. ; size, 14×9 cm. $(5\frac{1}{2} \times 3\frac{1}{2}$ in.) ; text, 9.8×6.7 cm. $(4\frac{1}{3} \times 2\frac{7}{8}$ in.). It has 582 leaves (1 blank), and 1164 pages. It is in two volumes bound in one, the first of which ends with the Psalms. It is illuminated throughout in blue and red. There are 143 illuminated capitals, of which 85 have also miniatures. The first chapter of Genesis has eight miniatures, representing the creation, with a crucifixion at the bottom. It contains the entire Bible without mutilation, with prologues and the Apocrypha, but without the appendices or definitions of Bible names. On a prefixed leaf is a memorandum in English, discussing the costumes, head-dresses, etc., found in the miniatures, and this remark: "From Cardinal Fesch's collection Coll^d & Perfect." On the first parchment leaf is inscribed, in rather faded ink: *Ex Bibliotheca Nigconensi Ordinis Minimorum.* Examined by favor of the librarian.

THE HARVARD UNIVERSITY MANUSCRIPTS
Cambridge, Mass.

GREEK.—(1.) *Cursive of the Gospels* No. **666** (Scrivener, 899), of cent. **XII.** or **XIII.**; size, 21.7 × 15.2 cm.; parchment, 4to; having 295 leaves, with 1 column, and 23 or 24 lines to a column. It has the chapter-tables, chapters, and titles: section ἀ–κβ′ in Matthew; ornamented. The church reading-lessons and subscription are added at the end of John by a later hand. [It is neatly written, in black ink, the letters depending from the ruled lines; capitals in vermilion; initials and headings of the Gospels ornamented, and each Gospel preceded by a (badly blemished) portrait of the evangelist.] A later scribe, of the XIVth century, has supplied sundry *lacunæ*; viz., John iii.4–18; v. 12–vi. 7; vii. 2–xxi. 25. It came from Albania. It was purchased by the library through Dr. C. R. Gregory. Its place in the Harvard Library is *A. R. Show-case.*

(2.) *Lectionary of the Gospels* No. **296** (Scrivener, 483), cent. **IX.** or **X.**; size, 31 × 22 cm.; 6 leaves of parchment in the UNCIAL character, having 2 columns and 19 lines to the page. A fragment of an *Evangelium* (Matt. iv. 25–v. 13; 36–45; John xiv. 27–xv. 3; xvi. 18–33; xvii. 1–13, 18). This MS., together with *Evangelium* **277**, and the *Lectionary of the Apostolos* No. **75**, were purchased by Edward Everett in 1819, when he was Eliot Professor of Greek in the University [through Mr. Cartwright, the British Consul-General at Constantinople]. Its library designation is *Dr. 69.* It was collated by Edward A. Guy, and numbered by him (**1**^h). See Amer. Acad. of Arts and Sciences, series 1, vol. iv., pp. 409–415. Harvard Library location, *A. R. Show-case.*

(3.) *Lectionary of the Gospels* No. **297** (Scrivener, 484), cent. **XII.**; 4to, parchment; size [text], 21 × 14.5 cm.; 230 leaves, [2] columns, [23] lines. Collated by E. A. Guy (**2**^h). Harvard Lib. location, *A. R. g 3.10 : Tom. I.*

(4.) *Lectionary of the Gospels* No. **298** (Scrivener, 485), cent. **XIII.**; size, 31.5 × 24.5 cm. [text, 24.5 (or 23.5) × 19.5 (or 18.5) cm.]; parchment, of 202 leaves, with 2 columns, and 25 or 26 lines to the page. Eleven parchment *palimpsest* leaves and one of paper are added by a later hand. [Red musical notes throughout, Hoskier.] Collated by E. A. Guy (**3**^h). Luke vii. 6 (in accord with ℵ B), omits πρὸς αὐτόν. Harvard Lib. location, *A. R. g 3.*

(5.) *Lectionary of the Apostolos* No. **75** (Scrivener, 70), cent. **XII.**; size [text], 21 × 14.5 cm.; parchment, 281 leaves (pp. 562), 2 columns, 25 lines. Collated by E. A. Guy (**2**^h). Harvard Lib. location, *A. R. Case, g 3.10 ; Tom. II.*

The collations of E. A. Guy, above referred to, were never published. The items above (additional to those derived from Greg.) are furnished by favor of W. H. Tillinghast, assist. librarian of Harv. Univ.

Mr. H. C. Hoskier, now of New York city, in Appendix H. to his *Collation of the Greek cursive codex Evangelium 604* (London, 1890), gives an interesting account of his visit to Cambridge in 1887, and his notes on these MSS. While there he copied the whole of the uncial (fragments) *Lectionary of the Gospels* No. **296** (12 pages), and describes with great care the condition of the leaves, size and shape of the letters, and forms of the breathings and accents. He has noted the following "various readings," *i. e.*, readings which vary from the *Textus Receptus:* Matt. v. 4, παρακλιθησονται; v. 11, διωξωσιν, ειπωσιν, πονηρων; v. 12, ουτως; v. 39, σιαγωνα; v. 42, *init.* +ειπεν ο κυριος; v. 43, *init.* ηκουσατο (*pro* ηκουσατε); John vi. 5 (*ante* επαρας *init.*) +τω καιρω εκεινω; vi. 5 —ουν; vi. 5 (*post* οφθαλμους)+αυτου εις τους μαθητας αυτου ειπεν. "Then follows (immediately after ειπεν, and leaving vi. 5 unfinished) John xvii. 18, in which we note (*ante* εμε)+συ πατερ." John xiv. 28, εστιν; xiv. 30—τουτου; xiv. 31, ουτως; xv. 2, αιρει *pro* αιρει. John xvi. 23 (before αμην αμην)+ειπεν ὁ κυριος τοις εαυτου μαθηταις. [This last and the other similar interpolations, as in John vi. 5, are not unusual in *Lectionaries*, as introducing a new lection. Scholars will notice that several of the above readings, though varying from the T. R., are now found in the Revisers' Text.]

The following list of Latin MSS., taken from the catalogue of the Harvard College Library, has been verified by the personal inspection of Rev. Dr. Geo. E. Merrill, of Newton, with additional notes by him.

(1.) LATIN.—(Catalogue No. 38, 158.) *Latin Vulgate*, cent. XIII. "*Biblia Sacra Latina cum prologis,*" ff. [425] *cir.* 3 × *cir.* 4⅔ in.; 2 col., 43 l. *G. L.* Beautifully written in minute characters on very thin vellum, ornamented with many initial letters in gold and colors, in the centre of the greater part of which are little miniatures finely painted. In binding, the tops of some of the pages were cut too close. Stamped on the back cover are the arms of some cardinal; the stamp on the front cover is indistinct. An iron ring is attached to the top of the back cover. [An alphabetical explanation of Hebrew names is appended, followed by a table of festivals. The volume came to Harvard by bequest of Charles Sumner, April 28, 1874.—G. E. M.]

(2.) (Catalogue No. 38, 157.) "*Biblia Sacra Latina cum prologis,*" cent. XIII., ff. 628, *cir.* 3 × *cir.* 4⅔ in.; 2 col., 45 l. *G. L.* Beautifully written on fine vellum, with illuminated capital letters, and a large initial to the book of Genesis, occupying the length of the page and containing eight separate miniatures, the lowest one a crucifixion. There are many MS. marginal annotations, and the back fly-leaves are covered with writing. On the first back fly-leaf is the presentation inscription in Latin, dated 1476, of Marcus de Bononia to Jacobus de Bononia; to this leaf is attached a modern transcription of the same. But, "notwithstanding the earliness of the Italian ownership, the MS. is evidently of French execution. A printed notice is pasted on the first front fly-leaf. The initial letter F to Maccabees ii. 1, is wanting. This MS. is from the library of the Duke of Sussex. [The printed notice referred to, as well as the lettering on the back of the cover, put the date at the XIVth century. The book came to the library by the bequest of Charles Sumner. The order of the N. T. Books places Acts after Hebrews.—G. E. M.]

(3.) [An incomplete copy of the Vulgate text] 4to, ff. 258. MS. coarsely written on paper, in black and red ink, the number of lines on a page varying from 29 to 41. The contents are arranged in the following order: 1 and 2 Maccabees, Acts, Canonical [sic] Epistles, Apocalypse, the Epistles of Paul in customary order, except that Thessalonians precedes Colossians, Ecclesiasticus beginning with ch. 19 middle of v. 20; Job, Tobit, Judith, Esther, Ezra, Nehemiah ii [iii.], Esdras iii. [iv.], Esdras to ch. 3 middle of v. 31.

(4.) (Cat. No. 38, 157.) [*Novum Testamentum*] (Vulg.) cent **XIII.** or **XIV.**, ff.

95, *cir.* 3 × *cir.* 4⅝ in. ; 2 col., 51 l. *G. L.* Beautifully written in minute characters on vellum, of most beautiful texture, with rubricated and ornamental letters. Printed notice pasted on the first front fly-leaf. On the back it is lettered *Sæc.* XIII. The Catholic Epistles and the Apocalypse precede the Epistles of Paul. The famous passage, 1 John v. 7, 8, has been rewritten by a later hand. Many other passages have been similarly altered. On the inside of the front cover is pasted the book-plate of Willett Lawrence Adye.

[Another Harvard MS. of the Vulgate, not in the library catalogue, has recently come to light, the following description of which is furnished by the kindness of Dr. Thayer of the Harvard Divinity School.]

(5.) *Biblia Sacra Latina* (Vulgate), cent. XIII., ff. 433. Size, 10 × 6 in. (25 × 16 cm.), 2 columns, 52 lines. Prefixed is a table of church-lessons, followed by (Jerome's) prologue, and at the end of the volume the interpretation of Hebrew proper names. At the bottom of the last page is a record of its purchase by a certain "Andreas Justus, for 34 francs, from the heirs of the late Simon Boceella de Luca," corroborating other indications that the MS. was of Italian origin.

The biblical text begins with Gen. ii. 12—the first leaf having been torn out, as have ff. lxxxxvii. (beginning of 2 Kings), cxxviii. (1 Paralip.), clxxvii. (Job), ccxxii. (Ecclesiastes).

It is elegantly and compactly written, with well-executed initials and miniatures (several of which have been cut out), wide margins, containing many careful annotations (from Jerome, *et al.*), occasional interlineations in a very fine hand.

The Ep. to the Laodicæans is added in a smaller hand at the bottom of p. 403, *verso* (after Col. and before 1 Thess.), but it exhibits no reading not noted in J. B. Lightfoot's collation (*Com. on Col. and Philem.*, 7th ed., p. 287, sq.), except that it begins "*Paulus et Siluanus et Thimotheus non ab hominibus*," etc.

[Dr. Gregory's addition to Tischendorf's list of manuscripts of the Vulgate version, referred to on page 224 (see *Prolegomena*, p. 993), opens with three MSS., which are said to be at Harvard University. Their brief description is as follows:

AMERICA

1. *Cantabrigiæ in Provincia Massachusetts Universitatis Harvardensis, olim Ludovici Cass. Sæc.* **XII.**, *N. T., Textus est bonæ notæ. Notitiam codicis ab Ezra Abboto accepi.*

2. ———— ————, *Harvardensis.—Sæc.* **XIII.** *vel* **XIV.** : *Biblia integra : textus non est bonæ notæ : Notitiam codicis accepi ab Ezra Abboto.*

3. *Harvardensis olim Hawteianus. Sæc.* **VIII.** : *lectionarium : textus bonæ notæ Notitiam codicis accepi ab Ezra Abboto.*

This (No. 3) is 105 of George Livermore's Library Catalogue, and was sold, with two others, in 1894, to J. O. Wright, of New York (see below). It appears to be the MS. mentioned by Luther Farnham in *A Glance at Private Libraries.* Boston, 1855, p. 62. It is possible that No. 2 corresponds to the No. (2) described by Dr. Merrill above. No. 1 seems to be missing.

THE GEORGE LIVERMORE MANUSCRIPTS

(*Extract from the Catalogue of Geo. Livermore's library.*)

(103.) *Manuscript Bible* cent. XIIth *Bib. Sac. Latina*, well written in small Gothic characters, in 482 leaves of fine vellum, arranged in 2 columns. The initials are all illuminated in red and blue, and several containing small miniatures. Some of the initials are very finely executed ; at the end of the initial to the Book of Genesis, representing the work of creation in seven compartments, is a drawing of the crucifixion. The mother of Jesus is standing on one side of the cross and St. John on the other. At the end of the MSS. the interpretations of proper names used in Scripture are arranged in 5 columns, on 30 leaves, 11 in. × 7¼ in. Small folio, calf (covers broken). Dated 1150. From the library of the Duke of Sussex. See *Bib. Sussexiana*, vol. i. p. lxxii.

(104.) *Manuscript Bible* XIIIth cent. *Bib. Sac. Latina.* MSS. written in small Gothic characters, in double columns, on 622 leaves of fine, thin vellum, 8¼ × 5¼ in. Some of the principal capitals illuminated, others merely in red and blue, and flourished. At end interp. of prop. names on 57 leaves. Thick 8vo, calf (one cover loose); Sæc. XIII. See *Sussex.* v. i. p. lxxii.

(105.) MSS. on vellum, cent. VIIIth, N. T. Gospels, Latin. An evangelistarium, or copy of the church lessons from the Gospels for the whole year ; double columns, 119 leaves, 4to, full morocco, gilt ; Sæc. VIII. Lettered on back, *Evangelia Quatuor.* MS. Sæc. VIII. The following note from Mr. Livermore : " Bought for me by Mr. Henry Stevens, at the sale of the library of Rev. Dr. Hawtrey, Provost of Eton, being No. 111 on the catalogue, and particularly described by the former owner. This is probably the oldest MSS. in America."

The above three manuscripts were sold at the sale of Mr. Livermore's library, in Boston, November, 1894, to J. O. Wright, Esq., of New York city. Their present locality is unknown to the writer.]

THE HAVERFORD MANUSCRIPTS

Haverford College, Penn.

From a printed catalogue issued by Prof. Robert W. Rogers.[1]

(1.) *Hav. 27.*—MS. on paper, much worm-eaten ; size of leaves 28.2 × 18 cm. (7 × 11 inches), 2 columns on the page, and 22 lines. Prefixed to the MS. proper are 10 pages, divided into squares, with curiously illuminated borders, containing, in colored ink (red, yellow, and black), directions for the lessons to be read on particular days. Then follows a page containing an illuminated cross. The text is in Syriac and Karshuni, and is accompanied throughout by embedded liturgical directions for church use. The character is Malkite. After the text is a finely written note concerning the composition of the four gospels.

(2.) *Hav. 28.*—A fine paper MS. of the XIIIth (?) century, in the Estrangelo character ; size of leaves 8½ × 6½ inches [21.8 × 16.7 cm.], each containing 2 columns, 26 lines to the page. It contains the whole New Testament, including the Anti-legomena Epistles. On the first leaf a later hand has written, " Simeon

---

[1] " The Haverford Manuscripts " as catalogued number about 50. of which 21 are Hebrew, 1 Heb -Samaritan, 6 Æthiopic, 8 Syriac, 5 Arabic, 3 Armenian, and 6 Latin. They were purchased in Egypt, Palestine, and the Lebanon, by Prof. J. Rendel Harris, and presented to the library by him and his friend, Mr. Walter Wood, " in the hope that they may become the nucleus of a more extended collection, and may furnish a stimulus to the study both of ancient documents in general, and of the Semitic languages in particular." The MSS. consist mostly of extracts from the Old Testament, with some Rabbinical writings and prayers. Beside the 4 New Testament [Syriac] MSS. here described, are 3 Syriac "service books" on *paper* [description not given], 1 Latin *paper* MS. of 123 leaves (cent. XV.), containing the "gospel," and 1 Arabic MS. containing all the books of the N. T. in the order : Gosp., Act., Paul., Cath., defective at the beginning to Matt. ii. 22.

The catalogue, with some additional items of information, have been kindly furnished by Prof. Allen C. Thomas, Librarian.

son of Joseph to Joseph son of Simeon." The rest of the quire is taken up with a list of lessons written in illuminated squares and circles. The table of chapters is prefixed to each gospel. The order of the Gospels is Matthew, Mark, Luke, John. The Acts of the Apostles is immediately followed by the Epistle of James. Then follow 1 Pet. and 1 John, and after them the Antilegomena Epistles in the order: 2 Pet., 2 and 3 John, and Jude. The Epistles of Paul follow as far as Heb. xi. 12. There is a *lacuna* from Heb. xi. 12 to xiii. 24. An ascription of praise to the Holy Trinity concludes the N. T. portion of the MS., the rest of which is occupied by several subscriptions, a statement of the doctrine of the Trinity, and other supplementary matter, including extracts from Mar Ephrem and Mar Jacob of Serug, and one contains an illuminated cross.

(3.) *Hav. 33.*—MS. of the four Gospels, on paper; size of leaves 32.1 × 20.6 cm. (12½ × 8 inches), each containing 2 columns, the right hand in Syriac, the left hand in Karshuni. The text of Matthew begins with the second ternion, at chap. ii. 21; the Gospel of John ends on the verso of 1st leaf of the 70th ternion. A later hand has added a subscription stating that the book was written in 1209 of the Christian era.

(4.) *Hav. 57.*—Selections from the Gospels according to the usage of Mosul, in Karshuni. A paper MS. containing 113 leaves, the margins sometimes ornamented with writing. Size of leaves, 30.1 × 20 cm. (7¾ × 11¾ inches); text enclosed in red ruled lines, 14.1 × 23.1 cm. (5⅛ × 9 inches).

THE IRWIN MANUSCRIPT
Oswego, N. Y.

No. **5** (Greg.) *of the Vulgate versions*, cent. **VIII.**, 14½ × 10½ inches, in large UNCIAL letters of gold, on 144 folio leaves, of purple vellum, in double columns of 30 lines each. "There is no division between the words in each sentence or clause. There are scarcely any headings. Those which occur are : *Secundum Mattheum*, in rustic capitals, and *Secundum Johannem*, in UNCIALS. There are only two 'explicit,' the one to Matthew in rustic capitals, and the other to John in UNCIALS. Mark and Luke have neither headings nor 'explicit.' The vellum is fine in texture, smooth and glossy, and is so pellucid that whenever there is a blank space on a page the letters show through it from the reverse. The letter-forms are Carlovingian, and very beautiful and simple. It cannot, on the one hand, be earlier than A.D. 700, while the absence of all decorative adjuncts in connection with initial letters, which are the special characteristic of Carlovingian calligraphy, shows that it is not later than A.D. 760–70." It was "bound in crimson morocco, extra, in the early part of the last century." The MS. was formerly catalogued as **Hamiltonianus 251**, having been for a long time in the collection of the Duke of Hamilton. At the sale of his collection it passed into the hands of Trübner, the German publisher of London, and then to Bernard Quaritch, who sold it to its present possessor.

Mr. Samuel Berger, of Paris, in his *Histoire de la Vulgate pendant les premiers siècles du moyen âge*, ch. ii. p. 259, says, in speaking of "The Chirographic School": *De ces manuscrits, le plus ancien est, sans doute le fameaux manuscrit Hamilton 251, qui apres avoir eté quelque tempes entre les mains de M. B. Quaritch, a eté acquis en* 1890 *par M. Th. Irwin, d'Oswego (Etat de New York).* Prof. William Wattenbach, of the Prussian Royal Academy of Sciences, declares his belief that

16

it is identical with the famous "Golden Gospels" which Archbishop Wilfred of York caused to be written for him about A.D. 680, and which was saved from the fate that awaited York library by being given to the monastery at Ripon [disputed by Berger, p. 259]. He considers that it was presented by Cardinal Wolsey in 1521 to King Henry VIII. The following dedication to the king appears upon the first leaf of the volume:

> " Fato servatus tibi sum, ter maxime princeps
> Te quoque servarunt aurea fata michi.
> Instaurata nitent per te sacra dogmata : per te
> Aureus est author Christus ubique meus!"

> "By fate, thrice greatest prince, I have been saved for thee;
> And thee, the golden fates have likewise saved for me.
> The holy rules of Faith by thee re-strengthened shine,
> And all the world knows Christ as golden Author mine!" [1]

THE LENOX LIBRARY MANUSCRIPTS

New York City

GREEK.—*Lectionary of the Gospels* (not in Scrivener's list apparently), lettered *Evangelia | Graece | Codex Chartar.* | Cent. XV. or XVI., on paper, 11¼ inches in height × 7½ in width, in cursive characters, 180 leaves (the folios not paged), in 2 columns, of 28 lines to a full column. The captions and initials are in pale red, and the text in pale black. It contains the full weeks for John, Matthew, and Luke. From leaf 140 onwards it is in confusion ; the leaves are to be read : 139, 172–179, 164–171, 156–163, 148–155, 140–147, 180. The manuscript is bound in maroon morocco, with the stamped crests and monogram of the Rev. Theodore Williams, whose books were sold at public sale in London in 1827. The next owner was the Duke of Sussex, and his book-plate is inserted, but it was acquired too late to be described in Pettigrew's *Bibliotheca Sussexiana.* After the dispersal of the Sussex collection in 1844 it was bought by Mr. Lenox. It is perfect.

LATIN (Lenox No. 1).—*Bible*, a manuscript on vellum, in Gothic characters, ascribed to the XIVth century. It contains 505 leaves, not paged, besides a blank leaf at the front and another at the end. The text is in 2 columns, of 54 lines to a column, the pages measuring 14 inches in height × 9 inches in width. It is bound in blue morocco, with the book-plate of the Duke of Sussex. In Pettigrew's catalogue of that library it is fully described, vol. i. pp. lxxv.–lxxx., from which the following extract is taken : "The initial letters of this MS. are highly ornamented, and very fancifully depicted ; many contain very fine miniatures, all in gold and colors of exceeding richness. There are 118 miniatures, besides illuminated letters, and every capital is written either in red or blue ink. The flourishes between the columns and in the margins are both fanciful and elegant. There is a written running-title, and the titles of the books and their prologues are in red. The number of the chapters is placed in the margin." The volume begins with the prologue of St. Jerome, and closes with the list of proper names and interpretations, in 36 leaves. Purchased by Mr. Lenox.

LATIN (Lenox No. 2). — *Bible*, manuscript on vellum, Gothic characters, XIIIth(?) century, 338 leaves, not paged, text in 2 columns, of 60 lines to a full

---

[1] This valuable manuscript is now the property of Mr. Theodore Irwin, Vice-President of the Second National Bank of Oswego, N. Y., who has kindly furnished the material for the above sketch.

column, the page $7\frac{13}{16}$ inches high $\times 5\frac{1}{2}$ inches wide, bound in blue morocco. It begins with the prologue of St. Jerome, and ends with the index of names in 23 leaves. The initial letters are ornamented; there is a running-title at the top, and the chapter numbers are placed in the margin. There are a few marginal notes in a later hand. At the top of the first page is the inscription: "Ista biblia ptīet ad locū scī Honustij apᵈ Guastuhaymonis." Purchased by Mr. Lenox.

LATIN (Lenox No. 3).—*Bible*, manuscript on vellum, small Gothic characters, XIIIth (?) century, 328 leaves, not paged, text in 2 columns, of 55 lines to a full column, the page $7\frac{7}{8}$ inches high $\times 5\frac{5}{8}$ inches wide. Bound in old mottled calf, with arms stamped on the sides. It is lettered: BIBLIA ‖ SACRA ‖ MS. ‖ SÆC. XIII. It has the book-plate of the Duke of Sussex, in whose catalogue (*Bib. Sussexiana*, vol. i. p. lxxii.) it is thus described:

" 7. *Biblia Sacra Latina, MS. in Memb. Sæc. XIII., Octavo.* Three hundred and eighteen leaves. Eight and a quarter inches by five and a quarter. Written in a very small Gothic character on thin vellum. The capitals are flourished, and some illuminated in red and blue. The chapters are numbered, and there is a running-title, the letters of which are alternately written in red and blue ink. The arrangement of the books corresponds with the preceding MS. [the ordinary arrangement], with this one exception in the Old Testament, in which the third book of Esdras is inserted. After the Revelation are two leaves containing a table of the Epistles and Gospels for the Sundays throughout the year."

The three following manuscripts were received by the Lenox Library with the Robert L. Stuart bequest in 1892:

LATIN (Stuart No. 1).—*Bible*, manuscript on vellum, Gothic characters, XIIIth (?) century, 414 leaves, besides 4 blank leaves between the third book of Esdras and Proverbs; text in 2 columns, of 51 lines to a full column, the pages measuring $8\frac{3}{8} \times 5\frac{1}{2}$ inches, bound in light brown morocco, gilt sides and edges, with case (by F. Bedford), and lettered: BIBLIA SACRA ‖ LATINA ‖ MS. ‖ CIRCA 1250. The prologue of St. Jerome is at the front, and an index of 31 leaves at the end. There are pictorial initial letters in gold and colors; the running-title at the top is in alternate red and blue letters; and the chapter numbers are set well out in the margin. At the top of the first page is the inscription : Biblia p̄ns̄: ē Mōasterij Diuæ Mariæ populo Romæ Sacⁱ orⁱˢ frm̄ hert Diui Augī. From the Libri collection.

LATIN (Stuart No. 2).—*Bible*, manuscript on vellum, small Gothic characters, XIIIth (?) century, 604 leaves, not paged, besides 2 leaves at the front containing the list of books, etc.; text in 2 columns, of 45 lines to a full column; $6\frac{13}{16} \times 4\frac{1}{2}$ inches on the page; bound in old stamped leather, apparently of the XVth century. It begins with the prologue of St. Jerome, and ends with an index of 44 leaves. Four leaves in Luke are supplied on vellum in a later hand. The initial letters are colored, and a few are pictorial; the running-headings are in alternate blue and red letters; and the chapter numbers, with a few exceptions, are set in the text. It has the small armorial book-plate of J. Gomez de la Cortina et Amicorum.

LATIN (Stuart No. 3).—*Bible*, manuscript on vellum, minute Gothic characters, XIIIth (?) century, 494 leaves, not paged, of which leaf 3 (containing the end of the prologue and the beginning of the first chapter of Genesis) is entirely gone, and leaf 448 is mostly lacking; text in 2 columns, of 53 lines to a full column; size of the page $5\frac{7}{8} \times 3\frac{3}{4}$ inches [text measures $4\frac{1}{16} \times 2\frac{1}{2}$ in.]; bound in blue morocco, full gilt, gilt edges, in case. It begins with the prologue of St. Jerome, and ends with the index in 39 leaves. There are pictorial and elaborately colored initials; the running-titles are in red and blue letters; and the chapter numbers are set in with the text. In the upper corner of the blank vellum leaf at the front are the initials " W. A. McV.", perhaps the Rev. William Augustus McVickar, at one time rector of the American chapel at Nice, who died in New York city in 1877. For facsimile, see Table VII.

Order of Books in the Lenox Latin Bible MSS.:
In Lenox No.1 and 3.—After Paralipomenon 2 come the books of Esdras 1, Esdras 2 (*i. e.*, Nehemias), Esdras 3, Tobias, etc. The Acta Apostolorum are placed after the Epistle to the Hebrews.
In Lenox No. 2.—After Paralipomenon 2 come the books of Esdras 1, Esdras 2 (*i. e.*, Nehemias), Tobias, etc. The third book of Esdras is omitted. The Acta Apostolorum follow directly after the gospels.
Stuart No. 1.—Paralipomenon 2 is followed by Tobias, while the books of Esdras 1, Esdras 2 (*i. e.*, Nehemias), and Esdras 3, are placed directly after the book of Psalms. The Acta Apostolorum come after the Epistle to the Hebrews.
Stuart No. 2.—Paralipomenon 2 is followed by Esdras 1, Nehemias, Esdras 2 [3 ?], Tobias, etc. The Acta Apostolorum follow the Epistle to the Hebrews.
Stuart No. 3.—Paralipomenon 2 is followed by Esdras 1, Nehemias, Esdras 2 [3 ?], Tobias, etc. The Acta Apostolorum come after the Epistle to the Hebrews.

For the above careful descriptions, as well as for many other courtesies, the author is indebted to Wilberforce Eames, Esq., the accomplished librarian of the Lenox Library.

THE NEWBERRY LIBRARY MANUSCRIPT
Chicago, Ill.

A cursive Greek MS. of the four Gospels, entire, of the XIIth (?) century, written on fine vellum, very well preserved; having 211 leaves, $3\frac{1}{2} \times 5\frac{1}{4}$ in., with 27 lines to the page. It has κεφάλαια (Matt. 68, Mark 48, Luke 83, John 18); sections (Matt. 357, Mark 239, Luke 342, John 232), " Amm." sect and Eus. canons, the latter in red ink, both in the ink and hand of the writer of the text. It has an unbroken division of the text into reading lessons, the beginning and end of every lesson marked by a rubric; and sometimes after the ἀρ. there is a word or two introductory to the section. The Gospels, too, are marked at the end: "end of the Gospel acc. to," etc.—all apparently in the same hand as the text. It has subscriptions (ὑπογραφαί) to the Gospels, quite simple; the longest at the end of Matthew; also a second summary, giving contents of each Gospel. It has the ὑποθέσεις at the beginning of the Gospels, the κεφάλαια of each Gospel sometimes preceding and sometimes following the ὑπόθεσις. (The κεφ. and ὑπόθ. to Matt. are missing.) It has references at top and bottom of pages to certain festival days. It is illuminated by initial letters of gold, touched with red or vermilion, and each Gospel has at the beginning a picture of the evangelist. The writing is small but clear. The dative iota subscript remains unnoted. Letters have some marks of antiquity.

The MS. is beautifully bound in red morocco, and lettered on the back Τα Ἁγια Ευαγγέλια χειρόγραφα. But little is known of its history. It was bought from the library of Probasco, Cincinnati, but no facts were given by him as to its origin. It was bound by F. Bedford. Its readings were collated a few years ago by Mr. Edward A. Guy.

The above data have been kindly furnished to this handbook as a result of personal inspection by Mr. C. E. Woodruff, of the Divinity School of the University of Chicago.

THE PRATT MANUSCRIPT
Boston, Mass.

In the Armenian Version. No. **1.** An illuminated parchment manuscript, containing the Gospels in Armenian from Malatia, Eastern Turkey ; the property of Mr. S. Brainard Pratt, of Boston, Mass. ; dated A.D. 1262 ; $7 \times 4\frac{1}{2} \times 2\frac{1}{2}$ inches. See Gregory (Tisch.), *Proleg.* p. 915.

THE PRINCETON MANUSCRIPT
Princeton Theological Seminary, Princeton, N. J.

Lectionary of the Gospels No. **303** (Scrivener, 491), cent. **XII.** or **XIII.** ; size, 31.6×27 cm. $1^1 + 338$ leaves, 2 columns, 22 or 23 lines ; containing the daily lessons from John, Matthew, and Luke. This *Evangelium* was written for use in Constantinople. "Perhaps in the XIVth century, Abul Fath, Presbyter, son of Presbyter Abul Badr, presented it to the church of Mar Saba, in the diocese of Alexandria, as Gregory, the patriarch, testifies in the manuscript. Afterwards it was in the monastery of the Iberi, at Mt. Athos, whence, in 1857, M. Sebastianoff brought it to Paris, where Firmin Didot bought it. At length, in 1885, it came to America."—Gregory. Comp. the *N. Y. Independent*, Oct. 18, 1888, and Jan. 24, 1889. Dr. Gregory examined it in Paris, 1885. Verified by Rev. J. H. Dulles, Librarian of the Seminary.

THE SYRACUSE UNIVERSITY MANUSCRIPT
New York

Cursive of the Gospels No. **668** (Scrivener, 1144), cent. **XII.** ; size [measurement made by the librarian], $20\frac{3}{4} \times 16$ cm., vellum, 201 leaves, 1 column to the page, 26 to 28 lines each, silver letters, chapter tables, titles, sections (the section No. 234 is at Mark 16, 9), canons, beginnings of the lessons noted in the margin, the synaxarion [συναξάριον] or calendar of daily lessons, the menology [μηνολόγιον] or table of festal or sacred days, with their appropriate readings, illuminated. It contains the four gospels in the order : Matt., Luke, Mark, John. By favor of Mr. Henry O. Sibley, librarian of the university, the following data are added : "The MS. has evidently been rebound. On the vellum fly-leaf of the *rebinding* appears the following : 'This MS. was purchased in 1885, in Constantinople, by Prof. Albert L. Long, D.D., of Robert College, Constantinople, and by him brought to America. It was purchased and presented to the library of the Syracuse Univ. by Mrs. Caroline S. Reid, May, 1886.' And at the end of the volume appears the following :

' *Index to the contents of the volume.*

The Gospel of Matthew, f.	1.	recto—f. 52 verso.		
" " " Luke,	f.	54.	" —f. iii. v. med.	
" " " Mark,	f.	113.	" —f. 145 v. med.	
" " " John,	f.	147.	" —f 187 v. med.	

1 "The leaf numbered 1 is from another more ancient manuscript, which John, the president (πρόεδρος), presented, with nine other books, βιουσ άϑλουσ τε μαρτύρων καὶ ὁσίων, to I know not what church or monastery."

Table of Chapters, or
In the Gospel of Matthew, f. 52 *v. med.*—f. 53 *v.*
" " " " Luke, f. iii. *v. med.*—f. 112 *v. med.*
" " " " Mark, f. 146 *v.*
" " " " John, f. 187 *v. med.*

' *Synaxarion*, or table of church lessons for the movable Feasts from Easter to Easter, as read in the Oriental churches f. 188 *v.*—f. 194 *v.*
' *Menologion*, or monthly calendar of church lessons from Sept. 1 to Aug. 29, f. 195—f. 201 *v.* The last leaf of the MS. is wanting. It contained the church lessons for Aug. 30 and 31, and probably also the usual invocation and colophon, with name of scribe, date, etc.' "

THE UNION THEOLOGICAL SEMINARY MANUSCRIPTS
New York City

(1.) *Cursive of the Gospels* No. **1**, Syriac Version, the property of Syrian Prot. College, at Beirût, Syria ; contains also No. **1** of Acts and Catholic Epistles, and No. **1** of Pauline Epistles, cent. **IX.**, on vellum, containing 203 leaves, with 2 columns, and chapters doubly numbered ; size, 27.5 × 18.7 cm. (10¾ × 7¼ inches) ; has the [so-called Ammonian ?] sections, lessons for feasts, and the ὑπογραφαί, or subscriptions. The contents are thus given in detail in the subscriptions :

	Matt.	Mark.	Luke.	John.
Kephalaia	70	49	83	20
Canones	360	240	348	232
Miracles	25	23	22	9
Parables	25	6	27	5
Testimonies	32	17	72	15
Lessons	74	40		48
Sections	23	12	23	20

The text of the Gospels is the Philoxenian or Harclensian. The Acts, James, 1 Pet., 1 John, and the Pauline Epistles, are from the Peshitto.
There are wanting, Matt. i.–xii. 19 ; xiii. 28–57 ; xvii. 20–xix. 12 ; xxv. 11–xxvi. 21 ; Mark iv. 2–35 ; Luke xix. 38—xx. 21 ; John viii. 31 (Syriac 20)–ix. 31 ; some part of 1 Tim., all of 2 Tim. ; Tit. i. 10–iii. 15 ; Philemon ; and, of course, John vii. 53–viii. 11 ; 2 Pet., Jude ; 1 John v. 7, and 2 and 3 John.
The MS. formerly belonged to another monastery in Tûr 'Abdîn. It was brought from Mardîn, in Asiatic Turkey, by 'Abd-ul-Messiah, who gave it to the American College at Beirût. It is now in New York. It has been collated by Prof. I. H. Hall. See *Journal of Amer. Oriental Society*, New Haven, Oct. 1877 ; and Gregory (Tisch.), *Proleg.* p. 828.
(2.) *A MS. of the Gospels, and Epistle of James* was obtained from Mardîn, in Mesopotamia, by Rev. Alpheus N. Andrus, and presented by him to the Union Theological Seminary, in March, 1872. It consists of 146 leaves of thick parchment ; binding much dilapidated ; size, 7½ × 5½ inches (19.1 × 16.5 cm.), 2 columns to the page, each 5½ × 1¾ inches (16.5 × 4.5 cm.). Writing in the old Jacobite character, circa XII. sæc. ; Estrangelo forms rare, except in the lesson numbers ; one line at bottom of C. 2, Fol. 98, is entirely in the Estrangelo, including three words of Luke xxii. 29. Vowels of Greek series are found, some *a prima manu*, others added by a later scribe. Titles and subscriptions are simple in form.
Text coincides with original Widmanstadt edition (1555), and those of the American Bible Society. John vii. 53–viii. 11, and Luke xxii. 17, 18, are omitted. Variations from the common type occur in the spelling of the equivalents for

Jews, Herod, Herodias, Rome, Peter, Soldier, Israel, Andrew, and other transliterated and foreign terms. The contents of the MS. in its present condition are : one, a fragmentary leaf, portions of Matt. xx. 22, 23, and xxi. 4–7 ; it really begins on Fol. 2 (Q. 4) at Matt. xxi. 10 ; a gap occurs Luke xxiii. 21–xxiv. 9, and another in the last quinio, representing John xxi. 17 to end of Gospel ; and Epistle of James, i. 1–ii. 2 (first part of the verse). The present ending is at James ii. 26, the remaining portion of which has been supplied by a later hand.

Writing careful and accurate ; ornamentation generally wanting. The Jacobite church-lessons are noted in vermilion letters, inserted in the body of the text. For full description of the MS., see I. H. Hall, *Journal of the Soc. of Bib. Lit. and Exeg.* for June and December, 1883.

(3.) *The Greek Lectionary of the Gospels* No. **929**, cent. **XIII.** ; a 4to, vellum MS., containing 25 leaves, 1 column, and 35 lines to the column. The text measures 17.3 + 11.5 cm. to 18 × 12—*i.e.*, it varies in size. The text is damaged slightly on two leaves. One page is also stained with green ink, erasing half of one line. [These points noted by C. R. Gillett, Librarian.] The same MS. contains *Lectionary of the Apostolos* No. **254.** See Gregory (*Proleg.*), pp. 777 and 791.

THE WILLIAMS MANUSCRIPT

Utica, N. Y.

A Syriac Manuscript of the Acts and Catholic Epistles No. **12** (and of the *Pauline Epistles* No. **13**), the property of Mr. Robert S. Williams, to whom it was sent by his brother, Rev. W. F. Williams, missionary to Mardîn. Dated **1471.** Size 26.2 × 18.7 cm. (10$\frac{1}{2}$ × 7$\frac{1}{2}$ inches), on cotton paper ; contains 151 leaves, having 2 columns and 25 lines to the page ; the written portion, 21 × 12.5 cm. (8$\frac{1}{2}$ × 5 inches). The leaves are arranged in quiniones and quaterniones, the last being a ternio. A later hand has added the numeration of the folios in Syriac numerals. It contains tables to find the movable feasts, and of the church-lessons from the Acts and the Epistles ; then the Acts and seven Catholic Epistles, followed by the Pauline Epistles, in which Philemon precedes Hebrews. The text is Peshitto, with the Antilegomena in Philoxenian. At the end are 132 verses in honor of the Trinity, apparently by a certain scribe from the Christians of St. Thomas in Malabar. The verses and text were copied at the expense of one David, the Syrian, from an older MS. in the possession of a certain Suleiman, residing in the castle of Husn Keifa, on the river Tigris.

There is a general introduction and prefaces to the Acts, the Catholic Epp., and to each of the Pauline Epp., taken from Gregory Bar-Hebræus. The church-lesson notes are in red, in the body of the text, and also numbered in the margin. This numbering shows that the so-called Antilegomena Epistles were (contrary to the usual practice) read in the churches. The text is much superior to that used by Pococke, and contains many readings suggested by him as emendations. The writing is fully and carefully vowelled ; and the marks indicating the hard or soft sounds of the *b-e-g-a-d-k-e-ph-a-th* letters are supplied in red. Numerous marginal notes, linguistic and grammatical, are found, many of them being from Gregory Bar-Hebræus. Dr. I. H. Hall has carefully examined it, and has collated much of it. He says : " On the whole, this MS. is very valuable for its texts and its notes ; not only as a carefully edited copy of the ancient text, but as a linguistic and grammatical treatise. Its place is high among MSS., although the date of its writing is not so very remote. It is easy to see, from

Pococke's version, that this MS. is every way superior to the Bodleian as a copy of the Antilegomena Epistles." See *Jour. Amer. Oriental Society*, Oct. 1884, pp. xviii.–xxi. ; also, an article by Dr. Hall in *Jour. Soc. of Biblical Literature and Exegesis*, Boston, 1885: Proceedings for June–Dec. 1884, pp. 37–49. See also Gregory (Tisch.), *Proleg.* p. 845.

THE WRIGHT MANUSCRIPT

The property of John Wright, D.D., St. Paul, Minn.

A *Latin copy of the Epistles of Paul*, complete, of the XIVth cent., size 12½ × 8½ inches, written upon thick paper. It is accompanied by Nic. de Lyra's Commentary. A rubric states that it was written either during Lyra's lifetime, or shortly after his death, which occurred at Paris, Oct. 23, 1340. The manuscript has a stichometrical notation and subscriptions to the several books. The chapters begin with a red letter, but there is no division of verses. There is an index of the contents of chapters on three pages.

The manuscript was for many years in the library of the Order of St. Francis in Italy. Dr. Wright, whose courtesy has furnished these particulars, has had it in his possession about ten years.

NOTE.—There is yet another Greek MS. of the New Testament in the United States, which has recently been presented by Dr. Caspar René Gregory to the University of Chicago, the full description of which, unfortunately, has not reached the author in season for publication here.

TABLE XII

ECCLESIASTICAL WRITERS

PART I.—Arranged according to the time they flourished.

PART II.—Alphabetical list with descriptive explanations.

TABLE XII

PART I

ECCLESIASTICAL WRITERS,[1] ARRANGED CHRONOLOGICALLY, ACCORDING TO
THE TIME THEY FLOURISHED

[*For explanations, see Part II.*]

DATE.	NAME.	DATE.	NAME.
A.D.		A.D.	
80	Cerinthus.	330	Marcellus Ancyranus.
95	CLEMENS ROMANUS.	330	Juvencus.
107?	IGNATIUS.	334	Theodorus Heracleensis.
108	POLYCARPUS.	340	Julius Firmicus Maternus.
110	PAPIAS.	341	Eusebius Emesenus.
120	Carpocrates.	342	Macedonius.
125	Basilides.	344	Orsiesius Ægyptius.
126	Quadratus.	345	Aphraates.
140	Marcion.	347	Serapion.
140?	Valentinus.	350	CYRILLUS HIEROSOLYMITANUS.
140	JUSTINUS.	354	HILARIUS PICTAVIENSIS.
160	Ptolemæus.	354	LUCIFERUS.
160	Heracleon.	356	Marcus Diadochus.
167	IRENÆUS.	359	Phœbadius.
168	Theophilus Antiochenus.	360	Meletius Antiochenus.
170	Apollinaris.	360	Zeno Veronensis.
170	Dionysius Corinthius.	362	Titus Bostrensis.
170	Hegesippus.	362	Victorinus (F. M.).
170	Melito.	368	EPIPHANIUS.
172	Tatianus.	368	Optatus.
177	Athenagoras.	370	Amphilochius Cappadox.
192	CLEMENS ALEXANDRINUS.	370	Apollinarius (or is).
192	Theodotus.	370	BASILIUS MAGNUS.
192	TERTULLIANUS.	370	DIDYMUS ALEXANDRINUS.
196	Polycrates.	370	Ephræm Syrus.
220	Ammonius Alexandrinus.	370	Gregorius Nazianzenus.
220	HIPPOLYTUS.	370	Gregorius Nyssensis.
230	ORIGENES.	370	AMBROSIASTER.
247	Dionysius Alexandrinus.	370	Pacianus.
248	CYPRIANUS.	373	Macarius Ægyptius.
251	NOVATIANUS.	374	AMBROSIUS.
254	Gregorius Thaumaturgus.	378	Diodorus Tarsensis.
260	Paulus Samosatenus.	378	HIERONYMUS.
270	Porphyrius.	379	Timotheus.
278	Archelaus.	380	Philastrius.
283	Theognostus.	384	Faustinus.
290	METHODIUS.	385	Theophilus Alexandrinus.
294	Lucianus Antiochenus.	385	Siricius.
294	Pamphilus.	387	Gaudentius.
301	Petrus Alexandrinus.	388	Evagrius Ponticus.
303	Dorotheus Tyrius.	390	RUFINUS TORIANUS.
303	Lactantius.	390	Tichonius.
315	Arius.	396	AUGUSTINUS.
315	EUSEBIUS PAMPHILI.	398	CHRYSOSTOMUS (Johannes).
326	ATHANASIUS.	400	Palladius.
328	Eustathius Antiochenus.	400	Cassianus.
330	Antonius Abbas.	400	Faustus.
330	Asterius.	401	Antiochus Ptolemaitanus.

[1] Writers most frequently cited are in small capital type.

DATE.	NAME.	DATE.	NAME.
A.D.		A.D.	
401	Marcus-Eremita.	502	Cæsarius Arelatensis.
401	Philo Carpasius.	507	FULGENTIUS.
401	Severianus.	513	Severus Antiochenus.
401	VICTOR ANTIOCHENUS.	514	CASSIODORUS (M. A.).
401	Chromatius.	520	Procopius Gazæus.
405	Pelagius.	523	Ferrandus (Fulgentius).
405	Prudentius (Aurelius).	535	Agapetus I.
407	Theodorus Mopsuestenus.	540	Apringius.
410	Nonnus.	540?	Arethas.
412	CYRILLUS ALEXANDRINUS.	540	Facundus.
412	Isidorus Pelusiota.	550	PRIMASIUS.
416	Orosius.	553	Liberatus.
417	Zosimus (?)	555	Victor Tununensis.
418	Marius Mercator.	561	Anastasius Sinaita.
420	Fastidius (Priscus).	581	Gildas Badonicus.
420	Julianus Hæreticus.	581	Eulogius.
422	Maximus Taurinensis.	589	Columbanus.
423	THEODORETUS.	590	Leontinus Byzantinus.
423	Cælestinus.	590	Gregorius Magnus.
428	Nestorius.	601	Hesychius.
430	Theodotus Ancyranus.	635?	Andreas Cretensis.
431	Eutherius.	640	Thalassius.
431	Capreolus.	645	MAXIMUS CONFESSOR.
431	Maximinus.	649	Martinus.
433	Chrysologus.	701	Beda Venerabilis.
434	Proclus.	730	DAMASCENUS (Johannes).
434	Eucherius.	770	Ambrosius Autpertus.
439	Socrates Scholasticus.	776	Paulinus Aquileiensis.
439	Valerianus.	785	Tharasius.
440	Nilus Abbas.	787	Elias Cretensis.
440	Sozomenus.	792	Syncellus.
440	Leo I. (Magnus).	813	Theodorus Studites.
440	Salvianus.	820	Claudius Taurinensis.
444	Prosper Aquitanus.	841	Haymo.
448	Basilius Seleucensis.	845	Hincmarus.
458	Ammonius Presbyter.	858	PHOTIUS.
458	EUTHALIUS.	980	Suidas Grammaticus.
458	Gennadius Constantinopolitanus.	990	ŒCUMENIUS.
460	Arnobius.	1007	Fulbertus.
462	Faustus Rejensis.	1040	Theophanes Cerameus.
470	Ruricius.	1077	THEOPHYLACTUS.
475?	Gelasius Cyzicenus.	1078	Michael Psellus.
484	Victor Vitensis.	1111	Rupertus.
484	VIGILIUS TAPSENSIS.	1116	EUTHYMIUS ZYGADENUS.
490	Avitus (Alcimus Ecdicius).	1118	Zonaras (Johannes).
495	Gennadius Massiliensis.	1120	Glycas of Sicily.
500	ANDREAS CAPPADOX.	1140	Antonius "Melissa."
500	Pseudo-Dionysius Areopagita.		

PART II

ALPHABETICAL LIST OF GREEK AND LATIN ECCLESIASTICAL WRITERS, WITH
THE TIME, FOR THE MOST PART ACCORDING TO CAVE, AT WHICH THEY
FLOURISHED

DATE.	NAME AND ABBREVIATION.	REMARKS.
A.D.	GREEK.	GREEK.
220	Ammonius Alexandrinus (Ammon.).	Reputed author of the Sections.
450	Ammonius, presbyter.	Commentator on John, the Acts, etc.
370	Amphilochius Cappadox (Amphil.).	Bishop of Iconium, Lycaonia.
561	Anastasius Sinaita (Anast.).	Bishop of Antioch, Syria (?).
500	ANDREAS CAPPADOX (And.).	Bishop of Cæsarea in Cappadocia.
635	Andreas Cretensis (Andr.).	Archbishop of Crete (or A.D. 850? Tisch.)
401	Antiochus Ptolemaitanus.	Bishop of Ptolemais, in Phœnicia.
330	Antonius Abbas.	Egyptian Monk.
1140?	Antonius.	Greek Monk.
370	Apollinarius (or is) Laodicenus.	Son of Bishop of Hierapolis.
278	Archelaus.	Bishop of Carrahæ, in Mesopotamia.
315	Arius.	Father of Arianism.
330	Asterius.	The Arian of Cappadocia.
326	ATHANASIUS (Ath.).	Bishop of Alexandria.
177	Athenagoras (Athenag.).	Athenian Philosopher.
370	BASILIUS MAGNUS (Bas.).	Bishop of Cæsarea.
448	Basilius Seleucensis (Bas. Sel.).	Bishop of Seleucia, in Isauria.
120	Carpocrates.	Gnostic of Alexandria.
178	Celsus.	Epicurean Philosopher.
80	Cerinthus.	Syrian Heresiarch.
398	CHRYSOSTOMUS (JOHANNES) (Chrys.).	Bishop of Antioch and Constantinople.
192	CLEMENS ALEXANDRINUS (Clem.).	Catechetical Teacher.
95	Clemens Romanus (Clem. Rom.).	Apostolic Father.
412	CYRILLUS ALEXANDRINUS (Cyr.).	Bishop of Alexandria.
350	CYRILLUS HIEROSOLYMITANUS (Cyr. Jer.).	Bishop of Jerusalem.
730	DAMASCENUS, JOHANNES (Dam.).	Presbyter of Damascus.
247	Dionysius Alexandrinus (Dion.).	Bishop of Alexandria.
500?	Pseudo-Dionysius (Dion. Areop.).	Called Areopagita.
170	Dionysius Corinthius.	Bishop of Corinth.
370	DIDYMUS ALEXANDRINUS (Did.).	Bishop of Alexandria.
378	Diodorus Tarsensis.	Bishop of Tarsus.
303	Dorotheus Tyrius.	Bishop of Tyre.
787	Elias Cretensis.	Bishop of Crete.
370	Ephræm (Ephr.).	Hymn writer.
368	EPIPHANIUS (Epiph.).	Bishop of Salamis, in Cyprus.
581	Eulogius.	Bishop of Alexandria.
341	Eusebius Emesenus (Eusemes).	Bishop of Emesa.
315	EUSEBIUS PAMPHILI (Eus.).	Bishop of Cæsarea.
325	Eustathius Antiochenus.	Bishop of Antioch.
458	EUTHALIUS (Euth.).	Bishop of Sulca (or ci).
431	Eutherius.	Bishop of Tyana, Cappadocia.
1116	EUTHYMIUS ZYGADENUS (Euthym.).	Monk of Constantinople.
388?	Evagrius (Ponticus) (Evagr.).	Archd. of Constantinople.
476	Gelasius Cyzicenus.	Bishop of Cæsarea, Palestine.
458	Gennadius Constantinopolitanus.	Presbyter of Constantinople.
495	Gennadius Massiliensis.	Presbyter of Marseilles.
1120	Glycas (Michael).	Of Sicily.
370	Gregorius Nazianzenus (Naz.).	Bishop of Constantinople.
370	Gregorius Nyssensis (Nyss.).	Bishop of Nyssa.
254	Gregorius, Thaumaturgus.	Bishop of Neo-Cæsarea.
170	Hegesippus.	Church Historian.
160?	Heracleon.	The Gnostic.

DATE	NAME AND ABBREVIATION.	REMARKS.
	GREEK.	GREEK.
A.D		
601	Hesychius.	Patriarch of Jerusalem.
220	HIPPOLYTUS (Hip.).	Bishop of Portus.
107?	IGNATIUS (Ign.).	Apostolic Father and Martyr.
167	IRENÆUS (Iren.).	Bishop of Lyons.
412	Isidorus Pelusiota (Isid.).	Presbyter of Pelusium, Egypt.
140	JUSTINUS (Just.).	The Martyr.
590	Leontius Byzantinus.	The Advocate of Constantinople.
294	Lucianus Antiochenus.	Presbyter and Martyr.
373	Macarius Ægyptius.	Macarius, Sr., surnamed the Great.
342	Macedonius.	Bishop of Constantinople (Arian).
330	Marcellus Ancyranus.	The Sabellian opp. by Eusebius.
140	Marcion.	The Heretic.
356	Marcus Diadochus.	Egyptian Bishop.
401	Marcus Eremita.	Egyptian Monk.
645	MAXIMUS CONFESSOR (Max. Conf.).	Monk of Chrysopolis.
360	Meletius Antiochenus.	Bishop of Antioch.
170	Melito.	Bishop of Sardis.
290	METHODIUS (Meth.).	Bishop of Tyre.
1078	Michael Psellus.	Byzantine Senator.
428	Nestorius.	Bishop of Constantinople.
440	Nilus Abbas.	Monk of Constantinople and Egypt.
410	Nonnus (Nonn.).	Of Panopolis, Egyptian by birth.
990?	ŒCUMENIUS (Œcu.).	Bishop of Tricca, Thrace.
230	ORIGENES (Or.).	Catechist of Alexandria.
400	Palladius.	Bishop of Heleuopolis.
294	Pamphilus (Pamph.).	Presbyter of Cæsarea.
110	Papias.	Bishop of Hierapolis.
260	Paulus Samosatenus.	Bishop of Antioch.
301	Petrus Alexandrinus (Petr.).	Bishop of Alexandria.
401	Philo Carpasius.	Bishop of Carpasia, in Cyprus.
858	PHOTIUS (Phot.).	Patriarch of Constantinople.
108	Polycarpus (Polyc.).	Bishop of Smyrna.
196	Polycrates.	Bishop of Ephesus.
270	Porphyrius.	The Philosopher.
434	Proclus.	Bishop of Constantinople.
520	Procopius Gazæus.	The Sophist.
160?	Ptolemæus.	The Valentinian Gnostic.
176	Quadratus.	Bishop of Athens.
347	Serapion.	Bishop of Thmuis, Egypt.
401	Severianus.	Bishop of Gabala, Syria.
513	Severus Antiochenus.	The Monophysite.
439	Socrates Scholasticus (Soc.).	The Church Historian.
440	Sozomenus (Soz.).	The Church Historian.
980	Suidas Grammaticus (Suid.).	The Lexicographer.
792	Syncellus.	Monk of Constantinople.
785	Tarasius (Taras.).	Patriarch of Constantinople.
172	Tatianus (Tat.).	The Syrian Sophist.
640	Thalassius.	Monk in the Libyan Desert.
423	THEODORETUS (Thdrt.).	Church Historian and Commentator.
407	Theodorus Antiochenus.	Bishop of Mopsuestia.
334	Theodorus Heracleensis.	Bishop of Heraclea, in Thrace.
813	Theodorus Studites.	Patriarch of Constantinople.
430	Theodotus Ancyranus.	Bishop of Ancyra, in Galatia.
192	Theodotus Byzantinus.	The Gnostic.
283	Theognostus.	The Catechist of Alexandria.
168	Theophilus (Thph. Ant.).	Bishop of Antioch.
385	Theophilus Alexandrinus.	Bishop of Alexandria.
1077	THEOPHYLACTUS (Theophyl.).	Archbishop of Bulgaria.
379	Timotheus.	Archbishop of Alexandria.
362	Titus Bostrensis (Tit. Bost.).	Bishop of Bostra, in Arabia.
140?	Valentinus.	The Gnostic.
401	VICTOR ANTIOCHENUS.	Presbyter of Antioch.
1118	Zonaras (Johannes).	Greek Historian.

DATE.	NAME AND ABBREVIATION.	REMARKS.
A.D.	LATIN.	LATIN.
535	Agapetus I. (Agapet.).	The Pope.
370	AMBROSIASTER (Ambrst.).	Pseudo-Ambr.
374	AMBROSIUS (Ambr.).	Bishop of Milan.
770	Ambrosius Autpertus, or Ansbertus.	Benedictine Monk.
345	Aphraates.	Bishop of Monastery, near Mosul.
540	Apringius (Apring.).	Bishop of Pax Julia, in Spain.
460	Arnobius Junior (Arnob.).	Semipelagian.
396	AUGUSTINUS (Aug.).	Bishop of Hippo.
490	Avitus (Alcimus Ecdicius) (Avit.).	Archbishop of Vienna.
701	Beda Venerabilis (Bede).	The Venerable Bede.
423	Cælestinus.	Bishop of Rome.
502	Cæsarius Arelatensis.	Bishop of Arles.
431	Capreolus.	Bishop of Carthage.
400	Cassianus (Johannes).	Founder of Western Monachism.
514	CASSIODORUS. M. A. (Cassiod.).	Senator, Prefect, and Consul.
401	Chromatius (Chrom.).	Bishop of Aquileia.
433	Chrysologus (Peter).	Bishop of Ravenna.
820	Claudius.	Bishop of Turin.
589	Columbanus.	Irish Monk.
248	CYPRIAN (Cypr.).	Bishop of Carthage.
434	Eucherius.	Bishop of Lyons.
540	Facundus.	Bishop of Hermiane.
420	Fastidius (Priscus).	Bishop of Britain.
384	Faustinus.	The Presbyter.
400	Faustus.	The Manichæan Bishop.
462	Faustus Rejensis.	Bishop of Rhegium.
523	Ferrandus (Fulgentius).	Pupil of Fulgentius, of Ruspe.
340	Firmicus, Julius.	*See* Maternus.
1007	Fulbertus.	Bishop of Chartres.
507	FULGENTIUS (Fulg.).	Bishop of Ruspe, Africa.
387	Gaudentius (Gaud.).	Bishop of Brescia.
581	Gildas Badonicus.	Abbott of Bangor (?).
590	Gregorius Magnus (Greg.).	Bishop of Rome.
841	Haymo.	Bishop of Halberstadt.
378	HIERONYMUS (Hier.).	Jerome, Translator of the Bible.
354	HILARIUS (Hil.).	Bishop of Poitiers.
845	Hincmarus.	Archbishop of Rheims.
412	Isidorus Pelusiota.	Bishop of Seville.
325	Jacobus, Nisibenus.	Bishop of Nisibis, Zoba.
420	Julianus Hæreticus.	Pelagian Bishop.
550	Junilius.	African Bishop.
330	Juvencus (Juv.).	The Spanish Poet.
303	Lactantius (Lact.).	The Christian Cicero.
440	Leo I. (Magnus).	Bishop of Rome.
553	Liberatus.	Deacon of Carthage.
354	LUCIFER (Luc.).	Bishop of Cagliari.
418	Marius Mercator.	Friend of Augustine.
649	Martinus.	The Pope.
340	Maternus, Julius, Firmicus.	Bishop of Milan (?)
431	Maximinus.	Bishop of Anazarb (?)
422	Maximus Taurinensis (Max. Taur.).	Bishop of Turin.
251	NOVATIAN (Novat.).	Roman Presbyter.
368	Optatus.	Bishop of Milevi, Africa.
416	Orosius, Paulus.	Presbyter of Tarragona, Spain.
344?	Orsiesius Ægpptius.	Abbot of Tabenna.
370	Pacianus, Hispanus.	Bishop of Barcelona.
776	Paulinus Aquileiensis.	Paul of Aquileia.
405	Pelagius (Pel.).	The English Monk.
359	Phœbadius.	Bishop of Agen, Aquitania.
380	Philastrius.	Bishop of Brescia.
550	PRIMASIUS (Prim.).	Bishop of Adrumetus, Africa.
444	Prosper Aquitanus.	Opponent of Pelagianism.
405	Prudentius, Aurelius (Prud.).	Christian Poet.

DATE.	NAME AND ABBREVIATION.	REMARKS.
	LATIN.	LATIN.
A.D.		
390	RUFINUS TORIANUS (Ruf.).	Presbyter and Monk of Aquileia.
1111	Rupertus Tuitiensis (Rup.).	Abbot of Deutz.
470	Ruricius, Senior.	Bishop of Limoges.
440	Salvianus (Salv.).	Presbyter of Marseilles.
385	Siricius.	Bishop of Rome.
192	TERTULLIANUS (Tert.).	The Montanist of Carthage.
390	Tichonius.	The Donatist of Africa.
439	Valerianus.	Bishop of Cimiez.
555	Victor Tununensis (Vic. Tun.).	African Bishop.
484	Victor Vitensis.	North African Bishop.
362	Victorinus, C. M. (Victorin.).	The African Philosopher.
484	VIGILIUS TAPSENSIS (Vigil.).	The African.
360	Zeno Veronensis.	Bishop of Verona.
425	Zosimus.	The Historian, Bishop of Rome.

TABLE XIII

LIST OF ROMAN EMPERORS

FROM AUGUSTUS TO CONSTANTINE, B.C. 31—A.D. 337

B.C. 31 to A.D. 14	AUGUSTUS, Caius Julius Cæsar Octavianus.
A.D. 14–37	TIBERIUS. (SEJANUS, *Consul*, 26–31.)
37–41	CALIGULA.
41–54	CLAUDIUS.
54–68	NERO.
68–69	GALBA.
69–	OTHO (Jan. to April). VITELLIUS (April to Dec.).
69–79	VESPASIANUS.
79–81	TITUS.
81–96	DOMITIANUS.
96–98	NERVA, *M. Cocceius.*
98–117	TRAJANUS, *M. Ulpius.*
117–138	HADRIANUS.
138–161	ANTONINUS PIUS, *T. Aurelius.*
161–180	MARCUS AURELIUS, *Antoninus.*
180–192	COMMODUS.
193–	PERTINAX (Jan. to March); JULIANUS, *M. Didius* (March to June).
193–211	SEPTIMIUS SEVERUS.
211–217	CARACALLA and GETA (211–212).
217–218	MACRINUS.
218–222	HELIOGABALUS (properly called AVITUS, or BASSIANUS).
222–235	ALEXANDER SEVERUS.
235–238	MAXIMINUS, *the Thracian.*
238–244	GORDIANUS.
244–249	PHILIPPUS, *M. Julius* (of Bostra, Arabia).
249–251	DECIUS.
251–253	GALLUS and VOLUSIANUS.
253–	ÆMILIANUS (three months).
253–260	VALERIANUS and GALLIENUS (254–260).
260–268	GALLIENUS.
268–270	CLAUDIUS II., *M. Aurelius.*
270–275	AURELIANUS, *L. Domitius.*
275–276	TACITUS, *M. Claudius.*
276–	FLORIANUS (three months), and PROBUS, *M. Aurelius.*
276–282	PROBUS, *M. Aurelius.*
282–283	CARUS, *M. Aurelius,* and CARINUS.
283–284	NUMERIANUS and CARINUS.
284–285	CARINUS and DIOCLETIANUS.
285–305	DIOCLETIANUS and MAXIMIANUS (286–305), *Augusti,* with GALERIUS and CONSTANTIUS (292–305), *Cæsars.*
305–306	GALERIUS and CONSTANTIUS, *Augusti,* with MAXIMINUS and SEVERUS, *Cæsars.*
306–307	GALERIUS and SEVERUS, *Augusti,* with CONSTANTINUS and MAXIMINUS, *Cæsars.*
307–324	CONSTANTINUS, MAXIMIANUS (307–310), and MAXENTIUS (307–312), in the West; GALERIUS (307–311), MAXIMINUS (307–313), and LICINIUS (307–324), in the East.
324–337	CONSTANTINUS, sole Emperor.

GLOSSARY

OF ABBREVIATIONS, SIGNS, AND LIBRARY DESIGNATIONS

A., Act. . . . . .MSS. of Acts and Catholic Epistles.

Adye. . . . . { Willett L., author of *The History of the Printed Text of the N. T.* (Lond. 1865).

Aedil. . . . . .Division in the Laurentian Lib. at Florence.

Ægina . . . . .Town and island in Saronic gulf, 16 m. S.W. of Athens.

æth. . . . . .The Æthiopic version.

Am. . . . ."Ammonian" sections. See p. 91.

Ambr. . . . . .The Ambrosian Lib. at Milan.

αναγνώσματα. . . . .Marks indicating lections, found in the margin of pages.

Angel., Angelic. . . .The Angelica Lib. in the church of St. Augustine, Rome.

Ap., Apoc. . . . . . { MSS. of the Apocalypse (*Tisch., Scr.*), for which our designa-tion is R. (Revelation).

Apl. . . . . .The Apostolos. Lectionaries of the Acts and Epistles.

Apost. . . . . .Scrivener's abbreviation for the *Apostolos*.

arab. . . . . .The Arabic version.

arm. . . . . .The Armenian version.

Arundel. . . . . .MSS. in the B. M. procured in 1646 by the Earl of Arundel.

Athens . . . . .The National Library at Athens, Greece.

Ath., Athos . . . . . .Mt. Athos, in the Greek Archipelago.

Auck. . . . . .Auckland, New Zealand, city library.

Barb. . . . . .Lib. of the Barberini Palace at Rome. Contains 7000 MSS.

Baroc. . . . . .MSS. in the Bodleian Lib. named after Francesco Barozzi.

basm. . . . . .The Bashmuric version.

Batop., Batoped. . .Βατοπαιδιον ("child of the bush"), a monastery on Mt. Athos.

B–C . . . . .MSS. in the lib. of the Baroness Burdett-Coutts, of London.

B.-C. H. . . . . { MSS. belonging to the Baroness B–C, but deposited in the lib. of Sir Roger Cholmely's School at Highgate.

bohem. . . . . .The Bohemian version.

Bolog. . . . . .Bologna (Italy) University Library.

"*bon not*". . . . . . ."*Bonæ notæ*," abbreviation of *Textus bonæ notæ* (Gregory).

Borg., Borgian MSS.Named from Stephen Borgia, Sec. of *Soc. de Prop. fide.*

Braithwaite . . . . . .MSS. bought at Athens by J. Bevan Braithwaite.

Brit. Mus., *B. M.* { The library of the British Museum, London. *Add.* signifies
Add. . . . . { "addition," a classification in the library.

Bur., Burney . . . { MSS. purchased by the British Museum from the heirs of Charles Burney.

Camb. . . . . { The university library at Cambridge, Eng. Add. = "Addi-tion."

17

Canon......... { Canonici (*Abbot* M. Aloysius), who sold certain MSS. to the Bodleian Lib.

capp., capp-t ..... chapters (κεφάλαια) or chapter-tables.

Carac............. Καράκαλλον, a monastery on Mt. Athos.

Carpentras....... The pub. lib., dept. Vaucluse, near Avignon, France.

Casanat......... Lib. at Rome founded by Cardinal Casanata, A.D. 1700.

chart. .... Indicates paper as the material of MSS. *Tisch. Scr.*

Chelten........ { Cheltenham, where a valuable collection of MSS., gathered by Sir Thos. Phillips, of Middle Hill, Worcestershire, are now in possession of Mr. Fitzroy Fenwick.

Chilian............ Χιλιανδάριον, a Slavonic monastery on Mt. Athos.

Chisian.......... The Bibliotheca Chisiana, belonging to Pal. Chigi, at Rome.

codd. opt........ The better of the known MSS. of versions (W–H).

Coislin, Cois...... Coislinianus, MSS. once in the lib. of Bp. Coislin at Metz.

Coll. Prop....... The college of the Propaganda at Rome.

col., coll......... A column or columns on the pages of MSS.

Coniston........ Residence of John Ruskin, in Lancashire, Eng.

Constan........ { Κωνσταμονίτος, a monastery on Mt. Athos, founded by Constans, son of Constantine the Great.

Constan........ } Constantinople.
Const'ple....... }

Conv. Sopp..... { "Conventi Soppressi," MSS. added to the Laurentian Lib. at the suppression of monasteries in 1810.

Copen............ Copenhagen Roy. Lib. Theol. dept. (Latin *Havnia*.)

cop. .... The Coptic version of the N. T.

Corsin......... { The lib. of Palazzo Corsini at Rome, founded by Card. Neri Corsini.

Cosin.......... { Cosinitsa (Cosinissa ?), a small island in the Greek archipelago; N. lat. 36° 36′, E. long. 25° 42′.

CPol., CPoli..... Gregory's abbreviation for *Constantinopolis.*

Cromwell....... Name of a Department in the Bodleian Lib.

Crum .... { W. E., M.A., editor of Coptic MSS. brought from the Fayoum by W. M. Flinders Petrie, Esq. (Lond. 1893).

Curzon.......... The lib. of Robt. Curzon, of Parham Park, Essex, Eng.

Cutlum........ { Κυτλυμοσ (Cutlumush), a Turkish family who founded a monastery on Mt. Athos.

"*Del.*"........ { Signifies that the MS. should be stricken from the catalogue.
"*Delendus est*".

Dion............ Διονύσιος (St. Dionysius), a monastery on Mt. Athos.

Doch., Docheiar... Δοχειάριος, a monastery on Mt. Athos.

Egerton .... { Francis Henry, 8th Earl of Bridgewater, who established a fund in the Brit. Mus. Lib.

Esc., Escurial..... The library of the Escurial, in Spain, near Madrid.

Esph., Esphig..... Ἐσφίγμενος, a monastery on Mt. Athos.

Este., Estensis.. { MSS. belonging to the Bibliotheca Estense transferred from Ferrara to Modena by the Duke Cæsare d'Este, 1598.

Evann........... Scrivener's abbreviation for Gospels (cursive).

Evl. .... Evangelia or lectionaries containing the Gospels.

Evst. .... Scrivener's abbreviation for Gospel lectionaries (evangelia).

Evv............Gregory's abbreviation for Gospels (cursive).
explicit..........A word placed at the end of a MS., to record its completion.

ff., fol., *foll.*......*folium, folia*, a leaf or leaves of MSS.
Flor. Lau.........See Laurent.
Fr., Fr.-on-O......Frankfort-on-the-Oder.
fr...............The Frankish version.
F-S............Facsimile of MSS.
F-S. Scr.........Facsimile found in Scrivener's 4th ed.

Gad...........﹛ Gaddianus, a designation of MSS. in the Laurentian Lib. at Florence; from Taddeo Gaddi, a Florentine architect (?).
Gb.............Griesbach's edition of the N. T.
georg...........The Georgian or Iberian version.
go..............The Gothic version (W–H).
goth............The Gothic version.
Greg., Gregory....Caspar René Gregory, editor of Tischendorf's *Prolegomena*.
gr.............﹛ Signifies the Greek Department in many libraries—often omitted in our list for lack of space.
Gronov..........John Frederick Gronovius, German critic, of Leyden.

Hack...........Hackney, London, res. of Lord Amherst.
Harl.........﹛ *Harleianus*, the Brit. Mus. Collection of MSS. from the Library of Robert Harley, Earl of Oxford.
Hebdomas.......*ἔβδ.* See p. 201 Lectionaries.
Heb. Tim. ....Indicates that Hebrews precedes the Pastoral Epistles.
ἐβδ., ἐβδομάς.....Lat. *hebdomas*, a week. See p. 201 of Lectionaries.
ἐωθ. ....﹛ *ἑωθινά*, eleven Gospels used in turn, one every Sunday, at Matins, beginning with All Saints day. (1) Matt. xxviii. 16–20; (2) Mark xvi. 1–8; (3) 9–20; (4) Luke xxiv. 1–12; (5) 12–35; (6) 36–53; (7) John xx. 1–10; (8) 11–18; (9) 19–31; (10) xxi. 1–14; (11) 15–25.
Holkham......﹛ MSS. belonging to the Earl of Leicester at Holkham (Norfolk), Eng.
Hoskier.........H. C. Hoskier, of New York, Banker.
Hunt...........Hunterian Museum at Glasgow.
Huthii ....MSS. named for Peter Daniel Huet, born at Caen in 1630.
Iber., Iberon, or ﹜ *τῶν Ἰβήρων*, a monastery on Mt. Athos.
Iveron ......
init.............*initia*, beginnings of church lessons.
Inst.............*"'L'Institut de France,"* including the *Bibliothèque Mazarine*.

Jer., Jeru., H. S...Jerusalem. Library of the ch. of the Holy Sepulchre.
Jer. Syr.........The Jerusalem Syriac version.

Kerameus ....Papadopulus K., of St. Petersburg, cataloguer of N. T. MSS.
Kosinitsa........see Cosin.

Laing ....Robert, a collector of MSS. now in Edinburgh Univ. Lib.
Lamb., Lambeth...Lib. of the Archiepiscopal palace in London.
Lamb...........Lambros, Spiridion P., Athens, author of catalogues of MSS.
"Latet" ....Gregory's sign for "locality now unknown."
Laura..........'Η Λαύρα, "*The* monastery," the largest on Mt. Athos.

Lau., Laurent... { Laurentian Library, founded by Cosmo de Medici and his grandson Lorenzo, at Florence.
Laud............MSS. in Bodleian Lib. from Abp. Laud.
Lazarus........ { Lib. of the Armenian Monastery of St. Lazarus, on the island of that name near Venice.
Leicester........The library of the town council of Leicester, Eng.
Linköp., Benzel. { Linköping, Sweden. MSS. once belonging to Eric Benzel, Abp. of Upsal.
Ln..............Lachmann's edition of the N. T.
Malatest....... { Bibl. Malatestianus, Cesena, Italy, founded by Domenico Malatesta.
Mangal..........Mangalemine church at Berat.
Mark, St. Mark, { Ducal Pal. lib. Venice. As *all* Venice MSS. are in this li-
Ven. M...... { brary, the designation Mark is often omitted.
me.............Memphitic or Lower Egypt (W–H).
Med., Medicæus...Belonging to the Medicæan Lib. at Florence.
men., menol......Menologium (μηνολόγιον), a table of saints day lessons.
Meermann...... { John Meermann, a Dutch scholar, b. 1873, whose library, sold at the Haugue in 1824, contained valuable MSS.
Melos., Milo......Μηλος, a Greek island in the Cyclades.
membr..........*membrana*, parchment or vellum.
Miller......... { Emmanuel, of Paris, author of *Cat. des MSS. grecs de la Bib. de l' Escurial*, Paris, 1848.
Miller...........Rev. Edward, editor of Scrivener's *Plain Introduction*.
Milo............See Melos.
Misc............*Miscellany*, a term specially used in the Bodleian Lib.
mon.............Monastery.
Mun.............Royal Lib. of Munich.
Mur., Muralt.....Edward de Muralt, the N. T. editor at St. Petersburg.
mus............Musical notes in MSS.
mut............Mutilated, by loss of cover or parts of MSS.

Nessel. ....Daniel de, the librarian of the Imperial Library at Vienna.
Nic. de Lyra.....Born in Lyre, near Evreux, Normandy, d. Paris, 1340.
Ottob.......... { Bibliotheca Ottoboniana, purchased by Pope Alex. VIII. (Ottobuoni) for the Vatican Library.
Oxf. Bodl. ....The Bodleian Library at Oxford, Sir Thos. Bodley, founder.
Ox., Oxf.........The University at Oxford, Eng.

P., Paul... .....The Pauline Epistles.
Pal............*palimpsest*.
Pal.,Vat.-Pal.....From the Library of Palatine, Elector of Bohemia.
Panticap....... { Panticapæum, the ancient Παντικάπαια; site near the modern *Kertsch*, Russia.
Pantocrat........Παντοκράτωρ, a monastery on Mt. Athos.
Pan., Pantel......Παντελεήμων, a monastery on Mt. Athos.
Parham.........The residence of Robt. Curzon, Lord de la Zouche.
Paris E. M.......MSS. brought to Paris by Emanuel Miller.
Paris Inst...... { The *Institut. de Paris*, to which belong the *Bibliothèque Mazarine*, which has 6000 MSS.

Paris, Par. Nat., ⎧ The National Library of France at Paris. MSS. belonging
P. N......... ⎨ here were formerly called *Regius.*
part. bis ....*Partim bis rescriptus,* "partly twice palimpsest."
Perron...........Cardinal (died 1618), who once owned G 91. Pesh. = G 299.
pers.............The Persian version.
pict.............Illuminated with pictures.
Philoth. ....Φιλόθεος, a monastery on Mt. Athos.
Phm. Heb...... ⎧ Indicates that Hebrews follows the Pastoral Epistles, as in
⎨ our English version.
Pickering........William, a London bookseller.
Prol. ....Contains prologue or ὑπόθεσις.
Prop......... ⎧ College of Propaganda, founded 1622 by Gregory XV. ; *ex-*
⎨ *tended* by Urban VIII.
Protat..........Πρῶτατον, a monastery on Mt. Athos.

Quaritch........(Bernard), the London bookseller.

Ravianus.........A codex in Berlin. A mere transcript of the Complutensian.
Regius .... ⎧ Former designation of MSS. belonging to National (once
⎨ Royal) Lib. at Paris. "*Paris*" now takes its place.
rescr.............*rescriptum,* "written over," palimpsest.
Reuss...........Edward W. E., of Strasburg (*Argentoratus*).
Riccardi....... ⎧ Palazzo R., the ancient Pal. of the Medici. Bibl. Riccardi-
⎨ ana, a lib. founded by the Riccardi ; 3500 MSS.
Roe...........MSS. brought to Oxford by Sir T. Roe about 1628.
rubr.............*rubrum,* red, the color of the ink used for MSS. *Tisch. Scr.*

σαβ. κυρ.........σαββατο-κυριακαί. See p. 201 of Lectionaries.
sah.............The Sahidic or Thebaic version.
Sak., Sakkel......Sakkelion, Librarian of the Athens Nat. Lib.
Salon...........Saloniki, the present Turkish name of Thessalonica.
sax. ....The Anglo-Saxon version.
Scr............ ⎧ Scrivener, F. H. A., the author of the Introduction to N. T.
⎨ Criticism.
S. Saba, Saba .. ⎧ The monastery of Mar Saba, near the Dead Sea. The MSS.
⎨ are now in the church of the Holy Sepulchre at Jerusalem.
Selden ....A dept. of the Bodleian Library given by John Selden.
Simop......... ⎧ Σιμόπετρα, the monastery on Mt. Athos, named from Simon
⎨ the Hermit.
sl.............The Slavonic version.
Staur., Stauron....Σταυρονίκητα ("the cross"), a monastery on Mt. Athos.
St. Genev. ....The Library of St. Genevieve in Paris.
St. Greg.........Γρηγόριος, a monastery on Mt. Athos.
στίχοι............" Lines or rows," an ancient measure into lines. See p. 88.
St. Pet..........The Imp. Library at St. Petersburg.
subs.......... ⎫ See ὑπογραφαί.
subscriptions... ⎭
sup., suppl. ......Supplementary, a library designation.
Synaxarion .... ⎧ συναξάριον, a table of daily lessons for the year, beginning at
⎨ Easter.
Syr^cu ....The Curetonian Syriac MSS. of the N. T.
Syr^p.........The Philoxenian version, also called Harclensian Syriac.

Syr.pesh............The Peshitto Syriac version.
syr. hl............The Harclensian Syriac (W–H).
syr. hr...........Jerusalem Syriac (W–H).
syr. vg............The Peshitto or "Vulgate" Syriac (W–H).
syr. vt............The old Curetonian Syriac version (W–H).

the..............Thebaic or Upper Egypt (W–H).
theot............The Theotisca version.
Thottianus.....{ MSS. in the Copenhagen Library named for Count Otto von Thott, a Danish financier; b. 1703, d. 1785.
Tisch..........{ The *Prolegomena* to Tischendorf's 8th ed. of the Critical Greek Test., prepared by Caspar René Gregory, of Leipsic.
Treg. ....Tregelles' edition of the Greek New Testament.

U., Unc..........Uncial MSS.
"*un. No.*"........" Unworthy of a number," in the judgment of Gregory.
ὑπογραφαί.......Subscriptions describing contents of N. T. books.
Urbino-Vat.......MSS. in the Vatican once in the Ducal Library at Urbino.

Vacat...........Sign that the No. has no corresponding MS.
Vall.............}
Vallicellianus .. } Lib. of Santa Maria in Vallicella at Rome.
Vat. Reg.......{ Codices Reginenses, or MSS. given by Christina, Queen of Sweden, to Card. Azzolini, and sold by him to Pope Alexander VI.
vg..............The Vulgate version.
Vien., Vienna.....The Imp. Lib. at Vienna.
Voss...........{ Vossius, Isaac, for whom are named MSS. in Leyden Acad. Lib.

Wake ....MSS. given by Abp. Wake to Christ Church, Oxford.
Wallerstein......The lib. of Prince Oettigen-Wallerstein, of Bavaria.
W-H ....Westcott and Hort's *Introd. to the text of the Gr. Test.* vol. ii.
W-H=.......{ Signifies here that the MS. is *of the same text with*, or that the No. is *applied to*, thus: "W-H=G 565," means Westcott and Hort have used this No. for *Gospels 565*. (See G. 81.)
Wisb............Wisbech, Eng., on the River Nene.
Wolfen..........Wolfenbüttel Ducal lib. (*Guelpherbytanus*).
Wordsworth......Dr. Christopher, Bp. of Lincoln.

Xeno., Xenoph....Ξενόφωντος, a monastery on Mt. Athos.
Xerop..........Ξηροπόταμος, a monastery on Mt. Athos.

Zittav..........}
Zittaviensis....} MSS. in Zittau, a city in Lusatian Saxony.

+..............Indicates addition of the words following.
>..............Omission of the words following.

INDEX

The numbers refer to pages. Descriptive titles in *italics*. Names of manuscripts and headings of chapters in SMALL CAPITALS.

THE END

THE GREEK NEW TESTAMENT

THE NEW TESTAMENT IN THE ORIGINAL GREEK.

Vol. I. The Text Revised by BROOKE FOSS WESTCOTT, D.D., Canon of Peterborough and Regius Professor of Divinity, Cambridge, and F. J. A. HORT, D.D., Hulsean Professor of Divinity, Cambridge. With an Introduction by PHILIP SCHAFF, D.D., LL.D., President of the American Bible Revision Committee. pp. xcii., 596. Crown 8vo, Cloth, $2 00. *Student's Edition*, Text only, $1 00. (*By mail*, $1 11.)

Vol. II. containing Introduction and Appendix by the Editors. pp. xxxiii., 512. Crown 8vo, Cloth, $2 00.

I venture to introduce the Greek Testament of Westcott and Hort with the modest assertion, *Hic habes textum omnium editionum antiquissimum et purissimum.* It is based exclusively on documentary evidence, and on the most careful comparison of all the ancient sources of the text as they have been collected and made available by the indefatigable labors of Lachmann, Tischendorf, and Tregelles. It embodies the results of the combined labors of more than a quarter of a century. It will, of course, not supersede the large editions which contain the whole critical apparatus; but it will take its rank at once among the best standard editions of the Greek Testament.---Dr. SCHAFF's *Introduction to the American Edition.*

By far the purest and best edition of the Greek Testament in existence.—*Christian Union*, N. Y.

The careful scholarship, the ample knowledge, the minute investigation, the acute analytical and classifying power displayed in the variety and treatment of very complex subject-matter, can hardly be overestimated.—*Westminster Review*, London.

THE REVISED GREEK-ENGLISH NEW TESTAMENT: Being Westcott & Hort's Revised Text of the New Testament in the Original Greek, and the Revised English Version of the New Testament printed on opposite pages. Together with Dr. Philip Schaff's Introduction to Westcott & Hort's "New Testament in the Original Greek." pp. civ., 540. 8vo, Half Leather, $3 50. (*By mail*, $3 78.)

PUBLISHED BY HARPER & BROTHERS, NEW YORK.

PRIMARY CONVICTIONS:

Being Discussions on Subjects Connected with the Evidences of Christianity (Columbia College Lectures, 1892). By WILLIAM ALEXANDER, D.D., Hon. D.C.L. Oxon., Hon. LL.D. Dublin, Lord Bishop of Derry and Raphoe. Crown 8vo, Cloth, Uncut Edges and Gilt Top, $2 50.

We think these discussions are even better as a book for study and reflection than as academic lectures, and that the more they are pondered the richer they will be found. . . . The title "Primary Convictions" states the subject in hand with precision. . . . The American Church is deeply indebted to the Bishop for his visit, and to Columbia College for inviting it.— *Churchman,* N. Y.

The book is a noteworthy one because of the fine erudition displayed by the author, his simple and gracious eloquence, and his felicity of allusion and illustration.—*Boston Beacon.*

They are clear, earnest utterances, sparkling with illustrations. People who have faith, but desire a tonic for it, will find this series of lectures both serviceable and acceptable. Readers who dissent from the author, either wholly or in part, will certainly be compelled to respect his earnestness and ability. —*Cincinnati Commercial-Gazette.*

A thoroughly evangelical sentiment pervades these lectures, and they constitute a strong and impressive defence and vindication of the Christian religion.—*Lutheran Observer,* Philadelphia.

Dr. Alexander's volume is very thoughtful, but not in the least "dry." He writes with a fluent and graceful pen, and in a style at once unconstrained and persuasive. His standpoint is that of the broad thinker, liberalized through culture, but unswerving in loyalty to fundamental verities.—*Philadelphia Bulletin.*

PUBLISHED BY HARPER & BROTHERS, NEW YORK.

☞ *The above work is for sale by all booksellers, or will be sent by the publishers, postage prepaid, on receipt of the price.*